D0034727

How "Natives" Think

LIBRARIES

How "Natives" Think

Marshall Sahlins

About
Captain Cook,
For Example

The University of Chicago Press
Chicago & London

Marshall Sahlins is the Charles F. Grey Distinguished Service Professor of Anthropology at the University of Chicago.

The University of Chicago Press, Chicago 60637
The University of Chicago Press, Ltd., London
© 1995 by The University of Chicago
All rights reserved. Published 1995
Printed in the United States of America
04 03 02 01 00 99 98 97 96 95   5 4 3 2 1

ISBN (cloth): 0-226-73368-8

Library of Congress Cataloging-in-Publication Data

Sahlins, Marshall David, 1930–
      How "natives" think : about Captain Cook, for example / Marshall Sahlins.
            p.   cm.
      Includes bibliographical references and index.
      ISBN 0-226-73368-8
      1. Obeyesekere, Gananath. The apotheosis of Captain Cook.   2. Cook, James, 1728–
1779. 3. Ethnology—Polynesia.   4. Hawaii—History—To 1893—Historiography.
5. Mythology, Hawaiian.   6. Ethnology—Hawaii—Philosophy.   7. Ethnologists—
Attitudes. /
      I. Title.
      DU626.0283S35   1995
      996.9'0072—dc20   94-34816
                                                                                              CIP

♾ The paper used in this publication meets the
minimum requirements of the American National Standard
for Information Sciences—Permanence of Paper for
Printed Library Materials, ANSI Z39.48-1984.

Contents

The art on the title page is taken from a petroglyph scene at Puakō, Kohala, Hawai'i Island, generally interpreted as a representation of the procession of the god Lono during the New Year Festival (Makahiki), with the size of the figures proportionate to their rank and a large image of the god adjacent. Other petroglyphs decorating this volume are as follows. *Chapter 1:* Lono figure from Puakō, Kohala, Hawai'i Island. *Chapter 2:* So-called Birdmen, from Kukui Point, Lāna'i. *Chapter 3:* Petroglyph understood to represent a birth scene, from Pu'uloa, Hawai'i Island. *Chapter 4:* So-called Paddle-men, from Puakō, Kohala, Hawai'i. *Epilogue:* Boxers from Kalailinui, Maui (cf. the boxing match in figure 1.3). The images are redrawn following the representations in J. Halley Cox with Edward Stasack, *Hawaiian Petroglyphs* (Special Publication 60; Honolulu, Hawaii: Bishop Museum Press, 1970).

Illustrations

Preface

When Gananath Obeyesekere published his book *The Apotheosis of Captain Cook* (1992), which attacked me and Captain Cook as agents (in our different ways) of Western violence and imperialism, I thought to let it pass. Pretending as a fellow "native" to speak on behalf of Hawaiian people against the calumny that they mistook Cook for their own god Lono, Obeyesekere had put together such a flimsy historical case, as it seemed to me, that it was sure to be taken apart by scholarly reviewers, who presumably would also be able to perceive the humbug he put out about my own work. I was wrong. On the contrary, the American Society for Eighteenth Century Studies awarded *The Apotheosis of Captain Cook* the Louis Gottschalk prize for 1992. To understand what this means and why I have felt an obligation to publish this book, you'll have to read it. All of it, though, footnotes and appendixes included.

At first I intended to write a pamphlet, and I still think of the work as belonging to that genre. It had a suitable eighteenth-century title: "'Natives' versus Anthropologists; Or, How Gananath Obeyesekere Turned the Hawaiians into Bourgeois Realists on the Grounds They Were 'Natives' Just Like Sri Lankans, in Opposition to Anthropologists and Other Prisoners of Western Mythical Thinking." But the essay kept getting longer (and the title shorter). It kept on turning up interesting theoretical issues: how in speaking for "native" others, one could deprive them of their own voice; how giving them our "practical rationality" left them with a pidgin anthropology; how spinning their history out of our morality ends up doing no one a favor. All these are vital issues for the human sciences. They justify our attention to the details in dispute. The bygone events and remote practices at issue in Captain Cook's death assume a certain interest for an anthropology sensitive to the character and variety of forms of life.

A number of people gave me good advice about this pamphlet while in manuscript. I especially thank Greg Dening, Peter Sahlins, Bill Sewell, Deborah Gewertz, and Rob Barofsky. To Dorothy Barrère I am as usual deeply indebted for comments on things Hawaiian and some arcane genealogical references. David Graeber gave important research assistance.

I do not use a computer or even a typewriter. Mr. James Bone turned out the finished manuscript.

Introduction

He was a man of conflicting qualities, but the worst of them got the better of him. Famous civilizer and secret terrorizer, Prospero and Kurtz, Captain Cook increasingly gave way to his darker aspect during his third voyage of discovery in the Pacific. And this, argues the anthropologist Gananath Obeyesekere in a recent work, led Cook finally to his downfall at Hawaiian hands in February 1779. Presuming that as a native Sri Lankan he has a privileged insight into how Hawaiians thought, Obeyesekere is able to defend them against the imperialist myths that have ever since been inflicted on them. He claims that for a long time now Western scholars have deceived themselves and others with the conceit that indigenous peoples, as victims of magical thinking and their own traditions, could do nothing but welcome their European "discoverers" as gods. Cook was not the only one; Cortés was another. The famous version of this colonial myth that concerns Cook is that Hawaiians perceived him as a manifestation of their returning year-god Lono, and the rituals in which he was then entangled played a critical role in his death. The nefarious side of the Western "civilizing mission," such contempt of the Other lives on in academic theory. And although one might think that between them Michael Taussig, James Clifford, and Francis Ford Coppola had scripted the heart-of-darkness metaphor to death, Obeyesekere would now also make Kurtz-work of my own writings on Captain Cook. He says that they add new dimensions of arrogance to the European myth of the indigenous people's irrationality.

So, in the pages of Obeyesekere's *The Apotheosis of Captain Cook: European Mythmaking in the Pacific* (1992) I am seen competing favorably with Captain Cook for the title of principal villain. This pamphlet is my answer to the honor. Initially, I admit, it seemed unnecessary to reply, given what a serious reader would most probably conclude about Obeyesekere's anthropological reasoning and his misuses of historical documents (not to mention his inventions of my work on Hawaii). More importantly, by the time Obeyesekere got through making ad hoc concessions to the historical data about Cook's divinity, there was virtually nothing left of the thesis that it was Europeans, not "natives," who apotheosized him.

For all his assertions about how Hawaiians were too rational to conceive of Cook as one of their own gods, Obeyesekere allows that this did not prevent them from deifying the British navigator after they had killed him. The people of Hawai'i island, he says, then made Cook a 'true god' (*akua maoli*) in the same sense and by the same rituals as they treated royal ancestors. Moreover, he says that during the first days of their acquaintance with Cook, they installed him as a Hawaiian chief of the highest tabus. Possessed of 'godly blood' (*waiakua*), such chiefs "partook of divinity," Obeyesekere again acknowledges: they were "sacred," and had "divine qualities" (Obeyesekere 1992: 86, 93, 197).[1] In fact, it will be easy to show that, in word and deed, Hawaiians received Cook as a return of Lono. Yet already one might ask what has become of the idea that the divinity of Cook was a Western invention rather than a native conception, because the Hawaiians had too firm a grip on empirical reality to so delude themselves? Unfortunately, judging from the generality of responses to *The Apotheosis of Captain Cook*, what is left is a rhetorical politics as appealing as its scholarly arguments are defective. I had forgotten Borges' warning that "the man does not exist who, outside his own speciality, is not credulous." Hence this reply.

A word first about the history of the controversy. The way Obeyesekere recounts it has the same quixotic air as his argument that Cook's divinity is a piece of Western ideology. It all began, he says, when a lecture I gave on Cook at Princeton in 1987 provoked his "ire":

> Readers will be curious as to how I, a Sri Lankan native and an anthropologist working in an American university, became interested in Cook. It is, in fact, precisely out of these existential predicaments that my interest in Cook developed and flowered. The apotheosis of James Cook is the subject of the recent work of Marshall Sahlins. . . . He employs it to demonstrate and further develop a structural theory of history. I am not unsympathetic to the theory; it is the illustrative example that provoked my ire.

1. Hereafter in parenthetical citations the abbreviation "Ob.," followed by a number, will indicate page references to Obeyesekere 1992.

When Sahlins expounded his thesis at one of the Gauss Seminars at Princeton University in 1987, I was completely taken aback at his assertion that when Cook arrived in Hawai'i the natives believed that he was their god Lono and called him Lono. Why so? Naturally my mind went back to my Sri Lankan and South Asian experience. I could not think of any parallel example in the long history of contact between foreigners and Sri Lankans or, for that matter, Indians. (Ob. 8)

The Gauss lectures I gave at Princeton in 1983 (not 1987) did not concern the apotheosis of Captain Cook. They were about the "Polynesian War" of 1843–1855 between the Fijian kingdoms of Bau and Rewa. Obeyesekere's ire must have been cooking since 1982, when I presented a version at Princeton of the Sir James Frazer lecture, "Captain James Cook; or the Dying God." By 1987, the Frazer lecture had been out for two years, published as a chapter of *Islands of History* (Sahlins 1985a). This chapter elaborated on the pages devoted to Cook and the Hawaiian festival of the New Year (Makahiki) in *Historical Metaphors and Mythical Realities* (Sahlins 1981). Perhaps it is ungrateful of me to say that *Islands of History* and *Historical Metaphors* are not, however, "two major books on this subject [of Cook's apotheosis]," as Obeyesekere describes them (Ob. 202n.12). The Frazer lecture on Cook's life and death as a manifestation of Lono was but one of the five chapters of *Islands*; whereas, in *Historical Metaphors*, a major book of 84 pages in all, substantially less than half is given to this topic.

While elevating these texts to the status of major works, Obeyesekere's criticisms of them pay scant or no attention to the other articles I had written that are most relevant to the objections he raises. These neglected works show that there is nothing basically new in the debate between us. In 1988 I had discussed a similar attempt to lay on me the brilliant idea that history is governed by the unthinking reproduction of cultural codes (Sahlins 1988; Friedman 1988). Obeyesekere does not refer to that discussion. An essay that appeared in the succeeding year, "Captain Cook at Hawaii" (Sahlins 1989), is the most extensive and best-documented argument I have published about Cook as an actualization of Lono. Very rarely does Obeyesekere notice this piece either, and then only in confused and confusing ways. He neglects to mention that it is a sustained response to a series of criticisms just like his own that had previously been raised by a group of Danish scholars (Bergendorff, Hasagar, and Henriques 1988). They also thought Hawaiians could not have made the elementary "mistake" of confounding Cook with their own god Lono; that there could be no detailed correspondence between the events of Cook's visit and the ceremonials of the New Year (Makahiki) because this festival of Lono's return as we know it is a later invention; and that the notion of Cook being received as a Hawaiian god is a Western-inspired myth, promoted largely by Christian missionaries and their chiefly converts after 1820. So I went ahead and showed, for example, the detailed correspondences between the events of Cook's visit, as described in contemporary documents, and classic ethnographic accounts of the Makahiki festival written by Hawaiian intellectuals in the earlier part of the nineteenth century. This empirical demonstration is represented by Obeyesekere as the absurd presupposition on my part that the Makahiki had not changed since 1778–79. Likewise, specific observations in this work that would seem to demand consequential refutation are simply stonewalled by Obeyesekere. From him, one would never know that certain rituals Cook was put through by Hawaiian priests match precisely and in detail the standard ethnographic descriptions of the ceremonies for welcoming the image of Lono at the New Year. Such omissions at least are consistent with his habitual reliance on the logical fallacy of converting an absence of evidence into the evidence of an absence: if the British (with certain notable exceptions) do not explicitly say that the Hawaiians received Cook as Lono, this must mean that he was not Lono. But there will be more than a decent number of occasions to discuss Obeyesekere's scholarly dispositions in the pages that follow. More interesting is the broader anthropology of his criticisms.[2]

To go back to the original moment of the dispute, there is also something less here than meets the ire, or at least Obeyesekere's original irritation seems historically and anthropologically undermotivated. He could not recall, he says, a single South Asian deification of a European, pre mortem or post mortem, though it is possible that colonial officials were sometimes treated "very much like native *chiefs*" (Ob. 8). One might reasonably question whether the comparison is anthropologically pertinent, let alone a sufficient cause to take offense. There is no a priori reason to suppose that the cultures or cosmologies of South Asians afford a special access to the beliefs and practices of Polynesians. If anything, the Indo-European speakers of South Asia are historically more closely related to native Western anthropologists than they are to Hawaiians. And why should the reactions of South Asian peoples to European colonials—South Asians, who have been dealing with diverse and exotic foreigners for millennia—why should they

----

2. Other articles relevant to the Makahiki and Cook's apotheosis not considered by Obeyesekere include Sahlins 1977 and Sahlins 1985b.

be the basis for knowing Polynesians who, for just as long, had been isolated from any such experience? The underlying thesis is crudely unhistorical, a not-too-implicit notion that all natives so-called (by Europeans) are alike, most notably in their common cause for resentment.

This anthropology of the universal "native" is in fact an explicit notion—and a moral appeal. You could say Obeyesekere is no Thucydides for any number of reasons, including that his book was not meant to be a treasure for all times but was indeed "designed to meet the taste of an immediate public" (*Pelop. War* I.22). Time and again Obeyesekere invokes his native experience, both as a theoretical practice and a moral virtue, claiming on both scores the advantage over the "outsider-anthropologist" (Ob. 21–22). We shall see him explicating Hawaiian concepts of divinity by the memories of a Sri Lankan childhood. Relying on such insights, he accepts the role of defender of preliterate Hawaiian natives, who could not otherwise speak for themselves, against the scholarly purveyors of the imperialist delusion that these people would have groveled before the White Man as before gods. But just where does the idea come from that this was demeaning? The irony produced by the combination of a dubious anthropology and a fashionable morality is precisely that it deprives the Hawaiians of their own voice. In an immoderate display of question-begging, virtually every time a Hawaiian is recorded to have said or implied that Cook was an appearance of Lono, Obeyesekere attributes the report to the White man who made it; or else to other Haole (White men), such as missionaries, who are supposed to have put the idea into the islanders' heads. Hawaiians thus appear on the stage of history as the dummies of Haole ventriloquists. Still, this is not the greatest irony of a book that pretends to defend the Hawaiians against the ethnocentric Western scholars by endowing them with the greater measure of bourgeois rationality.

If the underlying argument is that all "natives" are alike, the superimposed argument is that they one and all enjoy a healthy, pragmatic, flexible, rational, and instrumental relation to the empirical realities. Reflecting rationally (and transparently) on sensory experience, they are able to know things as they truly are. Given this inexpungable realism, Hawaiians would never come to the objectively absurd conclusion that a British sea captain could be a Polynesian god. According to Obeyesekere, such "practical rationality" is a universal human disposition—Western mythologists evidently excepted. Indeed, it is a physiological capacity of the species. It follows that, on the basis of a common humanity and a shared sense of reality, Obeyesekere has the possibility of immediately understanding Hawaiians, without regard for any cultural particularities or presuppositions. Presumably, then, he need not have resorted to his Sri Lankan experiences. In principle he could have appealed directly to Christianized Europeans to reflect on the evident fallacy of supposing God could appear on earth in the form of a human being. On the other hand, if it were really Christian missionaries who set the Hawaiians to thinking that Cook was Lono, this would have required, as a historical prerequisite, that the islanders accept as truth about Jesus Christ what they could not spontaneously believe of Captain Cook. But then, for all their empirical good sense, the Hawaiians on their own had worshipped certain anthropomorphic images—having the guise of ordinary Hawaiians but also strangely unlike them—which they must have known were merely made of wood, since they had carved and erected these gods themselves. Their idols were "even the work of men's hands; they have mouths and speak not; eyes have they and see not." What is the big difference, in terms of empirical reason, between worshipping such images and according divine honors to Captain Cook?[3]

Still, the alleged divinity of Cook will seem a slander so long as one follows Obeyesekere in reducing the veridical to the objectivity of the instrumental. The appeal is not simply to our moral sense but to our common sense. Obeyesekere's "practical rationality" is a common or garden variety of the classic Western sensory epistemology: the mind as mirror of nature. As it happens, his defense of Hawaiian rational capacities—like their ability to perceive that Cook was just a man or that Britain was not in heaven—is an affected anti-ethnocentrism that ends by subsuming their lives in classic Occidental dualisms of logos and mythos, empirical reason and mental illusion.

Distinguishing the practical from the mythical in the same way that the observable is different from the fictional, these oppositions are as foreign to Hawaiian thought as they are endemic to the European habitus. For Hawaiians, the notion that Cook was an actualization of Lono was hardly an unreflected, nonempirical proposition. It was construed from, and as, perceived relations between their cosmology and his history. Hawaiian thought does not differ from Western empiricism by an inattention to the world but by the ontological premise that divinity, and more generally subjectivity,

3. I say "honors" advisedly, thinking of Lévi-Strauss's belle pensée to the effect that, though the Spanish took the Indians for less than human, the Indians regarded the Spanish as gods, thus posing the question of who gave more credit to the human race. And why should it be that the Westerners alone have such a "veil of ideas" before their eyes? For all he says about the universality of the so-called practical rationality, to believe Obeyesekere, the Europeans were unable to recognize empirically their own simple humanity in the Indians' (or Hawaiians') view, even as they were simply unwilling to view the Indians as human.

can be immanent in it. For his own part, in a fanciful psychoanalytic moment, Obeyesekere remarks that the politics of Cook's fitful dispensations of grog to his crew worked on the symbolic significance of the brew as "the milk of the father" (Ob. 45). This is surely no less remarkable than the Hawaiian appreciation of Cook as Lonomakua, 'Father Lono,' the particular form of the New Year god. Nor is "the milk of the father" any less grounded in an empirico-meaningful logic, even if unconscious, as Obeyesekere implicitly supposes in speaking of certain analogues of discipline and the perceptual pun that "milk makes you groggy."

Such pensées sauvages, as nearly every anthropologist knows, require a disciplined empirical disposition. They entail sustained, intensive, and imaginative reflection on experience, on the properties and relations of things. But for all that they do not everywhere constitute experience in the same way, according to the dictates of a universal practical rationality. Again, Obeyesekere speaks in theory of the mix, in any people's beliefs, of natural common sense and cultural presupposition. The latter presumably opens the possibility that they will lapse into mythical thinking. We are not, however, given the theoretical principle that explains when one or the other of these contradictory dispositions will take over, only the practical demonstration that they can be invoked at the analyst's convenience.

Perhaps this is no great matter, since the antithesis of reason and custom invites us to abandon the anthropology of the later twentieth century for certain philosophical advances of the seventeenth. Sir Francis Bacon likewise had seen in empiricism a redemption from the error of inclining before false idols, such as custom and tradition, whose hold on men's minds represented the intellectual consequences of original sin. An obstacle to the right use of the senses, inculcated by nannies, teachers, and preachers (of the wrong religion), custom continued to be, for famous English empiricists, an unwanted social interference in the acquisition of knowledge. Someone imbued with "Romanist" beliefs from infancy, said Locke, was prepared to swallow the whole doctrine of transubstantiation, "not only against all Probability, but even the clear Evidence of his senses" (*Essay* IV.xx.10).[4] Hence, in contrast to Obeyesekere, one might have imagined it some evi-

---

4. From *An Essay concerning Human Understanding:* "The great obstinacy, that is to be found in Men firmly believing quite contrary Opinions, though many times equally absurd, in the various Religions of Mankind, are as evident a Proof, as they are an unavoidable consequence of this way of Reasoning from received traditional Principles. So that Men will disbelieve their own Eyes, renounce the Evidence of their Senses, and give their own Experience the lye, rather than admit of any thing disagreeing with these sacred Tenets" (Locke, *Essay* IV.xx.10).

dence of progress in anthropological sensitivity that, since Locke, the exotic cultural presuppositions of other peoples have achieved a certain epistemological respectability. I do not mean simply the role of cultural conception in sensory perception: the seeing eye as an organ of tradition. Insofar as cultural knowledge is a relation of empirical intuitions to local propositions, rather than to objects as such, some relative claims to truth had to be awarded to custom. But now comes Obeyesekere's regressive opposition between a universal empirical reason and particular cultural constructions. Even apart from the Hawaiians' treatment of Cook, the coexistence of these opposed dispositions makes a great embarrassment out of their ordinary existence. From the perspective of a practical rationality the deification of Cook would be far from their worst empirical blunder. A much greater scandal attends their daily pragmatic relations to nature. For, in the Hawaiian view, many natural things, including the foods they produce and consume, are 'bodies' (*kino*) of various gods, Lono included. With eyes to see, brains to think, and stomachs to feed, how could they believe that?

In the final analysis, Obeyesekere's anti-ethnocentrism turns into a symmetrical and inverse ethnocentrism, the Hawaiians consistently practicing a bourgeois rationality, and the Europeans for over two hundred years unable to do anything but reproduce the myth that "natives" take them for gods. I say "bourgeois rationality" because, as we shall see presently, ever since the seventeenth century the empiricist philosophy in question has presupposed a certain utilist subject—a creature of unending need, counterposed moreover to a purely natural world. The sense of reality that issues from the perceptual process does not refer to objects only but to the relations between their attributes and the subject's satisfactions. Objectivity entails a certain subjectivity. In the Hobbesian and Enlightenment versions, which are still too much with us, objectivity was mediated by the body's sense of pleasure and pain. Hence the close relation, acknowledged also in Obeyesekere's version, between what he calls "practical rationality" and economic utility. But, while Sri Lankans and Hawaiians are able to achieve this bourgeois sense of reality, Westerners presumably have been incapable of freeing themselves from the myths of their own superiority. In this respect they would act out their own archaic parodies of the "pre-logical mentality." Beginning with Christian missionaries and colonial apologists, a long lineage of Europeans who have reflected on Cook's death have mindlessly reiterated the arrogant tradition of his divinity. Even those who pretend to make a profession of reality checks, the academic historians and anthropologists, prove to be prisoners of the myth. So the inversion of "native" and bourgeois is complete. In the name of anti-ethnocentrism, the Hawaiians are endowed with the highest form of Western mentality, while Western scholars slavishly repeat the irrational beliefs of their ancestors. This is the central critical vision of Obeyesekere's book.[5]

The ironic result of an irreproachable moral inspiration, this critical vision, consistently and relentlessly applied, has equally paradoxical scholarly effects, amounting in sum to an anti-anthropology. In negating Hawaiian cultural particularity in favor of a universal practical rationality, Obeyesekere subverts the kind of ethnographic respect that has long been a condition of the possibility of a scholarly anthropology. The negation has a double aspect. One has already been mentioned: the erasure of Hawaiian discourse, its attribution instead to Western mythical thought. Directly or indirectly, subtly or overtly, the "natives' point of view" is metamorphosed into European folklore, especially when it has the inconvenience of identifying Captain Cook with Lono. In the following pages, we will see that this transfer is mediated by another discourse, which is precisely a recurrent rhetorical appeal to Western logic and common sense. Obeyesekere invites the reader to find this historical mention "strange" or that one "hard to believe," some hypothetical he proposes instead being "more natural to suppose," and so forth. He willingly substitutes our rationality for the Hawaiians' culture. From this follows the second aspect of a critical anti-anthropology: the generation of historical and ethnographic fables. Again and again in Obeyesekere's book we are confronted with an invention of culture, as Hawaiian rituals are given commonsense significance or historic events are refigured in ways that we know a priori how to understand.

The debate over Cook, then, can be situated in a larger historical context, an intellectual struggle of some two centuries that probably has greater significance for most readers than the petty academic blood sports. As an accomplished student of Western culture and society, Obeyesekere would turn its own classic mode of intelligence against it by awarding the corner on "practical rationality" to the so-called natives. But in thus supporting an intellectual version of the Western civilizing mission, the Enlightenment

5. Clearly this is a polemical vision, developed for the immediate purpose. The notions of reality and illusion, or of the West and the rest, in *The Apotheosis of Captain Cook* are not the same as those of *The Work of Culture* (Obeyesekere 1990:65–69, 217, and passim). On the other hand, the character and tone of *The Apotheosis* seem to echo some remarks of Obeyesekere on styles of intellectual debate in Sri Lanka (Obeyesekere 1984:508).

project of the perfection of man by empirical reason, Obeyesekere's anthropology has more in common with Cook's voyage than his uncompromising criticism of it suggests.

Cook, of course, was one of the Enlightenment's great "philosophical travellers," an incarnation of its rationalizing project in the scientific sense as well as in the registers of technological improvement and commercial development. An expert cartographer, mathematician, and seaman, Cook's machine-like competence, together with his rise from humble origins to high rank and world fame, made him a personal icon of the developing capitalist-industrial order of which he was also the global agent (Smith 1979). There was a curious correspondence, too, between the character of Cook's ethnographic science and the rationalizing effects of his voyages. In opening new trade routes and markets for Western enterprise, Cook proved to be the agent as well of a transformation of the customs he carefully observed to the all-round rationality he thus practiced. The same antagonism of inductive reason to the "idols of the tribe" that was promulgated in Europe as a philosophical attitude was realized abroad as colonial history, that is, by the civilizing of the "natives." Hence the link between Obeyesekere's project and Cook's own, the one and the other prepared to dump a bourgeois sense of practical rationality on the Hawaiians—as a helpful and compassionate gesture. Imperialism thus works in mysterious ways. We have noted that in Obeyesekere's book it unites Hawaiians and Sri Lankans in a common nativism that is historically and culturally adventitious, based on a remotely analogous common experience of Western domination. But what they can then be expected to have most in common are cultural exports of Western "civilization."

"Civilization" was a term coined in France in the 1750s and quickly adopted in England, becoming very popular in both countries in explication of their superior accomplishments and justification of their imperialist exploits (Bénéton 1975; Benveniste 1971:289–96; Elias 1978). The meaning was not the same as the sense of "culture" as a way of life that is now proper to anthropology. Among other differences, "civilization" was not pluralizable: it did not refer to the distinctive modes of existence of different societies but to the ideal order of human society in general (Stocking 1968, chap. 4; 1987, chap. 1). The lack of synonymy between "civilization" and "culture" is interesting in light of the academic memories currently in vogue to the effect that anthropology was born of the Western colonial experience, as handmaiden to imperialism—a complicity with power from which it has never intellectually freed itself. The moral attractiveness of these memories, however, need not blind us to their historical selectivity. For, "culture" of the modern anthropological persuasion originated in Germany, also in the late eighteenth century, but precisely in defiance of the global pretensions of Anglo-French "civilization" (Berlin 1976, 1982:1–24, 1993; Berlin and Jahanbegloo 1991:99–108; Elias 1978). In contrast, the Age of Discovery had not actually discovered "culture" so much as "barbarians" and "savages" (cf. Padgen 1982). As a general rule, Western Europeans lacked what Todorov (1984:189) calls "perspectivism"; for them, the indigenous others were stages in a unitary scale of progress whose apex was their own "civilization." Nor did the philosophers of this civilization seem to notice that such contemplation of the self in, and as, negative reflexes of the other contradicted the principles of inductive reason by which enlightenment was supposed to be acquired. For the philosophes and their intellectual heirs, human nature was one—and perfectible by the exercise of right reason on clear and distinct perceptions. Rousseau apart, the inferior stages of human development were seen as burdened with superstition and other irrational impediments to earthly progress. There was little room here for cultural distinction except as the mark of inferiority or the survival of delusion—and the watchword was, "Ecrasez l'infâme!"[6]

For the German bourgeois intellectuals, however, bereft of power or even political unity, cultural differences became essential. Defending a national *Kultur* at once against the rationalism of the philosophes and a Francophile Prussian court, Herder (most notably) opposed ways of life to stages of development and a social mind to natural reason (Herder 1968, 1969). Unlike "civilization," which was transferable between peoples (as by a beneficent imperialism), culture was what truly identified and differentiated a

---

6. It was not among the Western European imperialist nations—Spain, Portugal, Holland, England, or France—that an appreciation of cultures as distinctive modes of experience and existence was born. True, a certain number of skeptics and critics of "civilization" and its pretensions came forth, defending the virtues, the customs, and sometimes the rights of its colonial victims (see Padgen 1982; Vyerberg 1989). But rarely did they achieve a true "perspectivism" or "pluralism" (Berlin 1991). On the contrary, if Montaigne, Rousseau, Raynal, or Diderot celebrated exotic others for living closer to nature than Europeans did, the "nature" they thus celebrated was a European invention. The judgments remained absolute in form and Western in provenance. In their simplicity, liberty, bravery, or sexuality, the Indians might be better able to live up to these European values; even as, on the other hand, Europeans were surpassing the noble Indians "in every form of barbarity" (Montaigne 1958:156). Such local reversals of the ideology notwithstanding, it was precisely the global contrast of civilization and barbarism that imperialism put on the anthropological agenda (see also Rousseau 1984, Montesquieu 1966, Diderot 1972, and Wolpe 1957). The best approaches to perspectivism, it seems, were the fictional parodies of Swift (*Gulliver's Travels*) and Montesquieu (*Persian Letters*).

people (as from the superficial French manners of the Prussian aristocracy). Culture came in kinds, not degrees; in the plural, not the singular. Nor could there be any uncultured peoples as there were uncivilized ones. "Only a real misanthrope," Herder said, "could regard European culture as the universal condition of our species" (in Barnard 1969:24n). Each people knows their own kind of happiness: the culture that is the legacy of their ancestral tradition, transmitted in the distinctive concepts of their language, and adapted to their specific life conditions. It is by means of this tradition, endowed also with the morality of the community and the emotions of the family, that experience is organized, since people do not simply discover the world, they are taught it. They come to it not simply as cognitions but as values. To speak of reasoning correctly on objective properties known through unmediated sensory perceptions would be epistemologically out of the question. Seeing is also a function of hearing, a *judgment*, and in the economy of thought—what Herder (1969:163–64) once spoke of as "the family or kinship mode of thought"—reason is invested with feeling and bound to imagination. It follows that the senses are culturally variable: "The North American can trace his enemy by the smell. . . . the shy Arab hears far in his silent desert. . . . The shepherd beholds nature with different eyes from those of the fisherman" (Herder 1968:38–39, 1969:300). Such counter-Enlightenment discourse could be summed up by noting that what was *error* for the empirical realists, the transubstantiation one swallowed along with the holy wafer, became *culture* for Herder (see Dumont 1986; Berlin 1976, 1991: 70–90; Manuel 1968; Barnard 1969; Lovejoy 1948).

The anthropological concept of culture as a specific form of life thus emerged in a relatively underdeveloped region, and as an expression of that comparative backwardness, or of its nationalist demands, as against the hegemonic ambitions of Western Europe. What could it mean to be German in the absence of a country? "Culture" defined the unity and demarcated the boundaries of a people whose integrity was politically equivocal (Elias 1978:5–6). At the same time, the term articulated a certain resistance to economic and political developments that threatened the people's past as well as their future:

> *Kultur* theories can be explained to a considerable extent as an ideological expression of, or reaction to, Germany's political, social and economic backwardness in comparison with France and England. . . .
> These Kultur theories [Russian as well as German] are a typical ideological expression—though by no means the only one—of the rise of

backward societies against the encroachments of the West on their traditional culture. (Meyer 1952 : 404–5)

Speaking likewise of the German reaction "to the dominant cosmopolitan French culture" by the assertion of their own identity, Dumont (1986 : 590) describes this as "perhaps the first example of a peripheral culture acculturating to modernity on the ideological level."

Now, two hundred years later, a marked self-consciousness of "culture" is reappearing all over the world among the victims and erstwhile victims of Western domination—and as the expression of similar political and existential demands.[7] This culturalism, as it has been called, is among the most striking, and perhaps most significant, phenomena of modern world history (Dominguez 1992; Turner 1993; Appadurai 1991; Sahlins 1993). Ojibway Indians in Wisconsin, Kayapō in Brazil, Tibetans, New Zealand Maori, Kashmiris, New Guinea Highland peoples, Zulus, Eskimo, Mongols, Australian Aboriginals, and (yes) Hawaiians: all speak of their "culture," using that word or some close local equivalent, as a value worthy of respect, commitment and defense. A response to the planetary juggernaut of Western capitalism, their struggles recreate, if on a wider scale and in more critical form, the opposition to bourgeois-utilitarian reason that first gave rise to an understanding of cultures as distinct forms of life.

But the modern struggles are also unlike the old, since all kinds of new cultural entities, processes, and relationships are in play—transnational cultures, global flows, ethnic enclaves, diasporic cultures. Eclipsing the traditional anthropology-cultures, this planetary reorganization of forms expresses itself in a postmodern panic about the concept of culture itself. All that is solid seems to melt into air. So, at this transitional moment, the notion of culture is in jeopardy: condemned for its excessive coherence and systematicity, for its sense of boundedness and totality. Just when so many people are announcing the existence of their culture, advanced anthropolo-

---

7. The modern self-consciousness of "culture" is not intellectually discontinuous with the Herderian original, inasmuch as the latter, too, was sustained by anticolonialism: "No Nimrod has yet been able to drive all the inhabitants of the World into one park for himself and his successors; and though it has been for centuries the object of united Europe, to erect herself into a despot, compelling all nations of the Earth to be happy in her way, this happiness-dispensing deity is yet far from having obtained her end. . . . Ye men of all the quarters of the Globe, who have perished in the lapse of ages, ye have not lived and enriched the Earth with your ashes, that at the end of time your posterity should be made happy by European civilization" (Herder 1968 : 78; cf. Berlin 1976 : 168–72).

gists are denying it. Menaced by a hyperrationality on one side, the regard for cultural difference or the possibility of diverse human worlds is thus beset by an exaggerated irrationality on the other. Nor are these the only abuses the noble culture must suffer. For, inside the academy, the word has altogether escaped anthropological control—along with "anthropology" itself—and fallen into the hands of those who write liberally about "the culture of addiction," "the culture of sensibility," "the culture of autobiography." "Culture," it seems, is in the twilight of its career, and anthropology with it.

May the owl of Minerva take wing at dusk. It is with these afflictions of "culture" in mind that I write of our rationality and Hawaiian belief, and of the remote ideas entailed in the remote death of Captain Cook. Just to prove Obeyesekere mistaken would be an exercise as picayune in value as it would be in difficulty. What guides my response is a concern to show that commonsense bourgeois realism, when taken as a historiographic conceit, is a kind of symbolic violence done to other times and other customs. I want to suggest that one cannot do good history, not even contemporary history, without regard for ideas, actions, and ontologies that are not and never were our own. Different cultures, different rationalities.

This book is organized to answer to the larger issues of comparative rationality and complementary questions of cultural order raised by the narratives and interpretations of Captain Cook's apotheosis in Hawaii. Rectifications of Obeyesekere are generally placed in a peripheral relation to the text: briefer responses in footnotes and more extended comments in appendixes. (The latter will be referenced as A.1, A.2, A.3, etc., in the margins of the main text, adjacent to the discussion to which they are apposite.)[8] The first two chapters concern Cook's career as a form of the year god Lono, respectively in life and after death. Here I rehearse many interpretations made previously, in a way that will give some idea of the historical issues to those unfamiliar with them, while at the same time emphasizing those that have been disputed. The third chapter considers Obeyesekere's alternative theories of Cook's life and death at Hawaii, with an eye toward how an appeal to a universal empirical rationality turns Hawaiian history into pidgin anthropology. The fourth and final chapter is mainly an exami-

8. Too many of Obeyesekere's criticisms have the quality of bad character references, in that they have nothing to do directly with the issue of Cook's godliness but endeavor to show that even in regard to minor and tangential historical details my work is not to be trusted. I am thus obliged to document that Obeyesekere's charges and insinuations of this sort are false, which will require considerable space in footnotes and appendixes.

nation of Hawaiian concepts of rationality and of what there is, especially in the matter of gods and their worldly manifestations, compared to common-sense or common-"native" versions of Hawaiian belief. This chapter also discusses well-documented cases of the treatment of Europeans as spiritual beings in the Pacific, up to and including the apotheoses of modern anthropologists. Such deification is no European myth, either in New Guinea, the Cook Islands, or in Hawaii. The work concludes with a brief epilogue, again concerned with rationality, or the pseudo-politics of historical interpretation.

ONE

Captain Cook
at Hawaii

einrich Zimmermann heard it directly from Hawaiians: Cook was Lono.[1] J. C. Beaglehole, the great historian of Cook's voyages, characterized Zimmermann as "the jack of all trades from the Palatine who liked to wander and wrote a little book about the voyage and the great captain" (1967: lxxxix). An ordinary seaman aboard the *Discovery*, Zimmermann kept some abbreviated notes in German on his experiences, which he managed to hold on to despite the Admiralty's attempt to sequester all shipboard records of the expedition. The Admiralty's intention was to prevent other accounts from reaching print before the officially sponsored version (Cook and King 1784). Zimmermann, however, was able to forestall the official publication with his own *Reise um die Welt mit Capitaine Cook.* This appeared in 1781, the year after the return of the expedition (there was no English edition until 1926). Undistinguished for its accuracy or knowledge, Zimmermann's slim volume is of little value according to Beaglehole, except for its lower-deck impressions of Cook. Yet it also sets down some Hawaiian impressions of Lono-Cook—in a decipherable transcription of the Hawaiian language.

The first vernacular quotation appears in Zimmermann's discussion of the gods. The Hawaiians, he says, "have a great many . . . which they name after their king and chiefs" (Zimmermann 1988:95). The seaman thus reverses Hawaiian naming relations between gods and chiefs (cf. Valeri 1985: 145), a mistake he repeats when speaking of the connection between Cook and an image of Lono:

---

1. As has become customary in Hawaiian studies, the glottalized form "Hawai'i" refers to the island of that name, while the unmarked "Hawaii" and "Hawaiian" refer to the entire archipelago.

They made a god of Captain Cook on the Island of O-waihi and erected an idol in his honor. They called this "O-runa no te tuti," "O-runa" meaning god and "tuti" Cook. This god was made after the pattern of the others but was adorned with white feathers instead of red, presumably because Cook being a European had a fair complexion. (Zimmermann 1988:95–96 [1781:77])

The phrase "O-runa no te tuti" is reasonably glossed as 'Cook is indeed Lono.' It occurs again in Zimmermann's second citation of Hawaiian speech. Here Zimmermann refers to the occasion when Lieutenant King led a large party towards the shore of Kealakekua Bay for the purpose of negotiating the return of Cook's body.[2] King was kept waiting nearly an hour for a response, during which time the other boats approached the shore and entered into conversations with Hawaiians there. Zimmermann's text indicates he was present—"We held the five boats at a short distance from the land"—and reports one of the interviews. The Hawaiians, he wrote,

showed us a piece of white cloth as a countersign of peace but mocked at ours and answered as follows: "O-runa no te tuti Heri te moi a popo Here mai" which means: "The god Cook is not dead but sleeps in the woods and will come tomorrow." (1988:103 [1781:88])

The Hawaiian here is again decipherable, but it is more straightforward than Zimmermann's translation: "Cook is indeed Lono; he is going to sleep; tomorrow he will come"—no death, no woods. The apparently curious statement fits into the range of European accounts of the incident, all of which cite Hawaiians to the effect that Cook would be returned the next day, while describing his existing condition as anywhere from dead and cut to pieces, to alive and sleeping with a young girl (Anonymous of Mitchell 1781). Mr. King speaks only of the dismemberment and the message from the Hawaiian king, Kalani'ōpu'u, "that the body was carried up the country; but that it should be brought to us the next morning" (Cook and King 1784, 3:64; cf. Beaglehole 1967:554). David Samwell attributes the statement

2. Zimmermann incorrectly recollected this episode as occurring on 15 February 1779, the day after Cook's death; by the accounts of Mr. King and others, it took place in the late afternoon of 14 February. The rest of Zimmermann's report of the affair is consistent with the general record.

that Cook was not dead to the royal emissary Hiapo, and describes it as part of an attempt to lure Lieutenant King to shore (Beaglehole 1967:1206). An analogous report by an unknown party, apparently also a participant, confirms that Zimmermann's version is not aberrant:

> after waiting some time Mr. King began to doubt the sincerity of there [sic] promise of bringing the Body and again put the question to this he was answered that Capt Cook was not Dead and desired Mr. King to come on shore and see, but being again told that we knew he was they gave for answer that we would not have it before Morning being a great distance up the Country. (Anonymous of NLA Account, 11)

Obeyesekere writes: "If Cook was the god Lono arrived in person, it is strange that the ship's journalists, in spite of constant probing, could not find this out; or that Hawaiians, in response to constant probing, could not state this as a fact" (Ob. 95).[3] Something is indeed "strange," since Obeyesekere cites Zimmermann's text on idols, and even "O-runa no te tuti," although he does not translate the sentence or refer to its second mention. He also allows that this text—as well as a passage in Rickman's journal about Cook as "their E-a-tu ah-nu-ah" (*akua nui*, 'great god')—would give the captain the status of Lono. So did they or didn't they say it? No, they did not. According to Obeyesekere, this kind of talk was just shipboard gossip. "O-runa no te tuti" was Haole scuttlebutt: "It is virtually certain that Zimmermann's idea that Hawaiians thought of Europeans as immortal, or that Cook was a god, comes from their own shipboard traditions" (Ob. 123). This means the fo'c'sle hands are gossiping about Cook in Hawaiian—which is at least a greater show of respect for their linguistic capacities than Obeyesekere usually accords them. On the other hand, the Hawaiians' words have been taken from them.[4]

It will be useful to keep an on-going catalogue déraisonné of Obeyesekere's arguments, as he comes up with some original additions to the known fauna of historiographic fallacies. The example in the previous paragraph

A.1

What the Sailors Knew

---

3. The idea that Cook was Lono "in person," as contrasted to an actualization of Lono, is neither a Hawaiian concept nor mine, although Obeyesekere often alleges it is mine and does not investigate theirs (see below, chap. 4 and 196n).

4. "The Hawaiian versions of Cook's apotheosis came from accounts of native scholars and missionaries after the Hawaiians had overturned the tabu system in 1819, and the first American evangelical missions had begun to arrive (the following year)" (Ob. 49–50).

might be christened "double-bind question begging." It consists of two propositions. First, the absence of a European mention that Cook = Lono means that for Hawaiians Cook was not Lono. And second, the presence of a Hawaiian mention of Cook = Lono is an indication of the European myth to that effect. In other words, the European non-assertion is evidence of Hawaiian realities, while the Hawaiian assertion is evidence of European beliefs. Obeyesekere's thesis is thus confirmed when the Haole do not say what they are supposed to say, or else when the Hawaiians say what they are not supposed to. More species in due course.[5]

The remainder of this chapter reviews the events of Cook's visits to Hawaii in 1778 and 1779, with an emphasis on the documentary evidence that he was greeted in Hawai'i island as a personification of the New Year god Lono. It will be impossible to rehearse all the details; the reader may wish to consult earlier works I have offered on the subject as well as the major historical sources cited therein: Sahlins 1981, 1985a, 1985b, 1988, and 1989.[6] But first, to situate the reports penned by Zimmermann and many

5. A coda to Zimmermann's "They made a god of Captain Cook on the Island of O-waihi and erected an idol in his honor." Something like that actually happened to the fur trader, Nathaniel Portlock. In June 1786, when Portlock was at Ni'ihau, the ruling chief "Abbenooe" ('Ōpūnui) asked for an armchair from the cabin of the *Queen Charlotte,* ostensibly for the wife of his superior, Kā'eo of Kaua'i. On a second visit, in February of 1787, 'Ōpūnui escorted Portlock on a tour of the Waimea area in Kaua'i:

> After gratifying my curiosity amongst the plantations my friend accompanied me to a large house situated under hills on the west side [of] the valley, and about two or three miles from the sea beach. . . . on the left side of the door was a wooden image of a tolerably large size, seated in a chair, which nearly resembled one of our armed chairs; there was a grass-plot all round the image, and a small railing made of wood; beside the chair were several to-e's [adzes, which traders fashioned in iron, on the model of Hawaiian stone adzes] and other small articles. My friend informed me that this house had been built with the to-e I had given them on my first calling at Oneehow [Ni'ihau], and that the other articles were presents that I had made him at different periods, *and that the image was in commemoration of my having been amongst them.* Few people were admitted into this house. (Portlock 1789: 192–93; emphasis added)

6. Obeyesekere also cites a reprinted version (Sahlins 1982) of the first article I did on the Cook/Lono issue, "The Apotheosis of Captain Cook" (Sahlins 1978), which includes certain interpretations I had abandoned by 1980 (cf. Sahlins 1981). In a note to the chapter on Cook in *Islands of History* (which was scheduled to appear first in French) I referred to the French translation of that original article (Sahlins 1979), and warned that my "ideas of Cook's presence and death in Hawaii, and of the nature of the Hawaiian New Year Festival (Makahiki) have been substantially altered by subsequent research" (Sahlins 1985a: 104n). Understandably, the complex history of translation and republication of this piece of juvenilia escaped Obeyesekere's notice, as apparently did my warning against identifying positions stated there with later reflections on Cook.

others of Cook's company, I present a general outline of the Hawaiian New Year ritual, the Makahiki festival. It will also be necessary to discuss the correlation between the Hawaiian lunar calendar, by which the Makahiki was ordered, and the Gregorian calendrical coordinates of the Cook visit.

Captain Cook and the Makahiki Festival, 1778–79

The issues presented by Captain Cook's appearance off Maui and Hawai'i island late in the year of 1778 were cosmological. It was the time of the Makahiki, the annual rebirth of nature configured as an elemental cosmic drama. From early December to mid-January, the *Resolution* and *Discovery* circumnavigated practically the whole of Hawai'i in a clockwise direction, reproducing the procession made on land, along the coast, by the image of Lono during this season. Writing to the Admiralty Secretary about Cook's death at Hawaiian hands some weeks later, Captain Clerke observed that even on that fatal day the famous navigator "was received with the accustomed respect they [the Hawaiians] upon all occasions paid him, which more resembled that due to a Deity than a human being" (Beaglehole 1967: 1536). The British were well aware that "the title of Orono [Lono], with all its honours, was given to Captain Cook" (Cook and King 1784, 3:159). They understood "Orono" to be some sort of abstract status—not just a personal name as Obeyesekere contends—for they frequently allude to Cook as "the Orono" (with the article) in their journals, as if the Hawaiians were speaking thus. The seamen were given to referring to Hikiau temple, where Cook had undergone certain rituals on first landing, as "Cook's altar." Indeed from many circumstances it was clear to Mr. King that the islanders held the British as a lot in extraordinary estimation: "they regard us a Set of beings infinitely their superiors" (Beaglehole 1967: 525). But for all that, the Haole had not fathomed what "the Orono" meant to the Hawaiians; nor did they know that their visit had fallen within the special months of the Makahiki (see appendix 1).

This makes the detailed correspondence between the incidents they naively recorded and particular observances of the New Year festival all the more remarkable. On the other hand, probably because it was so extraordinary, the coincidence of Cook and the Makahiki was not unknown to the old folks around Lahaina and elsewhere whose recollections of the events were recorded in the 1830s by Hawaiian students of the American mission high school. Arranged and piously embellished by Rev. Sheldon Dibble, these accounts were published in 1838 under the title of *Ka Mooolelo Hawaii*

(Hawaiian History).[7] They say Hawaiians had considered Cook—or "Lono" as they still knew him—the returning god of the Makahiki time (Kahananui 1984:17–23, 171–75).

A festival of four lunar months in all, the Makahiki was marked at a certain point by the reappearance of the exiled god cum deposed king Lono. The god was embodied in a wooden image and a manifestation called Lono-makua, 'Father Lono' or 'Lono the Parent.' The name is a metaphor of the god's seasonal existence. Circuiting Hawai'i for the better part of the lunar month Welehu, the last month of the Hawai'i island year, Lono effected the regeneration of nature together with the renewal of the kingship and human society. As in cognate ceremonies in other Polynesian islands, the beneficial passage of the returned god is associated with the reappearance of the Pleiades on the horizon after sunset in late November—an event that in 1778 occurred a few days before Captain Cook appeared off Maui.[8] This was also the period of winter rains in Hawaii, rains which mediate a double transition of nature resonant with cosmological significance: from "the dying time of the year" to the time when "bearing things become fruitful," and from the season of long nights ($p\bar{o}$) to the season of long days (ao) (Beckwith 1932).

Initiated each year by the winter solstice, the turn from night to day, $p\bar{o}$ to ao, replicates the succession in the famous cosmogonic chant, Kumulipo, from the long night of the world's self-generation ($p\bar{o}$) to the ages of day or the world of mankind (ao). Midway through the creation, at the eighth of fifteen periods, the gods and men appear. Born together, as siblings, they are destined to be locked in fraternal strife. The first god, Kāne, and the first man, Ki'i, are rivals over the means of their reproduction: their own elder sister, La'ila'i. The struggle is presented as the condition of the possibility of human existence in a world in which the life-giving powers are divine. Man

7. Obeyesekere does not consider the *Mooolelo Hawaii* a credible source of Hawaiian memories of Cook on grounds that the book was arranged and edited by the missionary Sheldon Dibble, who must have had it in for Cook for playing god. This issue is discussed further along in the present chapter.

8. New Year rituals in other Polynesian islands and Fiji entailed the same general scenario of the return of the ancient god or the ancestors to inseminate the land, and had a number of specific resemblances to the Hawaiian Makahiki. These similarities are discussed in a previous article (Sahlins 1989:394–96) in response to the assertion—with which Obeyesekere is in agreement—that the Makahiki as we know it was constituted by Kamehameha around the turn of the nineteenth century. Still another work (Sahlins 1985b) shows the detailed correspondances between Hawaiian Makahiki ceremonies and the rituals of the Maori agricultural cycle. The former represents a hierarchical version of the latter, the king in Hawaii taking the encompassing role of warrior man, thus capturing the benefits of the god's passage. Obeyesekere does not take notice of these discussions.

wins a victory of a certain kind, although it needs to be constantly renewed. The end of the eighth chant thus announces the human era, day *(ao)*: "Man spread abroad, man was here now, / It was day" (Beckwith 1972:98). This indeed was the triumph annually repeated over Lono, the fertilizing god, at the New Year: representing humanity, the king retook the bearing earth.

In the Kumulipo creation chant, the same drama is played out between the triad of Kāne, Ki'i, and the one who mediates the transfer of powers between them, La'ila'i. The older sister of god and man, La'ila'i is the first-born and heiress of all the earlier eras of divine creation. She personifies the pivotal role of woman; she is uniquely able to transform divine into human life. In Hawaiian descent ideology, women function analogously: they transfer sacred tabus from one descent line to another—hence the critical role of strategic marriages in contests of rule. So, in the Kumulipo, the issue in the struggle of the brothers (god and man) to possess La'ila'i was cosmological in scope and content, and political in form. Yet, since the man's name, Ki'i, means 'image' while Kāne means 'man,' everything has already been said. The first god is 'man' and the first man is 'god' (the image). Hence, in the sequel the statuses of human and divine are interchanged by La'ila'i's actions. To the rage of Kāne, who has prior claim on her, La'ila'i illicitly takes Ki'i as a second husband, and her children by the upstart man are born first. The children of man become senior to the god's progeny:

> Kane was angry and jealous because he slept last with her,
> His descendants would hence belong to the younger line,
> The children of the elder would be lord,
> First through La'ila'i, first through Ki'i,
> Children of the two born in the heavens there
> > Came forth.

> > > (Beckwith 1972:106)[9]

9. In a curious statement, Obeyesekere asserts: "Nowhere in the *Kumulipo* is there any reference to an original triad in Sahlins's sense" (Ob. 232n.14). This is patently false. Obeyesekere simply disregards the drama constituted by chants 8 to 10, part of which is quoted here, together with Beckwith's (1972:99–100) explication of the text. The struggle devolves on three characters appearing in chant 8: the first-born woman La'ila'i, the original man Ki'i, and the first-born god Kane. As the succeeding verses explain, La'ila'i "sat sideways," meaning she took a second husband, Ki'i, and their children became superior to Kane's offspring by La'ila'i. Obeyesekere merely cites the lines of the eighth chant that tell of the successive births of La'ila'i, Ki'i, Kane, and Kaneloa, also a god—thus proving there were more than three! This curious irrelevance is part of a more general sidetracking of the same sort concerning an observation I had made about Cook's death scene: the parallel between the aforementioned cosmogonic trio and the moment on 14 February 1779 when the king's wife intervenes on his side pleading with him not to go off with Lono (Cook) to the *Resolution* (see appendix 10). This is repudiated by

All the same, man remains dependent on the god for life. Without the generative intercession of the god, people can accomplish neither their own reproduction nor the production of the natural means of their existence. Everything happens as if these Polynesians were condemned to suffer their own version of Zeus's vengeance (for the famous deception practiced by Prometheus). As Vernant describes it, Zeus's fury was likewise the consequence of human hubris: the duplicitous sacrifice prepared by Prometheus (in Gordon 1981:43–79). Having offered the god the inedible portions of the ox, while reserving the delicious food for themselves, men were thenceforth and forever destined to exhaust themselves filling their bellies. In Polynesia the theft of the bearing earth (woman) made men forever dependent on the ancient, transcendent and divine powers of procreation.[10] Polynesians were ever and again engaged with the divine in a curious combination of submission and opposition whose object was to transfer to themselves the life that the gods originally possess, continue to detain, and alone can bestow. By successive rituals of supplication and expropriation, the god is invited into the human domain, to give it life, and then banished that mankind may take possession of the divine benefits. "Man, then, lives by a kind of periodic deicide" (Sahlins 1985a:113). Hence the annual rehearsal in the Makahiki of the victory described in the Kumulipo. Respectively represented by Lono and the king, the original struggle of god and man was repeated with the sovereignty and possession of the earth at stake. Hawaiian traditions make the same connections with the foreigner they called Lono: on first landing at Kealakekua during the Makahiki period (of 1778–79), Captain Cook was escorted to the great temple of Hikiau where, it is said, the Kumulipo was chanted before him, in his honor (Beckwith 1972:9).

The Kumulipo had been composed for the tabu chief Ka'I'imamao, a previous ruler of Hawai'i island, whose son Kalani'ōpu'u was the king known to Cook. In the chant, the royal child is called "Lono of the Makahiki" (Lonoikamakahiki), which is also the name of a famous kingly predecessor of Ka'I'imamao in the capacity of Lono. Hawaiians relate very similar traditions of the god Lono, the original King Lonoikamakahiki, and of Ka'I'imamao: traditions that have structural analogies both with the cosmogonic ri-

---

saying that "The idea of an *original triad* is, I think, influenced by Christian ideas" (Ob. 181; emphasis in original).

10. One possible reading of the succeeding chant 11, where Ki'i's descendants are subject to usurpation by a warrior stock (the cock on the back of Wakea), to a flood, and to death, is that this is the punishment of man's original hubris. As excessive potency to the exclusion of the gods was the crime, impotency without divine concourse is the effect.

valry of god and man and with the historic fate of Captain Cook. Telling of the usurpation and banishment of the god by a more humanized warrior figure, these several stories are linked by interchangeable personages and episodes—notably the seduction of the sacred woman by the god-king's human rival.[11] They are in turn linked to Cook not only by the analogies of myth and history, but by the fact that, taken in chronological (or genealogical) series, they convey just this sense of transformation from the one to the other. The effect is something like the observation Dumézil (1948) made about the contrasts between Indian mythology and Roman dynastic legends. Traditions of the early Latin kings repeat the mythical feats of the Indic gods, but precisely in a humanized form and a quasi-historical register. It is interesting that Martha Beckwith (1919:301–4) had already come to a similar conclusion about the progression from divine to human, the miraculous to the historical, within the body of Hawaiian traditions. Here the royal heroes prove to be the true successors of the gods by duplicating the divine exploits on the plane of earth: that is, in the compass of the Hawaiian islands and as deeds of political and intellectual prowess. Politics appears as the continuation of cosmogonic war by other means. Beckwith writes (1919:304):

> Gods and men are, in fact, to the Polynesian mind, one family under different forms, the gods having superior control over certain phenomena, a control which they may impart to their offspring on earth.

Just so with the several human manifestations of Lono: passing from the Kumulipo to Ka'I'imamao and Cook, the same stories are told. The triumph of the warrior associated with human sacrifice over the peaceful and productive god represents the appropriation by man of the fructified earth.

But the initial cosmic statements of this theme appear in later versions as struggles over sovereignty between legitimate kings of the blood, whose

11. Such transpositions of characters and events are common devices of Hawaiian and Polynesian mythology. Indeed, they are common the world over. But Obeyesekere understands them—particularly the episodes that identify the god with the first Lonoikamakahiki, and both with Cook—as confusions elaborated in the early 1820s by the English missionary William Ellis if not actually introduced by him (Ob. 157). Ignoring the recurrent structures in the several Lono traditions, Obeyesekere is thus able to preserve a certain innocence of the relationship between the god and his human actualizations: a relationship that neither exhausts the being of the former nor the humanity or individuality of the latter. The redundancies in the legends of the various Lono figures have been discussed elsewhere (Sahlins 11a:19854–15, 20b:19856–9). Obeyesekere also disregards these discussions. Too bad: as they speak of the movement from the mythic to the historic within the Lono tradition, they are of some value in understanding the Hawaiian reception of Cook.

superior tabus bespeak divinity, and warrior-usurpers whose junior rank indexes their (relative) humanity. The protohistorical Ka'I'imamao suffers the abduction of his wife by a rival who is his father's sister's son. In the ensuing battle, this king is banished, killed, or commits suicide, according to the version. If Cook, who by Hawaiian tradition had a liaison with the sacred woman of Kaua'i, met an analogous fate, he was not even the last of the historical Lonos. In O'ahu, the story will be repeated of local kings, in connection with successive conquests by Maui and Kamehameha of Hawai'i (Sahlins 1992, chap. 1).

The temple in which Cook was received on the 17th of January 1779—with ceremonies said to have included a recitation of the Kumulipo—was the one from which Lono departed in his annual circuit of the island, and to which he returned twenty-three days later to be greeted by the king. Hikiau temple at Kealakekua was one of the royal shrines (*luakini*) dedicated much of the year to the rituals of the war god Kū, with whom the king was specifically associated. However, during the period of the conjunction with the procreative aspect of the godhead, the season of Lono, the military god is in abeyance. Now the normal temple rites centering on Kū are suspended. The Makahiki season lasted nearly four lunar months, but the twenty-three day span of the Lono tabu, when the image of the god was abroad, was the climax of the ceremonies. It was a time of great popular festivities, of feasts, games, and amusements. Apart from certain tributary rites, all the other ceremonies of the Makahiki took place in the principal temples and thus concerned high chiefs and priests alone.[12] But the time of the god's appearance was one of general celebration: not only because of the feasts and amusements, but in virtue of the special *aloha* between the people and Lono. In certain myths, Lono is the original god, even as he is the major figure in

12. Repeating an error that had been made by previous commentators on Cook's reception at Hikiau temple, Obeyesekere finds it "strange" that if Cook were Lono, the god should be invited "to this place antithetic to his persona" (Ob. 83; cf. Sahlins 1989:397–98). This is a characteristic example of an appeal to Western common sense—what one finds "strange"—in preference to an examination of Hawaiian ethnography. A temple in the care of Lono priests, from which the god departs at the New Year, Hikiau was hardly antithetical to Lono. In the classic descriptions of the Makahiki, the king offers a pig to Lono in the temple at the end of the god's circuit of the island (Malo 1951:150; Kelou Kamakau 1919–20:44–45). Hence the fact that Captain Cook was escorted directly to Hikiau upon coming to anchor, where he was the object of the ceremonies that paralleled the formal reception of the Lono image (*hānaipū*) and the offering of a pig, afford evidence to the opposite effect of that imagined by Obeyesekere.

the domestic cult. His annual return, coinciding with the return of the sun and the revival of nature, is the occasion of collective joy.[13] It appears, moreover, that the Makahiki image of Lono is born of a symbolic union between the god and the women of the people, just as in some myths Lono descends from the heavens to mate with a beautiful woman of Hawaii. So, when Cook descended on Kealakekua Bay during the Makahiki season, the young women, observed David Samwell, were spending most of their time singing and dancing—in a certain marked manner, as he collected two lascivious hula chants in point (Sahlins 1985a: 15–16). The New Year was the great period of hula on Hawaii, even as the patron of the dance, the goddess Laka, is described in ancient chant as Lono's sister-wife.[14] The night before the Makahiki image is seen, there is a ceremony called 'splashing water' (*hiʻuwai*). Kepelino relates that sacred chiefs are carried to the water, where the people in their finery are bathing. In the excitement, "one person was attracted to another, and the result," says this Catholic convert, "was by no means good" (Beckwith 1932:96). When the people emerged at dawn from their amorous sport, the image of Lonomakua was standing on the beach (fig. 1.1).

The image is a tall, cross-piece affair, about three meters high, with white tapa cloth and skins of the *kaʻupu* bird suspended from the horizontal

13. The term *Makahiki* in early European sources almost always refers to the public ceremonial climax, the period of the Lono circuit; hence, the festival is typically described in this literature as lasting about one month. In the Hawaiian, "Makahiki" is used in several senses: its general meaning is "year," and it is also applied to the four-month New Year cycle as well as the specific twenty-three days of the Lono procession and celebrations. The last, by all evidence and for evident reasons, is the unmarked, popular acceptation of "Makahiki." So Malo, for example, speaks of the preparation of feast foods just before Lono's appearance as provisioning "against the coming of the Makahiki" (1951:143). I have discussed all this previously. Obeyesekere neglects this discussion and uses historical reports of a one-month ceremony—and one aberrant notice of a ten-day ceremony—to draw the incorrect conclusion that the Makahiki was more variable than I admit (Ob. 99–100). From historical notices I have plotted the timing for all Makahiki celebrations from 1778–79 to 1818–19, so far as possible, and made these determinations publicly accessible (see Sahlins 1989: 414n.1). The evidence shows substantial continuity and regularity of the celebrations. Obeyesekere does not acknowledge or discuss this data. His misunderstanding of the relation between public and temple events in the Makahiki, and of the correlation between the Gregorian calendar and the Makahiki rituals of 1778–79, is also the basis of his presumption that the British should have reported the unusual festivities—and of his reliance on the absence of such report again as a report of absence. The British finally landed thirteen days after the Lono procession was completed and saw (and reported) only a few terminal rites (see appendixes 4 and 5).

14. Handy (1927:210) makes the point about analogous Marquesan rituals that the dance would arouse the god, implying a Frazerian sacred marriage between the earthly women and the divine progenitor.

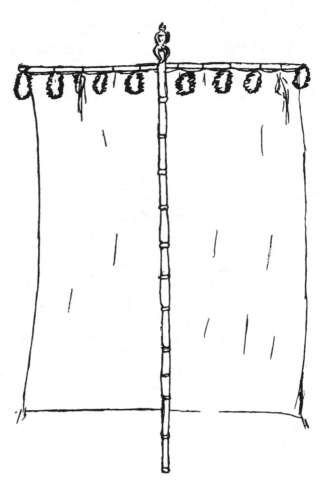

Fig. 1.1 Makahiki image.
(From Malo 1951. Repro-
duced courtesy of the
Bishop Museum,
Honolulu)

bar.[15] Its appearance on the beach initiates the tabu of Lono, which will last
for the twenty-three-day circuit. Peace is prescribed by the tabu, and putting
out to sea in canoes, as for fishing, is interdicted. "Peace" entails a suspension
of normal human occupations and of human control over the land, for the
god now marries or takes possession of it. His dominion will be signified by

15. S. M. Kamakau (1961:52–53) makes the specific connection between the emblem of
the Lono king, Lonoikamakahiki, and the Makahiki image, from both of which *ka'upu* birdskins
hung. The *ka'upu* is almost certainly the albatross, a migratory bird that appears in the western
Hawaiian chain—the white Lanyon albatross at Ni'ihau—to breed and lay eggs in October–
November, the beginning of the Makahiki period. Cross-piece images of the Makahiki sort

the tributes offered to the Makahiki image at the boundaries of each district *(ahupua'a)*. By contrast, the sovereignty of the king lapses while the god is abroad. The ruler is immobilized by the rule that he cannot leave the place where he began the Makahiki celebrations, at least until the completion of certain purification rites following the return and dismantling of the Maka-hiki image. But, while the king stays put, the principal image of Lonomakua, accompanied by certain gods of sport, undertakes its clockwise or "right circuit" of the island—that is, with the land on the right. A right circuit "signified a retention of the kingdom" (S. Kamakau 1976:5). Indeed, the food and property offered to the god in each district was collected the same way as royal tributes, through the local land stewards *(konohiki)*. Lono re-claims what was once his. But immediately after they make the offerings that acknowledge the god's dominion, the people of the district enter into ritual combat with those in Lono's retinue. Apparently the local people gain the victory, since the god's tabu is lifted: the fertilized land may now be entered. In contrast to the popular joy that now begins, however, the image of Lono is carried out of the district facing backward, "so that the 'wife' can be seen" (Ii 1959:72).[16]

The god fructifies and then cedes district after district, a process that is generalized and encompassed at the end of the circuit by a climactic en-

---

were used in the Marquesas and Tahiti as signs of truce or peace, hence analogously to the Lono figure, whose appearance inaugurates a prescribed time of peace.

Handy (1927:131) makes a general observation regarding Polynesian New Year rituals and the breeding of migratory birds: "It is possible that the observed departure and return, or pas-sage, of migratory birds at certain seasons had something to do with the idea of the departure and return of ancestral deities and gods of fertility in the Fall and Spring, and the presence or absence of the gods at certain seasons."

16. Aside from the main Makahiki image, also known as the 'long god,' *(akua loa)*, there were one or more 'short gods' of similar form *(akua poko)*—apparently one in each major chief-dom division *(moku)*—which traveled left along the shore and returned to the temple of origin on an inland path (Malo 1951:148–49; Anonymous of Kohala 1916–17:192–217). Not much more is known about these images. Obeyesekere falsely alleges that "Sahlins omits the reverse circumambulation of the 'short god'" (Ob. 64), footnoted by the observation that, although Sahlins has written about land-sea oppositions in Fiji, "yet he does not apply them to Hawai'i" (Ob. 212n.44). I have discussed the opposition between the long god and the short god of the Makahiki in a work to which Obeyesekere often refers, *Historical Metaphors* (Sahlins 1981:19, 73), as well as in a work to which he never refers (Sahlins 1985b:216). In the former, I offer the interpretation that the opposition of circuits represents the contrast between Lono's ascen-dancy and the king's submission at this time. For, the short god not only travels to the left, but, from John Papa 'I'i's (1959:75–76) description relative to O'ahu in the early nineteenth cen-tury, it apparently travels to the king's personal lands (Kailua and Kaneohe, sites of important royal estates according to Māhele land records). Obeyesekere often alleges I failed to say things I did say—and just as often attributes statements to me that I did not say.

gagement with the king. Resuming all local battles, the king achieves the final victory for mankind. This ritual conflict is called *kāli'i*. The term can be glossed 'to strike the king,' 'to act the king,' or 'to be made king'—all of which now happen. Returned from its progress and defended by a great body of armed warriors, the image of Lono stands on the shore before the temple from which it departed (Hikiau temple at Kealakekua, in the Hawai'i island tradition). The king, also with a warrior host, had beforehand gone out to sea, and now comes in by canoe to meet the god. (The scene is a reenactment of the foreign origin of Hawai'i rulers: kings of human sacrifice who came from Kahiki, foreign lands beyond the horizon, and displaced the original dynasty of tabu chiefs; see Sahlins 1992, chap. 1.) The king lands, preceded by a warrior champion who is expert at parrying spears. The

champion deflects the first of two spears aimed at the ruler. But the second spear, carried on the run, touches him. It is a symbolic death, or the king's death as a foreign being, which is also his rebirth as an Hawaiian sovereign. The tabu on him is lifted, and his warriors charge ashore to enter the lists against the defenders of Lono in a massive sham battle. The transformation of the king from outsider to sovereign is achieved through, and as, the encompassment of the ancient deity and legitimate king, Lono. Conqueror becomes ruler through the appropriation of the productive and indigenous god. Assuming the attributes of his divine predecessor, the king will soon reopen the temples to normal rituals, including the major temples and fishing shrines of Kū, and the therapeutic and agricultural houses of Lono. It deserves reemphasis that the renewal of the kingship to the benefit of mankind, if at the expense of Lono's reign, coincides seasonally with the rebirth of nature. In the ideal ceremonial calendar, the *kāli'i* battle follows the annual appearance of the Pleiades by thirty-three days: precisely, in the late eighteenth century, the twenty-first of December or the winter solstice. The King returns to power with the sun.[17]

Whereas, over the next two days, Lono plays the part of the sacrifice. The Makahiki effigy is dismantled and hidden away in a rite watched over by the king's "living god," Kahoali'i or 'The-Companion-of-the-King,' the one who is also known as 'Death-Is-Near' (Kokekamake). Close kinsman of the king as well as his ceremonial double, Kahoali'i swallows the eye of the victim in ceremonies of human sacrifice—a condensed symbolic trace of the cannibalistic "stranger-king." The man-god Kahoali'i passes the night prior

17. The calculations on which this conclusion is based are explained in Sahlins 1985a: 119n.

to the dismemberment of Lono in a temporary house called "the net house of Kahoali'i," set up before the temple structure where the image sleeps. In the myth pertinent to these rites, the trickster hero—whose father has the same name (Kūka'ohi'alaka) as the Kū-image of the temple—uses a certain "net of Maoloha" to encircle a house, entrapping the goddess Haumea, even as Haumea (or Papa) is a version of La'ila'i, the archetypal fertile woman, and the net used to entangle her had belonged to one Makali'i, 'Pleiades.' Just so, according to Malo, the succeeding Makahiki ceremony, following upon the putting away of the god, is called "the net of Maoloha," and represents the gains in fertility accruing to the people from the king's victory over Lono. A large, loose-mesh net, filled with all kinds of food, is shaken at a priest's command. Fallen to earth, and to man's lot, the food is the augury of the coming year. The fertility of nature thus taken by humanity, a tribute-canoe of offerings to Lono is set adrift for Kahiki, homeland of the gods. The New Year draws to a close. At the next full moon, a man (a tabu transgressor) will be caught by Kahoali'i and sacrificed. Soon after, the houses and standing images of the temple will be rebuilt: consecrated—with more human sacrifices—to the rites of Kū and the projects of the king.

Now, the question here is, how does the Makahiki cycle, known from descriptions penned by Hawaiians in the earlier part of the nineteenth century, including some who participated in the ceremonies at a mature age, and confirmed in various details by Western historical accounts going back as far as the late 1780s, how does this Makahiki scenario articulate with the events of Captain Cook's second visit to the Islands from 26 November 1778, when he came off northeastern Maui, to 14 February 1779, when he fell at Kealakekua Bay? An empirical issue for the most part, to be settled by comparing the Cook documents with the later Makahiki corpus, the question entails, however, a preliminary correlation of the Hawaiian lunar calendar with the Gregorian dates of the British visit, for the classic Hawaiian texts recount the sequence of Makahiki ceremonies by the dates of the Hawai'i island year. They describe a punctuated series of rites extending from the last months of the lunar year, 'Ikuwā and Welehu, into the first two months of the new year, Makali'i ('Pleiades') and Kā'elo. The climactic circuit of Lono would begin on 24 Welehu and end on 16 Makali'i, the day of the *kāli'i* battle between the king's partisans and the god's. The phases of the moon for Gregorian dates of 1778 and 1779 can be calculated by a known formula. But as a lunar year is only 354 days, it remains to be determined which Hawaiian months are indicated by these phases and thus correlated

A.4

Historiography of the Makahiki

Table 1.1

Optional Calendars of Major Makahiki Events, 1778–1779

	2 Ikuwa	24 Welehu	16 Makali'i	15 Kā'elo
	Makahiki begins	*Lono appears*	*End of Lono's circuit*	*End of Makahiki*
"November Makahiki"	22 Sept 1778	14 Nov 1778	6 Dec 1778	3 Jan 1779
"December Makahiki"	21 Oct 1778	14 Dec 1778	4 Jan 1779	2 Feb 1779

All Gregorian dates are c. ± 1 lunar. From Sahlins 1989:405.

with these Gregorian dates. To keep the lunar calendar in a rough correspondence with the sidereal year requires the intercalation of a lunar month three times over an eight-year span. This Hawaiians were known to do in the late eighteenth–early nineteenth centuries, but in an irregular, improvised fashion rather than by strict rule.[18] Still, the known historical variation can be useful in relating the Cook voyage to the Hawai'i calendar, as it sets the limits of possible correspondences between the two.

Within the limits of documented historical variations (from 1787 to 1819) in the Makahiki period, there are two reasonable options for 1778–79, which I hereafter call the "November Makahiki" and the "December Makahiki" (table 1.1). By the first possibility, the Makahiki would have begun on September 22, 1778, the procession of Lono occurring from the 14th of November to the sixth of December. In the December Makahiki, the season begins October 21, 1778, and the god's circuit runs from December 14 to January 4, 1779. These are the only reasonable options, because they already lie near the early and late extremes of the Makahiki as historically documented, and to push the dates another month either way would situate the ceremony beyond normal precedents (Sahlins MS). These options, again, are analytic possibilities for correlating dated Cook accounts with the

18. Evidence of the improvisational character of Hawaiian intercalation practices in the period 1779 to 1819 may be found in Sahlins (MS). In this manuscript—which has been publicly available since 1989, when notice of its archival deposit was published (Sahlins 1989: 414)—there is a detailed discussion of known political manipulations of the Makahiki calendar and rituals during these four decades. (See below, appendixes 4 and 5, for the relevance of this discussion to Obeyesekere's misunderstandings of the Makahiki calendar, the history of the ceremony, and my treatments of these issues.)

rites described by Malo *mā* (Malo 'folks') in terms of a Hawaiian lunar calendar: they do not refer to optional datings by Hawaiians or to my sudden discovery of such a possibility (as Obeyesekere has written).

By either of the possible correspondences, Captain Cook's second visit to the Islands in 1778–79 would overlap the period when the Makahiki god was abroad. In neither case could Cook's movements around Hawai'i (from 2 December 1778 to 17 January 1779) be synchronized precisely with Lonomakua's—a claim I have never made. But as we shall see, the parallels between incidents recorded in the Cook annals and specific rituals in the sequence described by Malo *mā* definitely favor the December Makahiki.

A.5
Calendrical
Politics

The Procession of Lono, 1778–79

"God is in the details"
—Mies van der Rohe

The *Resolution* (Captain James Cook) and the *Discovery* (Captain Charles Clerke) appeared on the horizon off northeastern Maui on the 26th of November, 1778, some ten months after their initial "discovery" of the Hawaiian Islands. About a week before, the Pleiades had appeared on the horizon at sunset, an event that normally precedes the advent of the Makahiki gods and their New Year circuit of the island (Ii 1959:72). Approaching Maui, the British ships first moved westward along the north coast, entering into some contact with Hawaiians coming off the island, and over the next few days they doubled back eastward, making for northwestern Hawai'i island on the first of December (maps 1.1 and 1.2). As recorded in the British journals, the encounters of the Haole with Hawaiians at Maui closely match the traditions of "Lono" (that is, Cook) collected by the students of the mission high school at Lahainaluna (Maui) in the mid 1830s. These are the traditions published in the *Mooolelo Hawaii* (Hawaiian History) which issued from the mission press in 1838 (Kahananui 1984:9–21, 167–75). Taken together, the British and local texts confirm that the Hawai'i islanders knew Captain Cook as "Lono" before they set eyes on him, and that his visit coincided with the (December) Makahiki festival.[19]

Captain Clerke's log entry for 26 November 1778 reads: "The first man on board told me he knew the ship very well, & had been on board her at

---

19. One should not be misled by the English section of the *Mooolelo Hawaii* (Kahananui 1984), which consistently translates the "Lono" of the Hawaiian text as "Captain Cook."

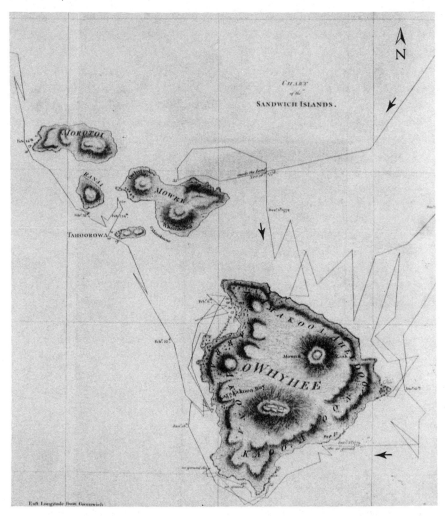

Map 1.1 Cook's track off Maui and Hawai'i, beginning 26 November 1778, and arriving at Kealakekua Bay on 17 January 1779. (From Cook and King 1784, vol. 3)

A tou I [Kaua'i] & related some anecdotes which convinc'd me of his veracity." According to Lieutenant King, the Hawaiians knew that the British had killed a man at Kaua'i in January; but all the same, if their manner was now "humble & fearfull of offending," they "appeard transported with joy" when they learned the British meant to stay a long while (Beaglehole

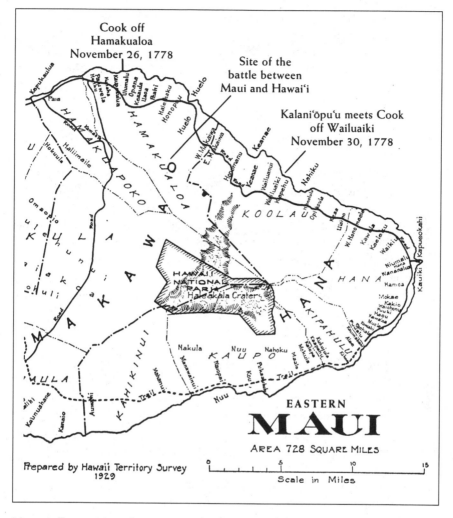

Map 1.2 Eastern Maui, showing sites of Kalani'ōp'u's battle (Hamakualoa) and the encampment (Wailuaiki), to which the king had retired, and from which he came out to Cook's ships. (From *Indices of Awards*, 1929)

1967:497). Midshipman Edward Riou describes the Hawaiians' great and general pleasure on the second day off Maui:

> This day our decks have been crowded with the Natives expressing the greatest joy & pleasure at the most trivial things that first repre-

sented itself to them, dancing and singing was all that could either be seen or heard. Many of the women scrambled up the Ship's side and was as soon turned away, when they abused us (finding that nothing could be done by fair word) most sincerely. (Riou Log, 28 November 1778 [P.M.])

I have elsewhere suggested that not enough attention has been paid to such testimonies of Hawaiian attitudes, gestures, and emotions when it comes to determining what Cook's visit meant to them. There is here a "whole history of popular desire and delight that parallels the chroniclers' descriptions of incidents and events" (Sahlins 1989:412). Recall that Lono is a popular god—the god of the men's domestic cult—and his annual progress around the island is a general fête. The pleasure recorded in the Haole accounts, moreover, is consistent with the news of the first British visit that had been transmitted from Kaua'i to Maui, according to the *Mooolelo Hawaii*. The news was that this was a visitation of Lono and a company of extraordinary *akua*, 'gods' (Kahananui 1984:10, 14). And this traditional notice again enters into a dialogue with the documentary evidence from late 1778 to indicate that indeed the Hawaiians at Maui *were already on the look-out for Lono*.

On the afternoon of November 30, a large sailing canoe bearing a man with a red feather cloak—hence, by the canoe and feather cloak, a chief (*ali'i*)—came out from northeastern Maui to the *Discovery*. This notable, according to the master Thomas Edgar, "Ask'd for our Arrona or Chief" (Edgar Log, 1 Dec 1778 [P.M.]; "Arrona" would be "O Lono," indicating a proper name). Edgar's naive report thus complements Hawaiian recollections as well as the historical testimonies of their pleasure: the return of the British to the Islands was immediately understood as a return of Lono.

Moreover, the people on Maui who so knew Cook in late November 1778 were actually warriors from Hawai'i island, led by their king, Kalani-'ōpu'u. On the same day (30 November) that Edgar was asked for Lono's whereabouts, Kalani'ōpu'u visited the ships—although the British did not then know he was the ruler of Hawai'i, and would not find out until he met them again at Kealakekua on the 25th of January following. Both British and Hawaiian sources confirm that Kalani'ōpu'u was on Maui fighting for the control of that island. Moreover, the details of that fighting, on which the Cook journals and *Mooolelo Hawaii* also corroborate each other, are consistent with the Makahiki calendar as classically described, supposing the December concordance was in effect. The *Mooolelo* indicates Kalani'ōpu'u had conquered the east coast prior to Cook's arrival and then fought further westward at Hāmākuloa (map 1.2). But, before Cook's arrival, he had retired eastward again to Wailua Iki, which is where the Hawai'i islanders met the British (Kahananui 1984: 13–16, 169–70). The Cook documents confirm this with some exactitude. William Ellis, surgeon's mate of the *Discovery*, reported that Kalani'ōpu'u fought a series of battles on Maui, "the last of which happened near the latter end of November, the time we first discovered the island" (Ellis 1782, 2:186). Moreover, the *Resolution* and *Discovery*, after earlier passing westward near the battle site of Hāmākuloa, first encountered Kalani'ōpu'u and his Hawai'i warriors on the last day of November further eastward, in the vicinity of Wailua Iki.[20] Now, during the circuit of Lono, the tabu of the god is in effect, interdicting warfare. By the earlier possible dating of the Makahiki of 1778–79, any fighting after mid-November would be a violation of the tabu; but Kalani'ōpu'u's withdrawal from battle in late November would be appropriate for the December Makahiki, as the god's progress was yet to come (table 1.1). According to the classical rules, moreover, the king is immobilized during the circuit of Lono, being released after certain purificatory ceremonies analogous to those of the ten-day seclusion of a royal heir following the death of his predecessor. We shall see that Kalani'ōpu'u's movements followed just that ritual schedule: he and his army remained in Maui during Cook's circumnavigation of Hawai'i; but they arrived in Kealakekua some eight days after the British, or at a date corresponding to the king's release from the Makahiki tabus (Sahlins 1989: 410–11).[21]

To resume the narrative of the circumnavigation, the *Resolution* and *Dis-*

20. Cook describes this encounter as taking place in the afternoon of the 30th "off the NE end of the island" (Beaglehole 1967:476). This must have been quite close to Wailua Iki, since the island of Hawai'i was not yet in view. It came in sight that evening (ibid.).

21. Obeyesekere attempts to argue that Kalani'ōpu'u was fighting on Maui during the time the Lono tabu should be in effect (from 14 December 1778 through 4 January 1779), indicating either that there was no such tabu or that the Hawai'i king was pleased to violate it (Ob. 80–81). His evidence for the dates of the fighting on Maui rests on a single statement by Lieutenant Rickman—a source he otherwise disparages on grounds of linguistic incompetence (Ob. 81, 72–73). On 17 January 1779 Rickman reported Kalani'ōpu'u was in Maui "settling the terms of peace," and that he would come into Kealakekua in about ten days. The latter observation corresponds to the scheduled ritual prescriptions of the Makahiki (Sahlins 1989:410–11), even as the former, if it were true, does not necessarily mean that there was fighting between 14 December and 4 January. Willing, nevertheless, to believe this is what Rickman's testimony indicates, Obeyesekere dismisses a priori the lieutenant's notice of Kalani'ōpu'u according Cook the status of "E-a-thu ah-nu-eh" (*Akua nui*, or 'great god'), as well as his report of a Ni'ihau or Kaua'i chief's idea that on leaving the Islands the British would visit the sun (Rickman 1966 [1781]:298, 332; Ob. 71–73).

covery came off the Kohala coast of Hawai'i island on the second of December, whence they would laboriously beat eastward against the wind. Long tacks sometimes took them out of sight of the land; at other times they might stand in to shore to "trade" for provisions (map 1.1). For awhile, also, the two ships lost touch, but they rejoined off the south coast of the island on January 6, 1779, and anchored together at Kealakekua on January 17. Concerning the trade with Hawaiian canoes, there is good evidence that coming out to sea was ritually prohibited at this time, which is also good evidence that the December Makahiki was on—and that, all the same, with a certain inducement from the British, the Hawaiians knew how to overcome their ritual scruples (Sahlins 1989:406–8).

Recall that during the 23-day procession of the god, the sea is in principle tabu. No canoes are allowed to venture off, as for fishing (with a certain exception to be noted presently).[22] Hence, if Cook were really the Lono of the Makahiki and this were indeed the period of the god's circuit, establishing contact with the British ships would pose an evident ritual dilemma. And it happens that the recollections of the old-timers recorded in the *Mooolelo* speak precisely to this problem.[23] Even more important here, they speak to

22. In Kepelino's account of the Makahiki (HEN 1:113–25), it is noted that the gods on circuit "passed either inland or by canoe." As I have indicated before (Sahlins 1989:416n.14), despite the descriptions by Malo *mā* of a progress by land only, this statement makes sense: if certain passages were effected by canoe, the journey could be done in 23 days, perhaps a difficult accomplishment otherwise. Also, if the god did take to the sea between certain districts (*ahupua'a*), Cook's circumnavigation would not be so unusual either.

23. With his usual scrupulousness, Obeyesekere alleges that "Sahlins implies" the *Mooolelo Hawaii* "was a product of the traditional priests of Kamehameha's time" (Ob. 159). This statement is not annotated for the good reason that I have not said or implied anything of the kind. He knows, and I know, that the information in the *Mooolelo* was gathered by the Lahainaluna high school students from Hawaiian old-timers—the "world's first oral history project" it has been called (see Finney et al. 1978). Sheldon Dibble in two places describes the method of compilation. In the preface to his own history, based on the *Mooolelo*, he wrote:

The method which I took to collect facts was as follows: I first made out a list of questions, arranged chronologically according to the best of my knowledge. I had continual occasion afterwards to add to the questions, to vary and to change them. I then selected ten of the best scholars of the Seminary, and formed them into a class of inquiry. I met them at an appointed hour, gave them the first question and conversed freely with them upon it, that they might understand fully and distinctly what was sought for. I then requested them to go individually and separately to the oldest and most knowing of the chiefs and people, gain all the information they could on the question given out, commit each his information to writing and be ready to read it on a day and hour appointed. At the time of meeting each scholar read what he had written—discrepancies were reconciled and corrections made by each other and then all the compositions were handed to me, out of which I endeavored to make one connected and true account.

its resolution: the ability of Hawaiians to flexibly and reflexively surmount an empirical contradiction in their own cultural terms—that is, without jettisoning their own concepts or constructions in favor of a universal perceptual realism (such as Obeyesekere recommends):

> At the time Lono (Cook) [this parenthetical "Cook" is not in the original Hawaiian, only "Lono"] arrived the people could not go out to sea in their canoes because it was the time for the annual gift giving ceremonies called the Makahiki. But because Lono had arrived by sea the people assumed it was perfectly proper for them to go out to sea in their canoes. The people were convinced Lono was really a god [*akua*] and his vessel was a temple [*heiau*]. (Kahananui 1984:171, cf. p. 17; also cited in Sahlins 1989:406)

As this passage in the *Mooolelo Hawaii* follows upon a discussion of Cook's entire circumnavigation, it implies the tabu was in effect during that period and thus supports the December dating of the Makahiki. Reciprocally, the Cook chronicles support the *Mooolelo's* account of tabu violations. On two occasions while off Hawai'i the British reported seeing white flags being waved at them from shore: a sign that a tabu was in effect—not a flag of truce as some of Cook's company believed. This happened at northern Kohala on 2 December 1778, or 12 Welehu by the December Makahiki calendar, which would be a scheduled temple rite (Malo 1951:142; cf. Ii 1959:72); then again near Cape Kumakahi on 19 December, being 29 Welehu, thus during the Lono tabu and procession (Riou Log, 2 Dec 1770; Cook in Beaglehole 1967:482–83; Roberts Log, 19 Dec 1778). On the second occasion (19 December) the British ships moved off before any canoes could reach them. However, Cook's own journal entry for the incident of December 2 is altogether consistent with the affirmation of the *Mooolelo* that,

---

Thus we proceeded from one question to another till a volume was prepared and printed in the Hawaiian language. (Dibble 1909:iii–iv)

Aside from noting that he added some ideas of his own, Dibble, in the shorter preface to the Hawaiian edition, indicates that stories of more recent years were written by adult students from their own recollections (Kahananui 1984:157).

Obeyesekere prefers to hold Dibble responsible not only for the obvious Christian interpolations in the *Mooolelo* but for the Hawaiian recollections of Cook. The basis of this critical assessment is the argument he also wishes to prove: that any such description of Cook as Lono is a European myth—notably promoted by missionaries. The debating technique is begging-the-question-squared: denying both what is said and who said it on the basis of a *petitio principii*.

because this was Lono, the people decided the tabu could be violated. Indeed, they were actually prevailed upon by the British to bring out provisions, after their initial hesitation:

> As we drew near the shore, some of the Natives came off to us ["throwing out white streamers," wrote Roberts, "as emblems of peace"]; they were a little shy at first, *but we soon inticed some on board and at length prevailed upon them to go a shore and bring off what we wanted.* Soon after these reached the shore we had company enough, and as few came empty, we got a tolerable supply of small pigs, fruit and roots. (Beaglehole 1967:476; my emphasis)

Lieutenant King's journal confirms that "the Natives were shy in their first approaches," and adds further particulars again consistent with the *Mooolelo's* sense of a visitation of Lono. "They were exceedingly happy in being sufferd to come on board," King noted, "& were very humble & humiliating [*sic*] in their outward actions" (Beaglehole 1967:501).

I open a parenthesis here on the "rationality" of these Hawaiian responses to Cook and more generally on the historiography of the *Mooolelo Hawaii.* For, the incidents related in the *Mooolelo* about violating the Makahiki tabu by going out to Cook's ships epitomize an interesting difference regarding the Hawaiian construal of empirical discrepancies between this Lono and their traditions, on one hand, and Obeyesekere's thesis of a biologically grounded, objective rationality on the other. Where the Hawaiians say they adaptively altered the tabu by rationalizations consistent at once with their old traditions and the new appearances—that "Lono [Cook] was really a god and his vessel was a temple"—for Obeyesekere the gross literal differences between a White man circling Hawai'i on two curious ships and the image of Lonomakua being carried around the coast had to be perceived by Hawaiians as the contradiction to the received beliefs that it really was. Reflecting on the differences, they would necessarily conceive Cook in realistic terms—which also turn out to be terms like ours, "ordinary human being," "from Brittanee" (Great Britain), "chief" of the "ship," and the like. Supposing the Hawaiians must resolve empirical contradictions to their traditions into universal objective perceptions, the theory thus presupposes that the people cannot deal with these perturbations by means of their own cultural resources. They revert to a kind of conceptual tabula rasa, on which experience inscribes itself in an unmediated and objective way.

Thus does Obeyesekere discover ways to suppress Hawaiian culture, as an alternative to acknowledging its historicity. And even as he censors the reflections of Hawaiians in such works as *Mooolelo Hawaii*, he claims to be championing them against the Western academics:

> One of the disconcerting features of the contemporary scholarship on Cook, and this applies to Beaglehole's work, is the cavalier manner in which bits and pieces from the missionary and *Mooolelo Hawaii* narratives are taken to prove the hypothesis of the apotheosis. I think these procedures are endemic to the scholarship pertaining *to nonliterate peoples who cannot strike back.* (Ob. 154; emphasis added)

But of course, Obeyesekere's dismissal of indigenous testimonies in the *Mooolelo Hawaii* by attributing them to the missionary editor Sheldon Dibble is precisely a way of silencing Hawaiian people. For Obeyesekere, the foregoing discussion of mutually corroborating parallels between the Cook records and the *Mooolelo* would be a historiographic scandal. Because the book was put together under missionary auspices, it can only be trusted to perpetuate the Haole myth of Cook as a Hawaiian god. Had not Sheldon Dibble "added some ideas of his own" to the stories collected by his Hawaiian students? The stories recorded by the ten Hawaiian students "from the oldest and most knowing of chiefs and people" cannot be admitted in evidence on the ad hominem ground that Dibble was responsible for their presentation. He must have invented the traditions about Cook and the Makahiki—if some other missionary had not already gotten to the old people. In Obeyesekere's view, then, the morality of using the *Mooolelo* as a historical source is proportionate to the inequity that can be heaped on Dibble as a missionary bigot. So he proceeds to heap it on, battering the book in the borrowed darkness of Dibble's contemptible attitudes. These are the critical methods about which he modestly adopts a scholier-than-thou attitude.

In evidence, Obeyesekere quotes the condemnation of the *Mooolelo* by the respected student of Hawaiiana, John F. G. Stokes. He does not tell us that Stokes's (1931) criticism did not extend to a denial of the notion, repeatedly expressed in the *Mooolelo*, that Cook was conceived to be a manifestation of the Makahiki god Lono. On the contrary, Stokes was convinced that the priests sincerely believed this to be so, and that Cook was generally so received.[24] He took the occasion of criticizing Dibble's Christian inter-

24. In a commentary on this issue written for another purpose, Stokes subscribed also to the *Mooolelo's* version of the tabu-breakers: "The *tabu* was undoubtedly present on account of the New Year services when Cook arrived. That *Lono* should break the *tabu* would have been a matter for him to decide in the people's mind [that is, according to the people's opinion] if they thought Cook was Lono" (quoted in Carruthers 1930:108).

polations in the *Mooolelo* to denounce as well the colossal ignorance of Cook's people for failing to recognize the divine esteem in which Hawaiians held the British navigator:

> Their ignorance of what was going on was colossal. None of them even recognized the significance of the name Lono, applied to Cook. To them it meant "chief" as shown in all the journals. Ledyard uses it in his hypothetical system of rank, as the highest class. Even when shown "Eatooa aronah" (namely, Akua Lono—The God Lono) they translated it as "The chief of the gods!" (Stokes 1931:92–93)

Not to defend Dibble's character either: that is precisely *not* the historiographic issue. Even if the report of Cook as Lono could be attributed to Dibble—despite that in arcane local details it obviously came from Hawaiians—all the strictures on his personal morality and religious interests would have no necessary bearing on the validity of the assertion. It is an elementary rule of logical argument that the truth or falsity of an idea pertains to its intellectual substance, not to the character or dispositions of its proponent. Nor can one legitimately assume that an author who may be suspected of lying on grounds of interest or ideology therefore *is* lying—not even a Christian missionary. Furthermore, to throw out the report of Cook as a manifestation of Lono on the a priori basis that this is a European myth—which Obeyesekere does not only for Dibble but a whole set of nineteenth-century sources that so quote Hawaiians, secular as well as missionary—is simply to make a conclusion out of a premise. Having supposed that the equation of Cook with Lono is a missionary falsehood, Obeyesekere feels entitled to dismiss anything that Dibble might publish to this effect as false. Still, the idleness of Obeyesekere's ad hominem and petitio principii arguments about the *Mooolelo Hawaii* is less significant than the ethnographic consequences. For, again, by swallowing up Hawaiian ideas in pretended missionary prejudices, such arguments obliterate the cultural traces of "people who cannot strike back."

There can be little mistake about who is speaking in various passages of the *Mooolelo*. It is no great task to prove that when the text reports that before the Haole came the Hawaiians were led by Satan and living in sin, it is not based on concepts of Polynesian origin. Yet something else is involved when specific Makahiki forms such as Lonomakua and the tabu on the sea during the procession of the god are described, or when Kalani'ōpu'u's movements are recorded in terms of little-known local place names, and these details then find complements in incidents of the Cook voyage as the

British reported them. This is not Dibble's work. Indeed, from certain mistakes in Dibble's own history concerning the course of Cook's vessels, Stokes thought "Dibble had not read, or had ignored, the authorized accounts of Cook's voyages" (1931:77). We need not follow Obeyesekere, then, in supposing the Hawaiian narratives of the *Mooolelo* are only the echoes of Reverend Dibble's satanic voices.

But apart from the question of who is speaking here, there is another historiographical issue posed by such quotative texts, which is the historical value of what is said. The latter problem is again complex. A report may be historically inaccurate, or not factually supportable, yet still structurally revelatory. By all available information, Captain Cook did *not* sleep with the daughter of the Kaua'i ruling woman, as the *Mooolelo* alleges. But the tradition that he did—"then Kamakahelei gave her own daughter as companion for Lono" (Kahananui 1984:168)—entails a conception of Cook that is consistent with the visitation of the Makahiki god. This cultural dimension would be missed by a strictly literalist relation to the texts.

End of parenthesis: return to the *Resolution* and *Discovery* making their way around Hawai'i island.

The trade of these vessels with the islanders says a lot about the ceremonial activities going on at the time. In particular, the varying patterns in the supply of fish, pigs, and feast foods from the Hawaiian side indicate that the Makahiki as classically described (by Malo *mā*) was under way. Precise details of the trade also confirm the December concordance of the Hawaiian and Western calendars.

Some fourteen or fifteen of Cook's people were making observations on the traffic with Hawaiians from the time the ships reached Maui until they anchored at Kealakekua. Certain of them—notably Bayly, Burney, Clerke, Cook, Edgar, Ellis, King, Roberts, and Samwell—were often more than perfunctory, taking care to record the kinds of foods and goods brought off by Hawaiians and some idea of the quantities.[25] Taken together, they indicate a remarkable pattern in the exchange of fish for British trade goods. Both the on-off timing in the supply of fish and the species offered correspond to canonical rules of the Makahiki.

Cook's people got fish from the Hawaiians in late November and again

25. The major sources on trade during the circumnavigation of Hawaii are Bayly (MSa, MSb); Burney (MSa, MSb, 1819); Clerke (Log); Cook (Log; also Cook and King 1784); Edgar (Log, Journal); Ellis (1782); King (Log; also Cook and King 1784); Riou (Log); Roberts (Log); Samwell (Beaglehole 1967:987–1300). See also Sahlins MS, on the daily activities of the British.

in early January, but evidently none in the time between. The combined indication of the journals, without exception, is that Hawaiians offered no fish whatever from November 26, 1778, when a variety of species including squid were obtained at Maui, to January 4 and 5, 1779, when some fish, probably albacore, were brought off the South Point of Hawai'i. This record is consonant at once with the December Makahiki and with the tradition (as recorded in the *Mooolelo*) that Cook's circuit incorporated Lono's—for recall that when the god is abroad putting out to sea (and a fortiori fishing) is tabu. (The pattern of trade is incompatible with a November Makahiki, however, insofar as the provision of fresh fish on 26 November would imply a violation of the Lono tabu, while the absence of like transactions during the next six weeks could have no evident reason.) And then, the appearance of the albacore at a certain date in the Cook annals is congruent with a specific fishing ritual that takes place toward the end of the Lono tabu, according to received accounts of the Makahiki, called "the fires of the Puea." An affair of the king and chiefs exclusively, this fishing rite runs from 28 Welehu to 11 Makali'i, in Malo's description, after which the sea is again tabu until the end of the Lono circuit, 16 Makali'i (1951:149–50). From Kelou Kamakau (1919–20:42) we learn that the fish concerned is the *ahi*, the albacore (*Thynnus thynnus*)—not to be confused with the *aku*, the bonito (or skipjack, *Katsuwonus pelamys*). The king himself goes out to catch *ahi* on 3 Makali'i. Now, according to the December Makahiki concordance, the relevant Gregorian dates would be:

> 28 Welehu (beginning of albacore fishing) = 18 December 1778
> 3 Makali'i (king fishes for albacore) = 22 December 1778
> 11 Makali'i (end of ritual fishing) = 30 December 1778
> 12–16 Makali'i (sea is tabu) = 31 December 1778–4 January 1779

Just so, on January 5, 1779, while nearing South Point, Surgeon Ellis and Midshipman Riou of the *Discovery*, for the first time in six weeks, report that fish were obtained in trade—which they unequivocally identify as "albacore" (Ellis 1782, 2:80, 144; Riou Log, 6 Jan 1779). We need to be careful about the identification because in late-eighteenth-century English texts the yellow-finned albacore is not always distinguished from the generally smaller bonito, which is the object of a different and later fishing ritual (see Beaglehole 1969:336n.1). But Surgeon Ellis seems reliable on this score, as he does consistently differentiate the two species—which makes it probable that Roberts, too, was speaking of albacore when he described the fish received on the *Resolution* in the same general location on the afternoon of 4 January as "bonneatoes, & one of them the largest that most of our people had ever seen" (Log, 5 Jan 1779). Moreover, Ellis noted that the albacore was obtainable only at South Point or, as he described it, "only at a small town, situated in a very barren spot, not far from the east point, nor was there any salted fish offered to sale but at this place, at A'tou'wi [Kaua'i] and O'neehoa [Ni'ihau]" (1782, 2:144). Again this evokes the *ahi* rituals, for the southern coast was specially frequented for albacore fishing, while the settlement at South Point was a seasonal fishing camp of the chiefs set on the seaside edge of an old lava flow (Titcomb 1972:521). Ellis even obliges us by recording that precisely seven albacore were brought that day to the ship; whereas we know—from the analogous *ōpelu* or mackerel rites (K. Kamakau 1919–20:32)—that seven is the number of fish ritually offered to the god as the first catch of the season.

Malo writes that in the days before the appearance of the Makahiki god (which in 1778 would be 14 December) the people are preparing feast foods. The special foods include "preparations of coconut mixed with taro or breadfruit, called *kulolo*, [and] sweet breadfruit pudding, called *pepeiee*" (1951:143). Just so, Ellis again tells of receiving "puddings of mashed breadfruit" off Maui on the 30th of November, and puddings once more off Hawai'i on the second of December (1782, 2:71, 74). Then there were the small pigs, always small pigs: ceremonially correct perhaps as offering to Lono but not so highly esteemed by the British, who wanted big hogs, and took pains to make their more practical preferences known to the Hawaiians (Cook and King 1784, 2:544). On December 13, the *Resolution* got 130 to 150 pigs (Trevenan Log, 14 Dec 1779); again, on December 23, 163 pigs (Bayly MSb, 23 Dec). One of the most important of Lono's myriad bodies (*kino*), the pig was likewise one of the tributes offered to the Makahiki image as it traveled through the districts (K. Kamakau 1919–20:42; Anonymous of Kohala 1916–17:204; S. Kamakau 1964:21). Indeed, the rules about eating pork during the Makahiki amounted to a culinary code of the season's cosmic relationships. The Lono priests and sometimes the people in general indulged in it but, except for a few occasions, pork was proscribed for the kings and *ali'i*. Insofar as Lono takes possession of the realm, this prohibition on the king seems appropriate, just as his ceremonial resumption of pork-eating at the end of the Makahiki would signify his incorporation of the god. Ledyard is not the most reliable of the Cook chroniclers, but he does notice that in late January 1779, Kalani'ōpu'u refused to eat pork.[26] Indeed, if we suppose that the December Makahiki dates were in effect, many of the king's doings during Cook's sojourn become intelligible.

We know that in late November 1778 Kalani'ōpu'u broke off fighting in Maui, which is consistent with the coming Lono tabu (of 14 December, though it would not be correct in a November Makahiki). On the 30th of November, he came aboard Cook's ships. But there followed a pattern of royal movements, or the lack thereof, that might seem curious given the evident significance of Cook's advent—were it not that this was the season of Lono's advent. Whereas Cook came to anchor on the 17th of January at Kealakekua, Kalani'ōpu'u did not arrive there until the 25th; nor had the British any sight of him since they left Maui. But we know the rule on the king's travel during the Makahiki from Vancouver's experiences with Kamehameha in 1793 and 1794: the king cannot leave the place where he has celebrated the Makahiki until he goes through certain ceremonies of purification. Malo discusses these ceremonies. They take place on 26 and 27 Makali'i and involve the consecration of certain ritual structures by the king, "in order to purify himself from the pleasures in which he had indulged before he resumed his religious observances" (Malo 1951:152). The dates of 26–27 Makali'i would correspond to January 14–15, 1779, or ten days before the king shows up at Kealakekua. Now, on the strength of a note by Emerson and normal ceremonial practice, Valeri (1985:227) concludes that the royal purification would last for a ten-day ritual period or *anahulu*—which is to say, until precisely January 24 or 25, 1779. And here again the Cook documents offer a curiously detailed confirmation. They report that the local authorities at Kealakekua foretold exactly when the king would be coming, and they turned out to be correct. This is the kind of precision one might expect only from ritual prescriptions. Edgar, for example, had called it exactly: on January 21 he was told the king would come four days hence (Log, 22 Jan 1779 [P.M. = 21 Jan]; cf. Roberts Log, 20 Jan 1779). So he did.

But already at Kealakekua Cook had received, if not a royal welcome, certainly something quite extraordinary. Probably it was the most generous reception ever accorded a European "voyage of discovery" in the Pacific Ocean (Brossard 1966:281). People on shore must have been following the progress of the ships around the island, for there were at least ten thousand

26. Malo seems to make too broad a statement about the interdiction of fresh pork for the *ali'i* (chiefs) during the Makahiki season, since no pigs could be consecrated in normal temple sites *(haipule)*. There are several pig sacrifices at the great temple during the Makahiki, at which time the chiefs evidently could consume pork (Malo 1951:150; K. Kamakau 1919–20).

on hand when they got to Kealakekua, several times the normal population. Later, when Cook landed, he was announced as "Orono" (Lono) by four men preceding him and bearing tabu ensigns. In this connection, Lieutenant King observed that "Captain Cook generally went by [that] name amongst the natives of Owhyhee" (Cook and King 1784, 3:5n). As "Owhyhee" specifically meant Hawai'i island to the British, King's comment is consistent with the Haole and Hawaiian reports that Cook was already known as "Lono" before he reached Kealakekua, indeed (as we know) from the moment he appeared at Maui.

Cook's arrival had epiphanal dimensions. This helps account for the tumultuous scene the British witnessed when they came into the Bay. "Anchored in 17^{fms} black sand," went Midshipman Riou's log (17 Jan), "amidst an Innumerable Number of Canoes, the people in which were singing & rejoicing all the way." It was pandemonium. Hundreds of canoes filled the waters of the bay—500 was the lowest number noted by chroniclers who purported to count them—as well as shoals of people swimming about and "all the Shore of the Bay was covered with people" (Beaglehole 1967:491). Not a weapon could be seen, Cook remarked. Rather the canoes were laden with pigs, breadfruit, sweet potato, sugar cane—with all the productions of the island. The women, said the surgeon William Ellis, "seemed remarkably anxious to engage themselves to our people" (1782, 1:86). They were well represented among the people who, in great numbers, clambered aboard the ships. And on board as well as in the water, on the shore and in their canoes, people were singing, dancing, shrieking, clapping and jumping up and down. They were jubilant.[27]

What did it mean? Everything suggests it meant the welcoming of Lono—which is the tradition of this day recounted by the nineteenth-century historian, S. M. Kamakau:

> when Captain Cook appeared they declared that his name must be Lono, for Kealakekua was the home of that deity as a man, and it was a belief of the ancients that he had gone to Kahiki and would return. They were full of joy, all the more so that these were Lono's tabu days

27. The firsthand descriptions of the welcome at Kealakekua were summed up this way by the naval historian, Richard Hough (1979:185): "But neither the thieving [which soon broke out], nor the unprecedented numbers, accounted for the hysterical element which grew rather than diminished as this day of noise and pandemonium wore on. It was rather as if the ships had by chance arrived at some culmination in the lives of this community, a climax that would affect their destiny. Polynesian excitement was one thing, and they were familiar with that. In this bay the whole population gave the impression of being on the brink of mass madness."

[i.e., the Makahiki]. Their happiness knew no bounds; they leaped for joy: "Now shall our bones live; now *'aumakua* [ancestor-spirit] has come back. These are his tabu days and he has returned!" This was a great mistake. He was a long-tailed god, a scorpion, a slayer of men. What a pity! But they believed in him and shouted, "Lono is a god! Lono is a god!" (Kamakau 1961:98–99)[28]

Kealakekua: 17 January–4 February 1779

The *Resolution* and *Discovery* came to anchor between the two villages of the Bay, Ka'awaloa on the northern headland and Kealakekua on the southern side (fig. 1.2, map 1.3). Separated by a steep precipice that fell directly to the shore, the two settlements, the one chiefly and the other priestly, were differentiated, too, in political character. Kealakekua, literally 'The Path of the God,' was the site of the great temple of Hikiau, from which the image of Lono traditionally departed on its Makahiki circuit. The village was home to a group of Lono priests who had the charge of Hikiau temple as well a characteristic temple or House of Lono (*Hale o Lono*). Ka'awaloa, on the other hand, was the village of the ruling chiefs of southwestern Hawai'i, the Kona district. Here resided the powerful Moana people, renowned as the king's war leaders, led now by one Kekuhaupi'o. The owning chief of Ka'awaloa, Keaweaheulu, would soon achieve fame as a henchman of the conqueror, Kamehameha. When Kalani'ōpu'u, the king of Hawai'i, came into the bay on the 25th of January, he took up residence with Keaweaheulu. Indeed all of the warriors returning from Maui with the king, some 500 of them, settled into Ka'awaloa. But the old priest, Ka'ō'ō, who likewise arrived with the king, was head of the Lono order—"the Bishop," the British called him—and he went to live with his fellow religious at Kealakekua. (Ka'ō'ō governed the *ahupua'a*, or district, in which Kealakekua was situated, and provided guides and a laissez-passer to British parties who made excursions inland.) Of course, Ka'awaloa also had its temples and priests, but it was dominated by *ali'i* (chiefs) and took on the character of a military camp during Cook's visit; whereas Kealakekua was primarily a ceremonial center, notably devoted to Lono and under the control of the "regular society" of

28. Obeyesekere discounts S. M. Kamakau's relations of Cook as Lono—though not those writings of Kamakau congenial to his own thesis (see, e.g., Ob. 149)—on grounds of their Christian inspiration: witness the Biblical allusion of "our bones shall live" in this passage, and the criticism of Cook (supposedly borrowed from missionary attitudes). Kamakau was one of the ten Lahainaluna students who compiled the *Mooolelo Hawaii* from the stories of the old folks.

Lono priests (Cook and King 1784, 3:159). Moreover, the British would soon discover that there were clearly "party matters subsisting between the Laity and Clergy," respectively domiciled at Ka'awaloa and Kealakekua (Clerke in Beaglehole 1967:543).

The personage who came out to the *Resolution* the first day and took Captain Cook ashore to Hikiau temple at Kealakekua was appropriately enough from Ka'awaloa. "Koah," an old priest and once a distinguished warrior, was a king's man, not one of the Lono priests from Kealakekua. When Kalani'ōpu'u arrived some days later, Koah went off to attend him; and after Cook's death, the same Koah was a main negotiator with the British on behalf of the king's party. In fact, the Lono priests distrusted and detested him (Cook and King 1784, 3:69 and passim; Beaglehole 1967:543; Edgar Log, 16 Feb 1779; Law Log, 16 Feb 1779). But for all that it was appropriate that Koah would put Cook through certain complex rites of welcome to Lono at Hikiau temple on the first day. For according to the classic descriptions of the Makahiki, upon the return of the god from his circuit the king enters the temple *(luakini)* to welcome him with the offering of a pig (K. Kamakau 1919–20:44–45; Malo 1951:150).

It was, of course, thirteen days past the scheduled return of Lono.[29] And the king himself was absent. But Koah, from the time he came on board the *Resolution*, began to construct Cook into the image of the Makahiki image. First wrapping Cook in a red tapa cloth, Koah then stepped back and made an offering to him of a small pig, accompanying the gesture with a long recitation. The act, as Lieutenant King observed, was exactly analogous to the way Hawaiians sacrificed to their "idols":

> This ceremony was frequently repeated [for Cook] during our stay
> at Owhyhee, and appeared to us, from many circumstances, to be a
> sort of religious adoration. Their idols we found always arrayed with
> red cloth, in the same manner as was done to Captain Cook; and a
> small pig was their usual offering to the *Eatooas* [*akua*, 'gods']. Their

29. According to Obeyesekere, "Sahlins says that every single event that occurred since Cook's arrival in Hawai'i in January 1779 can find a parallel in the ritual actions of the Makahiki" (Ob. 52; and again on 57). This statement is characteristically undocumented, for the reason (also too characteristic) that it is untrue. It is an imputation of the kind that might be called "hyper-ventriloquating," which is putting words in another's mouth that make him sound like a dummy. All the discrepancies, improvisations and the like mentioned in the present text have already been discussed in previous published works, especially Sahlins 1981, 1985a, and 1989; see also Sahlins MS for a day-by-day account of correspondences and differences between Cook's activities and Makahiki rites. Anyhow, as I recall, my thesis about Cook's death depended on his transgressions of the calendrical and political stipulations of the Makahiki.

Fig. 1.2 View of Kealakekua Bay, showing H.M.S. *Resolution* and *Discovery*. A small portion of Hikiau temple mound may be seen at the lower right. (From Cook and King 1784, vol. 3)

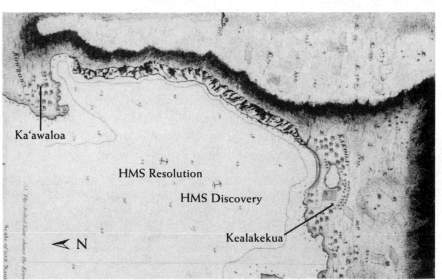

Ka'awaloa

HMS Resolution

HMS Discovery

Kealakekua

N

Map 1.3 Kealakekua Bay. (From inset accompanying map 1.1)

speeches, or prayers, were uttered too with a readiness and volubility that indicated them to be according to some formulary. (Cook and King 1784, 3:5)

Lieutenant King's observations are paralleled in the reminiscences of old Hawaiians from Kaʻawaloa itself, as related to Rev. William Ellis in 1821:

> As soon as Captain Cook arrived, it was supposed and reported that the god Rono had returned; the priests clothed him with the sacred cloth worn only by the god, conducted him to their temples, sacrificed animals to propitiate his favour, and hence the people prostrated themselves before him as he walked through the villages. (Ellis 1833, 4:104)[30]

30. Still another parallel appears in the *Mooolelo Hawaii* of 1838: "Because the people believed Lono [Cook] was a god they worshipped [*hoʻomana*] and exalted him. They gave him hogs and vegetables, clothing and all sorts of things in the same manner they gave to their gods. The priests bowed low when they approached him, placed a [red tapa cloth] on his shoulders, drew back a little, gave hogs and this and that thing, spoke slowly, spoke rapidly.

The wrapping of Cook in tapa cloth was indeed a token of idolization, as it entailed the consecration of persons and objects regarded as actualizations of the divine (Valeri 1985: 300–302). Cook had already made the connection between such wrapping of persons in tapa cloth and something religiously set apart during his earlier visit to Kaua'i, as a result of seeing temple images, a temple tower—the *anu'u*, a means of communication with the god—and his own person so adorned. Speaking of the tower in a main temple at Waimea, Cook wrote:

> Some part of it was, or had been covered with a very thin light grey cloth, which seemed to be consecrated to Religious and ceremonious purposes, as a good deal of it was about this Morai [Tahitian, 'temple'] and I had some of it forced upon me on my first landing. (Beaglehole 1967: 270; cf. 271)

A.6
Cook Wrapped

Thus rendered invisible (or partly visible) and abstract, a man or an image becomes a realization of the god's presence, even as the wrapping or binding signifies the human appropriation and domestication of divine powers. On the first day at Kealakekua, Cook was not only twice enveloped in tapa cloth, but incorporated in ceremonies at Hikiau temple that the British again described as "adoration" and Hawaiians recollected as "worship."[31] As if he were indeed to be transfigured, Cook's journal ends as Koah escorts him to these ceremonies: "In the after noon I went a shore to view the place, accompaned by Touahah [Koah, Ko'a'a], Parea, Mr King and others; as soon as we

---

That was prayer and worship" (Kahananui 1984: 173; the English translation speaks of placing a feather cape on Cook's shoulders, but the Hawaiian text [p. 18] explicitly says *kapa 'ula'ula*, a 'red tapa cloth').

Cook's own journal, which ends on the 17th of January, likewise generalizes about these prestations: "Among our numerous Visitors was a man named *Tou-ah-ah*, who we soon found belonged to the Church, he intorduced himself with much ceremony, in the Course of which he presented me a small pig, two Cocoanuts and a piece of red cloth which he wraped around me: in this manner all or most of the chiefs or people of Note interduce them selves, but this man went farther, he brought with him a large hog and a quant[it]y of fruits and roots all of which he included in the present" (Beaglehole 1967: 491).

31. Obeyesekere is apparently careless in writing that Cook "was escorted to the temple, 'worshipped and adored,' according to Sahlins[20]" (Ob. 53). The reference (20) is to Sahlins 1981: 21, which reads: "Upon landing, Cook was immediately escorted to the great temple at Hikiau, where he allowed himself to be led by priests through an elaborate set of rites, characterized in both British and Hawaiian accounts as 'adoration' or 'worship.'" On "adoration" see King (Cook and King 1784, 3: 5, 6; Beaglehole 1967: 509); on the Hawaiian *ho'omana*, usually translated as "worship," see the *Mooolelo* (Kahananui 1984: 19, 173). My intention in referring these terms to the historic sources was to indicate that I did not invent them; whereas, attributing them to me pretends that I did.

landed Touahah took me by the hand and conducted me to a large Morai [Hikiau], the other gentlemen with Parea and four or five more of the Natives followed" (Beaglehole 1967:491).

Cook fails to mention the four men bearing tabu ensigns who met them on shore and preceded them to the temple. Mr. King noted that in the phrase cried out by these escorts, the British could recognize the name "O Lono"—upon hearing which the Hawaiians on their course fled to nearby houses or prostrated themselves on the ground (ibid., 504).

In the temple, Cook went through a complex series of rituals involving four distinct episodes. Although it has been plausibly suggested that some of this ceremony was improvised for the occasion, at least two episodes are closely analogous to Makahiki rites, both concerned with the reception of the Lono image. Indeed, the very first ceremonial moment looks like a repetition of the sacrifice offered by the king upon the god's return from his progress. Cook was taken to the offering stage in front of the principal images. On this stage a pig had been placed some time before and was now rotting away. As it were, the remains were re-presented to Captain Cook. Having placed Cook under the offering stage, Koah "took down the hog, and held it toward him; and after having a second time addressed him in a long speech, pronounced with much vehemence and rapidity, he let it fall on the ground" (Cook and King 1784, 3:7). Note that in the rite of welcome appropriate to this time, following the battle royal with the god (*kāli'i*), the king offers a single pig in sacrifice, praying to Lono in his encompassing aspect, Lononuiakea: "This is for your tired feet from visiting our land, and as you have returned watch over me and over our [*kaua*, dual inclusive] land" (K. Kamakau 1919–1920:44–45). Note too that Cook had just completed a near-circuit of Hawai'i and was being offered a pig by a king's man (Kalani'ōpu'u being absent). So, was this "stinking hog" of 1779 the very one prescribed in the canonical accounts? By the December Makahiki, a pig would have been sacrificed to Lono on 16 Makali'i, or less than two weeks before Koah offered the putrid beast to Captain Cook.

The next ritual episode took place at the *anu'u* tower, the rickety scaffolding at the rear of the temple platform by which communication is effected with the god. Koah took Cook to the tower, which they both climbed. As they were thus precariously perched aloft, a procession of ten men led by the Lono priest Keli'ikea came in carrying a large piece of red tapa cloth and a hog. The procession stopped and prostrated themselves. Keli'ikea carried the tapa cloth to Koah, who swathed Cook round with it. The Lono priest then handed the pig up to Koah, and with Cook still above

A.7

**Lono at
Hikiau**

"in this awkward situation," the two priests "began their office, chanting sometimes in concert, and sometimes alternately." This lasted "a considerable time," after which Koah let the pig fall and he and Cook descended (Cook and King 1784, 3:7). King's personal journal adds that the priests "many times appeard to be interrogating" (Beaglehole 1967:505).

This episode, with Cook aloft in the temple tower, has proven wide open to interpretation. The main issue is whether Cook was the sacrifier (through the medium of Koah, as sacrificer) or the beneficiary (the god). Although from the dialogue between the priests and their relative positions, the latter seems most plausible, it should not be forgotten that Lono's entrance into the temple at the end of his progress is also the end of his ritual ascendancy. Or at least it is the beginning of the end. Having retaken the sovereignty in the battle on the shore *(kāli'i)*, the king will thenceforth by stages re-install the worship of Kū, with whom he is personally identified. In the annual ceremonial cycle, moreover, this ascension of Kū is a condition of the possibility of the restored worship of Lono (in agricultural and therapeutic rites). Hence the possibility of Valeri's alternative interpretation, to the effect that Cook was here sacrifier to Kūnuiākea (Kū in his encompassing aspect), as preliminary to his own ritual recognition as Lonomakua.[32]

This sequence, from the acknowledgment of Kū to the consecration of Lono, is certainly entailed in the final two episodes at Hikiau, although that which concerns Kū has its own ambiguities. Having descended from the

---

32. Valeri's interpretation of the Hikiau welcome of Cook is as follows:

Two things are clear. First, Cook was considered divine, just as a king was considered divine: he was a human manifestation of the god; he was both king and god. Secondly, Cook could not simply *be* Lono; he had to *become* Lono by first being connected with Kūnuiākea. Apparently, only his transformation could fully establish his identity as the god of the Makahiki—that is, establish it in a ritually controlled way, not as an unmediated and uncontrolled fact, as was the case before Cook's arrival at Kealakekua bay, while he was still circling the island. (1991:134–35)

Valeri's interpretation is consistent with his general thesis on cyclic transformations between Kū and Lono. It is also partly dependent on the fact that both Cook and the Kū image at Hikiau were swathed in red tapa cloth. But the red tapa was specific neither to this occasion nor to this god. Cook was so wrapped in other contexts, before, after, and outside of Hikiau. Also, if the following statement of Ellis's represents what he learned of *anu'u* rituals, it suggests that Cook's position in the tower was that of the god: "In the Sandwich Islands, the king, personating the god, uttered the responses from his concealment in a frame of wicker-work" (1833, 1:285).

Obeyesekere simply supposes that in the first two episodes at Hikiau, Cook—as a chief, a status that for Obeyesekere is different from divinity—is being "introduced" to the Hawaiian gods. His main argument is that this is "reasonably clear" (Ob. 84).

tower, Koah led Captain Cook to the semicircle of images around the sacrificial platform. As Lieutenant King described the episode in his journal:

> Koah led him [Cook] to different images, [and] said something to
> each but in a very ludicrous & Slighting tone, except to the Center
> image [of Kūnuiakea, encompassing form of Kū]; which was the only
> one covered with Cloth [red cloth, in the official *Voyage*], & was only
> three feet high, whilst the rest were Six; to this he prostrated himself,
> & afterwards kiss'd, & desird the Captⁿ to do the same, who was quite
> passive, & sufferd Koah to do with him as he chose. (Beaglehole 1967:
> 505–6)

   Although there can be no doubt of the homage to Kū, the description
of what it consisted in is a perfect amphiboly. The commas in King's text
make it uncertain whether Cook merely "kiss'd" the image or also prostrated
before it as Koah had. The only other extant description, contributed by
King to the official account, has the same problem: "Before this figure he
[Koah] prostrated himself, and kissed it, desiring Captain Cook to do the
same; who suffered himself to be directed by Koah throughout the whole of
this ceremony" (Cook and King 1784, 3:8). So, unless some new text is
discovered, we will never know what actually happened. Scholars have read
King's passage both ways. Valeri and Conner and Miller, for instance, speak
only of Cook's kissing the image (Valeri 1991:134; Conner and Miller 1978:
129). Others, including myself, have read it that Cook prostrated as well
(Sahlins 1985a:121; Besant 1890:149–50; Brossard 1966:297). The matter
is perhaps of no great significance, except that Obeyesekere has made a
great deal of the supposition that Cook humiliated himself by prostrating
before a Hawaiian god-image, and this played an important role in the
irrational behavior that led to his death (see below, appendix 14). But this is
permanently questionable. Besides, "kissing" in the Hawaiian manner means
pressing one's nose to another's nose or cheek while inhaling. For all we
know, then, Cook just sniffed at it.

   There can be little uncertainty, however, about the final and most pro-
tracted ritual that day at Hikiau. It was an unmistakable performance of the
hānaipū, the ceremonial 'feeding' or reception of Lono by the principal men
on the course of the god's progress. Cook indeed became an idolized man.
Lieutenant King and Koah held his arms outstretched, so that he appeared
as a living form of the cross-piece Makahiki image of Lonomakua. In this
posture, Cook was put through a series of formalities that corresponded in
precise details to the *hānaipū* rite described in Hawaiian accounts of the

Makahiki (Kelou Kamakau 1919–20:40–43; John Papa Ii 1959:73–75;
Malo 1951:147–48). Aside from the imitation of the Makahiki icon, the
agreements include certain choral dialogues, the specific foods offered, the
prestation of kava, anointing Lono with masticated coconut and feeding the
image (that is, the bearer or, in 1779, the English bearers). I juxtapose Lieutenant King's account of the episode at Hikiau and the well-known received
texts on the *hānaipū:*

We now were led near the Center of the
Area, where was a space of 10 or 12 feet
square, dug lower by 3 feet than the
level of the Area[.] On one side were
two wooden Images; between these the
Captain was seated; Koah support'd one
of his Arms, while I was made to do the
same to the other. At this time a second
procession of Indians carrying a baked
hog, Breadfruit, sweet Potatoes, plantains, a Pudding & Coco Nuts with Kiri-
keeah at their head approachd towards
us, he having the pig in his hand, &
with his face towards the Capt" he kept
repeating in a very quick tone some
speeches or prayers, to which the rest
responded, his part became shorter &
shorter, till at last he repeat'd only two
or three words at a time & was answerd
by the Croud repeating the Word
Erono. When this Offering was concluded, which I suppose lastd near a
Quarter of an hour, the Indians sat
down fronting us, & began to cut up the
hog, to peal the Vegetables, & break the
Coco nuts; whilst others were busy in
brewing the Yava by chew[ing] it in the
same manner they do at the other Islands. The Kernel of the Coco nut was
chewd by Kaireekeea & wrapped in a

And when the long god arrived at the
king's place, the king prepared a meal
for the said god. The attendants were
then under restriction for a short time.
As the god was brought out of the
king's house and the eyes of the king
beheld the image, they were filled with
tears, and he cried for his love of the
deity. And the king and all the people
who were in house, cried out, "Be thou
feared, O Lono"; and the attendant
people answered for the deity's greeting, saying: "Is it mine?" and they answered, "Here is the king's greeting
[aloha] unto you, O Lono." The people
outside replied, "Here is Lono's greeting
[aloha] unto your majesty." After these
things the deity with his attendants entered the king's house while certain
priests who came with him offered
prayers which were followed by the
king's priest. Then the king offered the
deity an ivory necklace, placing it
around the god's neck. The king then
fed the man who carried the idol, he
was the image's mouth, and ate the
pork, the uhau, taro and coconut pudding and awa. This service was called
hanaipu.

After this the deity went outside

piece of cloth with which he rubbd the
Capt⁽ˢ⁾ face, head, hands, Arms, &
Shoulders, & did the same to M⁽ʳ⁾ Bailey
& myself, Pareea also was just touchd &
Koah. These two now insist'd upon
Cramming us with hog, but not till after
[tasting] the Kava; I had no objection
to have the hog handled by Pareea, but
the Capt⁽ⁿ⁾ recollecting what offices
Koah had officiated when he handled
the Putrid hog could not get a Morsel
down, not even when the old fellow
very Politely chew'd it for him. (Beaglehole 1967: 506)

[to] the hanaipu of all the chiefs who
worshipped the deity. The deity did not
eat their pork, but the man who carried
it; he was its mouth who ate its food.
(K. Kamakau 1919–20: 40–43)

While the games were going on, the
akua loa (long god) was brought to the
gate of the enclosure surrounding the
house of a chief of *ni'aupi'o* rank. . . .
The person bearing the image said,
"Greetings." Those from within the enclosure replied, "Greetings, greetings to
you, O Lono." Then the bearer of the
image came in and stood by the door-
way of the house, where he was handed
an ointment made of masticated coconut wrapped in a bundle for the annointing of the stick, accompanied by
the words, "here is your annointing, O
Lono"; but the actual annointing was
done by someone from within the
house.

In the meantime, foods were prepared for the wooden god, to be eaten
by the man who carried it. They consisted of a cup of *'awa* [kava] and banana or sugar cane to remove its bitter-
ness, and some *'a'aho*, a pudding made
of coconut and pia [arrowroot] starch
thickened by heating with hot stones.
This food was laid on ti leaves to be
eaten after the other foods. Then a side
of well-cooked pork was given him with
some poi. The chief fed the carrier of
the god with his own hands, so that the
hands of the carrier did not touch any
of it. After this feeding of the god, the
bearer was ready to depart and said,

"Farewell, O friends." Those of the
household answered, "Farewell, O
Lono." Then the whole company left
the *hale mua* and went to the field to
wait for the chiefess of *ni'aupi'o* rank to
present her gift to the god. (Ii 1959:
73–75) [33]

The *hānaipū* ceremony was repeated more than once in the following
days, beginning with a performance on January 19 at the Lono temple of
Kealakekua—which Cook again suffered with outstretched arms (Burney
MSb, 18–19 Jan 1779; Cook and King 1784, 3:15). In Samwell's understanding, Cook was thus "invested by them [the Lono priests], with the Title
and Dignity of Orono [Lono], which is the highest Rank among these Indians and is a Character that is looked upon by them as partaking something
of divinity" (Beaglehole 1967:1161–62). According to Samwell, after the
ceremony of 19 January at Kealakekua, two priests conducted this Lono to
a place five miles distant, where he again went through the same honors. We
are probably justified in supposing this was the Hale o Keawe, the temple of
royal ancestral remains at Honaunau. Here is Samwell's description of the
rituals of 19 January:

> These People pay the greatest attention to Captn Cook, having a very
> high opinion of his Station & Quality, which he every where main-
> tains by his happy method of managing Indians which never fails of
> obtaining their Friendship and Esteem. To day a Ceremony was per-
> formed by the Priests in which he was invested by them with the Title
> and Dignity of Orono, which is the highest Rank among these Indians
> and is a Character that is looked upon by them as partaking something
> of divinity; The Scene was among some cocoa nut Trees close by

33. These parallel columns are reproduced as published in Sahlins 1989, pages 401–2. The
citation from 'I'i left out the final part of the rite, concerning the gifts of a chiefly woman
to Lono made subsequently and outside the chief's shrine (*hale mua*). Malo's description of
the *hānaipū* might also be noted here for corroborating parallels to the rites accorded Cook.
Malo (1951:147–48) records that when the bearer of the god entered the house of a chief,
after a prayer by a priest, the chief "fed the carrier of the image with his own hands, putting
the food into the man's mouth," after which the image was taken outside to be girded in a loin
cloth by a woman chief. We also have an actual notice from 1788 of the bearer of the image of
'Great Lono' (*Lono Nui*) at O'ahu being given kava in the manner described by John Papa 'I'i
(below, 90).

Ohekeeaw [Hikiau temple], before a sacred building which they call 'Ehare no Orono' [Hale o Lono] or the Temple of Orono. Captⁿ Cook attended by three other Gentlemen was seated on a little pile of Stones at the foot of an ill formed Idol stuck round with rags and decayed Fruit, the other Gentlemen sat on one side of him and before him sat several Priests and behind them a number of Servants with a barbequed Hog. As an introduction he who appeared to be the Chief Priest took a small Pig by the hinder Legs and struck it's head against the Ground, after which he held it over a blaze without the Circle till it expired. He then laid it at Captⁿ Cook's feet and put his own foot upon it, singing a Song in which he was accompanyed by all except the Servants who were carving the barbequed Hog. The Officiator had wrapt up some cocoa nut meat chewed in a clean Rag which he applyed to Captⁿ Cook's Head, Hands & feet, & wou'd have anointed his Cloaths with it but that he begged to be excused, he likewise applyed it to the Heads of the other Gentlemen. The Song was all this while kept up, interrupted now and then by short Speeches made by the Priest, which were sometimes repeated after him, at other times assented to by short responses from the Under Priests and Servants. One of the Priests rose & made an Harangue while the Chief Priest held Captⁿ Cook by the Finger. After this the Priests dined on the barbequed Hog; when they had done the Company dispersed except two of the Priests that took Captain Cook to another part of the Island about 5 Miles off, where much such another Ceremony was gone through. In their Way thither a Herald went before them singing, and thousands of people prostrated themselves as they passed along and put their Hands before their Faces as if it was deem'd Vilation or Sacrilege to look at them. (Beaglehole 1967:1161–62)

One only need add some details of this performance mentioned in other accounts, again consistent with the classic *hānaipū* rite. In the first part of the ceremonies at the House of Lono, Lieutenant King once more supported Cook's arms (Beaglehole 1967:510)—just as in the latter part, by Samwell's testimony, the "Chief Priest" (probably Keli'ikea) held Cook "by the finger." Burney notes the actual feeding of Cook with pork: "The first mouthful was chewed by the Priest and put into Captⁿ Cooks Mouth" (Burney MSb, 19 Jan 1779). God is in such details—more specifically, Lonomakua is.

I digress once more from the narrative to reflect on Obeyesekere's treatment of the *hānaipū* or ritual 'feeding' of Captain Cook. It is an example of how one makes a pidgin anthropology—which is at the same time a pseudo-history—by substituting a folkloric sense of "native" beliefs for the relevant Hawaiian ethnography. As a preliminary move, the project entails depreciating the ethnography one way or another. In Obeyesekere's case, he simply ignores the published observations, including the parallel-column arrangements of British and Hawaiian texts reproduced above, that indicate Cook was put through the customary reception of the Makahiki image (Sahlins 1989:400–403, 1981:21). One might think this argument substantial enough to require some refutation, or at least explicit recognition. But Obeyesekere does not discuss the *hānaipū* as such or its specific parallels to the rituals of January 17 and 19, let alone refer his readers to the pertinent sources. Rather, he raises the issue in the following manner and without annotation: "Sahlins, it should be noted, has an elaborate point-by-point description of the concordance between this ritual and the predications of the Makahiki calendar [sic]" (Ob. 82; no reference cited).[34]

The way cleared of Hawaiian custom, Obeyesekere finds himself at liberty to interpret the historical events by notions concocted out of common-sense realism and a kind of pop nativism. We are offered a certain Western version of how the "natives" really think—a main condition (and virtue) of which being that they should not think of Cook as a manifestation of Lono. Instead of the *hānaipū* of Lonomakua, Cook was the subject of an "installation ritual" that made him a tabu high chief by the name of Lono—not the god Lono, who rather thus became Cook's "guardian deity" (Ob. 82–87). Yet Obeyesekere rightly doubts that Hawaiians had any such installation ritual; so he suggests they invented one for the occasion (Ob. 217n.61).[35] The occasion evidently was Obeyesekere's defense of the objectivity of Hawaiian thought against the imperialist myth that they venerated White men. Accordingly, they endowed Cook with a status that had "divine qualities" (Ob. 86). This "plausible alternative" to Cook's divinity to one side, the translation of the *hānaipū* into folkloric anthropology proceeds by way of another oblique (and undocumented) allusion:

34. Or, more vaguely, referring to the whole set of Hikiau performances, in a statement that is again misleading as well as unannotated: "These rituals [according to Sahlins] exactly paralleled the Makahiki rites for Lono" (Ob. 53).

35. Obeyesekere's translation of the *hānaipū* into an "installation ritual" is part of a larger alternative theory, which is considered here in due course (pp. 123–38). The only thing remotely like the kind of installation ritual Obeyesekere has in mind would be the legitimation of a *usurping* chief in a name chant. Even so, a usurper would not acquire the tabus of divine descent such as the *kapu moe*, or prostration privilege (cf. Kamakau 1961:429–30).

Sahlins says that the ritual action where Cook's arms are supported by Koah and King is an attempt to imitate the crossbar by which Lono is represented. This is quite implausible: If Cook was the god Lono himself, it is strange that he should be asked to imitate his own form as the god of sports. The raising of arms is a standard attitude of praying in Hawai'i. Cook naturally was ignorant of this and he is therefore *made* to pray to the Hawaiian gods, the priests uttering "speeches or prayers" on his behalf. Cook is given the name Lono after the god Lono who is, to borrow a term not strictly applicable to Hawai'i, a kind of "guardian deity" to him. (Ob. 85)

Note the "it is strange" invocation of the common wisdom. Of course it is strange that Cook should be made to imitate the Makahiki image of Lono—in the capacity of Lonomakua ('Father Lono'), not as the gods of play (*akua pā'ani*) who also appear in separate images—only on the naive notion, equally insensitive to Hawaiian ideas, that "Cook was the god Lono himself." Cook was a living manifestation of the god: not your customary Makahiki image—and no less himself for it. It is thus testimony to Hawaiian empirical reason, as well as the flexibility of this indigenous rationality, that they remade Cook into the perceptual form of their own concept. This was with arms horizontally outstretched. The pretense that Cook was in the "standard attitude of praying," from which Obeyesekere imagines him praying to Hawaiian gods, is false. The "standard attitude" of praying is with arms raised vertically overhead "to the place of the god in the heavens" (S. Kamakau 1976:142; Valeri 1985:321). Aside from the improbable gymnastics—in the Hale o Lono version, at least, we know that Cook's arm-bearers were also sitting; or the evident implications of the description—"Koah support'd one of his arms, while I was made to do the same to the other"; we have Samwell's testimony at the *hānaipū* of 19 January that during the choral dialogue the head priest held Cook by the finger. Cook was not praying with upraised arms. Again, the supposition that a high chief named after a god acquires the latter as a "guardian deity" (as opposed to a substantial affinity) is what I mean by pop nativism. A lot more conjecture of Hawaiian culture then follows, when Obeyesekere speaks of the application of coconut oil to Messrs. Bayly and King:

If this ceremony repeats the anointing of the Lono image with coconut oil as in Makahiki (as Sahlins thinks), it is strange that King and Bayly were also thought of as incarnations of Lono! The ritual just described uses the pre-masticated kernel of the coconut—the milky sap of fertility, I would guess. Sahlins's view that Cook was anointed with *oil* is of course a continuation of the Western canonization of the great explorer. The culmination of the ceremony, where the priest Koah feeds the three Englishmen with food and kava blessed by Lono, indicates that the English are in a sense reborn as the children of the Hawaiian gods. It is likely that the installation ceremony had the effect of imbuing Cook with the mana of the war god Kū himself. Because Hawaiian chiefs do possess such "divine qualities," it seems natural for them to impart these to the English chief, particularly in the context of the political motivations sketched earlier. James King, in his official journal, recollected people telling him that the little image at Hikiau was that of Kū, and "it was Terreoboo's [Kalaniʻopuʻuʻs] God; and that he [Kū] also resided in us." It is therefore entirely possible that the installation rituals helped effect this "residence," both in Cook and in the other gentlemen present, thereby converting them into Hawaiian chiefs, though of varying degrees of ritual status and mana. (Ob. 86)

One gets a sense from this passage of how deeply quixotic is Obeyesekere's denial of the calumny that Hawaiians welcomed the Haole captain as an actualization of an Hawaiian god. It was not that at all. He was simply accorded the Hawaiian persona (Lono) of a chief with the prostration tabu, the privilege of those of "godly blood" (Ob. 191). And not only had Cook "divine qualities" in Hawaiian eyes, but the god "resided in him," a residence that these "installation rituals" helped to effect. However, it was the god Kū who thus resided in Captain Cook, not Lono, as an arrogant anthropology has presumed. This also helps explain why a month later, after his death, the Hawaiians could worship the Englishman as a "real god" (Ob. 91). Again, the passage shows the ethnographic contortions and distortions necessary to achieve this saving interpretation of Obeyesekere's thesis that Hawaiians were too practical and empirical to take Captain Cook for one of their own deities. When I say the distortions amount to a "pidgin anthropology," I mean that they have the quality of ad hoc fabrications based on a sort of generic primitivism, like Fenimore Cooper Indians. They appeal to a popular sense of common average "native" thought. But the crooked tree in the tall pine forest has spoken with a forked tongue.

"Strange" should be the beginning of anthropological wisdom rather than a way of putting an end to it. Regarding the anointing of Lieutenant King and William Bayly, and also the touching (symbolic anointing?) of

Koah and Palea, which Obeyesekere in the above passage finds "strange," these people were in Cook's ritual party, just as there were other notables (including gods of play) in Lono's train. It is thus relevant that Cook was so honored first. Moreover, in the case of the wooden image at *hānaipū* rites, the "attendant people" act for the god, and the bearer in particular eats for him. The honors done to James King and the astronomer Bayly might have seemed less strange if King's preamble to the fragment about Kū living "in us" had also been quoted by Obeyesekere:

> It has been mentioned, that the title of Orono [Lono], with all its honours, was given to Captain Cook; and it is also certain, that they regarded us, generally, as a race of people superior to themselves; and used often to say, that great Eatooa [*akua*, 'god' or 'gods'] dwelled in our country. (Cook and King 1784, 3:159)

By Hawaiian concepts, it would certainly be less strange that Cook's followers should be included in his being than that, by this ritual, the English were "in a sense reborn as the children of the Hawaiian gods." This sheer invention of ethnography is only balanced by the irony that if the English were made children of Hawaiian gods, they were indeed being deified. In turn, the irony is only surpassed by Obeyesekere's attempt to extract himself from the apparently compromising notion that the Hawaiian god was said to reside "in" Captain Cook & Co. It is surpassed because Hawaiians to whom Lieutenant King referred did not say the royal god "resided in us." This is a misquotation. The official journal says that the king's god "also resided *amongst* us" (Cook and King 1784, 3:160; emphasis added) and the counterpart passage in Lieutenant King's personal journal reads, the god "also liv'd *with* us" (Beaglehole 1967:621; emphasis added). Undaunted, however, by the possibility that Hawaiians could believe their god lived in the persons of Haole, Obeyesekere proceeds to offer an ethnographic justification of his mistake. A phony Hawaiian culture comes to the rescue of a historiographic lapse: it is "entirely possible" that the so-called installation ritual—that is, the *hānaipū* of Lono—"helped effect this 'residence' [of the king's god], both in Cook and the other gentlemen present, thereby converting them into Hawaiian chiefs, though of varying degrees of ritual status and mana" (Ob. 86). To summarize: as against the Western "myth" that Cook was received as a manifestation of an indigenous god, and in support of Hawaiian empirical realism, Obeyesekere is prepared to defend the mistaken notion that the god Kū lived in the Englishman's body.

Or, as an alternative to this pidgin anthropology, Obeyesekere contrives Hawaiian practices out of a sort of self-evident common sense, if again at the expense of the documentary descriptions. This is the case of the herald whom the British called "the tabu man." He was one of the priests of Lono—or a man of the officiating Lono priest, Keli'ikea—assigned to accompany Cook. Preceding the captain and at least sometimes waving a tabu ensign, he cried out "Lono" to warn of Cook's coming, at which people immediately fell to the ground. Lieutenant King, concluding his description of the events of 17 January at Hikiau, provided a general account of the tabu man:

> During the rest of the time we remained in the bay, whenever Captain Cook came on shore, he was attended by one of these priests, who went before him, giving notice that the *Orono* had landed, and ordering people to prostrate themselves. The same person also constantly accompanied him on the water, standing in the bow of the boat, with a wand in his hand, and giving notice of his approach to the natives, who were in canoes, on which they immediately left off paddling, and lay down on their faces till he had passed. Whenever he stopped at the observatory [at Hikiau, tabu to the populace], Kaireekeea [Keli'-ikea] and his brethren immediately made their appearance with hogs, cocoa-nuts, bread-fruit, &c. and presented them with the usual solemnities. It was on these occasions that some of the inferior chiefs frequently requested to be permitted to make an offering to the *Orono*. When this was granted, they presented the hog themselves, generally with evident marks of fear on their countenances; whilst Kaireekeea and the priests chanted their accustomed hymns. (Cook and King 1784, 3:14)

Samwell and Ledyard spoke of the tabu man's functions in the same terms.[36] Obeyesekere, however, obfuscates these respects accorded to "Lono" by making out that the herald was actually Cook's protocol guide, some kind of handler. By his telling, instead of announcing the advent of Cook in public places so that proper deference would be paid, the tabu man was detailed to the foreigner in order to ensure that he conformed to Hawaiian customs:

36. Ledyard, who can be fairly characterized as one of Obeyesekere's privileged journalists, has a long and comical description of the landing of Cook at Kealakekua, through a throng of canoes, on 17 January. The tabu man (whom Ledyard calls "a chief") "cried out in their language that the great Orono was coming," at which the people in the canoes inclined and covered their faces with their hands; when Cook got ashore the multitude prostrated as he passed, then jumped up to follow him, only to fall again when he looked around (Ledyard 1963:104–5).

Here, as in Tonga, the tabu man or herald accompanied Cook everywhere, for the same reason: Hawaiians knew that Cook was unaware of their customs, and the tabu man had to ensure that Cook conformed to them, especially in sacred spaces. (Ob. 83; see also 88)

It perhaps needs to be said that a herald would be unnecessary in "sacred spaces"—that is, the major temples *(luakini)*—since the populace is not admitted to them.

Why, then, this stonewalling in the face of the textual evidence? Probably because Obeyesekere's main debating game is a negative one, as we shall see over and again, the object being to cast doubt. Or, perhaps more fully, it is to cast doubts down on "outsider" scholars from the moral highlands of anti-imperialism. *In the event, Obeyesekere repeatedly confuses the option of suggesting a "plausible alternative" with defiance of the documentary record.* The alternative is either some commonsense realism or a universal nativism. But as the "plausible alternative" thus appeals to homemade reasons, while the defiance conceals indigenous customs, the historiographic problems are compounded by the moral contradictions of such politics of interpretation.

Meanwhile, back at Kealakekua, there was another politics of interpretation in play, with its own contradictions, notably between the Hawaiian chiefs and the priests, and possibly also between these ruling groups and the common people.[37] For it need not be supposed that all Hawaiians were equally convinced that Cook was Lono, or, more precisely, that his being "Lono" meant the same thing to everyone. Concerning the women of the people cohabiting with the sailors on board the British ships, Antigonus's famous remark on his own deification may have been more appropriate: "that's not my valet's opinion of me." Lieutenant King speaks of the special enthusiasm of the old folks at seeing the British (Cook and King 1784, 3: 130), a delight that may not have been shared by the entire population, especially the people working priestly estates on the rich agricultural zones upland of Kealakekua. The priestly herald preceding Cook and making everyone prostrate at the cry of "Lono" was not the only indication that the Hawaiian powers-that-be had unique possibilities of objectifying their own interpretations. They could bring a whole set of structures to bear in support of their cosmological opinions, including the controls on land and people that eventuated in a great flow of offerings—presented always in the appropriate ritual form—to Cook, as well as provisions to his company. Whatever

37. The discussion of different Hawaiian interpretations of Cook closely follows that in the Frazer lecture (Sahlins 1985a: 121–25).

the people in general were thinking, they were thus made practically and materially tributary to the religion of Lono of which the priests of Keala-kekua were the legitimate prophets.

This normalization of interpretations by the Hawaiian authorities de-serves some emphasis. For, the social differences of opinion which are ap-parent in the historical documents can hardly exhaust the indeterminacies and perplexities, let alone the disagreements, that in all likelihood marked the initial Hawaiian understandings of Cook. The British journals record the "surprise and astonishment" of Kaua'i people during the first days of contact in January 1778 (e.g., Beaglehole 1967:265). The *Mooolelo* expresses the counterpart in the people's wonderings at the nature of "the remarkable thing standing off-shore," which someone said was "a forest that has moved into the ocean" (Kahananui 1984:167). But the same text also demonstrates the hierarchical organization of interpretation that soon sets in, as the Kaua'i chiefly woman declares of Cook that this is "our god," and that Lonomakua should be placated rather than fought as some wished to do (ibid., 168). So the news of "Lono" traveled to the royal Hawai'i island party at Maui— a view that echoes in Edgar's notice of the chief who came out and asked for "our Arrona"—and by the time Cook came off Hawai'i his ship was a floating temple (ibid., 171). Finally, at Kealakekua, the priests and king are ceremoniously "worshipping" this Lono (ibid., 173). So again, even apart from the a priori authority of their opinions, the ruling powers pragmati-cally engage the people in the service of this interpretation. "Equality in condition," observed Mr. King, "was not the happiness of this island" (Beaglehole 1967:605).

Neither was equality in condition the theory or practice of Hawaiian history. Not all the disagreements were historically significant. The differ-ences of opinion upon which the events of Cook's stay would pivot appeared in the ruling class. They distinguished the Lono priests living near Hikiau temple at Kealakekua, in close contact especially with the British who estab-lished an observatory and hospital in the precincts of the temple, and the warrior chiefs of Ka'awaloa. These "party matters subsisting between the Laity and the Clergy" became increasingly evident from the time of King Kalani'ōpu'u's arrival with a large fleet of warriors on the 25th of January. Yet, even before this, the British on shore at Hikiau temple had experienced the opposition—and were themselves aggravating it:

We on shore soon found that there was a great difference between these Priests [of Lono at Kealakekua] & Koah & Koho the Chief of this district, which is call'd Akona [Kona]; Kireekeea [Keli'ikea, the Lono priest] telling us, that it was not to these [Ka'awaloa people] but to a Chief named Kao [Ka'ō'ō, the head Lono priest] who would come with Terreeoboo [Kalani'ōpu'u] to whom we were oblig'd for all provisions, that we in the tents received; Kireekeea was however conscious of his inferiority, by not testifying his dislike, & which was the reason that one of these two [Koah or Koho], or Pareea [Palea, also a king's man, *aikane*] who generally being by when the Capt" came on shore, got all the presents that certainly ought to have been given to Kireekeea, who doubtless was the Giver of all the hogs & Vegetables. . . . We began to attach ourselves the more strongly to the Priests, whose behaviour was remarkably obliging & modest; without however giveing any offence to the other Chiefs, who were very usefull on board the Ships by Keeping the Natives in order. (King, in Beaglehole 1967:510–11)

Note the multiple contrasts between the chiefs maintaining order, mostly aboard the ships, and the priests liberally providing provisions, especially to the British on land.[38] Along with these generous provisions, the priests also gave the shore party under Lieutenant King an uninhibited view of their dislike of Kalani'ōpu'u and his chiefs:

It has been often mentiond the very extraordinary marks of attention & disinterest'd proofs that the fraternity of Priesthood had paid the Captain, & we who liv'd on the shore, there always appeard in their conduct however some dislike to Terreeoboo, although very careful in treating him with Respect; but to many of the Chiefs about Ter-

38. The everyday provisioning of the British at Hikiau was accompanied by a sacrificially offered pig:

It is customary with the 2ᵈ Priest of this place, whose name is Kaireekea [Keli'ikea] & whom we call the Curate, to bring every day a barbequed Hog to the Tents in procession with a number of Priests singing in concert with him. The Ceremony lasts above half an hour, they sing sometimes all together, at other times in responses till near the Conclusion, which is wound up entirely by Kaireekea; his song lasts about 10 minutes, after which they fall to & eat the Hog, as we have so many that we do not stand in need of it. (Samwell, in Beaglehole 1967:1169)

Keli'ikea would be acting on the part of Ka'ō'ō: "This very benevolent old man sent us regularly in the morning more than sufficient to keep our parties & whenever the Capt" visited us, he as regularly headed his brethern, presented him baked hogs, breadfruit, Sweet potatoes &c &c. & after the Ceremony of giveing them was ended, went back to his Calm retreat" (King in Beaglehole 1967:515). Ka'ō'ō also daily sent Cook "vast daily supplies of Vegetables and barbecued hogs" and supplied excursion parties inland as well (ibid., p. 564).

reeoboo they openly declard to us their hatred but they were afraid to
do it publickly before them. (Ibid., 560)

The most dramatic proofs of this disaffection, and the priests' corollary
attachment to the British, would come after Cook fell at Ka'awaloa at the
chiefs' hands. In the ensuing hostilities the Kealakekua priests remained
loyal to Lono's people. Daily they sent supplies of food to the ships, while
warning the British more than once against the duplicity of Koah and
his fellows of Ka'awaloa. Midshipman Roberts' reflections on the division
among the Hawaiians are typical of many British journalists:

> . . . from the beginning of this fury with these people we have found
> two separate divisions among them. Those in our favour where [sic]
> the priest who performed the great ceremony to Capt. Cook at the
> first arrival of Keree-Oboo, whose name was Ka-oa [Ka'ō'ō], and his
> party, who has every [sic] been steadfast and faithful. . . . Two of them
> this night, at the risk of their lives, came on board the Ship and
> brought us a part of the sad remains of our unfortunate Captain. . . .
> They informed us of the ill designs of their countrymen [the
> Ka'awaloa people] against us, strictly cautioning us against placing in
> them any confidence or trust. (Roberts Log, 16 Feb 1779)

Other accounts specify that the two Lono priests were careful to advise the
Haole "to be on guard gainst Brittanee [Koah] who they said was implacable
and would take all opportunity to destroy us" (Anonymous of Mitchell
1781); or more generally, they "cautioned us against the treachery of the
People of the north Town" (Watts Proceedings, 16 Feb 1779). The priests
also made it clear that it was as much as their life was worth if the Ka'awaloa
people learned of their contact with the *Resolution.* [39]

Well before this, on the 26th of January, King Kalani'ōpu'u and Ka'ō'ō,
the high priest of Lono, had played out with Captain Cook a complex exchange of objects and courtesies—an "occasion of state" as Samwell called
it—that expressed the categorical differences between all three parties. [40]
The exchanges were preceded by a royal welcome rather different from the

39. For further notices of the relations between Ka'awaloa chiefs and Lono priests, see
King (Beaglehole 1967:514, 515, 559–60, 564); Cook and King (1784, 3:14–16 and passim);
Trevenan (Log, 16 Feb 1779); Roberts (Log, 16 Feb 1779); Samwell (Beaglehole 1967:1218);
Harvey (Log, 14 Feb 1779); Clerke (Beaglehole 1967:543); Anonymous of Mitchell (1781).
See also below, 85–86, and appendix 14.
40. The occasion of state is described in more or less detail in the official account (Cook
and King 1784, 3:16–19) as well as in the journals of King (Beaglehole 1967:512–13); Edgar

hānaipū feeding of Lono (though it was of a kind that would be repeated by Kamehameha for Vancouver). In large sailing canoes, the king and the Lono priests (with feather gods) went out and circled the ships, accompanied by chanting, and then returned to shore at Kealakekua. Here ensued the series of diacritical exchanges. Kalani'ōpu'u rose and put his own feather cloak and helmet on Cook, and in the British commander's hand the fly-whisk emblem of royal status. He also spread five or six similar cloaks on the ground, and his attendants brought four large hogs together with sugar cane, coconuts, and breadfruit. If the king had represented Cook in his own social image as a divine warrior, the "bishop," Ka'ō'ō, represented his own temple image as a divine Cook. Led by Ka'ō'ō, the Lono priests came up in a long procession bearing large hogs, plantains and sweet potatoes.[41] As described in the official account, Ka'ō'ō

> had a piece of red [tapa] cloth in his hands, which he wrapped round Captain Cook's shoulders, and afterward presented him with a small pig in the usual form. A seat was then made for him next to the king, after which, Kaireekeea and his followers began their ceremonies, Kaoo and the chiefs joining in the responses. (Cook and King 1784, 3:18)

King Kalani'ōpu'u also exchanged names with the Captain, thus again recognizing Cook in his royal persona. Later the Hawaiian ruler received from Cook a linen shirt and the latter's naval sword. The vice versa movement of regalia and personae was thus a microcosm of the transfers of sovereignty that mark the Makahiki festival—the denouement of which is the king's encompassment of the powers of Lono. In a correlated transaction of this occasion of state, the high priest unilaterally gave King Kalani'ōpu'u a number of iron adzes that had been collected by his fellow Lono priests in return for their generous hospitality to the British. If this again implied a *royal* appropriation of Lono's benefits (at the priests' expense), it was also a

---

(Journal, 27 Jan 1779); Roberts (Log, 27 Jan 1779); and Samwell (Beaglehole 1967:1169), among others.

41. The opposition of foods in the royal and priestly prestations—sugar cane, coconut, and breadfruit in contrast to sweet potato and plantain—seems significant inasmuch as the first are notably feast-pudding ingredients. (In Fiji, the first would indeed be 'chiefly' [*vakaturaga*] and the second 'land' or 'border' [*vanua, vakabati*]). Regarding the statement above that Kalani'ōpu'u took Cook in his image of a divine warrior, the *Mooolelo Hawaii* says: "Kalani'ōpu'u was kind to Cook ["Lono" in the Hawaiian text]; gave him some feather cloaks and feather standards—*kāhili*. Kalani'ōpu'u worshipped him [*Ua ho'omana nō o Kalani'ōpu'u iā ia*]" (Kahananui 1984:173, 18).

material paradigm of the evolving historic structure. The difference in the respective relations of King and Priest to Cook/Lono also entailed an opposition of practical interests.

"A royal feather robe has the chief, a newly opened bud, a royal child / The offering by night, the offering by day: it belongs to the priest to declare [the] ancient transactions." These lines from a celebrated eighteenth-century chant, the perfect caption to the intricate exchanges of the "occasion of state," speak to the difference that continued to distinguish the conduct of the Lono priests toward Cook from that of the warrior chiefs. Projected into history, the difference is that the sense of the totality and immortality of the society conveyed in the priests' transactions with the British was in the chiefs' case conflated with lineage and their own interest. By contrast to the Lono priests, "in all our dealings with the [chiefs]," wrote Mr. King, "we found them sufficiently attentive to their own interests" (Cook and King 1784, 3 : 15). The British catered to these interests so far as to suspend trade of iron implements in favor of the daggers affected by the Hawaiian nobility as insignia of their status—the kind of iron dagger that killed Cook. But the chiefs' interests were also dangerous because they were at times disposed to promote them by theft and chicane. In relation to the god, they knew how to play the trickster—the mythical and ancestral archetype of the usurper. The chiefly mode of exchange with the British alternated opportunistically between noblesse oblige and stealing. Cook, King, Ellis, and others remarked on the aristocratic vice from the day the ships entered Kealakekua Bay. The sudden outbreak of stealing could be traced "to the presence and encouragement of their chiefs": a Polynesian sociology derring-do that continued to plague the foreigners to the day of Cook's death—itself the consequence of the theft of the *Discovery*'s cutter, traceable by almost all accounts to the chief Palea. But then, the politics of the Makahiki was all about the aggressive seizure of Lono's gifts by the warrior chief.[42]

42. Mr. King contrasted the "quiet and humble" behavior the British had experienced in their circuit of Hawai'i with the losses to theft they had at Kealakekua, even before they could anchor. But in the previous days,

> Those who mostly came off, & often to a considerable distance, were evidently Servants or common fishermen; there was a meanness both in their figure & behaviour that distinguished them; If we began now [at Kealakekua] to be torment'd with a greater croud, it was from Many of good mein & appearance who were bold enough to steal our goods, & incourage others. (Beaglehole 1967 : 502)

See Obeyesekere's curious remarks on theft—"the Hawaiians did not practice theft" (Ob. 40)—and Kahananui (1984 : 9, 165).

We have to do with a certain "structure of the conjuncture": a set of historical relationships that at once reproduce the traditional cultural categories and give them new values out of the pragmatic context (Sahlins 1981, 1991). Chiefs, priests, and English were all following their received inclinations and interests. The result was a little social system, complete with alliances, antagonisms—and a certain dynamic. The British had been drawn into the schismogenic relation "between the Laity and the Clergy." In the existing ceremonial cum political circumstances, this was not necessarily to their advantage. For, the more the priests objectified themselves as the party of Lono, the more they intimated for Cook the destiny of the king's victim.

The opposition between the Lono priests and the king's party, which included priests of the war god Kū, had certain echoes in the O'ahu chiefdom of Kahekili several years later. Portlock and Dixon report an even more direct vilification of Kahekili on the part of an outspoken O'ahu priest.[43] Of course, since Kahekili's rule of O'ahu was by conquest, there might have been local resentments at stake. On the other hand, taking into account the displacement that the Ka'ō'ō crowd of Hawai'i were soon to suffer at Kamehameha's hand, one has to wonder if Cook had not entered into—and become the victim of—a long-term trend in the Islands analogous to the rise of the militant 'Oro cult in Tahiti or the similar Rongo cult in Mangaia. In the Hawaiian archipelago, a development of this sort under the aegis of the conquering Kū and his priests might help account for the intensity with which the Lono priests attached themselves to Cook's party.

But to turn again to historiographic reflection, one of the most interesting of Obeyesekere's attempts to substitute a "plausible alternative" for the textual evidence of the association between Cook and Lono concerns his treatment of the Lono priests of Kealakekua and their relations to the royal party at Ka'awaloa. Against all testimony, Obeyesekere denies that these were even priests of Lono, let alone that they had a "separate interest" from, or were in conflict with, the king and chiefs. On the contrary, according to Obeyesekere, these priests "were probably acting on Kalani'ōpu'u's orders" (Ob. 47). Indeed, it "is also clear from Lieutenant King's account" that

---

43. The opposition thus seems to have been recurrent, perhaps structural. The episode reported by Portlock and Dixon occurred in 1786. An apparently important priest came off to the *King George* and "kept repeating with great vociferation and for a considerable length of time, 'Terreterre poonepoone [Kahekili *punipuni*, 'liar'], Terreterre arreeoura [Kahekili *ali'i 'au'a*, 'stingy chief'?]' or that the king was a liar, scoundrel and deceitful person" (Dixon 1789:104; see Portlock 1789:161, 165, 166, for further complaints against the king by the same person).

Keli'ikea was one of the king's "servants," together with Koah (ibid.).[44] Obeyesekere's use of quotation marks makes it seem that Mr. King had said the two were royal "servants"; however, the passage of the journal to which the appended footnote refers says nothing about so-called servants. It is, rather, the text (just cited) where Mr. King talks about the "great difference" between the priests and chiefs, remarking how Keli'ikea was "too conscious of his inferiority" to testify to his disapproval of Koah and the chief Koho getting all the credit for presents that really came from the Lono priests.

The houses of these priests were grouped about a temple or "House of Lono," as Samwell had described; indeed, he spoke of their entire settlement as "some Temples or Houses consecrated to Orono" (Beaglehole 1967: 1169). Here lived Keli'ikea and Ka'ō'ō. This is the same place and "fraternity of Priesthood" (ibid., 560) that Mr. King identified as the only "regular society of priests" the British had encountered on the voyage. Omeah, who was called "Lono" and who was identified by King as the head of the whole order—he was more likely the bearer of the Makahiki image, as we shall see—also lived here:

> we had never met with a regular society of priests, till we discovered the cloisters of Kakooa [Kealakekua] in Karakakooa Bay. The head of this order was called *Orono;* a title which we imagined to imply something highly sacred, and which, in the person of Omeeah, was honoured almost to adoration. . . . Omeah, the *Orono,* was the son of Kaoo, and the uncle of Kaireekeea; which last presided, during the absence of his grandfather, in all religious ceremonies at the *Morai.* (Cook and King 1784, 3:159)

But Obeyesekere would rewrite the Lono priests out of existence, apparently because their differential relations to the British compromises his effort to dissociate Cook and Lono. Without any documentation (again) he asserts that Samwell and King "erroneously thought" the (Lono) priests in question "were opposed to the king" (Ob. 93). This correction is rounded off with an impostor genealogy that attempts to make the Lono order of Kealakekua into Kū priests and henchmen of the king by superimposing the names of a well-known Kū line on the names and kinship relations of the Lono priests described in the Cook chronicles—though not one of the names in these two sets of priests is the same, or can be shown to be so (see

44. This is the same Koah or "Brittanee" against whom the British had repeatedly been warned by the Kealakekua priests, including the two who came out to the *Resolution* on the night of 16 February and who were Keli'ikea's men (see appendix 11).

ibid.).[45] Perhaps the best that can be said for these historical fictions is that Obeyesekere demonstrates in his own practice what he is otherwise at pains to deny: that objective perceptions are ordered by a priori conceptions.

Returning to the scene of these developing relationships, there seem to have been no further ceremonies until a flurry of events in the last days of January and beginning of February. These began modestly with a tabu put on the sea by the Hawaiians in the evening of January 29 and the day of the 30th. Samwell alone seems to have noticed this tabu, although his supposition that it was due to the expected arrival of some chief turned out to be incorrect (Beaglehole 1967: 1171–72). The period of the full moon was approaching, however: February 1 would be the 14th day of the Hawaiian lunar month (± 1 day, depending on Hawaiian intercalation procedures for 29½-day lunar cycles). By the December concordance, this would be the full moon of the month of Kāʻelo, the time of the termination rites of the Makahiki (beginning 13 Kāʻelo). In this context, Mr. King's notice for the second of February in the published account appears most relevant: "Terreeoboo [Kalaniʻōpuʻu] and his Chiefs, had, for some days past, been very inquisitive about the time of our departure"—to which his private journal adds, "& seemd well pleas'd that it was to be soon" (Cook and King 1784, 3:26; Beaglehole 1967:517).

It is also in the context of the Hawaiian ceremonial calendar that Lieutenant King's subsequent remarks in the official *Voyage* might be understood. The Hawaiian questions about the British departure had made King curious to know "what opinion this people had formed of us." He took some pains to find out, but all he could learn was they thought the British had come from some country where provisions had failed and they came to Hawaii to fill their bellies. Stroking the sides and stomachs of the now-fattened sailors, the Hawaiians told them "partly by signs, and partly by words, that it was time for them to go; but if they would come again next breadfruit season, they should be better able to supply their wants."[46] King found it under-

A.8

Clark Gable for Cook?

45. What is involved in this genealogical creation is discussed below, in chapter 3 and appendix 13. Here it might be noted that the Lono priests of Kealakekua controlled the *ahupuaʻa*, or district, of that name stretching considerably beyond the village. Kaʻōʻo's daughter still had the say about access to Hikiau temple in Vancouver's time—and was still opposing the Hawaiʻi king (below, 133).

46. A connection between the Makahiki and the ripening of breadfruit in Hawaiʻi has not been noticed before, although this is quite possibly at issue here in the Hawaiians' remarks. On the contrary, Handy and Handy (1972:152) claimed that "the real bearing time for breadfruit" in Hawaiʻi island is from June through July only. But this is patently contradicted by data from the Cook chronicles: not only the report of Mr. King, but other accounts of trade for breadfruit from December into February while the British were circling the island or at Kealakekua (e.g.,

standable that the Hawaiians might want them off, considering the enormous amount of hogs and vegetables supplied to them (but see below,
141–43). On the other hand:

> It is very probable, however, that Terreeoboo had no other view, in
> his inquiries, at present, than a desire of making sufficient preparation
> for dismissing us with presents, suitable to the respect and kindness
> with which he had received us. For, on our telling him we should leave
> the island on the next day but one, we observed, that a sort of proc-
> lamation was immediately made, through the villages, to require the
> people to bring in their hogs, and vegetables, for the king to present
> to the *Orono* [Lono], on his departure. (Cook and King 1784, 3:
> 26–27)

In fact, the British were somewhat surprised by the sequel, for the substantial prestation of cloth, feathers, food, and iron trade goods, which they
were invited to see displayed at the house of the Lono priest Ka'ō'ō on February 3, was not directly for them:

> At first, we imagined the whole to be intended as a present for us, till
> Kaireekea [Keli'ikea, the Lono priest] informed me, that it was a gift,
> or tribute, from the people of that district [Kealakekua] to the king;
> and, accordingly, as soon as we were seated, they brought all the
> bundles, and laid them severally at Terreeoboo's feet; spreading out
> the cloth, and displaying the feathers, and iron-ware before him. The
> king seemed much pleased with this mark of their duty. (Cook and
> King 1784, 3:28–29)

Only afterwards, having reserved for himself about a third of the ironware
and feathers together with some tapa cloth, did the king present the food
and the rest of the cloth to Cook and King.

Note that the "tribute" was localized in origin and offered to the king.
In these respects it corresponds to the ceremonial offering that takes place

---

Ellis 1792, vol. 2 passim; Edgar Log, 4, 6, 8 Dec 1778, and elsewhere; Burney MSb, 20 Nov
1778, 27 Jan and 3 Feb 1779; Trevenan Log, 22 Dec 1778; Samwell in Beaglehole 1967:1152,
1158, 1215, 1216). The cognate New Year festival of Tahiti, likewise involving the return of
the ancestors, is associated with the ripening of the breadfruit (Moerenhaut 1837, 1:502, 517–
23; Oliver 1974, 3:259ff.). In Hawai'i, the breadfruit tree is a body of the god Kū, who is the
ultimate hero of the Makahiki. The goddess Haumea, another version of La'ila'i, disappears into
the breadfruit in certain myths involving a contest over her quite like the Kumulipo triad or
the Lono myths of the Makahiki (Beckwith 1970:97–99, 281–83).

precisely at this time, at the full moon of Kā'elo, according to the brief notice in Malo's (1951:152) account of the Makahiki cycle: "During the tabu period of Hua [13 and 14 Kā'elo] the people again had to make a *hook-upu* [offering] for the king. It was but a small levy, however, and was called the heap of Kuapola."

Another aspect of the termination rituals, as described by Malo, is also paralleled in the Cook chronicles of 1779. In Malo's account:

On the last day of the tabu period, the king and *kahuna-nui* [high priest], accompanied by the man who beat the drum, went and regaled themselves on pork. The service at this time was performed by a distinct set of priests. When these ceremonies were over the period of Makahiki and its observances were ended. . . . Now began the new year. (Malo 1951:152)

Just so, there was a ceremony at Hikiau on the night of February 2–3, corresponding to the 15th of the lunar month, or the end of the tabu period (of Hua):

Whilst Kao [Ka'ō'ō] was amongst the priests they were perpetualy offering sacrifices & prayers: before he left the place, which was at the time we first went out of Karakacooa bay [early morning of 4 February], they had during the preceding night many ceremonies upon the Marai [Hikiau temple], the Images were drest, the great drums, & large bundles of feathers, & of what Valuables they had collectd were placed under one of the Carv'd images; these things we understood Kao was to carry with him. (Beaglehole 1967:620)

This observation of King's has a double interest. It not only corresponds in date and certain particulars to Malo's Makahiki text, but it shows that, contrary to a certain historical tradition, the British had not desecrated the temple in the days preceding by burying old Willie Watman there or by carrying off the fencing for firewood.[47]

Watman's death bears an interesting relationship to the human sacrifice

---

47. The firewood incident is discussed at length in appendix 14, "On the Wrath of Cook." Hikiau was again the site of Hawaiian ceremonies on the 18th of February, Keli'ikea presiding (Burney MSb, 18 Feb 1779; Anonymous of NLA, 18 Feb 1779). This would be the beginning of a lunar month (Kaulua, by the reckoning adopted here), thus corresponding to the resumption of normal temple rites subsequent to the Makahiki (Malo 1951:152). The notion that the British had desecrated Hikiau temple is hardly supported by these reports of its continued use—at appropriate ritual dates.

prescribed in the final rituals of the Makahiki period. At the aforementioned tabu of the full moon, the king's human god-image, Kahoali'i, eats the eye of a sacrificial victim offered at the temple used in the principal Makahiki ceremonies (Malo 1951:152). No such sacrifice is reported in British accounts of the 1779 events. However, the old sailor Willie Watman died on the first of February, and was buried that afternoon in the Hikiau temple, the priests of Lono attending and participating—as Cook conducted the first public Christian ceremony in these Islands (see appendix 14). Indeed, it was *at the request of the Hawaiian authorities* that Watman's body was brought to Hikiau (for burial?). Lieutenant King says in one place the king desired it, in another place, the chiefs (Beaglehole 1967:517; Cook and King 1784, 3:24; see also Ledyard 1963:124). Led by the venerable Ka'ō'ō, the Lono priests followed the British service with their own ceremonies, expressing a wish to throw a dead pig, plantains, coconuts, and other offerings into the grave. They were "in some measure stop'd," but for three nights "Kao [Ka'-ō'ō] & the rest of them surrounded the grave, killd hogs, sang a great deal, in which Acts of Piety & good will they were left undisturb'd" (Beaglehole 1967:517; see also Ledyard 1963:125).[48] Everything thus suggests that the Hawaiians gave Watman's death a significance of their own, at a time and place that corresponded to the customary offering of a human sacrifice.

For that matter, these Hawaiian funerary ceremonies took place *after* the British had removed the palings and images of the semicircle at Hikiau for firewood—which supposed sacrilege had already been accomplished on the morning of Watman's death (Roberts Log, 1–2 Feb 1779; Beaglehole 1967:516–17; Burney MSb, 30–31 Jan 1779; Charlton Journal, 31 Jan–1 Feb 1779; Cook and King 1784, 3:25). Debate has raged among Haole ever since about whether taking the firewood provoked Hawaiian resentment—particularly on the part of the priests—and thereby Cook's death. Here it will suffice to repeat that, apart from Mr. King's explicit assurance that no offence was taken by the priests, it was Hawaiian notables who subsequently asked that Watman's death services be performed at Hikiau, that the priests voluntarily participated in these rites, that they used the temple

48. Among Obeyesekere's objections to the analogy between these events and the human sacrifice at the end of the Makahiki is the notion that Hawaiians would not have wanted a lower-class British type interred in their temple. This neglects the fact that human sacrificial victims were generally wrong-doers, rebels or so-called slaves (*kauwā*, generally war captives). There would be a point in supposing that the Hawaiians were asking that Watman's body be *brought* to the temple; burying him there was another, probably British, understanding. For a full discussion of this episode, see appendix 14.

for their own prescribed ceremonies on two subsequent occasions (3 February and 18 February), and that they continued to side with the British in the hostilities with Ka'awaloa chiefs that followed Cook's death (see appendix 14). Indeed, there could well be a valid motivation for dismantling Hikiau temple in the Hawaiian ceremonial calendar. At the conclusion of the Makahiki period, temples of this type *(luakini)* are refurbished for the resumption of normal rituals under the aegis of Kū. So it deserves notice in this connection that the British had seen Hawaiians carrying off posts from the temple fence; on more than one occasion also, Hawaiians had seemed to ridicule the temple images (except Kū). And finally the Hawaiians themselves burned down the houses on the temple platform, accidentally the British thought, the night the ships left Kealakekua Bay (see appendix 14).

But there was still another ceremony of this departure. On the first of February, and again the next day, the Hawaiians improvised a performance of the kind that marks the departure of Lonomakua from one district for the next in its procession round the island. Of course Cook's people thought these boxing matches were "entertainments" staged in their honor, that is, as courtesies for departing guests. The graphic and textual evidence suggests something else. In the Makahiki, when the Lono image passes on, its place is taken by images of the same form representing gods of play. These now preside over scenes of boxing, wrestling, and other popular amusements in celebration of the god's passage. (Actually, judging from the cognate Maori rites, the planted image together with the celebrating people could well be understood as the inseminating work of Lono's passage: see Sahlins 1985b.) So it happened on February 1: such Makahiki images watched over the boxing matches put on at Kealakekua by the Hawaiians with the British in attendance. Apparently the one drawn by Webber played the same role the next day (fig. 1.3). Since such images are seen at no other time of the year, their appearance now is substantial evidence that the Makahiki was indeed on—and that this conjuncture was informing the respects of Lono paid to Captain Cook.

By the same set of ceremonial circumstances, the British departure on the night of February 3 was well timed. It was the sixteenth day of the lunar month (of Kā'elo). According to the traditional calendar, the Makahiki was finished. In principle, the Hawaiian king would now rededicate Hikiau and other royal temples, and also—incorporating the benefits of the god's passage—reopen the agricultural shrines of Lono. Everything would be on ritual schedule, except that Cook, too, was visited by another manifestation

A.9
Blurred Images

Fig. 1.3 Boxing match
before Captain Cook at
Hawai'i, by John Webber,
showing Makahiki image
at left. (John Webber,
Bishop Museum)

of Lono, one of the severe Kona storms that coincide with the god's return, which disabled the foremast of the *Resolution*. Cook was obliged to return to Kealakekua for repairs. Sailing into the bay again on the 11th of February, the Great Navigator was now out of phase with the Hawaiian ritual cycle. Lieutenant King observed that there were not as many hundreds of people on hand at their return as there had been thousands when they first came into the bay. There was some kind of tabu in effect, which was ascribed to the king's absence but may have been a delayed bonito-fishing rite, marking the transition to the new ceremonial season. In any case, Cook was now

hors cadre. Unlike his arrival, his return was generally unintelligible and unwanted, especially by the king and chiefs. And things fell apart.[49]

In the mythopolitical crisis occasioned by Lono's inexplicable return,

49. The preceding paragraph and the next few to follow are adapted with little or no change from Sahlins (1985a: 127–28). Obeyesekere's gammon representation of my arguments concerning the disjunction between Cook's return and the Hawaiian ritual (cum political) cycle is as follows: "Sahlins's thesis that Cook was killed because he violated a tabu by returning at the inappropriate time has little merit. Cook and his crew were violating tabus from the very start" (Ob. 101).

the tensions and ambivalences in the social organization of the previous weeks were now revealed. The king, who came in next day, was said to be "very angry" with the priests for again letting the British use the ground near Hikiau temple (Beaglehole 1967:550). The priests reciprocated with a cordial detestation of the chiefs at Ka'awaloa, an attitude they did not trouble to conceal from their British friends. And to complete the triangle, the king and several chiefs were "very inquisitive . . . to know the reason of our return," Mr. Burney says, "and appeared much dissatisfied at it" (Burney MSb, 12 Feb 1779; see also Burney 1819:256–57). In retrospect, as Lieutenant King reflected, "it is not very clear, but that some Chiefs were glad of seeking an occasion to quarrel" (Beaglehole 1967:568). Actually, the chroniclers vary in their assessment of Hawaiian reactions, perhaps due to different experiences of the complex structure of the conjuncture. Samwell (1957:6), special friend to the priests, could find "the abundant good nature which had always characterized [the Hawaiians]" still glowing "in every bosom" and animating "every countenance." For John Ledyard (1963:141), it was evident from the people's appearance, "that our former friendship was at an end, and that we had nothing to do but to hasten our departure to some different island where our vices were not yet known, and where our extrinsic virtues might gain us another short space of being wondered at."

All along, the diverse and delicate relationships between the two peoples had been ordered by the one salient interpretation of Cook as the Makahiki god which the Hawaiian authorities were able to reify, and with which the Great Navigator could comply. Now that reality began to dissolve. For the king and chiefs, it even became sinister. "On our return to this place," observed one journalist, "great alteration was observed with respect to the conduct of the Natives, and the Chiefs and principal people were very importunate concerning the cause of our return" (Anonymous of NLA Account, 1). Lieutenant King records in his journal the touching empiricist belief that once the reasons for the return were explained to the chiefs, their noticeable disapproval would be dispelled (Beaglehole 1967:568; see also Gilbert 1982:104). But the problem was not just empirical or practical: it was cosmological—in which respect, the state of *Resolution's* mast was simply not intelligible:

The King, whose name was Keereiaboo ask'd Cap Cook what brought him back again. Cook said his mast was broken. The King told the Cap" that he had amused him with lies that went [*sic*] he went away he took his farewell of him and said he did not know he should ever come again.[50] It was plain the King suspected Cook had evil intentions and his Countenance changed towards him and we did not find the people so fond of us as before. They were constantly asking what brought us back for they could form no notion of our distress or what was the matter with our mast. (Anonymous of Mitchell 1781)[51]

Cook's return out of season would be sinister to the ruling chiefs because it presented a mirror image of Makahiki politics. Bringing the god ashore during the triumph of the king, it could reopen the whole issue of sovereignty. It is not for nothing that Cook's predecessors as Lono figures were in fact royals, rulers of Hawai'i island. In word and deed, the reaction of the king's party in 1779 confirms this political dimension of the Makahiki—the transfer of rule which sees the king in the role of the upstart and humanized warrior (Kū aspect) capturing the reproductive powers of the god (Lono aspect). Several of the British journal writers recorded Hawaiian fears that Cook *mā* had come back to take their country. Midshipman Gilbert, for example:

The Natives did not appear to receive us this time with that Friendship that they had done before. Our quick return seemed to create a kind of Jealousey amongst them with respect to our intentions; as fearing we should attempt to settle there, and deprive them of part if not the whole of their Country. (1982:104)

Lieutenants Burney and King likewise noticed the Hawaiian suspicions that the British intended to settle (Burney 1819:256–57; Beaglehole 1967: 568–69). And the direct complements in these and other journals are the descriptions of the thefts and violence that broke out upon the reappearance of the British, incidents that counterposed the foreigners to the chiefly crowd in particular.

"Ever since our arrival here upon this our second visit," wrote Captain

50. But see Cook and King (1784, 3:30), where it is said that Cook, in order to avoid the request of Kalani'ōpu'u and Ka'ō'ō that he leave his "son," Lieutenant King, with them, promised (à la Father Lono) to return the next year.

51. I say the problem of the mast was cosmological and not empirico-practical in the sense that Cook's return had a transcendent significance that was not exhausted by the technical explanation. The problem is analogous to the issues in Azande magic discussed by Evans-Pritchard: it may be the property of fire to burn down wooden structures, but it is not a property of fire to burn *your house*—or for that matter, to burn *property.* Obeyesekere's objection is typically literal: he finds it "hard to believe that the Hawaiians, experienced navigators that they were, could not understand the plight of the English forced to return to repair their ship" (Ob. 103).

Clerke, "we have observ'd in the Natives a stronger propensity to theft than we had reason to complain of during our former stay; every day produc'd more numerous and more audacious depredations" (Beaglehole 1967:531–32). The 13th of February, the day before Cook's fall, was notable for violent altercations with *ali'i*. Mr. Trevenen later blamed Cook's death on a chief thrown off the *Resolution* this day for stealing. Chiefs attempted to prevent some commoners from assisting the British who were loading water on shore, near the priests' settlement.[52] In a scuffle involving Palea, the one who was to arrange the theft of the *Discovery's* boat, two young officers (one of them George Vancouver) and several seamen were well and truly drubbed. That night, the ship's cutter was stolen. Cook, who had already shown in Tonga and the Society Islands that he would not suffer "the Indians" to think they had the advantage of him, decided after the skirmishes of February 13 that he would again be obliged to use force. So when he went ashore next day to take King Kalani'ōpu'u hostage against the return of the cutter, he made sure to land in the company of armed marines.

Just as Cook's return was something like a mirror image of the Makahiki, so the scene on the morning of the 14th of February at Ka'awaloa was reminiscent of the climactic ritual battle, the *kāli'i*, but played in reverse. The god Lono (Cook) was wading ashore with his warriors to confront the king. Rather than the reinstitution of human sacrifice by the king in celebration of the cult of the god Kū, news came to the Hawaiians gathered to protect Kalani'ōpu'u that Lono's people had killed one of the chiefs—this was Kalimu, shot by Lieutenant Rickman's blockading party at the north end of the bay. And certain other historical actors likewise assumed legendary roles. There were warrior champions like those of the *kāli'i* combat. Cook was accompanied everywhere by his second, lieutenant of the marines Molesworth Phillips, who indeed went before in the search for the king. On the other side, as best as can be made out, the man who struck the critical blow against Cook was one Nuha, a prominent Ka'awaloa warrior in the royal retinue (Sahlins 1985a:129–31). Just before, the king had been prevented

52. From Lieutenant King's journal: "In the Afternoon [of 13 February] the gentleman who was filling water out of the well on the other end of the beach for the Discovery came & acquaintd me, that a Chief had hindred the Natives whom he had paid from assisting him, & that he & others were very troublesome; he desir'd me therefore to let him have a Marine; I sent one with him accordingly, with his side Arms only; but Mʳ Hollamby soon returned, & said the Indians had now arm'd themselves with Stones, & were still more insolent, on which I took with me a Marine with a Musquet, upon seeing us coming they threw away their Stones, & upon speaking to some of the Chiefs present the mob was driven away, those who chose sufferd to assist in filling the Casks" (Beaglehole 1967:529).

from accompanying Lono-Cook by the intercession of his favored wife Kaneikapolei. For one brief and decisive moment, the confrontation returned to the original triad of the god (Cook), his human successor (Kalani'ōpu'u) and the woman (Kaneikapolei), with the issue again decided by the woman's choice.

The myths were not only Hawaiian. There was also the complementary British folklore characterized by J. C. Beaglehole as "the English search for a 'King.'" Hence Cook's ill-advised attempt to take Kalani'ōpu'u hostage—even though, by all accounts, the king was not implicated in the theft of the ship's boat. Given this melee of meanings, I may be permitted perhaps to give an anthropological reading of the historical texts.[53] For, in all the confused Tolstoian narratives of the affray—among which the judicious Beaglehole refuses at times to choose—the one recurrent certainty is a dramatic structure with the properties of a ritual transformation. During the passage inland to find the king, thence seaward with his royal hostage, Cook is metamorphosed from a being of veneration to an object of hostility. When he came ashore, the common people as usual dispersed before him and prostrated, face to the earth; but in the end he was himself precipitated face down in the water by a chief's weapon, an iron trade dagger, to be rushed upon by a mob exulting over him, and seeming to add to their own honors by the part they could claim in his death: "snatching the daggers from each other," reads Mr. Burney's account, "out of eagerness to have their share in killing him" (MSb, 14 Feb 1779). In the final ritual inversion, which however reproduces the ultimate fate of Lono, Cook's body would be offered in sacrifice by the Hawaiian king.

Cook was transformed from the divine beneficiary of the sacrifice to its

53. Ostensibly, the only approach to direct testimony available on Cook's death is that of Lieutenant Molesworth Phillips, as transmitted in Captain Clerke's journal (Beaglehole 1967: 534–36). Phillips was knocked down before Cook fell and did not see the end itself. There are many other notices in the public and private journals, including some from men in the boats offshore. Many of these may also have been constructed from the testimony of surviving marines, as well as from the ships' scuttlebutt, but only Phillips's account is in quotation marks. Lieutenant Burney, for example, prefaces his account, "the particulars of this Misfortune gathered from those who were on the spot, are as follows" (MSb, 4 Feb 1779). Alexander Home's and Mr. King's reports were likewise constructed (Home Log; Beaglehole 1967:555). J. C. Beaglehole has sifted through the various journals, and the present retelling generally follows his sensible rendering. But I tend to emphasize "symbolic" details in the accounts that Beaglehole ignored. Also, Beaglehole gave limited credence to information from Hawaiians, direct or indirect, earlier or later; whereas, I have found these data more useful in determining the Hawaiian personnel and, above all, the Hawaiian concepts necessary to interpret the fatal deed. Of course, many uncertainties remain: most important, the exact moment in the sequence of events when news of the death of the chief Kalimu reached the shore at Ka'awaloa.

victim—a change never really radical in Polynesian thought, and in their royal combats always possible (Valeri 1985). Every phase of the transformation had its own kind of offering: the shifting material signs of Cook's trajectory in cosmic value. In the beginning, as he went "to find the king," pigs were pressed upon him; and, as he waited for Kalani'ōpu'u to waken, more offerings of red tapa cloth—proving that the English captain was still the image of the Hawaiian god. The king came away willingly, and was walking by Cook's hand to the waiting ship's boat, when he was stopped by his wife Kaneikapolei and two chiefs, pleading and demanding that he not go on. By all accounts, British as well as Hawaiian, they told him such sad stories of the death of kings as to force him to sit upon the ground, where he now appeared—according to Lieutenant Phillips's report—"dejected and frighten'd" (Beaglehole 1967:535).

Nothing to this point had evoked the king's suspicions, and, likewise, it was only now, Phillips recounts, that "we first began to suspect that they were not very well dispos'd towards us" (ibid.). The transition comes suddenly, at the moment the king is made to perceive Cook as his mortal enemy. This is the structural crisis, when all the social relations begin to change their signs. Accordingly, the material exchanges now convey a certain ambiguity, like those Maori sacrifices that pollute the gods in the act of placating them. An old man offers a coconut, chanting so persistently that the exasperated Cook cannot make him lay off. A supplication begging the release of the king? Lieutenant Phillips considered that "the artful rascal of a priest" was carrying on to divert attention from the fact that his countrymen, gathering to the number of two or three thousand, were now arming to defend their king. About this time, the report comes that Kalimu has been killed by the British blockading the southern end of the Bay. The king is seen still on the ground, "with the strongest marks of terror and dejection on his countenance" (Cook and King 1784, 3:44), but he soon disappears from the scene. Events have gone beyond the power of anyone to control them. "Ye natives" are manifesting that disposition the English call "insolence." The final homage to Cook is tendered in missiles that include stones and clubs among the pieces of breadfruit and coconut. Each side thus responding violently to the perceived threats of the other, they soon reach "the fatal impact."

A.10
Cookamamie

TWO

Cook after Death

Within forty-eight hours of Cook's death, two priests from Keala-kekua came out to the *Resolution* under cover of darkness with a piece of the captain's "upper thigh." They were the men of "hon-est Keli'ikea," the Lono priest: one was the so-called tabu man who had always gone before Cook proclaiming the coming of Lono. They were re-turning this part of Lono as a gesture of solidarity with the British, a gesture they took care to conceal from the king's party at Ka'awaloa. In Hawaiian customary practice, the corruptible flesh of a royal sacrificial victim is thrown into the sea. The enduring bones are distributed among the victori-ous chiefs, the skull or lower jaw to the principal adversary of the defeated rival. So it was with Cook. The British learned that his skull had gone to the leading warrior of Ka'awaloa, Kekuhaupi'o, and his mandible to the king (Beaglehole 1967:1215; Cook and King 1784, 3:78; Anonymous of NLA Account, 13, 14). The charred remains the British later recovered are consis-tent with the Hawaiian tradition that the king had offered Lono in sacri-fice—a historical metaphor of the Makahiki ritual (Kahananui 1984:174).[1] Yet, even as Cook was thus being dismembered, the two priests on the *Reso-lution*—after one had "shed abundance of tears at the loss of the Erono"—asked a most "Singular question . . . & that was when the Erono would return, this was demanded afterwards by others, & what he would do to them when he return'd" (King in Beaglehole 1967:561).

---

1. Obeyesekere mistakenly claims that Cook's body was accorded the deification ritual of a deceased king. The abundant testimony from British and Hawaiian sources that Cook was treated as a sacrificial victim and adversary of the king is confirmed by the specific distribution of Cook's bones (see Malo 1951:104–5; Valeri 1985:338–39, 403). The differences between this treatment and the ritual for enshrining the bones of deceased royals are considered in the next chapter.

In the published *Voyage*, Lieutenant King adds that the idea of Cook's return "agrees with the general tenour of their conduct toward him, which shewed, that they considered him as a being of a superior nature" (Cook and King 1784, 3:69). Mr. Bligh, who hated King, dismissed the statement as another of the young lieutenant's absurdities, but Trevenan and others confirm it. "Some amongst them asserted that he would return in two months & begged our mediation with him in their favour" (Trevenan Annotations). Samwell's corroborative report—"The Indians have a Notion that Capt" Cook as being Orono will come amongst them again in a short time"—refers to another incident, a few days after the "singular question" of the two priests, when a man gave the midshipman on the guard boat of the *Resolution* "some burnt bones which he said belonged to the Orono" (Beaglehole 1967: 1217). The projected timing of the return in these accounts could have something to do with the reopening of the agricultural and therapeutic shrines of Lono, which came about two months after the end of the Makahiki. But the "extraordinary question" memorialized in an anonymous account of Cook's death "by an eyewitness" seems more directly associated with the Makahiki rites. The interrogator, again, was one of the priests who brought out Cook's flesh: "A most extraordinary question was asked by this Man which was, when Capt Cook would come back to the ship and resume his former station and if he would not appear in three days" (Anonymous of NLA Account, 14). After he is dismantled (it might be recalled), Lono sails back to Kahiki.

A.11
Priests' Sorrows,
Women's Joys,
and Sterotypic
Reproduction

Likewise, from the time of his death until some decades into the next century, Cook continued to figure as a form of Lono in Hawaiian popular belief and ritual practice. Among the numerous reports of this apotheosis, there is testimony that Cook's (purported) bones were carried in the annual Makahiki procession of Lono. The reports, it might be stressed, come mainly from Hawaiian people, as cited by this or that European chronicler. The provenance needs to be emphasized because the current politics of interpretation, as articulated by Obeyesekere, would have it that the idea really comes from Haole, whose myths the Hawaiians were mimicking for them (Ob. 50). Obeyesekere believes that if Cook's spirit was still abroad, it was as a ghost or as a deified chief by the proper name of Lono—because Hawaiians were too realistic and rational to suppose that a foreigner of strange appearance and incomprehensible speech could be one of their gods.

Cook as Lono in the Late Eighteenth Century

After Cook's death, no European ships touched at the Hawaiian islands for seven years, until 1786. Thenceforth, the early foreign visitors were mainly fur traders, and they recorded memories of Cook that were quite remarkable.[2] The demonstration of affection for "their beloved Cook" described in John Meares' account of 1787 will set the scene of our discussion:

> The numbers of them which surrounded the ship with a view to obtain permission to go to Britanee, to the friends of their beloved Cook, are incredible. . . . Presents were poured in on us from the chiefs, who were prevented by the multitude from approaching the vessel, and the clamorous cry of *Britanee, Britanee,* was for a long time heard from every part, without ceasing. (Meares 1790:9)

One is reminded of the celebration that greeted Cook when he first came into Kealakekua. Or again, of Kuykendall's (1968:206) observation that, from the time of Vancouver's last visit in 1794 to about 1825, "Great Britain held the highest place in the thought of Hawaiians about foreign countries; they considered themselves under the protection of that nation and frequently referred to themselves as *kanaka no Beritane* (men of Britain)." And if Meares' account suggests that the sentiment antedated Vancouver, the journals of the latter expedition can confirm that it was widespread in the Hawaiian population and mediated by the dead Cook. The memory of Cook, Lieutenant Puget wrote, "appears on all occasions to be treated with the Greatest Veneration by all Ranks of People" (Puget Log, 26 Feb 1793). Or even more, Cook had assumed a place in the general Hawaiian consciousness as a source of time, a frame of history, a position that the clerk Edward Bell connected with his status as Lono:

> The Natives seem to consider that melancholy transaction [Cook's death] as one of the most remarkable events in their History, almost every child able to prattle can give you an account of it, and in reckoning back to distant periods, which they do by memorable occurrences, and knowing the distances of time from one to another, this transaction seems to assist their calculations in a very great degree;— at that time they look'd up to him as to a supernatural being, indeed called him the 'Orono' or great God, nor has he to this day lost any of

2. The notices of the fur traders and other Haole concerning Cook and the Makahiki have been rehearsed in detail elsewhere (Sahlins 1989, 1991). The discussion here excerpts much of this previously published material.

his character or consequence with the Natives they still in speaking of
him style him the Orono and if they are to be believ'd, most sincerely
regret his fate. (Bell 1929, 1(6):80)[3]

Bell recounts these views of Cook in the context of a visit to Kealakekua
in March 1793. Obeyesekere gives this text a begging-the-question-squared
treatment, alleging that Bell (not Hawaiians as claimed) was the author of
the notion that Cook = Lono, Bell having taken the idea from the myth
to that effect promulgated by Lieutenant King and David Samwell—who
in fact, Obeyesekere also says, made no such identification of Cook with
the god.

Bell is . . . not conducting an interview with natives. He is adapting
the account of Cook's death in the 1784 official edition to accord with
his present experiences. Bell, following the official edition, says that
Hawaiians look upon [sic] Cook *as to* a supernatural being, clearly
showing the connections with the similes employed by King and Samwell. Yet Bell compares Cook to a supernatural being, the great god
Lono—a mistake that the earlier journalists never made. (Ob. 151)

The logic of this textual criticism is as follows. On the basis of a purported resemblance of Bell's similes to King and Samwell—that Hawaiians
looked "up to him [Cook] as to a supernatural being," a phrase that as such
does not occur in King or Samwell—Obeyesekere supposes that Bell came
to a conclusion his predecessors could not reach, namely, that Cook =
Lono. This proves that he got the whole idea from them and not from Hawaiians as he said. It also shows how Obeyesekere dispossesses Hawaiian
voices, simply taking their words from them and giving them to Haole. In
this case, the Haole Mr. Bell, in pretending to quote Hawaiians, must be
lying—to himself, in his own personal journal.

To return to the documents, a particular light is thrown on the relation
between Cook and Lono even before the Vancouver expedition in the experiences recorded by the fur trader James Colnett and his people in 1788
and 1791. In 1788, Colnett came upon an unmistakable Makahiki celebration at O'ahu. This was in January, hence at the appropriate time of the year.
Moreover it was well before Kamehameha's conquest, while the island was
ruled by Kahekili of Maui.[4] Colnett, in the *Prince of Wales*, was anchored at

3. On heroic calendrical reckoning in Hawaii, see Sahlins 1992, chapter 8.
4. The Makahiki image at O'ahu was abroad during the appropriate period of the Makahiki
at Hawai'i, as described by Malo *mā*: an inter-island regularity Obeyesekere considers a priori

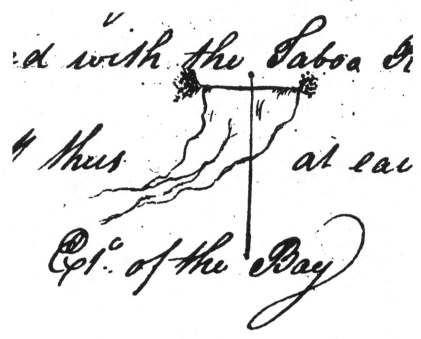

Fig. 2.1 Makahiki image drawn by James Colnett (Journal, 17 Jan 1788)

Waikiki on 17 January 1788. For two nights, he had observed fires burning and heard drumming on shore. Now a priest came off to the ship bearing a classic Makahiki image. We can be sure of this, and not merely because Colnett's verbal description resembles Malo's (1951 : 143–44) or John Papa 'I'i's (1959 : 70–72)—which in turn match the drawing made by Webber during Cook's voyage (fig. 1.3). We can be sure because Colnett likewise favors us with a small sketch, inserted directly into his journal entry (fig. 2.1). The entry reads: "one of the Chiefs that came of[f] was called a priest, attended with the Taboo Rods & a white Flag like a pendant with a stick on the Tack [?] part & seized to a long staff thus [see Colnett's sketch below] at each end of the pendant stick was a bunch of green Bows" (Colnett Journal, 17 Jan 1788). As we know, such images are not abroad outside of the Makahiki period. They are dismantled and housed in a temple after the circuit of Lono, to reappear at the next Makahiki.

---

improbable. It proved to be an image of Lono, though it appeared on O'ahu seven years before the regime of Kamehameha—who Obeyesekere thinks constituted the Makahiki as we know it. This observation has been in print for some years (Sahlins 1989, 1991).

But there is another, even more pertinent account of this incident, or rather two similar accounts, by a certain Andrew B. Taylor, who was sailing with Colnett as a passenger. Taylor's journal makes a significant triangulation of identities between the image, the priest in charge of it, and Captain Cook, as the first has the classic form of Lonomakua and the latter two are identified as "Great Lono." First, the episode of the priest:

On the 17th [of January, 1788] In the Morning we stood in the Bay. . . . At Noon we had a visit from the Orono-Nuez [Lono Nui, 'Great Lono'], a chief Priest, as they were pleased to call him. Twas evident he was a Priest of note among them by his retinue. He came in a large Double Canoe, in every respect well provided. One of the Chiefs of the Island attended the Great Man, but he was not of the smallest consequence compared with the Ecclesiastick. The Canoe wore [?] a large piece of red Cloth for Colours. When the consequential gentleman entered the Ship, the Chief came with him, and an attendant carrying A staff, eight feet high, on the top of which was a Cross piece of wood three feet long, and to this was secured a piece of Cloth, on the one side white the other black. This hung down the staff, and from the extremes of the cross piece hung bunches of dry Palm leaves, by way of tassel [?]. This I conjectured must be some mark of his consequence, order, or distinction[,] as the fellow stuck himself close at his heels where ever he went. Another attendant carried the Taboo stick, A branch of a Tree twisted, about three feet long and another of his attendants carried two small, brown, roasting Pigs. Those Three followed him Close as he viewed the Ship with the Captain, and took their Station close to him when he seated. His own Person was curiously ornamented, around his head he wore two rows of Feather necklace, and his body was covered with Cloth of different colours, except his breast which was naked. In respect to his Person he was rather low, but very stout, his Countenance clearly bespoke his own consequence, with a mixture of contempt for every other object. During his stay, I was gratified in a wish I had long entertained, of seeing them make their favourite Drink, called ava, used by the Priests, and Chiefs only. . . . The attendant who had gone through this operation, strained the liquor through a clean Plantain leaf and then held it with both hands, to the mouth of the Priest. . . . This Great man stood motionless. (Taylor Journals, 17 Jan 1788)

Note that the priest is himself called "Great Lono." The principle of identification of the priest and the god is elsewhere attested for Hawaii (Emerson in Malo 1951:80n; Kirtley and Mookini 1977:60; Edgar Log, 19 Jan 1779; Valeri 1985:130f.). Everything about the appearance and behavior of this "consequential gentleman" suggests he was manifesting the divine: the importance he assumed relative to the O'ahu chief, the way he drank kava without touching the cup, the red cloth (again) marking his canoe.

The counterpart of this priest at Kealakekua in Cook's time was Omeah (or Omeeah), the son of the old "bishop" Ka'ō'ō. Omeah was likewise known as "Orono" and treated with marked deference. As has been noted, Mr. King believed he was the head of the Lono order of priests and likened him to the Dalai Lama or the Japanese emperor—figures already known to Europeans in the eighteenth century as living gods.[5] The Lono image associated with the O'ahu priest described by Taylor also makes a reference to the ruling chief Kahekili, Kamehameha's rival and, at this time (1788), the most powerful figure in the Islands. Kahekili was tattooed down one side of his body, as were his warriors, and as was the tapa cloth hanging from the cross-piece Makahiki image. Finally, the Taylor journal allows us to close the circle by connecting these Makahiki manifestations of Lono with Captain Cook. For, Taylor learned that Cook also was known as "Orono nuez" (Great Lono) by the Hawaiians. Cook was so designated by one "Typowooah," a native of Hawai'i island—perhaps Kalaikoa, one of the Moana people of Ka'awaloa. On the 17th of February, Typowooah showed the people of the *Prince of Wales* a shirt purportedly worn by Cook the day he was killed. He said it was the "shirt in which ʸᵉ Orono nuez was killed in at Owhyhee" (ibid., 18 Feb 1788).

Colnett returned to Hawaii in 1791 in the *Argonaut.* His account of that visit not only attests to the persistence of the famous "singular question"—when will Lono return?—but shows that Hawaiians attributed powers to the dead Cook that were specific characteristics of the Makahiki god, Lonomakua. Colnett had been trading in the Islands in 1788, and now, in 1791,

5. Since Obeyesekere denies the contemporary British reports of the status of Omeah as a Lono priest (probably the image-bearer), does not take cognizance of the Taylor document about the O'ahu "Lono Nui," is unaware of the principle identifying the priest and the god, and does not get the allusion of incarnation in Lieutenant King's description of Omeah as "the Delai-Lama," he is free to disregard all of this in favor of the "plausible alternative" that Omeah was a high-ranking personage who happened to be named "Lono"—no (substantial) relation to the god—which is also all that was implied in the designation of Cook by the same name. This *suggestio falsi* is considered in the next chapter.

he was again at Kailua, Hawai'i. Embroiled in a dispute with the Spanish naval commander, Quimper, Colnett used the occasion to advance British interests at the Spaniard's expense. For this purpose he found the gunpowder he had offered to the Hawai'i chiefs,

> came very apropos, they being at war with the other Isles. Indeed they have constantly been at war since Captain Cook was kill'd, and also have had a deal of Sickness which never before this time afflicted them which they allege to having kill'd him. They made strict enquiry of me, if ever he would come back again, and when I saw him last, I told them: having constantly been in their part of the world, I could not tell, but this I knew, the Spaniards were coming to take their Country from them and make them Slaves. They enquired if Captain Cook had sent them, and how long he would be angry with them, and what they should do to get Captain Cook to entreat his area [ali'i, 'chiefs'] to send and assist them against the Spanish. Since I was here in the Prince of Wales [1788], two Volcanoes have open'd on the Lee Side [of] the Isle, which burn'd night and day with great fury and Tremendous Explosion which they say Captain Cook has caus'd. (Colnett 1968:220)

Colnett's notice is capital because of the association it makes between the returning Cook and the Makahiki deity, Lonomakua. Revenge and volcanic destruction are not inconsistent with this apotheosis; on the contrary, they are Hawaiian signs of it. Behind this is a complex logic of the relationship between celestial fires (of Lono, associated with thunder and lightning) and terrestrial fires (of the volcano goddess Pele), but we can make the case more directly by way of a text by S. Kamakau included in Thrum's manuscript on Hawaiian mythology—which will also motivate the feature of revenge in Colnett's report. According to this tradition, when a royal corpse was divided among major chiefs—as Cook's had been—the parts turned into dangerous fire gods, to whom were devoted certain prophets of Pele:

> The fault was that in dividing the body of an alii into several such gods, lava would come forth and destroy the land, and the fire prophets did not sanction such practice. Those prophets who did so were called destroyers and became a source of tribulation to the realm. That was the reason that the chiefs murdered Pele's prophets in older time. . . . If a great flow occurred and destroyed the land, the people

imagined that a great chief had been taken into the volcano. (Thrum, Mythology; for another translation, see Kamakau 1964:17)

Lonomakua, the Lono form of the Makahiki, is a member of Pele *mā*, 'Pele folks.' More than that, he is the keeper of the fire sticks of the volcano goddess, the deity who ignites Pele's eruptions (Beckwith 1970:40–41, 170, 206; Handy and Pukui 1972:337). An ethnographic notice from Kawena Pukui completes the logical connection between this terrestrial Lono and the celestial one:

> The most important male *'ohana* [family member] in the Pele clan was her uncle Lono-makua. . . . The name means Lono-the-elder. Lono (resounding) probably refers to thunder. It was he who kept the sacred fire of the underworld under his armpit. Vulcanism in Ka-'u is associated with heavy rain, thunder and lightning. Rain clouds were referred to in chants as "bodies" (*kino*) of Lono. (Handy and Pukui 1972:31)

Thus, by way of the Hawaiian cosmic scheme, a seemingly bizarre report such as Colnett's can be understood as a coherent synthesis of history (Cook's death), seismology (two volcanic eruptions) and theology (the return of Lono). That's what I mean by "mythopraxis" (Sahlins 1989:379–80).

Obeyesekere does not mention the foregoing exegesis of the Colnett text. He simply says that Colnett was obsessed by the Spanish and probably not "attuned to Hawaiian modes of thought." And even if some of his statements were true, they would not lend much support to "the thesis that Cook was the god Lono," because by this time "it is obvious that Hawaiians know that Cook came from 'Brittanee' and that he was under another chief (the King of England)" who would help them get rid of the Spanish. And as the Hawaiians had deified him *after* death (as a chief by the name of Lono), he was "alive" as a deity and "might even be a guardian of British sailors" (Ob. 141).

Obeyesekere's ideas about Cook's postmortem deification—from which follows the pidgin anthropology that Cook could be a guardian of British sailors, presumably reflecting a better resonance with Hawaiian modes of thought than Colnett's—will be considered later. In several contexts, however, Obeyesekere makes this argument about "Brittanee": that Hawaiians knew the foreigners came from "Brittanee" (Britain) and therefore could not have come from "Kahiki," the traditional homeland of Lono and other gods, of chiefly ancestors, and of many cultural good things. True, the foreigners came from "Brittanee." And where, and what, was that? One has to wonder what Obeyesekere thinks "Brittanee" meant to Hawaiians. His understanding of "Kahiki" does not give much confidence, as he repeatedly refers to it as a specific land, as if it could thus be contrasted with and different from "Brittanee" (Ob. 49, 61, and elsewhere). But Kahiki is a generic term for islands or lands beyond the horizon, of which there are many in various directions from Hawaii; also conveyed is a sense of distance in time. Out of sight, these invisible and godly places are in the sky—which is, incidentally, true to islanders' empirical experiences of things that lie beyond or come from beyond the horizon: they are in the sky (Beckwith 1970; Emerson 1893; Fornander 1916–20, 5:590–95; Makemson 1938:378–80; Kamakau 1976). There was no basis or reason for Hawaiians to suppose otherwise of "Brittanee." Already in Cook's time the Hawaiians knew the Haole were from "Brittanee"; but at that time they also knew that the great gods dwelt in the foreigners' "country" and that Lono was an invisible being who lived in the sky (Cook and King 1784, 3:5n, 159). Rickman (1966:332) cites a Ni'ihau chief who lamented he had not accompanied the British the first time they came, "and pointing to the sun, seemed to suppose that we should visit that luminary in our course, and that the thunder and lightning of our guns, and that which came from the heavens were both derived from the same source."[6] In any event, Obeyesekere's second critical dismissal of Colnett's report about the return of Cook confirms that Hawaiians continued to link Britain with Kahiki as late as 1809.

This second objection turns out to be so damaging to Obeyesekere's own thesis about the empirical impossibility of Cook being mistaken for a Hawaiian god that, had he reflected on it, he might not have written his book—and saved us all a lot of time and trouble. The second objection is as follows:

> Insofar as Kamehameha himself encouraged and gave a filip to possession and healing cults [but not as early as 1791; cf. Valeri 1991], one cannot rule out the possibility that in many contexts, including Colnett's interpretation, the "return of Lono" simply meant the return of his spirit, either in disembodied form (spirit transfer) or by possesion of someone else (spirit possession). A case of spirit transfer was reported by Campbell who lived in Oahu and wrote in 1809 about a Welshman, William Davis whom Hawaiians thought "had been one of

6. This statement of Rickman's, together with Obeyesekere's understanding of it, are considered below (pp. 174–75).

their own countrymen who had gone to Caheite [Kahiki] or England after his death, and had now come back to his native land." (Ob. 141; citing Campbell 1967 : 120)

Notice, first, the identity or at least equivalence of England and Kahiki as the place to which departed spirits travel and whence they return. Notice, second, that Hawaiians find it perfectly rational to suppose that a Welshman could be the manifest form of a departed Hawaiian spirit. And if Davis, why not Cook? The main argument of Obeyesekere is that Cook—not speaking Hawaiian, not looking Hawaiian, etc.—was empirically too different from Hawaiians or their god to be an incarnation of the latter. The corollary must be that Welshmen are more like Hawaiians than Yorkshiremen.[7]

Another account of Cook as a Lono figure from the eighteenth century is from one Joshua Lee Dimsdell, as set down by Captain James Barber (Dimsdell Account). Dimsdell is noticed in several voyaging journals, going back to Puget in 1794 (Puget Log, 27 Jan 1794). When Puget saw him, he was residing with the important chief Ke'eaumoku; Puget believed him to be an American. According to Barber's memoir, Dimsdell settled in Hawaii in July 1792, having visited the Islands several times before and acquired the language. Dimsdell recounted an interview with a certain "Pihore" who claimed to have killed Cook, "and added with tears that he hoped the Oroner [Lono] (so they term Cap'.C) would forgive him as he had built several Morais [temples] to his Memory & sacrificed a number of Hogs annually at each of them to this & other Devotional acts of his to the Oroner." Pihore also recounted the story of the death of "the Oroner." The manuscript continues thus:

It appears from further particulars related by Dimsdale that Cap Cook is now considered as their third God, which the Term Oroner intimates. There are a Variety of Morais built to his Memory in several parts of the Island & the Natives sacrifice to him in Common with their other Dieties. It is their firm Hope and Belief that he will come again & forgive them. He is never mentioned but with the utmost reverence of [?] Respect. After the affray they took the Body back about a mile amongst the rocks where they dissected it on a large flat Stone.

7. In the vein of so-called spirit transfer, Obeyesekere continues by referring to a chant (analyzed by John Charlot) in which the spirit of King Liholiho, who died in London in 1824, is asked to return from there to see his chiefs (Ob. 141). Obeyesekere apparently believes that this example of pragmatic rationality also substantiates his argument that the notion of Cook as a god who returns from Kahiki is a Western myth.

This Stone is still preserved with great Care. The flesh was even taken
by the Priests & the Bones were divided amongst the Chiefs. Those
that fell to Teriaboo and now in Possession of Tamamah [Kameha-
meha] his Successor Dimsdell has seen. They are preserved as Relics
& were shewn him as a great favour. These are perhaps ⅔ of the
Human frame or not quite so much. (Dimsdell Account)

Obeyesekere's critical reading of Dimsdell is a word of caution: it
sounds too Christian. Since we know that Lono does not mean 'third god,'
Dimsdell is "unconsciously, recasting the mythology of Cook in Eurocentric
trinitarian terms" (Ob. 145). So much for Dimsdell. And for whatever Pihore
and other Hawaiian people are reported to have believed and said. Once
more the argument that they did not say it is that only Europeans would
say it.[8]

Yet, Dimsdell's testimony is also interesting as testimony to a certain
cult of Cook/Lono. The mounting evidence of the next decades will show
that this was not an annual memorial feast for a deceased chief, of the kind
widely practiced in Polynesia (yet not documented for Hawai'i). The cult at
issue was the centralized or hierarchical Hawaiian version of the chiefly memorial, the Makahiki festival of Lono. During the Vancouver visit of 1793,
both Lieutenant Puget and Thomas Manby report that Cook's bones are
being kept at a temple whose location corresponds to Hikiau in Kealakekua.[9] Puget heard this at Ka'awaloa in connection with an account of Cook's
death he got from Kamehameha's brother Keali'imaikai (and apparently others): "They told us Capt Cooks Remains were in the Morai [temple] along
with those of Terreobo [Kalani'ōpu'u], which ,faces the place [Ka'awaloa
shore] where the above skirmish happened" (Puget Log, 27 Feb 1793).[10] The
day before, Puget had an interview with "the chief priest" at Kealakekua,
using a resident Haole (Isaac Davis) as interpreter:

Their gods he told us were numerous and Good. One he distinguished
as superior to the Rest, that always accompanied the King. It has the
same name as that given to Captain Cook, Orono. This Divinity

8. On indigenous Hawaiian triadic as well as quadratic notions of major gods, see Valeri
(1985:17–18, 1991:103–4).
9. Manby (1929:1[3]:39), speaking from Ka'awaloa, said that Cook's bones were under a
heap of stones at a marae one-fourth of a mile away.
10. "In effect, the Hawaiians were indicating that Kamehameha, who had slain Kalaniopu'u's heir in order to seize the rule, thereby acquired the victories and powers (bones) of his
predecessors. Or, as Mauss and Hubert put the principle: 'when one god vanquishes another,
he perpetuates the memory of his victory by the inauguration of a cult'" (Sahlins 1989:380).

(always *a mistake* accompanied the King) [correction in the document, may or may not be Puget's] on his Excursions. The Memory of Capt. Cook appears on all occasions to be treated with the Greatest Veneration by all Ranks of People, & his Name still mentioned with a Sort of enthusiastic Respect. (Ibid., 26 Feb 1793) [11]

Cook as Lono in the Nineteenth Century

From William Mariner's account, based on information initially received at Hawaii in 1806 from the resident Haole John Harbottle, the "veneration" of Cook at issue in earlier accounts can be identified as the Makahiki Festival. Harbottle had been in the Islands since 1793 and was for a long time in Kamehameha's service. Mariner met him when the ill-fated *Port au Prince* was on its way to Tonga, and afterwards recounted the interview in the context of his Tongan memories (compiled by John Martin). But Harbottle was not Mariner's only informant. He also knew certain Hawaiians living in Tonga.

> When Mr. Mariner afterwards understood the Tonga language, he conversed upon the subject with natives of Owhyhee [Hawaii], who were with him at Vavaoo; they corroborated everything that Harebottle [sic] had said and stated, moreover, that the natives had no idea that Cook could possibly be killed, as they considered him a supernatural being, and were astonished when they saw him fall. (Martin 1817, 2:66)

These Hawaiians are identified as a chief of middling rank and "the rest" of the lower order. They were young, and had not been eyewitnesses of Cook's visit or death, "but they spoke of these things as being universally known at the Sandwich Islands, and beyond all doubt" (ibid., 68). However, the most pertinent information that Mariner took the trouble to so confirm entails a reference to the presence of Cook's bones in the Makahiki procession of Lono:

> The people of the Tonga islands behaved towards Cook with every external demonstration of friendship, whilst they secretly meant to kill him; and the people of the Sandwich islands, although they actually did kill him, have paid, and still continue to pay him, higher honours than any other nation of the earth; they esteem him as having

11. Obeyesekere's answer to Puget is that since he said the god bore the same name as that given to Captain Cook, this implies "a clear separation of these two beings" (Ob. 145).

been sent by the gods to civilize them, and one to whom they owe the greatest blessings they enjoy. His bones (the greater part of which they have still in their possession!) they devoutly hold sacred; they are deposited in a house consecrated to a god, and are annually carried in procession to many other consecrated houses, before each of which they are laid on the ground, and the priest returns thanks to the gods for having sent them so great a man. (Ibid., 66)

The implication of Mariner's report is not simply that Cook was in the Makahiki (of which Mariner knew nothing), but that he has the appropriate ritual persona of Lono, whose annual visit is a restoration of natural fertility and human well being. All of this was stated in the *JPS* article, "Captain Cook at Hawaii" (Sahlins 1989). Obeyesekere alludes to that discussion but does not cite it. He ignores the reference to the Makahiki.[12] Indeed, he dismisses Mariner's whole discussion in one sentence as hearsay, and on the argument that his amanuensis, John Martin, lived in London when the myth of Cook as a god was popular: "Unfortunately, Mariner's is a piling up of hearsay accounts, complicated by the fact that Mariner 'communicated' his experiences in Tonga to his 'editor' John Martin in London, in 1811, at a time when the Cook myth was popular there" (Ob. 144). So once again, what Hawaiians say is dismissed a priori, even as it is supposed to be a Western myth on the grounds that it is already a Western myth—the reasoning being that Martin helped make up what Mariner heard from Hawaiians. Curious, however, that if this really is a compulsive Western myth about how "natives" misconceive Europeans as gods, neither Mariner nor Martin took the opportunity to make such an allegation about the Tongans' great regard for Cook. On the contrary, that Cook was deified is clearly denied for Tonga.

A notice by an American seaman, George Little, in 1809 is in the line of references to rituals of Cook dating back to the early 1790s. This was at Kealakekua:

I made a visit to the burying-place of Captain Cook, a beautiful, se-questered spot, of a circular form, surrounded with banana and cocoa-nut trees, the grave occupying the centre of the circle. The natives,

12. In general, Obeyesekere attempts to pass off such references to the ritual use of Cook's bones, notably in processions, as Western folklore, allusions to Christian cults of saints—except, of course, when he wishes to make the case that Hawaiians deified Cook only after death and as a chief, which traditionally required enshrinement of his bones.

on approaching this place, seemed to be awed into a profound reverence; and as two of our men, who had been at these islands several
times, spoke the language of the islanders,—in conversations with
them, they expressed unfeigned sorrow at the unfortunate circumstances which caused the death of this great chief, as they termed him;
they also informed us that, once in every year, all the natives assemble
here to perform a religious rite in memory of his lamentable death.
(Little 1843 : 131−32)[13]

Adelbert von Chamisso, the botanist and linguist of the first Kotzebue
voyage, in the Islands in 1816 and 1817, wrote of the Hawaiians and Cook:
"they adored him as a god, and still piously revere his memory" (in Kotzebue
1821, 3 : 236). The statement occasions one of Obeyesekere's more dazzling
critical readings. Unmindful that Chamisso was the author of virtually the
whole third volume of Kotzebue's *Voyage,* as is plainly indicated in the text,
Obeyesekere mistakenly attributes Chamisso's observation that Hawaiians
adored Cook as a god to Kotzebue. However, Chamisso also published a
separate edition of his work in 1836, an English translation of which appeared in 1986. Obeyesekere proceeds to use the corresponding sentence in
the 1986 edition as Chamisso's criticism of "Kotzebue's" assertion of 1821,
which is merely a slightly different translation of the same Chamisso text.
Ah, but the difference is momentous. Kotzebue (that is, Chamisso₁) had said
"they adored him as a god"; whereas, Chamisso₂ merely said "they honored
him like a god"—*like* a god.

The momentous difference is that between two English glosses of the
same German text: *wie einen Gott* (Chamisso in Kotzebue 1821, 3 : 239;
Chamisso n.d., 197). What is most impressive about this mistake, however,
is the fabulous history of Western thought Obeyesekere then proceeds to
concoct as the supposedly true source of the reported Hawaiian beliefs in
Cook's divinity:

13. I cite a longer passage here than I had previously (Sahlins 1989 : 381), as, in a rare
reference to that earlier work, Obeyesekere finds great significance in the fact that the clause
referring to "this great chief" was deleted (Ob. 73, 144). This is supposed to be an example of
my uncritical reading of sources, as if Little's understanding of Hawaiian great chiefship, and
still less the Hawaiians' conception, involved a radical contrast to their notion of *akua,* 'god,'
'divinity.' (Great chiefs of the prostration tabu [such as Cook] were *akua* in relation to the rest
of mankind, even as gods such as Lono took the forms of great *ali'i.*) Having made the point
that Cook was just a great chief, Obeyesekere deletes the rest of Little's text: "They also informed us that, once in every year, all the natives assemble here [at Kealakekua] to perform a
religious rite in memory of his lamentable death." This is another probable reference to the
Makahiki.

Kotzebue's statement [i.e., Chamisso₁] can be read as an efflorescence of the European dialogue that developed after the death of the great navigator [Cook] and the publication of the official journals. In other words, a *tradition* of Cook's apotheosis already existed in Europe, and later accounts, even the well-intentioned investigations of sea captains [Kotzbue], were easily contaminated by the tradition. What is therefore impressive is the persistence of views that qualified [*sic*] this tradition or differed [*sic*] from it. Thus, Adelbert von Chamisso, the naturalist on Kotzebue's ship the *Rurik*, often critical of Kotzebue, made an important qualification about his captain's account: "They honored him *like a god*, and they still honor his memory piously." (Ob. 142; italics in original)

Leave aside the grammatical non sequitur. Obeyesekere's flying in the face of evidence is describing ever-decreasing hermeneutic circles. Here is the myth of a European myth in the light of which all empirical testimonies to the contrary become mythical.[14]

After Chamisso, the next relevant notice of Cook's relation to Lono is a footnote in Freycinet's book about the voyage of *L'Uranie* that explicitly states Cook was received as a manifestation of the Makahiki god, here identified as a ruling chief of old, Lonoikamakahiki. Freycinet was in Hawaii in 1819, but he did not publish his *Voyage* until 1839. Hence Obeyesekere is certain that Freycinet's apparent triangulation of the identities of Cook, Lono the god, and the legendary king "is simply taken over from the missionary Ellis," who elaborated the mythical connection, if he did not invent it. This could be. But there are indications that something more, if not something different, is involved. One is that the pertinent myth was already a popular tradition in 1822, when Ellis arrived in Hawaii, as will be documented shortly. Secondly, Freycinet's text specifically connects Cook with the "chief god . . . Rono-ké-maka-ihi [Lonoikamakahiki]" (for which Freycinet provides the fanciful translation, 'Rono erupting suddenly to feed himself,' Freycinet 1978:73). But Ellis's account of this tradition does not include the proper name of the ancient Hawai'i king cum god, Lonoikamakahiki; it only links Cook with a king and god *"Rono or Orono"* (1833, 4:104–5). So,

---

14. Obeyesekere's argument about Chamisso's criticism of Kotzebue (= Chamisso) is doubled by the assertion that Kotzebue did not necessarily have Hawaiian sources for his identification of Cook with Lono "as Sahlins thinks." However, the issue of Kotzebue's sources in which Obeyesekere further entangles Chamisso's statement, "wie einen Gott," is not relevant to this voyage or time. It concerns Kotzebue's second voyage to the Pacific, touching at Hawai'i in 1824 and 1825.

the popular tradition of the 1820s, which was inscribed (we shall see) in the form of a *mele* or chant, was probably already in the air in August 1819:

> Rono was an ancient king of Owhyhi who, when on the point of leaving the island in a canoe, promised to return. Not seeing him reappear, the inhabitants began to worship him as a god. Later, when Captain Cook arrived on their shores, believing that it was their god Rono who had returned, the natives prostrated themselves at his feet." (Freycinet 1978:73n)

We come, then, to the time of the missionaries, the first contingent of which anchored at Kailua, Hawaii on the fourth of April, 1820. As we know, Obeyesekere believes that the American clergymen, following in a long-standing Christian tradition, were devoted to condemning Cook for playing god in the Sandwich Islands ("God is a jealous God," said the poet William Cowper, who is commonly cited as the source of the Christian contempt for Cook, having concluded that Cook was "content to be worshipped" upon reading the official *Voyage* in 1784. And how did Cowper do that?) Consequently any document implying Cook = Lono and bearing a missionary's hand can be rubbished on the historiographic principle that since the author belongs to a class of people with an evangelical interest in condemning it, the proposition must be untrue. Said otherwise, anyone who may be suspected of having an interest in lying must be lying. If the document cites local speech or tradition to the effect of Cook = Lono, it must mean the missionaries have succeeded in manipulating Hawaiian minds, myths, or memories. Or else, again, the attribution to Hawaiians is untrue; it is the missionary who is really speaking. This ventriloquism is all the more poignant because, according to Obeyesekere, there are no native Hawaiian testimonies of Cook's apotheosis before the missionaries: "The Hawaiian versions of Cook's apotheosis come from accounts of native scholars and missionaries after the Hawaiians had abandoned their tabu system in 1819, and the first American evangelical missions had begun to arrive (the following year)" (Ob. 49–50). Of course this is true of written "versions," since literacy came with Christianity; but are we thus entitled to forget that Hawaiian statements of Cook's career as Lono had been appearing repeatedly in European annals from 1779 on?

Nor can missionary texts that cite Hawaiian reminiscences of Cook be dismissed a priori because of what one may presume about the American clergy. Most especially the documents before the latter part of 1825, when Christianity was enjoying very indifferent success, as it had yet to be promoted by the Hawaiian powers-that-be (Sahlins 1992). In fact, the first such testimony of Cook's divinity came within two weeks of the missionaries' arrival. Samuel Whitney's journal for 13 April 1820:

> Kirooah [Kailua] is on the southwest side of Owhyhee. . . . A few miles south of this is Kanahkakooah [Kealakekua] the spot where the celebrated navigator Cook was killed. This person is still held in remembrance by some of the old men present. They say he was a god, and for a long time worshipped him as such. A man at Kirooah told one of our number that he had eaten part of Cook's entrails.[15]

The old-timers in Kailua and Kealakekua recounted such memories to many visitors throughout the decade. The LMS missionaries Tyerman and Bennet heard them in April 1822:

> In the course of our rambles, our guide pointed out the hollow, in the volcanic mass, where the body of Captain Cook was roasted, and, a little further on, the place where his arms and legs were submitted to the same process. This was, in fact, the highest honour that his murderers (with the inconsistency of savages) could show to his remains; the corpses of their kings and chiefs being prepared in a similar manner, that the flesh might be more easily separated from the bones, and the skeleton afterwards be put together and preserved, as an object not only of reverence, but even of religious homage. The relics of Cook were thus worshipped in a temple of Rono, one of the gods of Hawaii, of whom the people had a notion that the British navigator was the representative, if not the incarnation of him. (Tyerman and Bennet 1831, 1:376)[16]

Elisha Loomis, visiting Kealakekua in June 1824, reported: "All the natives agree in stating that Cook was considered as a God and, as such, was worshipped" (Loomis Journal, 12 June 1824). The Ka'awaloa chief, Naihe, gave Loomis an account of Cook's death. After profiting from the occasion

15. Since Whitney (as Ellis and others after him) was evidently talking to ordinary or middling people, the "worship" and "god" would not refer to a royal ancestor, the subject of a royal cult. Hence, this was not just the worship of the manes of a deceased tabu chief named Lono, as Obeyesekere argues.

16. Tyerman and Bennet were wrong about the disposition of Cook's bones at his death. By contemporary accounts, the bones were distributed to ruling chiefs as trophies; indeed the skull was separated from the long bones, so that bundled remains comprising these parts (ka'ai) could not have been constructed. However, at least from Dimsdell's time on (1792), we do have reports of an articulated set of Cook's bones involved in a Lono cult.

to reproach Cook for allowing himself to be worshipped, Loomis recounts the current tradition of the returning god:

> The natives had a tradition that one of their Gods named Rono or Lono had gone to a foreign country. When Capt. Cook arrived, it was supposed he was the identical Rono. This was the name they gave to him and the name by which he has ever since been known among them. (Ibid., 12 June 1824)

Obeyesekere does not consider any of these reports, perhaps because they are so many examples of missionary say-so. However, he does have something in general to say about the allegedly Hawaiian "notion" or "tradition" of Cook as an incarnation of Lono, namely that it is really missionary say-so. The missionaries, in the first place Hiram Bingham, were responsible for the idea that Cook's arrival was the reenactment of a certain myth of Lono's "returning to Hawaii in a triangular canoe" (Ob. 154). But, says Obeyesekere:

> This myth itself is suspect: First, it confounds the myth of Lono with that of a famous chief of Hawaiian legend, Lono-i-ka-makahiki and his wife Kaikilani; second the myth is quoted by a missionary, Bingham, who in turn obtained it from a compilation from the students of the Lahainaluna seminary in Maui and published it in 1838 as *Mooolelo Hawaii.* (Ob. 154)

First, to clear the decks, the myth in question—cited in two versions by Obeyesekere (Ob. 51, 158)—does not appear in the infamous *Mooolelo Hawaii* of 1838, a book which was not published by Hiram Bingham, but by Sheldon Dibble. Nor was the *Mooolelo* compiled "from" the students of Lahainaluna, but from interviews conducted by them with knowledgeable Hawaiian chiefs and elders (see above, 38n. 23). Second, missionary idea or no, the existence of this myth in 1778–79 was not a necessary condition of the reception of Cook as Lonomakua, the Makahiki form of Lono—an argument about the myth I have never made. The Makahiki itself was a sufficient condition of Hawaiian knowledge of Lono's annual appearance. The interest of the myth is in whether it throws light on the understanding of Lonoikamakahiki and Cook as instantiations of Lono, corollary to historical reports of the bones of both in the Makahiki procession of the god. Third, in this connection, the myth is not in fact a missionary invention or elaboration, whether by Bingham or Ellis (as Obeyesekere also claims a few pages later). The myth was a Hawaiian "popular tradition" first recorded about the *god* Lono in 1822, in the "Sandwich Islands Mission Journal" (ABCFM/MJ). The sources were important Hawaiian people, although the story was put into English. There is a Hawaiian-language version datable shortly thereafter, transcribed apparently by Bingham. The same myth and certain variants were set down by Kotzebue in 1824–25 and by members of the Byron voyage of 1825—all likewise as charters of Cook's identification with Lono. The alternative versions also transpose incidents and relations of the Lonoikamakahiki story to the original god Lono—such as the name of the former king's wife, Kaikilani-wahine-o-Puna, who appears here as the god's wife— thus representing on the mythical plane the interchangeable instantiations that (I argue) occurred in ritual and history.

The general journal of the American mission was kept by Bingham and one or more of his colleagues. On 19 September 1822, at O'ahu, it records that the missionaries were visited by the Ka'awaloa ruling chief Naihe and his wife Kapiolani, who came in the morning and stayed most of the day. They brought with them "Kepokulo, a priest of Tamehameha [Kamehameha], who formerly resided at Karakakua [Kealakekua]."[17] The priest gave the missionaries a list of Hawaiian gods, naming Maui as the greatest, Kairi [Kūka'ilimoku] as Kamehameha's principal god, and "Rono" as the Makahiki god. The text continues:

The following is a translation of a popular tradition of Rono. "In ancient time, Rono dwelt at the foot of a huge precipice near Kearakekua in Hawaii & hearing the voice of solicitation from the top of the precipice, in a sudden fit of anger & jealousy by a single blow he killed his wife Kaikiraniariiopuna [Kaikilani-ali'i-o-Puna]. He then carried her & placed her in a morai or house of worship, & wept over her in bitter regret and anguish. Then traversed all the Islands, boxing & fighting with every man he met. When the people demanded 'O Rono hehena nui e———?' Is Rono really crazy? he replied, 'I hehena hoi au ia ia.— I ulala hoi au i kona arohei.'—I am indeed crazy on her account. I am

17. Kepokulou or Kepookulou was in the suite of Naihe and Kapiolani (Kamakau 1961: 381). He is again identified as "former high priest of Kamehameha" by the missionary James Ely in 1824 (ABCFM Ely to Evarts, 11 Oct 1824). He held and distributed land in Kealakekua in 1819 and in Ka'awaloa in 1834. These land relationships are extremely interesting in light of the argument, to be made presently, that the Lono priests of Kealakekua were replaced by Kamehameha with his own henchmen. Indeed Kepookulou was a son of the famous Ka'awaloa warrior of Cook's time, Kekuhaupi'o—one of whose wives was a daughter of the Kū priest, Holoa'e (AH/GB 14:37,38).

wailing also for her love.' When he had gone through the islands he left them & fled to a foreign country in his Paimalau a triangular canoe of the God. His wife coming to life, searched the islands through in pursuit of him, & then went to a foreign country to seek her lost husband."

When Capt. Cook arrived the people took him to be their ancient God Rono, and worshipped him as such, while he not like Paul, encouraged the delusion & received the homage of this idolatrous people. But when they supposed themselves crowded upon by him, some doubted his divinity & tried the force of their weapons on his dis——ed person.

The story above may account for the institution of their annual games of boxing in honor of Rono, and also for the name of that annual celebration, called Muakeheiti as it is sometimes spoken by foreigners, derived from the words *Ma, ka, hiti* which signify, *to a foreign country* [sic]. (ABCFM/MJ, 19 Sept 1822)

The Hawaiian version of this is in the J. S. Emerson Collection of the Bishop Museum (HEN 1:648–52). A note indicates that it came to Emerson from Bingham's daughter (Mrs. Lydia B. Coan) and was written out by Bingham, apparently in 1824. The collection in fact includes two Hawaiian versions, one in the standard orthography and the other with archaic spellings, the first presumably Emerson's and the latter Bingham's. Although told of the god Lono, the legend again is better known as the story of Lonoikamakahiki, as confirmed by details appearing in this text but missed out of the 1822 journal entry, such as the name of Kaikilani's lover, "Hoakekoa." Apart from the details, the Hawaiian text differs in two interesting ways from the English. First, "Paimalau" (lit., the Portuguese man-of-war jellyfish) is the name of Lono's canoe—*Ua holo aku la i Kahiki maluna o ka waa. O Paimalu ka inoa o ka waa ana*—not, as in the missionary and subsequent English versions, a peculiarly shaped triangular canoe. (Obeyesekere makes a lot of this canoe, thinking he is scoring points by the realist assurance that Hawaiians could not mistake Cook's ship for a triangular canoe.) Second, the connection between the god's story and Cook's arrival is in the original Hawaiian, rather than appended to it as in the 1822 text. So the Hawaiian version ends:

Ua holo aku la hoi o Kaikilani-alii-o-Puna i Kahiki ma ka waa. A i hiki nei o Capt. Cook, manao na kanaka o Lono i hoihoi mai ai Olelo lakou, "Eia Lono e"

> Kaikilani-alii-o-Puna went to Kahiki [after Lono] on a canoe.
> When Captain Cook arrived, the people thought that Lono had re-
> turned. They said, "Here is Lono."

This story of Lono the god is, as I say, a transposed form of the tradition
of the king Lonoikamakahiki ('Lono of the Makahiki'), the ruler of Hawai'i
who appears in well-known genealogies some generations before Kamehameha. According to the tradition, his wife Kaikilani for a time ruled the
island, the first woman ever to do so. However, Lonoikamakahiki's children
did not succeed him, a loss of the rule which is one of many analogies between the lengthy royal legend and myths of the original god Lono. Others
include Lono's circuit of the island engaging in fights to test his prowess (and
his ability to rule), the liaison of his wife Kaikilani with an upstart Heakekoa
('Blood Sacrifice of the Warrior') and Lono's smiting of Kaikilani with a game
(*konane*) board, (Fornander 1916–20, 4:256–363). S. M. Kamakau's version
of the royal legend makes further and explicit connections to the Makahiki.
(This famous Hawaiian historian was a student collector of traditions in the
1830s for the *Mooolelo Hawaii* of the Lahainaluna school; his Lonoikamakahiki legend was first published in 1871.) As has been noted, in Kamakau's
text, Lonoikamakahiki's feathered ensign (*kahili*) is of the same form as the
Makahiki image of Lono:

> When Lono[-i-ka-makahiki] travelled, the large *kahili* was wrapped up.
> When it was set up the men in Lono's canoe prostrated themselves. In
> this way was the Makahiki god also honored. When Lono sailed from
> Hawaii, his emblem was erected, and on the tops of the masts hung
> *ka'upu* bird [skins] like banners. . . . When Lono-i-ka-makahiki, ruler
> of Hawaii, died, his children and his descendants did not become rul-
> ers of the government. His name was made famous through the Ma-
> kahiki god, Lono-i-ka-'ou-ali'i, and [he] was thus thought of as a god
> of the Makahiki celebration. The name Lono was combined with the
> word Makahiki, thus making it Lono-i-ka-makahiki. (Kamakau 1961:
> 52, 61)

Kamakau (1964:20) also says that Lonoikamakahiki—meaning the
ka'ai or bundled remains thereof?—was newly inserted into the Makahiki
procession by Kamehameha as one of the latter's 'created gods' (*ho'oakua*).
Kamakau's versions of tradition thus continue the interchange between the
god Lono and his royal namesake. Of course, the "authenticity," in the sense
of the antiquity, of Kamakau's particular renditions cannot be determined.

Nor would I give them any privileged status. What we do know is that they reproduce a set of transformations between Lono the god, Lono the ancient king, and Captain Cook that go back at least to 1822. More specifically, the forms of the 1820s are popular and abbreviated versions, adapted to the explication of the Makahiki, of what may be presumed to be esoteric royal traditions like that of Lonoikamakahiki, collected by Fornander. As myths, they are parallel to the reported presence in the Makahiki procession of Cook's bones as well as some representation of Lonoikamakahiki—if these were different! Rev. William Ellis's researches on Cook at Hawai'i island in 1823 develop these associations.

Ellis identifies his Hawaiian interlocutors on Cook's death as "a number of persons at [Ka'awaloa] and other places in the islands," with many of whom "we have frequently conversed" (1833, 4:101–2). Among these, was Kelou Kamakau, author of the excellent text on the Makahiki rites. Born about 1773, Kelou Kamakau lived at Ka'awaloa and was highly esteemed by Ellis for his knowledge and attainments. In his private journal, Ellis also mentions an interview on O'ahu with the ruling chiefs Kalaimoku, Ka'ahumanu, and "several others"—from which he concluded that Cook's bones were still in some temple in Hawai'i island "preserved as sacred relics" (Ellis Journal, 27 Feb 1823). Moreover, there are other Hawaiian voices behind this supposition:

> The missionaries in the Society Islands had, by means of some Sandwich Islanders, been long acquainted with the circumstance of some of Capt. Cook's bones being preserved in one of their temples, and receiving religious worship; and . . . every endeavour has been made to learn, though without success, whether they were still in existence, and where they were kept. All those of whom inquiry has been made have uniformly asserted that they were formerly kept by the priests of Rono, and worshipped, but have never given any satisfactory information as to where they are now. (Ellis 1833, 4:105)

As Hawaiians and LMS missionaries had both been in Tahiti since the late eighteenth century, this notice of Cook goes back to the time the Makahiki was celebrated.[18]

However, as the defender of "nonliterate peoples who cannot speak for

18. Turnbull noted in 1802–3: "A number of Sandwich Islanders have in different periods passed to Otaheite [Tahiti], where they find encouragement to settle from the young king Otoo, who, from their superior skill and warlike disposition, prefers them as attendants on his person" (Turnbull 1805, 2:67).

themselves," Obeyesekere is moved to attribute everything Hawaiians told Ellis about Cook as Lono to the Reverend William Ellis. For, he says, Ellis's "native informants, as in all works of this sort, are mostly nameless and featureless" (Ob. 157). And whereas Ellis says that Hawaiian accounts agree with Lieutenant King's, the latter (according to Obeyesekere) does not say that Cook was a god. Since Ellis does, "though briefly [sic]," he must have got his ideas from "an interpretation of Cook's death that is reflected in Cowper's work" (ibid.)—that is, the poet who got the idea that Cook was a god from reading Lieutenant King! Hence Obeyesekere concludes: "It seems very likely, therefore, that any informant statements regarding the complicated events that led to Cook's installation and deification would simply be fitted into the preconceived English view of his apotheosis" (Ob. 157).[19]

Having laid on Ellis the authorship of the statements he supposedly heard from Hawaiians, Obeyesekere does not go further into the English missionary's text except to dismiss the myth of Cook's advent as Lono's return. This part of the Ellis text concludes as follows:

As soon as Captain Cook arrived, it was supposed and reported that the god Rono was returned; the priests clothed him with the sacred cloth worn only by the god, conducted him to their temples, sacrificed animals to propitiate his favor, and hence the people prostrated themselves before him as he walked through the villages. But when, in the attack made upon him, they saw his blood running, and heard his groans, they said, "No, this is not Rono." (Ellis 1833, 4:104)

At this point, Obeyesekere breaks off his consideration of Ellis: "We no longer can take this account seriously" (Ob. 158).[20]

19. By "installation and deification" Obeyesekere is referring to his makeshift transformation of the *hānaipū* ceremony of welcoming Lono into the installation rite of a high chief named Lono, in which capacity (as distinct from the god Lono) Cook was supposedly deified by the Hawaiians after death. Note that even if this pidgin ethnography were true, it would still leave significant aspects of Ellis's reports of the historic association between Cook and the god Lono unexplained: such as the care of Cook's remains by Lono priests, and their use in the annual procession to collect tributes (i.e., the Makahiki circuit). These things, Ellis said, were told to him by Hawaiian people.

20. Obeyesekere gives several reasons why we can stop right here. First, the identification of Lono the god with the chief Lonoikamakahiki is problematic for Cook's time. Perhaps so, but the Lonoikamakahiki legend was a popular charter of Cook's apotheosis in the early 1820s; and its existence any earlier, during the functioning of the old religion, would fray the thread on which Obeyesekere's thesis is dangling, that a tabu chief named Lono is not the god, to a single insubstantial filament: well, maybe in the case of the tabu chief Lonoikamakahiki yes,

In the event, among the aspects of the account we are not to take seriously, hence that need not be mentioned, are local people's reports of the ritual respects paid to Cook's bones because of his identification with the god Lono, and the definite allusion to the Makahiki in their statements that these bones were annually carried around the island collecting tributes by priests of Lono. Ellis used quotation marks in parts of this discussion to indicate reported speech:

"After he was dead, we all wailed. His bones were separated—the flesh was scraped off and burnt, as was the practice in regard to our own chiefs when they died. We thought he was the god Rono, worshipped him as such, and after his death reverenced his bones." (Ellis 1833, 4:103)

A little further on, Ellis specifies the worship:

Some [people] . . . after [Cook's] death still supposed him to be Rono, and expected he would appear again. Some of his bones, his ribs, and breastbone, were considered sacred, as part of Rono, and deposited in a heiau (temple) dedicated to Rono, on the opposite side of the island. There religious homage was paid to them, and from thence they were annually carried in procession to several other heiaus, or borne by the priests round the island, to collect the offerings of the people for the support of the worship of the god Rono. The bones were preserved in a small basket of wickerwork, completely covered over with red feathers, which in those days were considered to be the most valuable articles the natives possessed. (Ibid., 104–5)

---

but not the tabu chief Lono-Cook. (We have already discussed the motivated transformations between the traditions of the several Lono god cum king figures.)

Obeyesekere's second objection to the myth is that, according to D. Barrère, the "peculiarly shaped canoe" was an invention of Kamehameha's reign. We have seen that this was a missionary mistranslation; it has no bearing on the antiquity of a canoe of Lono (or two such canoes) in the post-circuit phase of the Makahiki (Malo 1951:151–56).

Third objection: the (tapa) cloth in which Cook was wrapped was not a sacred garment, except by tautological deduction from the fact Cook was wrapped in it, and the notion that animals were offered Cook to propitiate him is at best a wild interpretation. The demur is based on a failure to investigate the practice and significance of wrapping images and other objects in which the god is realized—including priests and chiefs in certain ritual contexts (see appendix 6). Collected much earlier than the parallel observation in *Mooolelo Hawaii*, and outside of Maui, this information in Ellis provides independent support for Lieutenant King's contemporaneous notice to the same effect.

Lono collects the tributes of the districts during the Makahiki procession. The wickerwork basket described by Ellis is a *ka'ai*, which holds the deified remains of former kings and royals. Taken together with the references of Mariner, Dimsdell, the Vancouver people, Little, and others, Ellis's notices give us a consistent record of an annual ritual celebration involving Cook's (supposed) bones, identifiable as the classic Makahiki festival and going back into the 1790s, at least. This is what we should not take seriously.

What, then, to make of the interesting statement in the Ellis text to the effect that when the stricken Cook was heard to groan and even to bleed, the people said, "No this is not Lono?" The report is not unique to Ellis. It occurs in a number of sources dating from the 1820s onward (Judd 1966: 55; Kotzebue 1830, 2:180; Bachelot 1830:283; and Kamakau 1961:103, among others). Of two things, one is true: either it is an invention of the nineteenth century, contingent on the local success of the radical Western distinction between man and god (which I believe to be the case); or else, it was actually said, in which case the Hawaiians must have believed up to that moment—as they did again later—that Cook *was* Lono.

Obeyesekere's interpretations of this well-known statement are also two, and they likewise contradict each other. They confirm the impression (which the reader must by now share) that his book is a palimpsest of ad hoc arguments—here grasping at a straw(man), there inventing Hawaiian reasoning out of Western common sense or a pidgin "native" ethnography— put together willy-nilly at different times without much concern for coherence or reconciliation but on the scattershot principle of the more the better, as then maybe some will hit the mark. Just so for "No, this is not Rono." On the one hand, this should not be believed. It is a Western construction. (The same "Western mythologization," Obeyesekere writes, was already apparent before Cook's death when certain crew members speculated that Willie Watman's death destroyed Hawaiian beliefs in their visitors' immortality.) The idea that Cook's fall disproved his divinity "was probably attributed to Hawaiians by Europeans who had their own notions of body and spirit" (Ob. 158). Obeyesekere here would discard the episode because he realizes its implication: that until Hawaiians saw Cook bleed, while he was living among them, they must have thought he *was* Lono.[21] On the other hand,

21. This point about the purported remark of Cook's assailant—"it presupposes that, before the event, the people generally believed Cook to be Lono"—had already been made in a discussion to which Obeyesekere occasionally refers, although in this matter does not cite (Sahlins 1989:383). Here is another example: "Les naturels prirent Cook lui-même pour leur

not many pages earlier, the same exclamation about the dying Cook is credited by Obeyesekere. He accepts it as somehow supporting his argument
that the deification of Cook was only postmortem. Indeed the paralogism
can do double duty as historiographic criticism:

> What is striking about Sahlins's insistence is that the very "native"
> sources he approves unanimously [sic] state that at least when Cook
> died, they knew he was human and mortal. Thus, contrary to Sahlins,
> it is virtually certain that any elevation of Cook's ritual status must
> have occurred as a postmortem deification. (Ob. 147)[22]

But of course the only logical conclusion from the episode of "No, this is not
Rono" that is certain is that Cook had already enjoyed that condition in his
lifetime.

After Ellis, European accounts of the Islands continue to record Hawaiian memories of Cook's divine career, including many versions of the popular tradition linking him with the Lonos of ancient memory who promised
to return. The millennial dimensions of this cosmic Cook were already apparent in the beginning of the century, judging from Mariner's report, or
indeed they were already there in the annual renewal of life by the god (the
Makahiki). But one senses some decades of depopulation and cultural loss in
notices of Cook's coming such as this one from Byron:

> as they had confidently expected that the return of Orono was to con-
> fer some immediate and important benefit, they eagerly embraced the
> idea, that the blessed era was come, and that all the knowledge which

dieu Lono, dont je ne sais rien d'ailleurs. Il est toujours connu sous ce nom. Nous avons ici des
vieillards qui furent témoins de sa mort. . . . Quoiqu'il en suit, Cook cessa d'être un Dieu dès
qu'on le vit blessé et qu'on l'entendit se plaindre" (Bachelot 1830:283).

22. Of course, it is not a sequitur that Cook's deification must have been post mortem, any
more than it follows (in a Hawaiian sense) that his being human and mortal means he was not
a manifestation of Lono; or again, that Hawaiians saying so "at least" when he died means they
did not believe it before he died.

The same sort of clarity attends Obeyesekere's discussion of the return-of-Lono tradition
reported by Ellis. On the one hand, he says the myth is suspect because it confounds the god
and the chief (Lonoikamakahiki), and it comes from the Lahainaluna students via Bingham
(Ob. 153). A few pages later, noting that Ellis's earlier account of Lonoikamakahiki entails the
same confusion with the god, he writes: "This may not have been Ellis's own contribution to
the myth; it is more like a product of the Kamehameha reform. However, Ellis, more than
anyone else, fully incorporated the former into the latter and systematically rationalized it"
(Ob. 157). Yet Ellis was not responsible for this "popular tradition." Hawaiian people were. And
if a chief named Lono can be an instance of the god Lono at least since the 1790s. . . .

they believed, on the faith of tradition, they had lost should be restored, and new arts and new comforts taught them by the inhabitants
of the floating islands [i.e. Cook's ships]. (Byron 1826:27)

Kotzebue, whose visits of 1824 and 1825 bracketed Byron's, recorded a
myth of Lono's return in which the protagonist was the original deity. Kalaimoku, so-called Prime Minister of the time, was the source of the account,
and also of the observation that when Cook arrived he was supposed the
"Ekua Rono" (Akua Rono, 'God Lono') (Kotzebue 1830, 2:161–68, 179–
84). Byron's people of the *Blonde,* especially Richard Bloxam, set down a
considerable series of similar traditions and recollections.

Lord Byron (cousin to the poet) brought the body of the deceased king
Liholiho from London in 1825. The manuscript narrative of the voyage by
the Rev. Richard Bloxam contributed much to Byron's published account
(Bloxam Narrative). Like Kotzebue, Bloxam recorded versions of the Lono
myth—two different ones and a fragment of a third—that had to do with
the god (rather than the chief Lonoikamakahiki as in Ellis). These were
apparently given to Bloxam by "the missionary at Lahaina," probably the
knowledgeable William Richards. One is quite the same as that appearing
in the missionaries' general journal of 1822, except that Bloxam describes it
as "popular poetry" and records it in "poetical stanzas." When Byron published it (in English) he called it a "song" and set it as poetry or lyrics (1826:
20–21). One may conclude that this was not merely a "popular tradition" as
the missionaries said—in contrast to its epic version as the legend of Lonoikamakahiki—but also a popular chant *(mele).*[23] The interest of the second
version of the myth found in Richard Bloxam's narrative is that it is set in
Maui, or at least the god Lono, having descended from the heavens, lives
for a long time in a ravine on Maui subsisting on wild foods. The latter part
of the text, apparently translated by Richards, again makes the coming of
Captain Cook sequitur to the myth of the god's marital tragedy.

Lord Byron, Richard Bloxam, Bloxam's brother Andrew, and the artist
of the voyage, Robert Dampier, all report recollections of Cook by people
from Kealakekua and Ka'awaloa. The old-timers remembered Cook as the
god Lono. Richard Bloxam seemed surprised that although forty-seven years
had passed since Cook's death, "his memory is still revered by the
Natives. . . . Neither do they speak of him or know him by any other name

23. Ellis (1833, 4:65) tells of the dissemination of these popular chants relating the doings
of the Hawaiian great.

than Olono 'the God.'" Only a part of Cook's bones, Bloxam was told, had been returned to the British, "while a part still remain deposited in a Heiau near Toeaigh [Kawaihae] Bay" (Narrative, 14 July 1825). Andrew Bloxam, at Kealakekua, echoes the part about Cook being known "by the name of Orono the chief god." Several of the people they talked to, said Andrew, were old and remembered Cook (Bloxam Diary, 36; see also Byron 1826: 196). Naihe, the ruling chief at Ka'awaloa, was interviewed at that place. He claimed that the man who first struck Cook was from upcountry and was, as Dampier (1971:65) put it, "ignorant of Cook's attributed divinity." On another occasion, the aforementioned Kalaimoku was Byron's informant on these matters. "Of the respect, according to their notions, paid to his [Cook's] remains and of their belief, though once dead, he might, as their deity Orono, come again among them, Karaimoku's testimony is now hardly necessary" (Byron 1826: 123).

Obeyesekere says Dampier was attributing the words of Mariner and Lieutenant King to Naihe (Ob. 151). Kalaimoku's testimony he discounts because the man was quite Europeanized and apparently too willing to say anything *pour faire plaisir aux Blancs* (Ob. 143–44). Obeyesekere does not mention Richard Bloxam's narrative. Nor Andrew Bloxam's diary. As for the old-timers at Kealakekua Bay, he does not specify whether they were misquoted or deluded. It is enough that Byron's outfit was "influenced by missionary views, especially of Bingham and Ellis," to account for what they reported of Hawaiian views. Obeyesekere also ignores several other similar testimonies from the 1820s—Gilbert Mathison's, for example, who also learned of the association between Cook and the Makahiki procession:

It is generally well known, that after the death of Captain Cook the inhabitants repented them of the deed, and sincerely lamented a man whose previous conduct had been such as to secure their admiration and respect. To perpetuate his memory, therefore, they resolved to deify him; and accordingly made an appropriate image, which for many years was actually carried in procession round the island of Owhyhee [Hawai'i], under the appellation of the Wandering God. (Mathison 1825:431–32)[24]

Still another notice from the period quotes a Hawaiian worthy of some attention. The reporter is Laura Fish Judd, at Kealakekua in 1829:

24. Mathison evidently assimilated the presence of Kamehameha's human god Kahoali'i in the Makahiki with Cook's participation therein (see appendix 4).

Here I have made the acquaintance of the old queen, Kekupuohi, wife of Kalaniopua. She was close to Captain Cook when he fell, following her royal husband, whom the English were enticing on board the ship, to be detained as a hostage until a stolen boat should be restored. She says the natives had supposed that Captain Cook was their old god Lono, returned to visit them. They paid him divine honors, which he must well have understood. (Judd 1966:64–65)

So into the 1830s, similar reports continue, and not only in the *Mooolelo Hawaii,* with its detailed recollections of "the oldest and most knowing of the chiefs and people" (Kahananui 1984). Likewise, Varigny learned of the identification of Cook and Lono from an old-timer of Honaunau and Farnham from the "very aged" chiefly woman, Hoapili Wahine (Varigny 1874:18–23; Farnham 1846:37–38). But way up in the country, similar memories lingered, *notably in the rituals of the New Year.* The missionary Lorenzo Lyons recorded them in Waimea, Hawai'i:

January 1833. Last week the people having heard it was some where near the beginning of a new year thought that they must pay some regard to a feast held formerly on this occasion which was to eat abundantly of all such things as they chanced to have & pray to Lono (Captain Cook). They did not observe it exactly in the same way now— some of them collected together & read & prayed [i.e., to the Christian god]—when told we had no such thing they were quite astonished. (Lyons to Anderson, ABCFM/L, 6 Sept 1833)

This celebration in a remote Hawai'i island community in a double way disconfirms the thesis that Cook was merely apotheosized post mortem as a "guardian spirit" of Hawaiian chiefs. For, not only was this a New Year fête—or the 'New Makahiki' as Kawena Pukui called it (HEN 1:1294)— but, again, it was celebrated by the people in general, not the chiefs alone as an ancestral cult.

Who Is Speaking Here?

"O-runa no te tuti," Cook is Lono (Zimmermann). "The Indians have a Notion that Capt' Cook as being Orono will come amongst them again in a short time" (Samwell). From 1779 into the 1830s, Hawaiian people testified in direct speech, by their ritual practices, and in their myths that, for them, Captain Cook was an embodied form of their god Lono—of whom tradition has known other forms, human and not. Trouble is, even when quoted more or less verbatim from named people these testimonies have mainly been set down and reported by Haole. Now, Obeyesekere contends that Cook was not Lono "in person," but at best a tabu chief of that name who after death functioned as a royal ancestral god. He claims that the idea Cook was Lono (or more precisely, a form of Lono) is a long-standing myth of Europeans, a characteristic Western conceit that "natives" take them for gods. So someone is lying. Or at least some group, Hawaiian or Haole, is obsessively repeating certain prescribed scenarios of belief in the face of empirical realities to the contrary.

Happily, it is not the Hawaiians who are irrational. The concept of Cook as Lono was basically "created" by Europeans and essentially "perpetuated" by Europeans (Ob. 3, 50, 177). Discussing Maori versions of such "myths," Obeyesekere puts it as a general rule that "in an unequal power structure the white version triumphs and is eventually accepted by the subaltern culture" (Ob. 136). Still, even assuming with Obeyesekere that the idea of Cook's apotheosis is of European provenance, Hawaiians, who could not have traditionally believed it themselves, would have to have some strong inducements to rehearse it compulsively for the benefit of Western chroniclers. Perhaps here and there one might find an Uncle Komo, especially as time and acculturation march on—one ruling chief or another in the 1820s who for reasons of his or her own was willing to indulge the Haole fantasies about Cook. Yet it would be hard to sustain the claim that before the latter part of 1825, when American missionary doctrines began to be enthusiastically spread by ruling chiefs, Hawaiians were habitually repeating someone else's understandings of Captain Cook. How could they be so easily convinced of an identity of Cook and Lono that they were too pragmatic to believe on their own? Obeyesekere says that already by the time of Kalaniʻōpuʻu's death (ca. 1783) and Kamehameha's rise to power (at the latest, 1795), Hawaiians knew too much about the Western world to believe Cook was anything but an English sea captain (Ob. 146–47). True, their own religion was crumbling toward 1819, but that liberation might have made them more rational than ever. On the whole, then, this argument regarding the Hawaiian testimonies of Cook = Lono has more problems than the alternative that the Haole writers made them up. In general for Obeyesekere, with a few minor exceptions, it is not the Hawaiians being cited who are held responsible for what they are thus reputed to say. The Europeans doing the citing must be the ones at fault: Bingham, Ellis, Loomis, Whitney, Dibble, Kotzebue, King, Zimmermann, Rickman, Byron, Chamisso, Freycinet, Martin, Puget, Bell, Manby, Dimsdell, Byron, A. Bloxam, R. Bloxam, Dampier, Taylor, Colnett, and all the others of their ilk. They are doing the talking here.

The European chroniclers are prisoners of their own myths, and however they may refer these myths to Hawaiians, the words are theirs. The words are only ostensibly the "native's"; the Haole is the real source. This is the historiographic principle in Obeyesekere's critical readings of the texts. Again, there are two possibilities of ventriloquism. The European writer may lie outright. He may simply ascribe to the Hawaiians what he believed of them, something they never remotely said or intended. More charitable and more likely, however, the Haole misconstrues the Hawaiians because of his own conceptual predispositions. How could a European anyhow appreciate the finesse of a Hawaiian distinction between the chiefly Cook as a deified ancestor "Lono" and the deity Cook as a chiefly ancestor "Lono?" Especially when this Haole is convinced in advance that credulous "natives" have been known to take his kind for gods. In the event, Obeyesekere usually opts for the second alternative. The historical writers consistently misconstrue Hawaiian statements or actions to accord with their own belief that Cook was conceived as the god Lono. In this way, Obeyesekere systematically eliminates Hawaiians from their own history.

THREE

Historical Fiction, Makeshift Ethnography

O beyesekere attempts to improve his contention that the apotheosis of Captain Cook is a European fantasy by advancing a "plausible" counter-theory of the events of early 1779 at Kealakekua Bay. Unfortunately the "plausible alternative" is too often conceived as an alternative to what is explicitly described in the historical texts. Selectively ignoring or misrepresenting the primary documents, he constructs an implausible history out of a habitual combination of commonsense realism and pop anthropology. Suggestio falsi rushes in to fill the void left by suppressio veri.

Appropriately enough, Obeyesekere describes his project in the amphibolous terms of an effort "to provide the missing link" in the argument of Sir Peter Buck (Te Rangi Hiroa) that Cook was deified only after Hawaiians had killed him. Also appropriately, the missing link he provides is an undocumentable speculation about the motives of the Hawaii king, Kalani'-ōpu'u. The king presumably wanted to enlist Cook in his own wars. So he had the Englishman installed as a sacred Hawaiian chief—thus entitled to deification after death—which supposed alliance Cook supposedly declined. Obeyesekere believes that simply suggesting this plausible theory is enough to cast doubt on the notion that Cook was received as Lono, even though, as he allows, the "only confirmation would have to be in the lost journal of Captain Cook" (Ob. 87). Indeed, for him, "the very possibility of a plausible alternative interpretation" is sufficient criticism—since he represents incorrectly the thesis of Cook's apotheosis that he criticizes as entailing a "rigid interpretation of symbolic forms" (Ob. 82).

The converse of famous attempts to "fill a vital gap in the literature," Obeyesekere's confidence about what will be found in an unknown document has the same quality as his effort to supply the interpretation of Cook's fate with its missing link. As for doubt, Descartes proved it was possible to plausibly doubt everything and everyone, except oneself, by virtue of one's capacity to doubt. In other words, merely to be able to doubt is a self-reference that adds nothing to our knowledge of the world. Nor can plausibility consist in, or proceed from, doubt, but only from reason and evidence. In this case, the plausibility of Obeyesekere's counter-theory—that the king had Cook "installed" as a tabu chief named after the god and then deified post mortem—is undermined by reason, historical evidence and the ethnography of Hawaiian culture.

But one will have to make a distinction between the plausibility of an argument and its appeal. Obeyesekere's counter-theory has seemed attractive enough to too many professional reviewers of his book, let alone to those not familiar with Hawaiian history or culture. It is rather a scandal how many reviewers have been gulled into praising Obeyesekere's scholarship. Apart from the moral shakedown entailed in the contention that Cook's divinity is an imperialist ideology, I think the reason lies in the appeal to a Western sense of practicality and reality *at the expense of Hawaiian culture.* As we know, Obeyesekere repeatedly introduces or underlines his arguments with a certain distinctive rhetoric: phrases such as "it is hard to believe that," "it is puzzling that," "it is surprising that," "it is natural to suppose that." And "that" turns out to be some such common wisdom as "if Cook were already the god, why make him imitate the image?" or "if Cook were so important, Lono in person, how come the king and high priest were not there to greet him?" The clear function of this persistent rhetorical appeal is to substitute our good sense for theirs, more precisely our rationality for their culture. The method is precisely the opposite of a true heterology or science of the other, which begins, as Certeau says, just where the specificity of another society "resists Occidental specifications." It begins with the apparent incongruities of the voyaging account, the shocks to our own categories, logic and common sense:

> In the text of the ethnographic project oriented initially toward reduction and preservation, are irreducible details (sounds, "words," singularities) insinuated as faults in the discourse of comprehension, so that that travel narrative presents the kind of organization that Freud posited in ordinary language: a system in which indices of an unconscious, that other of conscience, emerge in lapses or witticisms. The history of voyages would especially lend itself to this analysis by tolerating or privileging as an "event" that which makes an exception to the interpretive codes. (Certeau 1991 : 223)

There is a kind of academic defense of the cultural integrity of indigenous peoples that, though well-intentioned, winds up delivering them intellectually to the imperialism that has been afflicting them economically and politically. I mean the paradox entailed in defending their mode of existence by endowing it with the highest cultural values of Western societies. So the Cree or the Maori or the Kayapó are supposed to be paragons of ecological wisdom. Or in this instance, the Hawaiians are the expert practitioners of Western intellectual virtues, such as the ability to accurately negotiate the dualism of received belief and objective reality. Indeed, in contrast to Western scholars and travelers who have been unable to see things clearly by virtue of the mythical scales before their eyes, the Hawaiians alone have systematically practiced a universal rationality—that had nothing to do with their own particular system of the universe. Such a defense of the peoples against imperialism seems rather to complete it by adding a moral and intellectual encompassment to a real-political domination.

Let me offer an example of this colonization by Western common sense which is also useful for understanding Obeyesekere's counter-theory. In two passages he asserts that Hawaiians could not possibly have perceived Cook as a manifestation of Lono because, in critical respects of appearance and language, the empirical discrepancy between the British captain and the indigenous god would make such an association absurd. This discordance is key for Obeyesekere, the epitome of the gap between reality and belief, percept and concept, that Hawaiians could never fall for:

> When James Cook arrived during the [Makahiki] festival in two large ships with a large number of people who neither looked Polynesian nor spoke the native language, the Hawaiians, it is said, thought he was the god Lono. By contrast, I argue in this book that Cook's arrival would *violate* Hawaiian commonsense expectations, though it could be consonant with European assumptions regarding native perceptions of white "civilizers." (Ob. 20; emphasis in original).[1]

1. The preceding sentences in Obeyesekere's text are marked by the kind of information that should prepare one for what follows:

For example [of discrepancies that Hawaiians would rationally reflect on], the normal beliefs of the Hawaiians were that their god Lono "arrives" at the Makahiki festival as an invisible presence when he is invited by priests. Furthermore, he is represented iconically in various ways in temple images. (Ob. 20)

The god does not arrive at the Makahiki when "invited by priests" or as "an invisible presence," but in the form of a cross-piece image, Lonomakua—which is a public and portable form, not a temple image. See also appendix 9.

In this passage and a later version Obeyesekere is wrong in everything he presumes about Hawaiian conceptions: the appearance of the god, the language of the god, the provenance of the god. Accordingly, he is wrong about who is dumping whose preconceptions on whom:

> It may be possible for Europeans to assume that a British naval captain could be a Hawaiian god, even if he spoke no Hawaiian and did not look Hawaiian. Unlike the European tradition that possesses such myths [i.e., that the "natives" take Europeans for gods] in its antecedent history, Hawaiians believed that their god Lono was a Hawaiian deity, and presumably looked like them, and spoke their language. Here then is another remarkable discordance that the scholarly debate has ignored totally: an English-speaking, un-Polynesian Lono with a smattering of Tahitian, accompanied by a large crew totally ignorant of the Hawaiian language and lifeways. (Ob. 61)

One of the more fascinating anthropological aspects of *The Apotheosis of Captain Cook* is that it contains no serious investigation into Hawaiian concepts of divinity. Rather, as we shall see, Hawaiian theology is understood on the basis of (alleged) Sri Lankan notions of gods and their worldly forms. Yet if the more relevant Polynesian ideas had been considered, they would throw this whole empiricist critique into turmoil, since the gods in their generic form are transcendent, and no one has any idea of their nature. They are transcendent, invisible, and originate in places beyond the horizon: Kahiki, or what is the same, the heavens. Lono is not in that sense a "Hawaiian deity" but, like the rest of the great gods—not only in Hawai'i but generally in Polynesia—he is foreign by origin.[2] And in his encompassing being, as distinct from worldly manifestations, Lono is unknown and unknowable:

> All of these gods, whether worshipped by the common people or by the *alii* [chiefs], were thought to reside in the heavens. Neither commoner nor chief had ever discovered their nature; their coming and their going was unseen; their breadth, their length and their dimensions were unknown. (Malo 1951:83)

2. As is well known, generally throughout Polynesia gods and people originate in an overseas land. The original home and place of the gods was another, fabulous land or island—most commonly named Hawai'i or some cognate thereof. Thus if Hawaiians came from Kahiki (or Tahiti), Tahitian gods stem from Hawai'i (Henry 1928:343, 394, 399), Maori from Hawaiki (Treager 1969:56–58), etc. Of Tikopia, Firth (1970:86) writes: "A theme which ran through much of the Tikopian conceptualization of their gods was their alien origin." Conversely, foreign lands are typically spiritual in Polynesia: "Any far distant land is, in Maori story, likely to be so confused with the spirit world" (Best 1924, 1:173).

One is reminded of the Tikopian response to the question of the gods' appearance: "We do not see them; how do we know what they look like?" (Firth 1970: 83).

The innocent Western positivist project—worthy of Locke or Hobbes and coming to us from them—of comparing Captain Cook with Lono to see if the percept matches the concept would here make no cultural sense (cf. Valeri 1985, 1987: 188). It makes no sense because the god as such has no recognizable form. Indeed, Valeri argues, I believe correctly, that inasmuch as what is divinized in Hawaii are the predicates of human existence, an anthropomorphic image is the most effective generic representation of the god (Valeri 1985: 9f.). And if we should ask, did Cook conform to the image of Lonomakua? the answer is clearly that he did. For even apart from indexical and analogical correspondences, such as his coming at the right season, circling the island, et cetera, the Hawaiians could be sure that he resembled the image of Lonomakua because they wrapped him in tapa cloth, held out his arms in the form of the Makahiki god, and made offerings to him.

The Hawaiians did not understand Cook's language. But, contrary to what Obeyesekere supposes—that Lono "spoke their language"—the gods were not intelligible to ordinary Hawaiians. The transcendence of the gods has its counterpart in incommunicability, or, as Valeri (1985: 148) names it for the comparable differentiation of chiefly speech, a "communicative invisibility." (Firth [1970: 244] quotes the Ariki Kafika referring to what is incomprehensible as "speech of the *atua*," as opposed to the speech of men.) We are fortunate to have an early attestation, from 1816, of the distinctiveness of the liturgical language on Hawai'i from an unimpeachable source, Adelbert von Chamisso:

> In the Sandwich Islands, the language of liturgy is a special language, which differs from the language spoken today. Commoners do not understand it; it is probably the unchanged ancient language of this people. . . . Information from Tahiti is in agreement on this point. (Chamisso n.d., 56–57)

In 1821, Reverend Whitney got a dose of the ordinary view of esoteric doctrine:

> It is astonishing to see what moral darkness covers their hearts. They told me that before they did not know what we meant by prayer, but supposed we meant telling long stories which neither we nor any one

knew what they meant, as was the custom of their priests. (Journal, 26 Jan 1821)[3]

There are numerous passages in *The Apotheosis of Captain Cook* where the failure to consider the Hawaiians' theological doctrines provides Obeyesekere with occasion to endow them instead with the dispositions of unreconstructed Western sensationalist philosophers. Most relevant is the relation between the major deities and their 'myriad bodies' (*kino lau*), which are the manifest forms the divine takes in the experiential world. As we shall see presently, human forms, representational and living, are among these varied embodiments, along with plants, animals, and other natural phenomena. Certain divine refractions of a god are given binomial designations, indicating a type-token relationship. The head term is the god in the generic sense, followed by a term or phrase signifying the attributes of the form in question. Thus the Makahiki body of Lono, Lonomakua ('Lono the Parent' or 'Father Lono'); or the ancient Hawai'i royal, Lonoikamakahiki ('Lono of the Makahiki'); or again, the war god of the Hawai'i ruler Kūkailimoku ('Ku Snatcher of the Island').

The bodies of the god represent its relationships to human activities; which means, conversely, that the object-conditions of human existence are endowed with subjectivity. The Cartesian condition of an objectified nature, which is the condition of the possibility of Obeyesekere's practical reason, is not the ontology of Hawaiian relations to the world. This does not mean that Hawaiians are unempirical—let alone that they privilege the "ideal" over the "real"—but it does mean that they draw conclusions of their own from their empirical experiences. Rev. William Ellis, in his personal journal, relates a conversation with Kalaimoku, the "Prime Minister," whose views of Lono (when recounted to Kotzebue and Byron) Obeyesekere found too Westernized to believe:

> Mr. Bingham and myself had a very interesting conversation with Mr. Pitt [Kalaimoku] as to the seat of the thoughts which he seemed to think was not the head. He also said, it was his opinion that all animated beings had thoughts and could deliberate and reason. He said it was also his belief plants, trees and all kinds of vegetables even the coral (which he considers a vegetable) had sense & feeling and

3. "But what particularly distinguished the Priesthood of the islands was that remarkable air of secrecy and mystery with which they concealed their doctrine from the community at large. No one except the King or highest Chiefs were permitted to enter even the sacred enclose where their temple stood" (R. Bloxam, *Narrative*, 144).

that they only wanted a mouth to make us fully acquainted with them.
(Ellis Journal, 24 Feb 1823)

This ontology of "spirit" involves an empiricism of a distinctive kind, a
sensory economy that passes by way of Hawaiian social practice (Valeri
1985; Durkheim 1947). The divine status of worldly phenomena is not an
unmediated empirical judgment, as of morphological resemblances and differences, some correlation between percept and archetype, or the lack
thereof—the way Obeyesekere decides that Cook could not have been
Lono. We have already seen that this sort of empirical judgment would be
impossible, since no one knows what Lono looked like. Moreover, a similarity of form does not characterize the myriad bodies of a major deity such
as Lono or Kū. All kinds of things and beings that are involved in, or con-
textually associated with, human activities in the domain of that god may
serve ritually as his manifestations (Valeri 1985:10–12). The dog and the
hawk are both forms of Kū, because Kū is the principle of male activities,
particularly warfare, and the characteristics of these animals evoke the warrior's fighting qualities. By the same associations, so are certain mountain
birds bodies of Kū—although they are quite unlike hawks—because they
supply the feathers of warriors' and chiefs' capes and of portable Kū images.
These are surely empirically based judgments, but they bring together a
variety of perceived relationships, for the judgments follow from a specific
world of cultural practice; they are not taxonomic classes of purely morphological attributes. Surely also, they are subject to debate and revision, such
as Obeyesekere sees as attending "practical rationality," but that is precisely
because they involve interpretive schemata and not the intuitions of the
senses alone. The sweet potato, the candlenut (*kukui*), and the pig are so
many forms of Lono. Obeyesekere claims that Cook could not be included
in this group because of the discrepancies between the empirical properties
of the English sea captain and the (presumed) characteristics of the god.
Does this mean that the sweet potato more closely resembled Lono than
Captain Cook did?

The Invention of Cook's "Installation"

For all his empirical defects, his un-Hawaiianness, Cook was installed as a
sacred Hawaiian chief on the day he landed at Kealakekua and again two
days later, according to Obeyesekere. He was endowed with the highest
tabus, the right of prostration—the holders of which, it turns out, are of

godly blood (*waiakua*) and deemed gods (*akua*)—and given the proper name Lono. The name probably had something to do with the Makahiki, Obeyesekere says, but it was Cook's name as a chief, which is to be distinguished (he thinks) from substantial affinity to the god Lono. The imputed motivation for these honors Obeyesekere goes to some length to describe, without however being able to show any evidence that it was actually a Hawaiian intention. The imputed motivation was King Kalani'ōpu'u's desire to enlist Cook's military aid in the wars he was fighting on Maui. This is argued on the analogy of attempts to engage Cook in local wars on the part of Tahitian chiefs—who did not, however, find it necessary to install him as one of their own. The description of the Hawaiian military situation Obeyesekere culls from Abraham Fornander's "superb and graphic account" (Ob. 78; Fornander 1969, vol. 2).[4] However, with regard to the supposition that this military situation was responsible for Cook's "installation" (and then, his postmortem deification), Obeyesekere writes: "The only direct evidence for this would have been Cook's logs and notes, but these have inexplicably been lost" (Ob. 78). But this neglects the direct evidence, to be considered in due course, that the Hawaiian king and chiefs were anxious for Cook to leave, not pleased when he came back, and angry with the priests for letting the British again take over the temple at Kealakekua—not to mention that the distribution of Cook's bones which Obeyesekere reads as deification was the way Hawaiians treated enemy chiefs. But then, the so-called installation of Cook as a high chief was patently something else, according to the plain

4. The historiography of this move is worth notice on a couple of counts. First, Fornander's informants: he talked to many old folks during his travels, most of whom he did not name, but among his major sources were S. M. Kamakau and Z. Kepelino (Davis 1979: 196–200). Kepelino was a Catholic, whose triadic notion of "the great godhead of the forefathers" (Beckwith 1932: 10) would surely have evoked Obeyesekere's blanket condemnation of his value as a historical source. Or perhaps this is the reason Kepelino is not mentioned by Obeyesekere. In contrast, S. M. Kamakau is one of those authors Obeyesekere knows how to use judiciously. Although Kamakau (1867) said he got his information about Cook from relatives who were there, Obeyesekere condemns the association with Lono as evangelical prejudice imbibed from the missionaries. On the other hand, Kamakau may be used without hesitation where he appears to support Obeyesekere's ideas. This kind of reading is also the second point about Fornander, who also goes on for a long time about Cook's earthly career as the Makahiki god Lono—based on Kamakau, *Mooolelo Hawaii,* and the Cook voyage accounts, primarily. But we only hear from Obeyesekere about the "superb and graphic account" of Kalani'ōpu'u's wars going on about the same time. Of course, Obeyesekere is right to use the sources judiciously and selectively. What is in question is the principles by which he is pleased to do so. The notion that a substantive statement can be ignored on the presumption that its author was directly or indirectly influenced by a priori missionary belief involves the fallacies of ignoratio elenchi and petitio principii as well as the presumption that Fornander lied about the source of his information.

evidence of Hawaiian ethnography: the canonical ritual for the reception of the image of Lono at the Makahiki. In any event it seems idle to argue that the empirical Cook could not be a Hawaiian god, that such is merely the standard European myth, and then make him a Hawaiian chief of "divine qualities" in whom the king's own god "resided."

If Cook were the god Lono, says Obeyesekere, if he was as important as Sahlins claims, how come the king and head priest were not at Kealakekua on the 17th of January 1779 to meet him? (Ob. 86) The answer is, the king was under Makahiki restrictions on royal movement, and his turning up on the 25th is powerful evidence that the Makahiki ritual calendar as known in the Kamehameha era was also in effect in the reign of Kalani'ōpu'u. So now one might reverse the question: where was Kalani'ōpu'u when Cook was (supposedly) "installed" as a high chief and potential ally on the 17th and again two days later? And why? Kalani'ōpu'u had in fact come on board Cook's ships on the 30th of November 1778, but in such unceremonious state that the British did not know until he sailed into Kealakekua Bay seven weeks later that they had already met the king of Hawai'i island. Cook, on the other hand, was known as "Lono" by Hawai'i island warriors *before* they met him—recall the chief who comes on board the *Discovery* off Maui asking for "our Arrona." By Lieutenant King's statement, Cook was apparently known as "Orono" all around Hawai'i island, and certainly from the moment he came into Kealakekua and was wrapped in red tapa cloth by Koah, the Ka'awaloa quondam warrior now priest. That very day he was "installed" as "Lono" (in Obeyesekere's characterization). Thenceforth he and his people were abundantly supplied by the priests of Lono at Kealakekua, in contrast to the dealings with the chiefly party at Ka'awaloa, who made themselves remarkable for theft and chicanery. What was the hurry about this "installation"? Why not wait until Kalani'ōpu'u came in, so that Cook would have some idea who he was supposed to help? And above all, how could Kalani'ōpu'u even know where and when Cook would come to land, to be forthwith inducted into the chiefship? The king was on Maui: no one has ever said otherwise. Meanwhile, for six weeks Cook was beating his way around Hawai'i, pulling close to shore now and then for trade. How could Kalani'ōpu'u guess what the Haole was up to: if, where and when he would come ashore so that he could be immediately fly-whisked away to his impromptu elevation as a chief of the highest order Hawaiians knew? Doubt?—doubt is easy.

Reasoning is harder. So on the one hand, Obeyesekere finds it illogical to suppose that Hawaiians could take Cook for one of their own gods, since the Englishmen did not speak Hawaiian, did not look Hawaiian, and did not come from Hawaii. Yet on the other hand, for Obeyesekere it is perfectly reasonable that, with all these same empirical deficits, the people immediately and without hesitation welcomed Cook as a Hawaiian chief. Not only a chief, but a chief with the tabus of those of 'divine blood' (waiakua). Indeed, Cook had the prostration tabu from the time he first stepped ashore at Kaua'i in January 1778—though no one ever "installed" him as a chief there—until the day of his death. Obeyesekere admits that such chiefs have "divine qualities" (the character of which he here invents as "the mana of Kū"), and Cook was likewise accorded them. It seems only "natural":

> Because Hawaiian chiefs do possess such "divine qualities," it seems natural for them to impart these to the English chief, particularly in the context of the political motivations [whose existence is revealed in the lost journals of Captain Cook]. (Ob. 86)

Cook, according to Obeyesekere, was installed as a chief named Lono in the same capacity as a certain "Omeah," who was also called "Lono." (Actually, we will see that Omeah was a high priest of Lono, and in that capacity an instantiation of the god.) Hence Samwell was right, Obeyesekere again allows, to say that Cook was looked up to as "partaking something of divinity," since Omeah likewise had "qualities of divinity" (Ob. 76, 93). Indeed, Cook would be, like Omeah, a "sacred person" (Ob. 94). Best reasoning of all, Cook would need to have the qualities of chiefs descended from the Hawaiian gods to be so highly considered. This he had or was given, Obeyesekere concludes from his misreading of the King text, as saying that Kalani'ōpu'u's god "resided in us" rather than "amongst us":

> I have . . . shown that in Cook's installation ritual priests told Lieutenant King that the akua "resided in us" [n.b.: not only should this citation read "resided amongst us," but it is not attributed by King to priests nor on the occasion of the so-called installation ritual; it occurs in the context of his general summation of the Hawaiian events]. If so, the installation ritual itself is to effect such a residence. One does not know how reliable King is for this kind of information, but it is not improbable that some kind of divinity did inhere in their most sacred chiefs, probably based on a notion of "godly blood" (waiakua). But this means that proper descent was absolutely essential, and it is likely that brother-sister marriage preserved "godly blood." . . . What is almost certain is that Hawaiians did not possess "divine kings" in the Frazer-

ian sense. Such a conception was perhaps applicable to Fiji but my reading of Maori, Marquesan, Tahitian, and Samoan ethnography does not warrant the assumption of an unambiguous divinity of kings. The "sacredness" of chiefs is primarily based on pan-Polynesian concepts of *mana* and *tabu*, rather than [*sic*] of divinity. (Ob. 197)

Thus, Hawaiian sacred chiefs of the kind that Cook became had some sort of inherent divinity, which was thought to be true also of Cook (the Hawaiian god dwelt "in" him); this sacredness was based on Polynesian conceptions of *mana* and *tabu* "rather than those of divinity." What can this convoluted reasoning mean—Hawaiian chiefs whose divinity was not based on notions of divinity but on *mana* and *tabu*? Andrews' 1865 Hawaiian dictionary reads: "Ma-na, s. Supernatural power, such as was supposed and believed to be an attribute of the gods" (1974:382). Likewise, more recent dictionaries: "mana. 1. Supernatural or divine power" (Pukui and Elbert 1957:217). Again, *kapu* (Hawaiian cognate of *tabu*): "1. Taboo, prohibition; special privilege or exemption from ordinary taboo; sacredness; prohibited, forbidden; sacred, holy, consecrated" (ibid., 123).[5] "So you see," said John Papa 'I'i, in 1841, commenting on the tabus of the *ali'i*, "our chiefs used to be gods" (Ii 1890:61). Obeyesekere does not tell us what *mana* and *tabu* signify. What he does say is that from the time Cook first set foot in Hawai'i he was considered a "sacred personage" of "divine attributes," in whom resided the most powerful Hawaiian god and before whom all must prostrate as is due to chiefs of "godly blood." From this we are enjoined to conclude that the idea the "natives" take Europeans for gods is a European myth, a "structure of the long run" in the Western-imperialist historical consciousness. Reasoning is harder.

The reason it is harder is that Hawaiian culture is not the universal—read "Euro-American"—commonsense rationality by which Obeyesekere would demystify it. And of course it should go without saying that Polynesian notions of god and godliness are not ours. To begin with, the Hawaiian

5. So, in Traeger's *Maori-Polynesian Comparative Dictionary* (1969:203):

Mana, authority; having authority, influence, prestige. . . . 2. Supernatural power; divine authority; having qualities which ordinary persons or things do not possess. . . . *Samoan*—mana, supernatural power. . . . *Tahitian*—mana, power, might, influence. . . . *Hawaiian*—mana, supernatural power, such as was supposed to be the attribute of the gods. . . . *Marquesan*—mana, power, dominion, divinity.

See also Traeger's summary of Polynesian uses of *tapu*, with meanings of 'sacred' and 'consecrated' throughout Polynesia (ibid., 472–73).

concepts of *akua* and *mana* do not occupy the far side of an ontological divide that irrevocably separates the divine from a world that (as St. Augustine was wont to stress) was made out of *nothing*. Akua is a relative category, notably when referring to ruling chiefs, as Polynesianists have stressed— and as Obeyesekere seems to realize when he speaks of degrees of divinity among living chiefs (Ob. 197). Accordingly, some *ali'i* of the highest tabus, closest to the gods by descent and nature, are *akua* relative to the rest of humanity. While generally true in Polynesia, the connection between chief and god had a more radical import in Hawaii by virtue of a genealogical discontinuity between these superior beings and the underlying population. Where Hawaiian tabu chiefs could articulate with a genealogy that ran more than 900 generations back to the origin of the universe (AH/GB 33 [Kamokuiki]; Beckwith 1972), ordinary people generally had no use for, and did not know their ancestry beyond their own grandparents (Sahlins 1992: 196–203). So perhaps even more than elsewhere, the high *ali'i* were to their people as the great *akua* were to the universe, the first also endowed with cosmic powers, as well as with the same epithets, obeisances, and respects as were due the gods.[6]

Chiefs entitled to the prostration tabu were offspring of brother-sister marriages: such a chief "was called *akua*, divine" (Malo 1951:54; cf. Ii 1890). Generally designated 'heavenly ones' *(lani)*, chiefs of the blood and great conquerors may also be deemed *akua*. In O'ahu tradition, one born ceremoniously at the inland temple of Kūkaniloko "was called an *ali'i*, an *akua*, a *wela*—a chief, a god, a blaze of heat"; such *ali'i* "were the *akua* of the land" (Kamakau 1991:38, 53). Kuali'i of O'ahu was a god, as his chant says *(he akua o Kuali'i)*, for he came from Kahiki (Fornander 1916–20, 4:395, 375). Lonoikamakahiki, the one we already know as an avatar of Lono, was a god *(akua)* relative to Kamamawalu of Maui, who was but a man: so Kamamawalu's priest said, in order to warn him off fighting Lonoikamakahiki (ibid., 4:338, 339). Valeri (1985:143–52) gives other textual examples. The very notion of 'godly blood' *(waiakua)* signifies the categorical assimilation of god and chief in Polynesian terms, inasmuch as the ancestor is to his descendants as a general class is to particular instances. Valeri argues that naming a chief after a god again means the same: a chief designated Lono would be a mani-

6. In 1790, a party of Tahitians offered a young plantain tree (ritual equivalent of a human sacrifice) and a suckling pig to a famous portrait of Captain Cook treasured by the Matavai rulers. The sacrificer hailed Cook as the chief of Matavai, and also "Chief of the Air, Earth & Water . . . Chief from the Beach to the Mountains, over Men, Trees & Cattle, over the Birds of the Air and Fishes of the Sea etc etc" (Morrison 1935:86).

festation of Lono.[7] And besides verbal practice, there is a large class of attributes believed to be common to tabu chiefs and gods, together with privileges and observances that unite them in distinction to ordinary people. Among these are insignia, tabus, actions or epiphanies that have effects on the cosmos, symbolic and communicative forms of invisibility, associations with celestial bodies, form-changing or the ability to take animal appearances, and others (ibid., 146–52). Finally, if chiefs are thus associated with gods, the converse is also true. In legends, *akua* are sometimes referred to as *ali'i*. And more generally, as was true of Captain Cook: "Gods are represented in Hawaiian story as chiefs dwelling in far lands or in the heavens and coming as visitors or immigrants to some special locality in the group sacred to their worship" (Beckwith 1970:3).

So what did Cook's "installation ritual" entail? Curiously, Obeyesekere did not "find it strange" from the point of view of practical rationality that the Hawaiians could *make* a chief of divine attributes, let alone do so out of such unlikely empirical material as an Englishman. Yet on ethnographic grounds this might have been legitimately doubted. For, the status of a tabu chief cannot simply be acquired. One cannot be given sacred tabus—like the prostration tabu, "equal" to the tabus of the gods (Kamakau 1961:4)—without the proper credentials of descent. There is no "installation ritual" that could do this. It becomes a contradiction many times over to say that Cook was too un-Hawaiian to be the manifestation of a god and yet was consecrated a chief of the highest tabu (*kapu moe*). Nor was Cook, who was already "Lono" before any Hawai'i islander had seen him, simply put through an improvised ritual, made up at the time for reasons of political expediency. What Obeyesekere calls the "installation ritual" was the reception of Cook at Hikiau temple when he landed at Kealakekua on 17 January, which notably included the customary ceremony for the reception of Lono at the Makahiki, as well as the repetition of the latter ceremony two days later by the priests of Lono. Recall that the proceedings of 19 January were described by Samwell as, "a Ceremony . . . performed by the Priests in which he [Cook] was invested by them with the Title and Dignity of Orono, which is the highest Rank among these Indians and is a Character that is looked upon by them as partaking something of divinity" (Beaglehole 1967: 1161–62). The ceremony was again repeated at a location about five miles

---

7. Some scholars who are not comfortable with Valeri's observations about the relations of chiefs and *akua* have been content to point out that Charlot (1987) has objected to them, as if the fact that an argument has been disputed means that it is dubious. See Valeri's response (1987).

away on the same day, thus probably at Honaunau, at the House of Keawe, where the bundled remains of royal ancestral deities were stored.

These rituals, we have seen, match in specific details the distinctive ceremonies (called *hānaipū*) by which the image of Lono-the-Parent is welcomed by Hawaiian notables at their respective personal temples *(mua)*, as described by Malo, K. Kamakau, and John Papa 'I'i. Ignoring this point—which has been repeatedly made in print—Obeyesekere simply substitutes his own version of Hawaiian ethnography, rechristening the *hānaipū* as an ad hoc "installation ritual" of a tabu chief, and claiming this to be a "plausible alternative interpretation":

> My alternative interpretation brings it [i.e., "the concordance between this ritual and the predications of the Makahiki calendar" *(sic)*] into serious question. The very possibility of a plausible alternative interpretation is at the very least a demonstration of the folly of attempting any rigid interpretation of symbolic forms. (Ob. 82)

The plausible alternative then entails a series of further historical and ethnographic fictions about the ceremonial events of 17 and 19 January—that is, the repeated performances of the *hānaipū*. As previously noted, these fabrications have Cook "being introduced to the Hawaiian deities," but not as the god Lono (Ob. 83); Cook praying (with arms overhead) to the Hawaiian gods—whereas his arms were supported in imitation of the Lono image; Cook being "given the name Lono after the god Lono who is, to borrow a term not strictly applicable to Hawai'i, a kind of 'guardian deity' to him" (Ob. 85); Lieutenant King and the astronomer Bayly being "in a sense reborn as the children of the Hawaiian gods" (Ob. 86); Cook being imbued "with the mana of the war god Kū himself" (Ob. 86)—indeed having the god take up residence in him (Ob. 86). Finally, after citing Samwell's description of the second *hānaipū* (19 January), Obeyesekere rounds off the series of spurious anthropological clichés by declaring: "I no longer need to analyze these ceremonies; basically Cook and his officers are now brought symbolically under the aegis of Lono, the god of the Makahiki" (Ob. 87).

These ad hoc notions with a suitably "native" ring to them turn out to be the first false turns in a labyrinth of similar interpretations required by the counter-theory of Cook as a (mere) tabu chief. Attempting to secularize what Hawaiians meant by the name and honors of Lono they bestowed on the Englishman, Obeyesekere constructs a tortuous exegesis of the ceremonies of January 19th, which turns out to be incorrect by all genealogical and ethnographic evidence. Some of the interpretive contrivances are required to keep out of sight the well-attested identification of the priest named "Omeeah" as a member of the Lono priesthood, indeed the head of that specialized order in Lieutenant King's estimation. Omeeah was likewise called "Lono," and "honored almost to adoration," King observed. Obeyesekere does not discuss these affinities with the god. He tries to make out that the meaning of calling Cook "Lono" is that "Lono" is an alternate chiefly name, just like Omeeah's. And since Omeeah was not an incarnation of the god Lono—although King likened him to the "Delai Lama" of Tibet—neither was Cook. Obeyesekere's "plausible alternative interpretation" comes as a complicated explanation of Samwell's text on the investiture of Cook with the appellation of "Lono." Or rather with this "Title and Dignity." The context of the statement, recall, was Samwell's description of the second *hānaipū* ceremony of greeting Lono, which took place at the House of Lono in front of a standing image of the god. For Obeyesekere, the meaning of this ceremony is as follows:

> The fact that Omiah was called Lono, plus the fact that other chiefs also have the name of Lono [none such in the Cook documents], led the journalists to assume that Lono was a category term. This is evident in Samwell's important statement that I shall quote once again: "Today a ceremony was performed by the Priests in which he (Cook) was invested by them with the Title and Dignity of Orono (Lono), which is the highest Rank among these Indians and is a character that is looked upon by them as partaking something of Divinity." This sentence has led to a great deal of scholarly misunderstanding, because Samwell's statement is taken to mean that either Cook was a character partaking of divinity or that Samwell was thinking of Cook in relation to the *god* Lono who partook of divinity. [The god who "partook of divinity?"] In fact Samwell is referring to the other Lono, Omiah; and he agrees with King that Omiah *partook* of divinity. The verb *is* clearly [*sic*] indicates that Samwell was using "character" in the sense defined in the Oxford English Dictionary as "a possessor of special qualities: a personage, a personality." Samwell was also correct in surmising that this was a ceremony of investiture. Furthermore, because Omiah was obviously not a god and yet called Lono, Samwell inferred that Cook was somehow or other being brought in line with Omiah, and his rank was parallel to the Omiah's. (Ob. 93)

Obeyesekere's metamorphosis of the *hānaipū* ceremony into the installation of a chief named Lono who partakes of divinity is the complement of a complex reinvention of the Lono priests as a well-known order of Kū priests, thus giving Omeeah and other Lono key figures new names and dissolving their connection to the god. Omeeah is identified as Pailiki— usually Pailili in Hawaiian accounts—the son of the king's high priest Holoa'e (Ob. 93). If this were indeed Pailiki, however, the thesis that Samwell was likening Cook to Omeeah-Pailiki (-Lono) would already be in some trouble. According to the source on which Obeyesekere here relies, Abraham Fornander, "native accounts" have it that Pailiki was with the king as the officiating priest on the Maui expedition (Fornander 1969, 2 : 173n).[8] Hence, Samwell would not have laid eyes on Pailiki until some days after the ceremony in question, if ever.

Obeyesekere effaces the distinct Lono order by affixing or superimposing a well-known genealogy of Kū priests in the service of the king to the Lono priests of Kealakekua whose relationships had been discerned by the British (Ob. 93). By this artifice, the names of Kū priests become aliases of the well-known Lono figures—Ka'ō'ō, Keli'ikea, Omeeah & Co. Thus, in Obeyesekere's rendition, the historical figure Ka'ō'ō appears as Holoa'e, who was the keeper of the king's gods and temples, primarily Kū gods—indeed, Kamakau (1964 : 7) and others call the Kū priesthood "the order of Holoae." But this identification (and its genealogical sequitur) is based entirely on a pure surmise or missing link supplied by Fornander. Fornander (1969, 2 : 183n) speculated that since Holoa'e was by all accounts the high priest of Kalani'ōpu'u, and yet the person who appears in that capacity in the Cook documents was called "Kaoo," "It is quite possible that Kaoo might have been another name or sobriquet of Holoae." (Some pages earlier in the note fixing Pailili on Maui, Fornander was even more uncertain: "There is no doubt that *Holoae* was the recognized high-priest of Kalani'ōpu'u; where he was, however, at the time of Cook's arrival at Kealakekua, is not easy to say" [ibid., 2 : 173n].) This possibly-might-have-been speculation, however, has no basis in the historical accounts or in the Hawaiian genealogical records. Of course it flies in the face of the clear determination of the Kealakekua "brethren" as a specialized order of Lono priests (and friends of Cook) in the chronicles of the voyage. We shall see that in a considerable genealogical corpus of the Kū order of Holoa'e—no doubt extant because Kamehameha's high priest Hewahewa was the great-grandson of Holoa'e—there is not a single name that matches the priests of Kealakekua mentioned in the Cook

8. Kamakau may have contributed one such account, as he wrote in an 1867 newspaper article, regarding Cook's appearance at Maui: "Pailili, son of Holo'ae, who had accompanied Kalani'ōpu'u, said, 'Life is ours! The god of our ancestors has returned'" (Kamakau 1961 : 97).

documents. Nor do any of these Kū names match the existing genealogical notices of the Ka'ō'ō *mā* (the 'Ka'ō'ō folks'). These are two entirely distinct sets of priests—and people. True, we know more about Holoa'e *mā*, and for good reasons: not only did they continue to serve as Kamehameha's Kū priesthood; Kamehameha seems to have sacked the Ka'ō'ō people in the 1790s.

When Vancouver visited Kealakekua in 1793, the relation between the royal town of Ka'awaloa and Kealakekua (site of Hikiau temple) had changed markedly from the conditions of Kalani'ōpu'u's time. Recall that in 1779 Kalani'ōpu'u took up residence in Ka'awaloa with the ruling chiefs of the Kona district. But Kamehameha's "palace" in 1793 was set in the area of the Lono priests at Kealakekua: on the grounds of what Samwell in 1779 had described as "some Temples or Houses consecrated to Orono" (Beagle-hole 1967:1169). The king's houses, observed Vancouver (who had been with Cook), were "situated in the same place where the habitations of the priests were destroyed, after the unfortunate death of Captain Cook" (1801, 3:199–200). Moreover, when Vancouver obliged Kamehameha to accompany him from Hilo to Kealakekua during the Makahiki of 1793–94, the king had a run-in with the surviving head of Kealakekua lands—a woman, daughter of Ka'ō'ō and wife to "the treacherous Koah":

> On this occasion I was surprized to find the King make some objec-tion to their [the British tents and astronomical instruments] being erected in the former situation, near the morai [Hikiau temple], giving us as a reason, that he could not sanction our inhabiting the *tabooed* lands, without previously obtaining the permission of an old woman, who, we understand, was the daughter of the venerable *Kaoo*, and wife to the treacherous *Koah* [of Ka'awaloa]. Being totally unacquainted before that the woman ever possessed the least authority over their consecrated places, or religious ceremonies, this circumstance much surprized me, especially as the king seemed to be apprehensive of re-ceiving a refusal from this lady; and which, after waiting on shore for some time, proved to be the case. (Ibid., 5:20–21)

Some peremptory action on Kamehameha's part settled the issue. At first the king asked Vancouver to put up his observatory elsewhere. But when the latter refused, Kamehameha "instantly assembled the principal priests in the morai, and after having a serious conference with them, he acquainted me, that we were at liberty to occupy the consecrated ground as formerly" (ibid.). The long-standing opposition between the king and the

Lono priests of Kealakekua—the famous "party matters subsisting between the Laity and the Clergy" as Clerke had put it in 1779—was still in evidence. Moreover, it seems to have culminated in the demotion of the Lono priests by Kamehameha early on in his reign. For, Byron's interesting remarks about Kamehameha coming down on the priests' power appear to refer to them, rather than the Kū priests of Holoa'e, who maintained their authority until the end (1819):

> In the early part of his [Kamehameha's] reign, finding that the great and separate power of the priests was dangerous to his authority, especially since he was often absent from his capital, then fixed in Hawaii near Kealakekua, he had taken upon himself the office of priest as well as king. (Byron 1826:72)

A.13

Priests and Genealogies

Everything indicates that the Lono priests of Cook's time were soon after consigned to the dust bin of history, leaving only their names in the British chronicles and a few genealogical traces in Hawaiian archives. In the person of the "high priest" Hewahewa (great grandson of Holoa'e), the Kū priests were still around to greet the missionaries in 1820 with the news of the overthrow of the old religion. This helps explain why Fornander—and after him Beaglehole (1967:510n), as well as Obeyesekere—guessed that Ka'ō'ō of Cook's time was Holoa'e (who goes unmentioned in the Cook texts). But Ka'ō'ō, his son "Omeeah," Keli'ikea, the "tabu man" (probably Kanekoa) and their colleagues of Kealakekua were Lono priests—which raises the question again of what the designation of "Lono" accorded to Omeeah meant, and why he enjoyed the deference worthy of a living god.

I say "living god" because, first of all, that is how, in effect, Lieutenant King described Omeeah. Recall what he said about the designation "Lono":

> Captain Cook generally went by this name amongst the natives of Owhyhee; but we could never learn its precise meaning. Sometimes they applied it to an invisible being, who, they said, lived in the heavens. We also found that it was a title belonging to a personage of great rank and power in the island, who resembles pretty much the Delai Lama of the Tartars, and the ecclesiastical emperor of Japan. (Cook and King 1784, 3:5n)

Since, for Obeyesekere, Omeeah "was obviously not a god," he finds this notice so "well stated" that he adopts it as a subheading: "The Other Lono: Omiah the Dalai Lama of the Hawaiians" (Ob. 92). Oops!—Obeyesekere might have thought better of so highlighting King's characterization of Omeeah had he realized that Europeans already knew well in 1779 that the Dalai Lama and the Japanese emperor were manifestations of gods.

Reported by Jesuit missionaries and others since the late sixteenth century (Japan) and the mid-seventeenth century (Tibet), the observations of the divine status of these Asian figures had become commonplaces of the popular voyaging literature in eighteenth-century Europe. Astley's *New Collection of Voyages*, for example, published in London in 1747, has this to say "Of the Dalay Lama, adored as a God incarnate":

> the Chief Object of worship in this Country, is the same which is in China called Fu, but by the *Lamas* in *Tibet, La.* This Prince, who was born one thousand and twenty-six years before Christ . . . gave himself out to be a God, assuming human Flesh; and when he died, it was pretended, that he only withdrew for a While, and would appear again in a determinate Time; as he actually did, if the testimony of his devout Disciples, the writings of the primitive Fathers amongst them, and, in short, the Tradition and Authority of the whole Church, from Age to Age, down to the present, are at all to be regarded as Proof. . . . So that the God *La* still lives, and is corporally present in the person of the *Dalay Lama*. In which Respect, the Church of *Tibet* has infinitely the *Advantage* of the Romish, inasmuch as the visible head of it is considered to be God himself, not his Vicar, or Deputy; and the incarnate Deity, who is the Object of divine Worship, appears alive in human Shape, to receive the People's Adorations: Not in the form of a senseless Bit of Bread, or playing at Bo-peep in a diminutive wafer, which would be too gross a Cheat to impose on the Understandings of Tibetans. . . . The Priests account for the several Incarnations of their Deity, from the Doctrine of the Soul's Transmigration, or passing from one Body to another; of which *La* was the first Inventor. (Astley 1747, 4 : 460–61; the like had been reported in Europe since 1665: see Lach and Van Kley 1993 : 734)

A literate man, engaged on a "voyage of discovery," Lieutenant King must have been aware of such well-publicized reports of the Dalai Lama. As for the "ecclesiastical emperor of Japan," the classical locus of this phrase is Engelbert Kaempfer's very popular account of that country, which also introduced the soi-disant title "Mikado" into the European tradition. (Sir James Frazer was indebted to Kaempfer's description of the "Mikado"—not to mention Gilbert and Sullivan.) First published in English translation in 1728, Kaempfer's work described the emperor as a living *kami*, in virtue of his descent from such deified men:

> the Mikados, or Ecclesiastical Hereditary Emperors, being lineal descendants of these great Heroes, and supposed heirs of their excellent qualities, are look'd upon, as soon as they have taken possession of the throne, as true and living images of their *Kami's* or Gods, as *Kami's* themselves, possess'd of such an eminent degree of purity and holiness, that no *Gege* [commoners] . . . dare presume to appear in their presence, nay, what is still more, that all the other *Kami's* or Gods of the Country are under obligation to visit him once a year, and to wait on his sacred person (Kaempfer 1728, 1:205–6).[9]

Obeyesekere's tortuous attempt to install Cook as a "sacred chief" by the name of Lono in the same capacity as Omeeah collapses in the very allusion to the Asian living gods. As a high priest or special priest of Lono, Omeeah was a human manifestation of the god. By the inescapable syllogism embedded in King's observation and unwittingly endorsed by Obeyesekere, Cook, in being likewise designated "Lono," was likewise treated as an actualization of that deity.[10]

But we need not go as far as Tibet for the evidence. Certain Hawaiians, notably certain priests, could be manifestations of their gods—in the local senses of such embodiment, of course. One of the earliest European notices

9. Kaempfer evidently held the emperor to be a living deity in virtue of his divine lineage, but not as the incarnation of ancestral gods as such. He thus distinguished the emperor from the celestial and terrestrial gods of the first ages, from whom the emperor descended in the senior line. Western descriptions of the Japanese emperor as a living deity go back at least to 1575, to the Jesuit Cosme de Torres (Cooper 1965:75). Characterization of the emperor as a living *kami* appeared as early as 1621 (ibid., 25; see also Montanus 1680:127). There is passing reference to the same in Purchas's collection of English observations, published in 1625 (Purchas n.d. [1625]:38). Lach and Van Kley (1993:1829, 1886) observe that probably no other Asian country was so frequently and thoroughly described by sixteenth-century Europeans as Japan; by the beginning of the next century it was perhaps the most familiar place in Asia.

In Tibet, of course, the doctrine of deification was different again: the transmigration of souls as described in the Astley Collection. This doctrine was reported by Bernier in a letter written from India in 1665 (ibid., 734); the German Jesuit John Grueber also described the Dalai Lama as a living god in the same decade (MacGregor 1970:53).

10. In appendix 1, I argue that King's elliptical explication of Cook's status as "Lono"—via Omeeah and Asian living gods—is rather the reverse of a European inclination to see themselves as gods in others' eyes: the reticence in King's formulation responds to an equal and opposite structure of an even longer run, the (original) sin of playing god—of which Mr. King was not easily disposed to accuse Cook.

of a Hawaiian priest refers to him as *he akua*, 'a god.' It is from the log of Thomas Edgar, master of the *Discovery*, at Kealakekua, 19 January 1779:

> a Man came on Board, who seemed to be an Eatooa or Priest, he brought in his hand a suckling Pig and a piece of Cloth he was pres- ent⁹ to the Capt" when he Jabbared something for about a Minute and Threw'd the Pig down before the Capt" who picked it up, he talked a little while Longer then Tied round the Capt"ˢ Neck the piece of Cloth.[11]

Certain of the people called "akua" were possessed by so-called sitting gods (*akua noho*) of which they were the ritual guardians (*kahu*) (Malo 1951:115– 17). Mentions of incarnations of Pele, goddess of the volcano, were com- mon into missionary times. William Richards tells at length of meeting one in July 1821 at Lahaina; she was called "Ke Akua Pele" ('The Goddess Pele') and attracted great attention (ABCFM/L Richards to Evarts, 13 Aug 1821). Reports of up-country hermits who were called gods, called themselves gods, and/or were prostrated to and treated as gods, were common in the early nineteenth century, and something similar was described in Cook's time (Cook and King 1784, 3:107–8; cf. Chamberlain Journals, 9 March 1831; ABCFM/L Coan to Greene, 17 April 1845; ABCFM/ML, E. Bliss to Lucia Lyons, 1 Mar 1839; *MH* 42:153, 1846).[12]

Another sort was Kohoali'i, who was a permanent incarnation of a god,

---

11. The captain in this case was Clerke (albeit "they considered us generally a race of beings superior to themselves"). John Law, the surgeon of the *Discovery*, has a virtually identical entry in his Journal for 18 Jan 1779. Edgar and Law both translate "Eatooa" as 'gods' in their later descriptions of the king's "visit of state" to Cook (Edgar Log, 27 Jan 1779; Law Journal, 27 Jan 1779).

12. One of the later notices of isolated country gods came from the missionary Timothy Hunt who, along with his colleague John Paris, encountered a "wild-looking" old man of the type in Ka'ū (Hawai'i island) in 1845. The incident also reflects an identification of the Ameri- can priests with their God—of a kind that may be found in more than one missionary report. As Hunt describes it, the old-timer had apparently not seen a missionary before:

> He answered our salutation and came out to observe us. He had no clothing, except a strip of native cloth about his loins. He looked strangely at us, and, after some inquiries put to him told us he was a god! After a little further communication, he exclaimed again, "I perceive you are Gods." Mr. Paris directed him to the only true God (*MH* 1846:153).

One is reminded of King Liholiho's retort to Hiram Bingham when the missionary remon- strated with Kamehameha's son for drinking too much, telling him God would not be pleased with such conduct. "I am God myself," the king replied, "what hell, get out of my house, go to your own house, God Damn" (Hammat Journal, 1 June 1823).

sometimes identified with the shark god brother of Pele, and performed important ritual offices on behalf of the king in royal temple rites. Vancouver saw him in 1794 when passing a night on Hikiau temple during a religious observance: Kahoali'i "was distinguished by the appellation of *Eakooa, no Tamaahmaah;* meaning the god of Tamaahmaah. This priest had been one of our frequent attendants" (Vancouver 1801, 5:37). The tradition of a certain Maui priest named for his deity Kanekehili, the god of Thunder, bears an interesting relation to Cook. They appear to have shared the same fate. Like Cook, Kanehekili's bones were worshipped after his death as the thunder god (Thrum 1909:48–49).

Now "Omeeah" was identified by Lieutenant King as head of the Lono priests at Kealakekua (the identification Obeyesekere neglects to notice). Not only was Omeeah "honoured almost to adoration," but his son, a lad of five, "was never suffered to appear without a number of attendants, and such other marks of care and solicitude, as we saw no other instance of" (Cook and King 1784, 3:159). Hence King's likening of Omeeah to the "Delai Lama." But if the transmigration of the god's soul to a little boy is not the Hawaiian doctrine, one might justifiably invoke the local identification of priest and god to account for Omeeah's designation as Lono. In relation to mankind, and notably in the commutations of sacrifice, the priest assumes the god's part. Nor would Omeeah be the only priest of Lono to be designated and treated as an appearance of Lono. We should not forget the 'Great Lono' (Orono Nuez) who came out to meet Colnett with the Makahiki image in his charge and who was repeatedly given kava by an attendant who held the banana-leaf cup to the priest's mouth, not allowing the latter to touch it. The "substitution of the *kahu,* or man who carried [or took care of] the idol, for the idol itself, was not an uncommon thing in the Hawaiian cult" (Emerson in Malo 1951:80n).[13]

---

13. In view of the seniority of Ka'ō'ō and the leading role he took among the Lono priests, it is more likely that he, rather than Omeeah, was the head of the order. Indeed, a number of the British thought so, and they generally called him "the Bishop." Omeeah, on the other hand, is a good candidate for the status of bearer or caretaker (*kahu*) of the Makahiki image. He and/or his young son appear to have accompanied Cook in some such function precisely on an occasion, the boxing entertainment of 2 February 1779, when the Makahiki image was on display. Law's journal reads: .

> I had the Opportunity of Seeing this Afternoon the respect Shewn to Capt. by the natives who was coming to view this sight attended by the High Priest & a Young Boy Nephew or Grandson to the King. Directly the Signal was given of his Approach which was done by the Continual Murmuring of the word *Orono* (signifying Chief) Every Body Layd down flat before him as he passed. He Entered Into the Ring and sat down

The Invention of Food Scarcity

The next defect in Obeyesekere's alternative interpretation develops in an attempt to resolve an implicit contradiction in his theory of the politics of Cook's death. On the one hand, Kalani'ōpu'u is supposed by Obeyesekere to have been desperate to engage Cook's aid for his war with Maui, even more desperate than Kamehameha would be some years later when he sought to enlist Vancouver in a similar project (Ob. 101). On the other hand, the Hawaiians were happy to see the Haole go at the beginning of February, and not pleased when they returned because of the *Resolution's* sprung mast a week later. Indeed, the ones who expressed the greatest relief at the initial departure of the British were their (supposed) would-be allies, the king and his chiefs. As noted earlier in another context, on 2 February, Lieutenant King wrote in the official account, "Terreeoboo and his chiefs, had, for some days past, been very inquisitive about the time of our departure," adding in his personal journal that they "seemed well pleas'd that it was to be soon, & that we would stop at Mowee" (Cook and King 1784, 3: 26; Beaglehole 1967:517). (Note that the inquiries began some days before the British—with Ka'ō'ō's consent and unconcern—had removed the palings from the fence at Hikiau, which Obeyesekere puts down as a significant factor in Hawaiian resentments against Cook.) Worse was the reception at the unexpected return to Kealakekua on 11 February.

A.14
On the Wrath
of Cook

Recall Captain Clerke's observation: "Ever since our arrival here upon this our second visit we have observ'd in the Natives a stronger propensity to theft than we had reason to complain of during our former stay; every day produc'd more numerous and more audacious depredations" (Beaglehole 1967:531–32, see also 568; Ellis 1782, 2:102; Home Journal, 7 Feb 1779). Again the chiefs promoted their desired alliance by being the worst offenders, as they had been from the 17th of January, the day the ships first entered Kealakekua Bay. They were also the most prominently featured in the altercations and violence that attended the British return. Several of the more acute journalists, including Midshipman George Gilbert, noted the Hawaiians feared the Haole had come back to settle the country:

when their was a kind of Song sung 3 or 4 times in a Chorus which I believe was in honor of him. (Law Journal, [22 Feb] 1779)

Obeyesekere has the idea that this was probably not for Cook, as Law says, but for Omeeah (whose presence would be a guess): "It is likely [*sic*] that people prostrated and were murmuring 'Lono' not primarily for Cook, but to Omiah who was accompanied by his son (not the king's son as Law thought)" (Ob. 94).

The Natives did not appear to receive us this time with that Friendship that they had done before. Our quick return seem'd to create a kind of Jealousey amongst them with respect to our intentions; as fearing we should attempt to settle there, and deprive them of part if not the whole of their Country. (Gilbert 1982:104)

The graphic account of Kalani'ōpu'u's displeasure by an anonymous correspondent—"The King told the Cap" that he had amused him with lies [when] he went away . . . and said he did not know he should ever come again"—has been cited in full on an earlier page (above, 80–81; Anonymous of Mitchell 1781). Lieutenant Burney likewise noted that Kalani'ōpu'u "was very inquisitive, as were several of the Owhyhee Chiefs, to know the reason of our return, and appeared much disatisfied with it" (Burney MSb, 12 Feb 1779). He too believed the Hawaiians suspected that the foreigners wanted to settle, given their long sojourn and their quick return (Burney 1819:256–57). And as we know, the king was also furious with the priests of Kealakekua for allowing the British to resume their occupation of the Hikiau temple precincts.

Obeyesekere does not explicitly confront the evident contradiction between the chiefs' attitude and their supposed interest in enlisting Cook's support. He does not find this "strange," "curious" or "puzzling." But he does in a way try to account for it, that is, by inventing a reason for Kalani'ōpu'u's behavior. He believes that Cook turned down the king's request that he intervene in the Maui wars. The testimony for this will be found in the same place as the evidence that Kalani'ōpu'u made the request: in Cook's lost journal. But the main contention is that the Hawaiians had grown hostile because their food supplies were depleted by the effort of supplying the two British ships—this would be a total of about 284 men—for 17 days (17 January–3 February 1779) in a politically centralized island of 100,000 people. Scarcity had set in among the Hawaiians, and they were thus anxious for their visitors to leave. Yet one can sense that this proposition—perhaps the weakest link in what turns out to be a missing chain of arguments—is in trouble from the way it is presented. For it is bracketed by the contradiction that, on one hand, the ordinary people (as distinct from the powers-that-be) were "starving themselves" and expectably showed a lack of warmth toward the Haole; whereas, on the other hand, these common folks showed no overt hostility to Cook *mā* when the latter returned due to the mast—on the contrary:

It therefore seems reasonable to assume that Kalani'opu'u did ask for Cook's aid and that Cook refused, as he almost always did, even if equivocally. For this and other reasons, including the depletion of food supplies—a critical problem for these islands—people were anxious to see the English leave. . . . The lack of warmth among ordinary people was expectable: To feed the British for an extended period of time meant starving themselves. People who, under the threat of constant warfare, were aware of the reality of food shortage must surely have been concerned over the demands made by chiefs to provide as many provisions as possible for the foreigners. The return of Cook's ship was a real threat to them as it was to Polynesian islanders everywhere. [A footnote here says there is evidence the problem had occurred in Tonga and elsewhere.] In spite of this, *there was virtually no overt hostility among the general population* and Samwell, who made a journey into the interior [*sic*], was impressed by the courtesy and hospitality of the people. (Ob. 88–89; emphasis added)[14]

Here again, as throughout, common sense—food supplies are a critical problem, they must have been starving, they must have been resentful—replaces ethnographic fact and thus generates historical fiction. The whole argument about scarcity is based on the combination of not knowing the ecology and productivity of the area above Kealakekua Bay, and ignoring the explicit British statements to the contrary.

Cook had landed in the region sustained by the famous "Kona field system," in its day probably the most extensive and productive agricultural complex in the islands of the Pacific basin (Newman 1970; Kelly 1983). Located on the mountain slopes some two to three miles above the barren Kona shore, this huge system extended northward from Kealakekua in a band approximately three miles wide and 18 miles long. Watered by unusual summer rains as well as the winter "Kona storms," the area was intensively cultivated in breadfruit, taro, sugar cane, bananas, sweet potato, and paper mulberry. Since Cook's time, when the fertility of the Kealakekua uplands was already remarked (by King, Edgar, and Ledyard), the Kona field system has been a marvel of the voyaging literature (see Kelly 1983). Archibald Menzies, botanist of the Vancouver expedition, set down a description of it in 1793:

14. See above, 79–81, on the differential responses among Hawaiians to Cook's return.

On leaving this station [Kealakekua], we soon lost sight of the vessels, and entered their bread-fruit plantations, the trees of which were a good distance apart, so as to give room to their boughs to spread out vigorously on all sides, which was not the case in the crowded groves of Tahiti. . . . But here the size of the trees, the luxuriancy of their crop and foliage, sufficiently show that they thrive equally well on an elevated situation. The space between these trees did not lay idle. It was chiefly planted with sweet potatoes and rows of cloth plant. As we advanced beyond the breadfruit plantations, the country became more and more fertile, being in a high state of cultivation. For several miles round us there was not a spot that would admit of it but what was with great labor and industry cleared of loose stones and planted with esculent roots and some useful vegetables or other. (Menzies 1920:75–76; see also 154–55)

Menzies' tour of the uplands allayed his and others' surprise at how Hawaiians had been managing to feed "in such abundance" the numerous visitors who had stopped at Kealakekua in recent years. (Indeed, the Vancouver squadron of three ships anchored there from 12 January to 26 February 1794, being "amply supplied" throughout, though when they arrived they found an American vessel that had already been in the Bay for six weeks [Vancouver 1801, 5:16].) But once Menzies was apprised of Kona's "vast resources," he spared the local agriculture no praise: "their fields in general are productive of good crops that far exceed in point of perfection the produce of any civilized country within the Tropics" (1920:81). Later descriptions by Gaimard in 1819, Ellis in 1823, and Wilkes in 1843 are in the same enthusiastic vein (Kelly 1983:57–58). The archaeologist, Stell Newman, sums up an analysis of the Kona field system:

The Kona Field System is without equal in Hawaii, and probably in the nation [U.S.A.] in terms of the extensiveness of a prehistoric modification of the land. It is quite comparable in terms of complexity and size with the well-known field systems of Central and South America. (Kelly 1983:73)

All this explains why the Cook annals include statements that directly contradict Obeyesekere's presumption that the people were starving, or even that Cook's ships had made any dent in the local food supplies. Why

Obeyesekere omits these statements is another question, especially considering that one of the most direct was penned by a favored source, George Gilbert—regarding whom he accuses Beaglehole and Sahlins of selective citation (since we did not take sufficient note of Gilbert's observations of Cook's irrationality: Ob. 203n.29). Of the ships' stay in Kealakekua, Gilbert (1982:102) wrote that they were surrounded with canoes every day and supplied "in the most plentiful and hospitable manner imaginable." Breadfruit, taro, and other foods, especially sugar cane, were "all in greater plenty than we had ever met with before" (ibid., 121). Pork, they salted enough of to last them back to England (ibid., 127). And all this *without* a perceptible effect on the supply, specifically *unlike* Tahiti and Tonga:

> The latter part of the time we lay in Matavai Bay in Otaheite [Tahiti] and at Amsterdam [Tongatabu], one of the Friendly [Tonga] Islands, being five weeks at each; we found supplies of all kinds began to grow scarce but that was far from the case here, *for everything was as plentiful the last Day, as when we first came in.* (Ibid., 103; emphasis added)

Likewise Captain Clerke, at the end of the Hawai'i stay: "We never saw, nor from what we did see, could we form any idea that any Isles whatever could have so much provision to spare and still themselves abound, which is the case here" (Beaglehole 1967:573). Lieutenant King confirms these glowing reports. Providing figures on the great amounts of pork consumed and salted down, most of which came from the Kealakekua area, he wrote, "and yet we could not perceive that it was at all drained, or even that the abundance had any way decreased" (Cook and King 1784, 3:118–19; see also Beaglehole 1967:619).

In sum, Obeyesekere's yarn about the political motivation for making Captain Cook a Hawaiian chief is insupportable. It is contradicted by the chicanery the Ka'awaloa chiefs practiced on the British from the beginning, by their increasing hostility, and by their resentment at the Haole's unexpected return. Obeyesekere's explanation of this resentment, that it was due to the scarcity, or indeed starvation, occasioned by the necessity of feeding the British, is not merely insupportable but made possible only by the tendentious suppression of explicit testimonies to the contrary. We can expect no better in logic or evidence from the last element of Obeyesekere's plausible alternative interpretation: that Cook was merely deified after death, as a tabu chief named Lono; but neither then nor while he was alive was he "mistaken" for the god.

The Invention of Cook's Postmortem (Only) Deification

Logic: what happened, again, to the empirical deficiencies of Cook as a Hawaiian god, or for that matter, to the certainty that making gods out of European explorers is a European myth? Cook anchored at Kealakekua on the 17th of January and was killed on the 14th of February. According to Obeyesekere, his remains were immediately put through the customary rites for deifying a deceased sacred chief. Yet, not a month before, he was empirically too grotesque to be considered a Hawaiian god: he didn't look Hawaiian, he didn't speak Hawaiian, he didn't act Hawaiian; besides, the English seamen were filthy (Ob. 65).

Obeyesekere takes his ideas about Cook's postmortem deification from Malo's description of the rites for deifying a deceased king—or more precisely making the king's bones an ancestral shrine (*'aumakua*) and his spirit or soul (*uhane*) a true god (*akua maoli*)—and from Sir Peter Buck's assertion that Cook was only so honored after death (Malo 1951 : 104–6; Buck 1945). Note that with regard to the supposed European myths of Cook's status, these honors are sovereign: "on the death of a king, one who was at the head of the government, the ceremonies were entirely different from those performed at the death of any other *alii* whatsoever" (Malo 1951 : 104). For his part in the analysis, Sir Peter lives up to his insider reputation as one who saw all other Polynesians in the image of New Zealand Maori. His contention was "that a living man was made a god does not accord with native custom and usage" (in Ob. 75). This is literally true, if one believes Hawaiians had some sort of regular ceremony for making living people into gods, which they had not. But if it means that there were no people walking about who were considered gods (*akua*) relative to other men, or who were not actualizations of specific gods, it is patently false, as we know already. The denouement comes in Sir Peter's next sentence: "If he [Cook] was thought to be a god, why should the heiau [temple] ceremony be conducted to make him one?" But the ceremonies at Hikiau did not "make" Cook a god. Insofar as they entailed the greeting of Lono by sacrifice at the end of the Makahiki procession and the rite for feeding the image, these were ceremonies for receiving the god in his annual passage. Cook was neither "made" a god nor "mistaken" for a god. He was recognized and honored as a form of Lono: Father Lono of the Makahiki.

Even if his corpse had been treated according to the royal deification procedure, this does not mean he was not an instantiation of the divine while he was alive. Malo describes a process for making the *remains* a godly embodiment, a transformation which is counterpart to the now transcendent state of the spirit—thus the 'soul' (*uhane*) is now a 'true god' (*akua maoli*). But in any event, this is not what happened to Cook's body. Cook was initially treated as a royal victim, not a royal ancestor. As Malo describes the deifi-cation of the dead king, the body is buried for ten days in a shallow pit over which a fire is kept burning. Prayers are recited continually during the pe-riod. Then, Malo says:

> After disinterment the bones were dissected out and arranged in order, those of the right side in one place, those of the left side in another, and, the skull bones being placed on top, they were all made up into a bundle and wrapped in *tapa*. (Malo 1951:105)

By all evidence, Cook's remains were not subjected to this procedure. Rather, Cook was treated as a sacrificial victim of the king, the customary fate of a royal adversary, and his bones were then shared out among the victorious chiefs. Lieutenant King thus had it from Hiapo, an emissary of the king and apparently a priest of Ka'awaloa:

> We learned from this person that the flesh of all the bodies of our people, together with the bones of the trunks, had been burnt; that the limb bones of the marines had been divided amongst the inferior Chiefs; and that those of Captain Cook had been disposed of in the following manner: the head, to a great Chief called Kahoo-opeon [Kekuhaupi'o]; the hair to Maia-maia [Kamehameha]; and the legs, thighs and arms to Terreeoboo [Kalani'ōpu'u]. (Cook and King 1784, 3:78)

That the body was burnt and bones distributed as trophies is confirmed in other British accounts, in some cases from other Hawaiian sources such as the priests who brought out the piece of Cook's flesh to the *Resolution* (Anonymous of NLA Account, 14; Beaglehole 1967:561, 1215; Edgar Log, 16 Feb 1779; Burney MSb, 15 Feb 79). Samwell also specified that the lower jaw of Cook went to the king, a detail of interest as this is the customary royal share of the sacrificial victim (Valeri 1985:339). Indeed, in every re-spect the disposition of Cook's remains conformed to the treatment of the slain enemy of the king. Valeri notes that the skull sometimes goes to one of the chiefs "especially it seems, to the one who has killed the man or taken him prisoner" (ibid.). Cook's skull went to the leading warrior of Ka'awaloa, Kekuhaupi'o. The distribution of the hair to Kamehameha is another indication of a sacrificial victim taken in battle, as is the burning (as opposed to baking) of the body (ibid., 338). Finally, and consistently, the Hawaiian tradition is that Kalani'ōpu'u offered Cook in sacrifice (Kahananui 1984:174).

What the British saw directly of Hawaiian attitudes toward Cook (and themselves) in the aftermath of his death was rage and contempt rather than veneration—the priests of Lono excepted.[15] If the Kealakekua "brethren," out of solidarity, returned a piece of Cook's "hind parts," the people of Ka'-awaloa were giving the Haole their own backsides, adding to their "insolence" by waving Cook's hat or other souvenirs of their triumph (cf. Samwell's notice, below, 243). It probably would have been difficult to convince the British that the Hawaiians were in the process of deifying Cook as a dead king:

> near some of the boats the Natives were extremely impudent[.] one of them figured away close to the boats in the Cloaths of one of the Mareens that were killed whilst another more impudent came and washed his bloody hanger intimating to us that he had been cutting the Body of Capt Cook, he showed many signs of insolence and contempt and frequently challenged us on shore and made signs that the Head, Legs and Arms of the Capt was separated from the Body. (Anonymous of NLA Account, 11)

They were not deifying Cook as a dead ruling chief named Lono—who should not be confused with the god—as in Obeyesekere's makeshift argument. They were carving him up and distributing the pieces. Skull, mandible, and long bones were shared out among the victorious chiefs rather than collected in a god-casket (ka'ai). Cook suffered the fate of a royal sacrifice and a trophy of war, not the funerary honors of the late king that Malo described. On the 20th of February, in response to pressure from the British, the Hawaiians reassembled and delivered to them Cook's bones (in tapa cloth covered by a feather cloak). The remains were at least in part identifiably those of Cook. They were confined to the deep in Kealakekua Bay.

All the same, as we have seen, from the early 1790s Hawaiians claimed to have Cook's bones in their possession. In the first decades of the nineteenth century, reports were they were kept in a temple and annually paraded around the island by priests collecting the tributes of the people. But if Cook thus returned to them, satisfying the "singular question" of the Lono

15. The Hawaiians suffered heavy losses on the 14th of February, when Cook was killed, and on succeeding days. A reckoning passed on to Mr. King on the 20th was thirty killed, including six chiefs, and about the same number wounded (Beaglehole 1967:567).

priests immediately after he had fallen, it should be noted that he was initially dismembered by the ruling chiefs. A moment of fatal opposition, the historical event was something like the ritual sequence leading up to the disappearance of Lono in the Makahiki period. The ceremonial of the night before, a prelude to the dismantling of the Lono image, is presided over by the king's companion and living god Kahoali'i, who is also known as 'Death is Near' (Kokekamake). In the Makahiki ceremonies, the king then goes into seclusion for ten days. After Cook's death, King Kalani'ōpu'u, who is said to have offered him as a sacrifice, "retired to a cave in the steep part of the mountain, that hangs over the bay, which was accessible only by the help of ropes, and where he remained for many days, having his victuals let down to him by cords" (Cook and King 1784, 3:66).

FOUR

Rationalities:
How "Natives" Think

A certain pseudo-politics of anthropological interpretation manages to express its solidarity with indigenous peoples by endowing them with the highest Western bourgeois values. Mr. Obeyesekere's version of this benevolent academic colonization, however, is unusual on several counts. Not many sympathetic anthropologists have dared to ascribe to Polynesians such a bourgeois relation to reality—in the guise of a universal human disposition to rational cum practical action. Yet Obeyesekere then doubles the compliment by reversing the usual prejudices: the "natives" are practical and the Westerners mythological. Moreover, he knows this to be true of Hawaiians because he is a Sri Lankan himself.

Objectivity and Utility

What does Obeyesekere mean by "practical rationality?" He introduces the concept in this way:

> In this book I focus primarily on an area of cognitive life where manipulative flexibility is readily evident. Following Max Weber, I emphasize "practical rationality," namely, the process whereby human beings reflectively assess the implications of a problem in terms of practical criteria. (Ob. 19)

People could not conduct their economic life or fight wars without such rationality, Obeyesekere explains. A footnote attempts to elaborate by calling attention to two significant meanings of "rationality" in Weber, emphasizing respectively "the systematic thinker's mastery over the world by means of his use of increasingly sophisticated concepts," and a "pragmatic rationality" proper, "where goals are achieved through technically efficient means, culminating in modern capitalism." Obeyesekere's not exactly crystalline position is that such "practical rationality, if not the systematization of conceptual thought, must exist in most, if not all societies, admittedly in varying degrees of importance" (Ob. 205n.48). This idea of rationality, however, is still too closely tied to instrumental activity. Obeyesekere wants to go beyond the strictly utilitarian and emphasize also the reflection and flexibility involved in practical rationality:

> The Weberian idea of pragmatic rationality has a utilitarian quality about it. I want to divest it of its utilitarian aura and expand it to include reflective decision making by a calculation or weighing of the issues involved in any problematic situation. Although practical decision making is also intrinsic to common sense, it is the reflective element that distinguishes practical rationality from common sense. (Ob. 20)

Perhaps one might salvage some intellectual value out of this unfortunate controversy by comparing this position on rationality to classical anthropological views of the humanization of nature and the pensée sauvage (Durkheim 1947; Lévi-Strauss 1966a). Hereafter I will use the expression "pensée sauvage" technically in preference to the so-called mythical thinking, the so-called totemism, the so-called primitive mentality, and other designations of that ilk. It is precisely to deny the implied opprobrium that Obeyesekere calls attention to a generic "practical rationality" which Hawaiians share with the rest of humanity. They share this rationality because it expresses universal biological processes of the species. In speaking of rational calculation and its objects, we are talking about "the physical and neurological bases of cognition and perception" (Ob. 60).[1]

It might be noted that this biologically grounded cognitive realism, which presumably kicks in when empirical circumstances do not match received concepts, then makes the theoretical place of the above-mentioned flexibility of responses rather uncertain. Or rather, the two problematics contradict each other. If the recognition of an event is based in a physiology characteristic of the species, there should be no cause for disagreement. If nonetheless the event is a source of difference and argument, then the per-

1. Very few people have taken seriously the two seminal articles by Geertz so ably contesting the culture/nature dichotomy as a stratified set of overlying and underlying determinants. On the contrary, Geertz persuasively argues, human nature in and of itself is fundamentally indeterminate, that is, without its various cultural specifications (Geertz 1973, chaps. 2 and 3).

cept as *experience* is socially constructed—that is, by relation to local knowledges and as sensitive to differential social powers. It is no simple expression of biology.

A more general anthropological issue is posed by a "practical rationality" that is a function of "the physical and neurological basis of cognition and perception." The practical and natural are then ontologically opposed to the cultural:

> The notion of practical rationality sketched above, I believe, links us as human beings to our common biological nature and to perceptual and cognitive mechanisms that are products thereof. These perceptual and cognitive mechanisms are also not "culture free," but neither is culture free from them. The fact that my universe is a culturally constituted behavioral environment does not mean I am bound to it in a way that renders discrimination impossible. (Ob. 21)

Every people, then, lives by some mix of nature and culture, rationality and . . . what, exactly? Obeyesekere works along the lines of a theoretical proportion in which the fourth term is rather unspecified: nature is to culture as practical rationality is to X. Since it contrasts with "practical rationality," which is flexible and responsive to empirical circumstances, X must be something like unreflected tradition (or symbolic formations, or mythical thinking). We can recognize the problematic, since for all the assertions of its ground in "native" experience, it is native to bourgeois Western social science. Take economics or development economics, for example, where the cultural factor so-called is "exogenous" to material rationality and typically conceived as an "impediment" to it, hence "irrational." Or in Weberian terms, the X in the above proposition would be nonrational values that are attached to means or ends and thus deflect action from *Zweckrätionalitat.*

But now we have sunk into a common average Western form of epistemic murk. By the logic of this argument, it is the natural and the rational-empirical which unite human beings, not the cultural and the symbolic, which presumably divide them. Hence it is on the former basis, the shared human sense of practical rationality, that one can know the Hawaiians. Pan-human practical rationality is the principle of an anthropological epistemology—*which is thus in principle independent of any specific cultural or historical knowledge:*

> The idea of practical rationality provides me with a bit of space where I can talk of Polynesians who are like me in some sense. Such spaces,

though not easy to create, are necessary if one is to talk of the other culture in human terms. (Ob. 21)

With a view toward understanding Obeyesekere's historiography, I will comment on his anthropological theory, taking the last point first and going back from there to the first premises. The exercise will help explain not only his historical methods but some of the more bizarre results thereof, such as the systematic elimination of Hawaiian discourse. It can also account for certain apparent contradictions, such as the one raised by the passage just cited, where it is claimed that a shared practical rationality, common to all human beings, is what gives the outsider access to the ways of Polynesians. If this does not contradict the special epistemological privileges Obeyesekere also claims as a "native"—hence like the Hawaiians on that score in contrast to the "outsider-anthropologist"—it certainly makes that distinction irrelevant. These arguments can only be reconciled if the "natives" generally think naturally, that is, pragmatically, while Western people remain bound by their cultural myths. And this is Obeyesekere's thesis, of course—the universal capacity for rationality notwithstanding.[2]

The inverted ethnocentrism has to end in an anti-anthropology. Obeyesekere asserts that a common practical rationality is what allows him "to talk of the other culture in human terms." Since he opposes this rationality to cultural particularity, the contention here is a pure negation of anthropological knowledge. It says that, apart from certain instrumental relations to sensory realia, Hawaiian culture is not accessible, at least not on "human terms." The anti-anthropology could perhaps be written off as a slip of the pen were it not Obeyesekere's settled custom to write Hawaiian history by an appeal to the reader's received reason in place of a study of Hawaiian cultural order. Hence the rhetoric of common sense we have already remarked: "It is hard to believe that the Hawaiians, or anyone for that matter, could ever have made the connection . . ." (Ob. 57); "I think it quite improbable that . . ." (Ob. 60); "I find it awfully hard to accept the scholarly view

2. This is Obeyesekere's position despite an occasional allusion to the possible "supervention" of biological thought process by culture. ("I am sympathetic to theories that can deal with similarity and difference constituted on the basis of a common human neurobiological nature" [Ob. 16].) There is something satisfying as well as seemingly judicious in the view that things are made up of contrary qualities: Prospero and Kurtz, culture and nature, rationality and mythology. For one thing, if the world is neither here nor there, but somewhere in-between, one can never be wrong about it, since whatever happens is explicable by one disposition or the other, as needed. Obeyesekere does not so much rely on this trusted psychoanalytic method, however. His history is more clearly segmented, if still dualistic, being made by "native" pragmatic rationalists on one side, and Western mythologists on the other.

that . . ." (Ob. 61); and numerous other statements of that kind. Without investigating Hawaiians' theological concepts, he can be sure they would not mistake Captain Cook for a god, since Cook didn't look Hawaiian or speak Hawaiian. Obeyesekere's intuitions of reality are taken and mistaken for the conditions of the possibility of Hawaiian history.

One might justifiably ask how in any event a Weberian practical rationality turns into a monopoly on empirical judgments, as if the alternatives, notably the pensée sauvage, were innocent of sensory discriminations and sustained reflection on experience. Yet such is Obeyesekere's claim. In a striking demonstration of his own discriminatory powers, Obeyesekere pretends that Lévi-Strauss's "science of the concrete" is of the same character as Lévy-Bruhl's "prelogical mentality." He writes: "Even those who explicitly try to counter the idea of a savage mind end up, as Lévi-Strauss does, with categorical distinctions not too far removed from the older models" (Ob. 15). But the argument of *The Savage Mind* is precisely that one does not have to be "rational" in the sense of "practical" in order to be "empirical." On the proliferation of species distinctions among so-called primitive peoples, Lévi-Strauss writes:

> The proliferation of concepts, as in the case of technical languages, goes with more constant attention [than would a concern for general names] to properties of the world, with an interest that is more alert to possible distinctions which can be introduced between them. This thirst for objective knowledge is one of the most neglected aspects of the thought of people we call 'primitive.' Even if it is rarely directed towards facts of the same level as those with which modern science is concerned, it implies comparable intellectual application and methods of observation. In both cases the universe is an object of thought at least as much as it is a means of satisfying needs. (Lévi-Strauss 1966a : 2–3)

Lévi-Strauss's argument is that, without sacrificing an empirical realism, the pensée sauvage dissociates it from practical rationality. Indeed, the relation between intelligibility and utility is often turned around: things generally become useful according to the way they are known, rather than vice versa, so that their "uses" by far transcend material-economic interests. I open, then, a seeming digression on the differences between "practical rationality" and the pensée sauvage, with a view toward the understanding of Hawaiian cosmology. It will seem less a digression, however, if I can show the historical specificity of the correspondence between practical rationality and empirical realism that allows Obeyesekere to segue so effortlessly from one to the other. The bourgeois subject is only part of the relevant metaphysics. At least as important has been the late Western invention of "objectivity," of a world of pure objects in themselves: "dumb objects" as they have been called, without either the meaningful values of a given cultural order or intersubjective relations to people (cf. Krieger 1994).[3] In turn, it may be argued that this Cartesian dualism of *res extensa* and *res cogitans* rests on a deeper Judeo-Christian conception of a contemptible world, created out of nothing, without immanent spirit or god.

But first, the native Western praxis theory of knowledge, which is not simply that we know things through their use but *as* their utilities.[4] What things are, is a function of their capacities to do people good or evil. Historically, the West has seen an epistemological union of the empirical with the instrumental, which together make up the rational, also known as the real or the objective, in contrast to the fictionality of the irrational. For all his distrust of experience, Descartes could be confident of judgments based on perceptions of pleasure and pain; for God would not have deceived us in this, but on the contrary gave us a decent sensory grip on the world for the sake of our own preservation (Sixth Meditation). The English empiricists such as Hobbes and Locke had even fewer reservations, and the materialist philosophes such as Helvétius, Holbach, and Condillac none at all. For all these Enlightenment types who were convinced that nothing was present to the mind that was not first present to the senses, the instrumental action of a subject in need of the world was the precondition of empirical understanding.[5] Their notion of empirical judgments presupposed a certain kind of sub-

---

3. "'Thus,' says Whitehead, in sardonic criticism of the 'characteristic philosophy' of the seventeenth century, 'the poets are entirely mistaken. They should address their lyrics to themselves, and should turn them into odes of self-congratulation. . . . Nature is a dull affair, soulless, scentless, colorless; merely the hurrying of material, endlessly, meaninglessly'" (in Bordo 1987:99).

4. Funkenstein (1986:290–93) calls this an "ergetic sense of knowing," knowing by doing, associating it with Descartes, Hobbes, and Vico, by well-known contrast to the contemplative ideal of many medieval and ancient philosophies. Or again, for Berman (1981:46), "the equation of truth with utility, the purposive manipulation of the environment," is the "Cartesian or technological paradigm."

5. The notion of objectivity as adaptation is surely endemic. Consider this prefatory remark by Peter Nidditch to *An Essay Concerning Human Understanding*:

The empiricism of Hobbes (1588–1679), Locke (1632–1704), and Hume (1711–76) should be seen as a compound of several doctrines, not all of them exclusively epistemological. Among these are, as a first approximation: that our natural powers operate in a social and physical world that we seek to adapt ourselves to, and that the variable

ject acting in specific relation to external objects. All of them began with what can only be called the bourgeois solipsism of an individual in need of the object, who accordingly comes to know the world by an adaptive process and as the empirical values of bodily self-satisfactions.[6]

Objectivity is mediated and oriented by subjective want. Its test is corporeal well-being. In such respects the initial stages of the Freudian "reality principle," involving the separation of ego from external objects (as from the mother's breast) by differentiated sensations of pleasure and pain, is a psychoanalytic version of the Hobbesian epistemology—as it were, a displacement of the pragmatic paradigm from the state of nature to the state of infancy. Certain passages of *Civilization* [*Der Kultur*] *and its Discontents* read like the opening chapters of *Leviathan*. Both refer to the same sensory economics of objectivity—not to mention the same antithesis between this species of individual rationality and the cultural order.[7] Apart from a few philosophers,

---

functioning of these powers in that environment is the agency by which we get and retain all our ideas, knowledge, and habits of mind; that our capacities of conscious sense-experience and of feeling pleasure or discomfort are primary natural powers . . . [etc.]. (Nidditch 1975:viii)

The same epistemological syndrome of a limited and suffering being (to use Marx's terms) framed the sensory metaphysics of the materialist philosophes. Helvétius, it has been said, had a genius for taking most arguments at least as far as their logical conclusions, but in respect of the corporeal grounding of empirical judgments he was altogether mainstream. Such judgments, he argued, suppose comparison of objects, comparison supposes attention, attention supposes some trouble, and trouble supposes a motive to take it. "If there were a man without desire, and such a man could exist, he would never compare any objects and pronounce no judgment" (Helvétius 1795, 7:196–97). So the motive of judgment is our love of happiness, and in the end it depends on nothing else than the body's sensibility to pleasure and pain (ibid., 204).

6. Compare the categorization of knowledge by Condillac's famous statue in the *Treatise on Sensations*, as the human form is progressively brought to life through the acquisition of the senses. Or Marx's "genealogy of conceptual thought" (in Schmidt 1971:110–11).

7. An infant, wrote Freud (1961:14), "must be very strongly impressed by the fact that some sources of excitation, which he will later recognize as his own bodily organs, can provide him with sensations at any moment, whereas other sources evade him from time to time— among them one he desires most of all, his mother's breast—and only reappear as a result of his screaming for help. In this way there is for the first time set over against the ego an 'object,' in the form of something which exists 'outside' and which is only forced to appear by a special action. A further incentive to the disengagement of the ego from the general mass of sensations—that is, to the recognition of an 'outside,' an external world—is provided by the frequent, manifold and unavoidable sensations of pain and unpleasure the removal and avoidance of which is enjoined by the pleasure principle, in the exercise of its unrestricted domination. A tendency arises to separate from the ego everything that can become a source of such unpleasure, to throw it outside and to create a pure pleasure-ego which is confronted by a strange and threatening outside. . . . In this way one makes the first step towards the introduction of the reality principle which is to dominate future development."

such as C. B. Macpherson (1962), I am not sure that Western academics, notably social scientists, have appreciated the cultural enormities of the proposition that we know the world as what makes us feel good: that "juger est sentir," as Helvétius said. The arbiter of what there is, the determinant of empirical properties, is a project of adaptation to nature. Hence the endemic Western association of reality and utility, and our commonplace view that practicality is the test of the truth, the proof of the pudding.

As a commonsense view of how others experience the world, however, such "objectivity" is doubly problematic: in the first place because it constitutes experience in a culturally relative way, which is not the only possible way; in the second place, because it nonetheless deems itself a universal description of things-in-themselves. "Every civilization tends to overestimate the objectivity of its thought," Lévi-Strauss remarks, "and this tendency is never absent." The observation apparently refers to an exaggerated appreciation of the practicality and necessity of one's categories, but then it can also be taken another way. People overestimate their objectivity because they are noticing only a fraction of the empirical characteristics of things, a selective attention and evaluation that corresponds to an act of categorization. Note that we are not dealing simply with physiological sensations but with empirical judgments. The biological mechanisms of perception are not in question, nor is their universality. At issue, rather, is the organization of experience, including the training of the senses, according to social canons of relevance. These canons, and therefore the distinctions people make among objects, vary even among "particular social groups in the [same] national society," as the *Encyclopédie* of the philosophes had already observed (Lévi-Strauss 1966a:2).[8] For, things are not only perceived, they are thereby *known*, which is also to say that they are classified. Hence people who are perceiving the same objects are not necessarily perceiving the same *kinds* of things—as happens, we shall see momentarily, in discriminations of "natural species." And conversely, people may agree about what certain images are, while perceiving them in entirely different ways—as happens to the red-green color blind.[9]

Western philosophy has been aware of the relativity of objectivity since the seventeenth century at least. Locke knew that it is impossible to exhaust the objectivity or empirical description of any object. He knew that in dif-

8. See Putnam (1975, chap. 12) on "the linguistic division of labor." The principle was discussed by Locke (*Essay* III.vi.30).

9. It is thus not even necessary that those who participate in a given cultural order have the same sensory experience of an object in order to agree about its identity, so long as they

ferent societies, or among different groups of the same society, people selectively and variously recognize only some of the possible attributes of things. Hence, from the same experiences they constitute different "sorts" of things. Empirical descriptions are inexhaustible, Locke observed, not only because an object presents numerous perceptible properties, only some of which are attended to, but because such properties are known through the relations or interactions of the given object with an indeterminate number of other objects.[10] Moreover, in many cases nature produces no clearcut distinctions between kinds, but only intercalary "Monsters" and thus "Grave Doubts"—as, for (a Lockean) example, whether a foetus is a human being or no. Hence Locke's famous (if blasphemous) revision of Genesis: "'Tis men who make the Species of Things." According to their interests, he says, and after the Manners and Fashions of the Country. And Locke was one of the all-time great empiricists.

---

are capable of making *some* kind of perceptual discrimination at the semiotically pertinent boundaries:

> Red-and-green color-blind people talk of reds and greens and all shades of it [*sic*] using the same words most of us assign to objects of the same color. They think and talk and act in terms of "object color" and "color constancy" as do the rest of us. They call leaves green, roses red. Variations in the saturation and brilliance of their yellow gives them an amazing variety of impressions. While we learn to rely on differences of hue, their minds get trained in evaluating brilliance. . . . Most of the red-and-green color blind do not know of their defect and think we see things in the same shades they do. They have no reason for sensing any conflict. If there is an argument they find *us* fussy, not *themselves* defective. They heard us call the leaves green and whatever shade leaves have for them, they call it green. People of average intelligence never stop to analyze their sensations. *They are much too busy looking for what these sensations mean* (Arthur Linksz, cited in Sahlins 1976:10).

10. We know things from the changes they make in, or receive from, other things—Locke's "mediated secondary qualities." We know the sun by its powers of melting and bleaching wax, even as we know wax by its melting in the sun and hardening in the cold, being divisible by a knife but unmarked by a feather; impervious to water and indigestible to people, and so on ad infinitum. Or as Locke (*Essay* IV.vi.11–12) had it: "This is certain, Things, however absolute and entire they seem in themselves, are but Retainers to other parts of Nature, for that which they are most taken notice of by us. Their observable Qualities, Actions, and Powers, are owing to something without them; and there is not so complete and perfect a part, that we know, of Nature, which does not owe the Being it has, and the Excellances of it, to its Neighbours; and we must not confine our thoughts to the surface of any body, but look a great deal farther, to comprehend perfectly those Qualities that are in it. . . . If this be so, it is not to be wondered, that *we have very imperfect* Ideas *of Substances*; and that the real Essences, on which depend their Properties and Operations, are unknown to us."

Humanized Natures

Ethnography shows that Locke's observations are true even of natural species, flora and fauna: they are known after the manners and customs of the country. This does not mean the people will not distinguish the species or genera recognized by Western scientific biology, as in some ways they often do, or that the distinctions they make are not empirical, as they characteristically are. Yet, as related respectively to different cultural orders, the same species can turn out to be beasts of entirely different intelligible *kinds*. They are identified by different perceptual qualities, which are not always or simply morphological, and thereby grouped with and distinguished from other forms in taxonomic arrays that may be, from some other point of view (notably that of systematic biology), curious indeed (Conklin 1962a, 1962b). For the Chewa of Malawi, certain mushrooms are in a class with game animals, as distinct from plants, on the basis of resemblances of the flesh. Again, domestic ducks are, as such, not "birds" let alone related in any way to wild ducks (Morris 1984).[11] Notice that the categorizations are empirical and objective. They are justified by observable distinctions, even if these distinctions are not ours (cf. Posey 1984 : 136). In a classic series of articles on the Kalam of Highland New Guinea, Ralph Bulmer repeatedly insisted on this point:

> The fact that folk-naturalists like the Karam see animals constituting "natural kinds" or "specimens" which bear some relationships to the species of the scientific biologist, does not mean there is a one-to-one correspondence between individual specimens and individual species. Conversely, the fact that folk-taxa do not correspond one-to-one to

11. Brian Morris explains (p. 49): "*Bakha* refers to the domestic duck, and besides being seen as outside the *Mbalame* (bird) category, is considered quite distinct from wild species such as *Chipweyo*, the fulvous tree duck and *Kalanga*, the Hottentot teal. Europeans often use *Bakha* as a generic term, but Chewa-speakers around Lake Chilwa were adamant that the term *Bakha* applied *only* to the domestic species."

The same for domestic ducks and chickens in Northern Thailand: "they are not birds (*nog*); the villagers do not invest them with the same values" (Tambiah 1969 : 439).

On mushrooms and animals: "Chewa women see a much closer association between mushrooms and meat (*Nyama*) [the life-form of edible quadrupeds] than between fungi and either plants or vegetables. . . . The association of fungi with animal life, rather than with plants (*Mtengo*), based as it is on *texture and edibility rather than morphology* is probably widespread in traditional culture" (Morris 1984 : 53, emphasis added; Morris cites Theophrastus and the Semai people of Malaysia on the last point).

scientific taxa does not mean that folk taxa are not necessarily "natural" units. (Bulmer and Tyler 1968 : 376)

But then, if the classifications of the same sets of organisms by different peoples so vary, even as they are equally natural (in the sense of empirical), it must mean that objectivity itself is a variable social value—an interested selection of relevant perceptible attributes out of all of those possible.[12] Indeed, the Kalam show that cultural repertoires of sensory discrimination are not the same. Giving the lie to the Western perceptual economy which accords affect to olfactory sensations and intellect to visual sensations, the Kalam differentiate frogs and other animals by odors—of which they habitually distinguish a considerable number:

> Some informants assert that all kinds of frogs have their distinctive odours, and all agree that certain taxa can be readily distinguished by these. . . . Karam are, on the whole, markedly conscious of odours, with a large number of terms in their vocabulary which are compounds of *kwy*—"smell," "stink" or "decay." They distinguish the scents of a number of plants and trees, in some cases explicitly using this as a key characteristic in identification, and say that most marsupials and large rodents have characteristic odours, which are sometimes noted in hunting. (Bulmer and Tyler 1968 : 355–56)

The big difference between this kind of sensory epistemology and the objective realism envisioned by Western science—and by Obeyesekere on behalf of Hawaiians—is that the first, the so-called folk taxonomy, is completely embedded in and mediated by the local cultural order, while the second pretends to be determined by things in and of themselves. The folk taxonomy is a cultural ontology, comprehending nature in terms set by human relationships and activities. But systematic biology would be the language of nature itself: a nomenclature of the world, each specific name in a

---

12. "Although many bird taxa," Bulmer (1968 : 634) writes, "do not correspond to biological species, they are nonetheless almost all firmly based on objectively valid biological observation." Once more this must mean that the differences and resemblances that are perceptually remarked are matters of cultural selection. Hence for the Kalam, the cassowary is famously not a bird, though it is such for many other New Guinea peoples (Bulmer 1967). Indeed, the cassowary is not classifiable with any other species. Its uniqueness as a taxon is a function again of a unique relation to humankind. By the Kalam values of its habitat and characteristics, the cassowary can be shown to be a representative of ancestors cum affines (i.e., in a cognatic order), as well as a sign of natural purity, whose annual capture is a ritual condition of the possibility of the reproduction of society.

one-to-one relation to what there really is—the self-expression of nature in the form of human speech. Indeed, scientific realism manifests its renunciation of the human order by naming the world in an unintelligible tongue; whereas, "native names of folk taxa always comprise a segment of the everyday vocabulary of a particular language" (Conklin 1962a:29). Accordingly, the folk classifications of plants and animals are integrated with many other aspects of human existence. The categories are factored by their relationships to persons and purposes as socially constituted—to local distinctions of groups and genders, habitats and directions, times and places, modes of production and reproduction, categories of kinship, and concepts of spirit. In brief, the creatures are embedded in a total cosmology from which it is possible to abstract them as things-in-themselves only at the cost of their social identities (Ellen 1986:101). The empiricism of the pensée sauvage consists rather of the discrimination of the creatures and features of nature according to the human values of their objective characteristics (cf. Feld 1982).

It is commonly said of folk taxonomies that the higher, more inclusive classes tend to be constituted on "cultural" criteria (although always perceptually distinct as well), while the lower order, terminal taxa reflect "natural" and/or "utilitarian" contrasts (Bulmer 1967:6; Bulmer and Tyler 1968:352, 378; Posey 1984:124). Yet, as we are speaking of hierarchical orders of being, this only means that the natural distinctions are instances of cultural forms, tokens of meaningful types. For the lower order, "natural specimens" must include in their own properties the cultural attributes that define the classes to which they belong—which also means that their "utilities," such as their edibility by certain categories of persons, are pragmatic aspects of their symbolic significance.[13]

---

13. It follows that the total structures of folk taxonomies are quite different from those of systematic biology. It also follows that when distinctions of species or genera are common to both, they occur nevertheless in different taxonomic loci (different ranks and levels; Berlin 1992, chap. 2). This makes attempts to show that folk taxonomies likewise constitute a true nomenclature of the world (reflecting what there really is) rather curious, since the positional values of any given species—the class in which it is included and the forms with which it is contrasted—vary radically from case to case and in comparison with scientific biology (cf. Saussure 1966:65–70, 111–22). One can say that, in many cases, the peoples recognize the same physical species, yet not the same *kinds* of species: the understandings of what these forms are, of their significant properties and relationships, are far from identical. The domestic duck named and distinguished by the Chewa may also be a species of systematic biology, but for all that it is not a species of "duck"—inasmuch as it is not of a kind with other "ducks" (as we know them).

The zoological schema of the Kalam people offers a good demonstration of the cultural organization of empirical objectivity.[14] On the highest levels, animal life-forms are grouped according to human life zones. The maximal classes are distinguished by their occupation of a series of habitats, themselves differentiated by their respective relations to human existence. Normally described as "natural habitats," these zones are indeed cultural distinctions of space, configured and evaluated from a human point of origin in the domestic group. More than that, they constitute a graded set of moral environments—or two sets, one horizontal extending from the household through garden land and open country to the mountain forests, another vertical from underground through terrestrial and arboreal zones to the empyrean—whose values are dependent on a Kalam theory of human reproduction. The lower and "cultural" spheres, in and around the household where life is lived out, are in that capacity spaces of degeneration. Here are entropic sites marked by the wastes of human existence: excrements, food refuse, menstrual "dirt," and rotting corpses (kept above ground near the houses until the flesh decays). However, just as the dead are progressively moved outward and upward as the perishable parts of the body rot away—until the clean bones are finally deposited in a tree at the forest edge—so higher and more distant reaches of the Kalam world acquire a positive and regenerative value. Metonymically the site of the ancestors (the bones) and metaphorically of affines (relative strangers), the distant, "natural" zones are where life is renewed. Annually, society is revived in a sequence of rites that involve, first, a return to a state of nature in the forest (where the cassowary is hunted), followed by grand ceremonies in the settlements which effect the growth of the taro crop, the initiation of young men and women, and the general fertility of the people.

To understand how this cosmography of social reproduction entails the empirical classification of animals, it needs to be added that women are associated with the households and the decay thereof, whereas the superior external and life-giving spaces are men's domains. The edibility, cooking, and categorizing of species then follows—indeed, if all else fails, the categorizing can be determined from the method of cooking. Animals living in and around the house, such as rats, geckos and lesser life, are generally not eaten because of their associations with domestic wastes (signs of anti-

14. The following analysis of Kalam animal classification has been derived from the works of Ralph N. Bulmer and associates: Bulmer 1967, 1968, 1974, 1979; Bulmer and Menzies 1972; Bulmer, Menzies, and Parker 1975; Majnep and Bulmer 1971. For some analogies in another (but distant) Highlands people, see Gell 1975.

life). However, birds and larger forest animals (the latter mainly arboreal) are freely eaten by all. These creatures are hunted by men and cooked in the superior fashion of above-ground steaming. By contrast, ground-living forms such as frogs, certain small marsupials, and rodents are considered "soft" foods, subject to decay and in that respect evocative of household dirt. Prohibited to young men undergoing initiation into manhood (reproductive status), these lesser forms are captured by women and children, and mainly eaten by them, upon being unceremoniously roasted in the fire. Thus, animals are divided into discrete kinds according to distinctions of cultural habitat that are at once perceptual and symbolic—notwithstanding the empirical "incongruities" these classes might entail from the perspective of an "objective" comparative morphology.

Just so, in the Kalam taxonomy, mammals belong to six different types—on the basis of their associations and distinctions of cultural habitat—which types, however, are unrelated to each other. In two of these classes, mammals are grouped with various nonmammalian species. Bats are of a kind with birds in a positive aerial category (*yakt*). Certain rodents are classed with frogs and small terrestrial marsupials, the "soft food" category (*as*). Household rats, however, are creatures apart (*kopyak*), and the large forest rodents are joined with arboreal marsupials, such as the cuscus, in the game animal category (*kmn*). Notice that rats (as we would consider them) are distributed among three distinct classes: "rats that are frogs" (to use Bulmer's phrase), the "dirty rats" of human habitations, and "giant rats" that are hunted. Bulmer observes that when confronted with the morphological resemblances among these three different kinds, Kalam will acknowledge the similarities, but not that the animals are therefore related or in the same general category. Rather, such criteria as dietary and culinary practices, together with hunting and collecting methods, "are the main factors sustaining this classification" (Majnep and Bulmer 1977:46). Other ethnographic inquiries revealed that these were hierarchically ordered as well as essentialized criteria. When Bulmer asked why frogs and small mammals were placed in the same, (*as*) category, Kalam first told him that all were found on or in the ground. When Bulmer objected that some frogs and small mammals were in fact found in trees, Kalam said all the creatures of this kind were collected by women whereas game animals (*kmn*) were hunted by men—which again, Bulmer notes, was an overgeneralization (Bulmer and Tyler 1968:352). The key turns out to be human-moral distinctions correlated with habitat and related specifically to the spirit world. For, as Bulmer learned with regard to the category of game animals, the operative distinction is in the mode of cooking, itself a ritualized practice associated with the propitiation of spirits. Speaking of game animals, Bulmer and Menzies (1972–73:490) observed, "what does appear to mark this taxon off precisely is that all *kmn* can be ritually cooked in propriation of the dead and of the nature demons *(kceky)*, and normally are prepared this way, whereas other marsupials and rodents [*as*] never are."[15]

In another dimension, then, the Kalam zoological system is infused with spirit, including the human dead and nature beings who—rather like the well-known Algonkian species masters—are in control of the animals, and who may be manifested in them, especially in intercalary forms. The cassowary would be one of the latter, and it shares a classificatory privilege with the two types of mammals yet to be mentioned, pigs and dogs. Each of these is a unique form, in a class by itself, and in an equally special relationship to Kalam, being treated as nonhuman kin of various types. But then, the whole system of animals is predicated on relationships to people, including the converse classificatory phenomenon distinguishing the categories of birds, game animals, and "frogs." By contrast to the unique species, these are structurally the most elaborated and differentiated classes, with the most varieties and subvarieties (or taxonomic levels). The elaboration would be related to the positive moral value of the general life form, the corollary of its habitation zone and the associations thereof with human existence. Edibility is only one such expression of moral value. One could easily imagine others. The knowledge of species in life-giving zones—be they birds or game animals, as in this case, or perhaps plants—is a virtue in itself: the kind of good that evokes intellectual inquiry and can lead to all sorts of applications, from the medicinal to the mythical, passing by way of the divinatory and the magical. "Nature taken abstractly, for itself—nature fixed in isolation from man—is *nothing* for man" (Marx 1961:169). But knowledge of the good is surely a virtue.

Empirical?—yes, the pensée sauvage is empirical. Does it involve universal human sensory capacities?—no doubt. But a sensory perception is not yet an empirical judgment, since the latter depends on criteria of objectivity

15. There are marginal overlaps between the *kmn* and *as* categories (game animals and "frogs") and also between domestic rats *(kopyak)* and certain feral rodents *(as)*. Bulmer and Menzies suggest that these come about because, as a matter of practicality or convenience, the animals in question may be cooked or consumed in the ways appropriate to one category or the other—which would confirm, post factum, the prescriptive character of the cultural differentiations (Bulmer and Menzies 1972–73:101).

which are never the only ones possible. One cannot simply posit another people's judgments of "reality" a priori, by means of common sense or common humanity, without taking the trouble of an ethnographic investigation. Anthropology, too, will have to be empirical. There is no other way of knowing what other peoples are knowing. Returning to the issue under scrutiny here, to say that it would be impossible for Hawaiians to perceive Captain Cook as an actualization of Lono because of the evident empirical differences between him and the god is to mark the end of our native wisdom, not the beginning of theirs. Better to adopt the attitude of Foucault when presented by Borges with a zoological classification from a certain Chinese encyclopedia,

> in which it is written that "animals are divided into: (a) belonging to the Emperor, (b) embalmed, (c) tame, (d) suckling pigs, (e) sirens, (f) fabulous, (g) stray dogs, (h) included in the present classification, (i) frenzied, (j) innumerable, (k) drawn with a very fine camelhair brush, (l) *et cetera*, (m) having just broken the water pitcher, (n) that from a long way off look like flies. In the wonderment of this taxonomy, the thing we apprehend in one great leap, the thing that, by means of the fable, is demonstrated in the exotic charms of another system of thought, is the limitation of our own, the stark impossibility of thinking *that*. (Foucault 1973:xv)

But there is still another dimension to the limitation of our own system of thought suggested by the contrasts of a pensée sauvage: not only the relativity of our notion of "objectivity" but the absolute sense of a world-in-itself that lies behind it. The evident difference between common average Western empirical judgments and Hawaiians' or New Guineans' is that ours suppose a world from which spirit and subjectivity were long ago evacuated. (Or at least where subjectivity is confined to the Kantian a prioris of pure reason that make experience possible, that is, as an intuition of universal predicates of objects.) Happily for the present discussion, Augustine developed just this distinction in the course of an unwitting reproach of Polynesian theology, the basic concepts of which he invented as the reductio ad absurdum of the "irreligious" idea that the world is the body of god. "And if this is so," he said, "who cannot see what impious and irreligious consequences follow, such as whatever one may trample, he must therefore trample a part of god, and in slaying any living creature, a part of god must be slaughtered" (*De Civitate Dei* IV.12). Of course, the classical paganism—

more precisely the Platonic cosmology—was the target of Augustine's contempt. But perhaps not coincidentally, given the resemblances of the Greek
and New Zealand creation myths, Augustine most accurately describes the
predicament of the Maori who tramples the Earth Mother Papa, attacks the
god Tāne in cutting down trees or killing birds, and consumes Rongo (cognate god of the Hawaiian Lono) when he harvests and cooks the sweet potato.[16] Augustine and his Western descendants, however, were spared such
blasphemy because God made the world out of *nothing*.

Nothing divine is in the world, which is to say, it is devoid of any humanized attributes, any anthropomorphic subjectivities. Like the Hebrew
people before them, Christians viewed the "deification of nature" as the essence of a paganism from which they sought to distinguish themselves (Funkenstein 1986:45).[17] "But what is my God?" asks Augustine in a well-known
passage of the *Confessions* (X.6). "I put the question to the earth. It answered,
'I am not God, and all things on earth declared the same.'" This world is in
itself pure materiality, without redeeming spiritual presence: made contemptible and resistant to our efforts, besides, by Original Sin. The cosmology is the metaphysical ground of the instrumental rationality just discussed, with the same implication of a suffering humanity alienated from an
impersonal nature. Adam was indeed the prototypical Economic Man, condemned, as Genesis, Augustine, and modern economists agree, to a per-
petual condition of need by temporal ends always greater than his means.
"We have been turned out of Paradise," wrote Lionel Robbins:

16. These effects are corollary to the descent of all things and persons from the common
ancestors, Heaven and Earth (Rangi and Papa): "Above all, [the Maori] held the belief that all
things, animate and inanimate, are descended from a common source, the primal parents, Rangi
and Papa. This belief had a considerable effect on the native mind, for, when the Maori walked
abroad, he was among his own kindred. The trees around him were, like himself, the offspring
of Tane; the birds, insects, fish, stones, the very elements, were all kin of his, members of a
different branch of the great family. Many a time, when engaged in felling a tree in the forest,
have I been accosted by passing natives with such a remark as: *"Kei te raweke koe i to tipuna i a
Tane"* (You are meddling with your ancestor Tane)" (Best 1924, 1:128–29; on certain ritual and
conceptual implications, see Sahlins 1985b).

17. Henri Frankfort repeatedly and clearly insisted that the ontological divide between
God and man distinguished the religion of the ancient Hebrews from other Near Eastern the-
ologies: "The absolute transcendence of God is the foundation of Hebrew religious thought.
God is absolute, unqualified, ineffable, transcending every phenomenon, the one and only
cause of all existence. . . . Consequently, every concrete phenomenon is devaluated. . . . To
Hebrew thought nature appeared void of divinity. . . . God was not in sun and stars, rain and
wind; they were his creatures and served him (Deut. 4:19; Psalm 19). Every alleviation of the
stern belief in God's transcendence was corruption. In Hebrew religion—and in Hebrew religion alone—the ancient bond between man and nature was destroyed" (Frankfort 1948:343;
see also Frankfort and Frankfort 1946).

We have neither eternal life nor unlimited means of gratification. Everywhere we turn, if we choose one thing we must relinquish others which, in different circumstances, we would not have wished to relinquish. Scarcity of means to satisfy ends of varying importance is an almost ubiquitous condition of human behaviour. (1952:15; compare Deane 1963:45, on Augustine)

Although the world was merely natural, purely corporeal, and humanity was related to it pragmatically, for a long time there could be no strictly natural history (Foucault 1973). Contemptible as this world was, or because it was contemptible, a system of Providential science linked its disparate elements by secret resemblances, independent of their radical empirical differences.[18] The resemblances were signs of the Absolute. They were traces of God's hand, signifying the hidden affinities of things that were otherwise perceptually distinct, and mediating the opposition of nature and humankind for the benefit, or at least for the edification, of the latter.[19] Yellow and green stones could cure jaundice and liver ailments. Red stones were for stopping hemorrhages. The walnut resembles the brain: it is good for headaches. Like a Hawaiian science of the concrete, such connections now surprise us. The salience they accord some singularity of resemblance violates our common sense of identity and difference.[20]

But the critique of similitude in the seventeenth and eighteenth centuries opened the way for this common sense of empirical reality. Securing once and for all the autonomy of nature, as Foucault says, it introduced a positivist natural history (which is also Obeyesekere's *episteme* of Hawaiian history). The instrumental epistemologies of the empiricist philosophers, having the same ground, appear at the same time. So does the English term "objective":

18. "The world, objectionable in itself, became acceptable by its symbolic import. For every object, each common trade had a mystical relation with the most holy, which ennobled it" (Huizinga 1954:206).

19. Eco (1986:56–57) quotes John Scotus: "In my judgment there is nothing among visible and corporeal things which does not signify something incorporeal and intelligible." LeGoff (1988:343) alludes to Dante: "To go and recover the hidden truth . . . on the other side of deceitful earthly reality was the major preoccupation of the men of the middle ages. Medieval art and literature were full of *integumenta* or veils, and intellectual or aesthetic progress in the middle ages was above all an unveiling."

20. Foucault (1973:51) highlights the Cartesian critique of what was then a fading, preclassical science: "'It is a frequent habit,' says Descartes in the first lines of his *Regulae*, 'when we discover several resemblances between two things, to attribute to both equally, even on points in which they are in reality different, that which we have recognized to be true of only one of them.'"

1. *Philos.* Pertaining or considered in relation to its object . . . —1675.
. . . b. Opp to *subjective* in the modern sense: that is the object of
perception or thought, as dist. from the perceiving or thinking subject; hence, that is regarded as a 'thing' external to the mind; real
(1647). (*OED* 1937:1350)

Objects became nothing more or other than their perceptible attributes
and relationships. Calibrated by empirical differences, the taxonomies of
things were representations of their distinctive identities, of which there
could be no confusions. A wind was only a wind, a sweet potato was only a
sweet potato, a man was only a man, and a good cigar was a smoke. Yet
according to the Hawaiian historian's rendition of Captain Cook's advent,
when his people "saw the strangers smoking they said, 'There are Lono-pele
[god of the volcano] and his companions breathing fire from their mouths'"
(S. Kamakau 1961:99). But then, for them the southwest Kona wind was
also a body of Lono, the sweet potato was a body of Lono, and Captain
Cook . . .

The Multiple Forms of Hawaiian Gods

Hawaiians, too, lived in a humanized cosmos whose empirical domains included a certain subjectivity. Recall the conversation between the missionaries and the chief Kalaimoku:

it was his opinion that all animated beings had thoughts and could
deliberate and reason. He said it was also his belief plants, trees and
all kinds of vegetables and even the coral (which he considers a vege-
table) had sense & feeling and that they wanted a mouth to make us
fully acquainted with them. (Ellis Journal, 24 Feb 1823)

The more recent ethnography echoes the older in this respect:

The subjective relationships that dominate the Polynesian psyche
are with all nature, in its totality, and all its parts separately ap-
prehended and sensed as personal. The Sky-that-is-Bright-and-
Wide (Wakea), the level Earth (Papa), were primordial Father and
Mother. Thunder is Kane-hekili (Male-in-the-form-of-gentle-rain),
and Ka-poha-'ka'a. . . . The rain-laden clouds over the Breast (Ka-'u)
of Earth (Papa) are Lono Makua [the Makahiki god], one of whose
forms is [the pig god] Kamapua'a. . . . Pele is vulcanism in all its forms,
while her sisters are rainbows seen at sea. . . . sweet potato and *kukae-*

pua'a [pig excrement], a native crab grass, and various other forms are "myriad body-forms" . . . of Kamapua'a; Ohi'a-lehua-a-Laka [Laka's 'ohia tree] . . . and the hawk, Io, were forms of Ku. . . . All the lizards (mo'o) are "bodies" of the legendary giant Mo'o Kiha-wahine, who is ancestress likewise to certain lineages. (Handy and Pukui 1972: 117–19; cf. Handy 1968; Kamakau 1964:57ff.; Valeri 1985:10–12; Kahiolo 1978; Beckwith 1970; Malo 1951)

This humanization, involving the specific doctrine of the god's 'myriad bodies' (kino lau), expresses the organization of natural or phenomenal species by social considerations: in accord, that is, with the being and activities of mankind. The Hawaiian schema of things can be understood as a unitary system of two dimensions. On one dimension are the folk taxa of various kinds: winds, divisions of the landscape, divisions of the ocean, colors, directions, meteorological phenomena, fish, land animals, rocks, wild and cultivated food plants, celestial bodies and heavenly space, not to neglect social persons. These classes are variously divided and subdivided into specific and subspecific levels: the food plants—including taro, yams, bananas, and sweet potatoes—notably so (Handy 1940). It is said Hawaiians knew some 300 varieties of taro (Handy and Handy 1972:83). Varieties of taro were most commonly named and distinguished by color differences in the corm or parts of the plant, but also by shape, locality, mode of growth, resemblances to other kinds of plants, resemblance to certain fish, taste, and a variety of idiosyncratic associations, such as the taro named after the Maui king who preferred it. Directly or indirectly, many of these distinctions already reflect the presence of the second classificatory dimension, which groups beings of different phenomenal kinds into unitary classes as 'bodies' (kino) of the one god. The winds, directions, colors, food plants, fish, and the like are each divided by the affiliations of specific varieties with divine forms that generically include them. In other words, the phenomenal series is cross-cut by the series of gods. So while certain fishes, winds, or crops may be bodies of Lono (or his pig-form, Kamapua'a), others are embodiments of Kū, Kane, and so forth.

This is not a (so-called) totemic system, since the classificatory operators are encompassing major gods. Yet, as the gods are at once individuals and inclusive classes, some of the same general sorts of totalizations and detotalizations are here possible, linking together phenomena of different kinds and levels as manifestations of the one being (cf. Lévi-Strauss 1966a: chap 5). Among the god classes, the more immediate human ancestors ('au-

mākua)—which also have particularizations in animals as well as persons—are distinguished from what we have called the major gods. As shall be noted momentarily, the two god series are associated genealogically, ritually, and eschatologically. But they are most fundamentally linked on a common ground of humanity, inasmuch as the major *akua* represent so many kinds of human beings, their respective attributes and activities, and the natural phenomena associated with them or their activities. The principle of the divine series, as Valeri (1985) has spelled out and abundantly documented, is the projection of human subjects and their predicates onto phenomena that are empirically connected with them or evoke them.

The four major male gods, Kane, Kū, Lono, and Kanaloa—especially the first three—constitute so many major classes of phenomena as their respective bodies. Lesser deities are designated usually by binomials consisting of the major god's name and an attribute referring to a particular function or character—thus the Makahiki god Lonomakua, 'Father Lono,' or the volcanic god who is keeper of Pele's firesticks, Lonopele. Then there are the various phenomenal embodiments, which are particularizations of the god insofar as the latter represents a specific kind of human being or aspect of human life. "There are thousands and thousands of names," wrote S. Kamakau (1964:58), "that are separated (*mahae 'ia*) into names of the same form. There is only one form ('*ano*) and the names only fit the work done."[21]

Determined on empirical grounds, these identifications of *akua* and their *kino*, gods and their bodies, are not for all that the judgments of unmediated perceptions. So far as this plant, that wind, or this person is a particularization of Lono, the empirical connection has been constructed through considerations independent of the object: in the most general terms, the judgment is mediated by the conceptions of a specific way of life. In the event, all sorts of resemblances and differences, temporalities, and contiguities connect features of nature and elements of culture to one or another of the great *akua*. As previously noted, the hawk, the dog, and certain game fish are bodies of Kū, since this god is the ideal male and these species evoke the warrior's qualities. Plants used in men's technical activities are likewise particularizations of Kū, such as the *koa* tree, from which canoes

21. Kamakau explains (p. 59): "Regarding the *'aumakua* [term here used generically, including the main *akua*] previously said to be Kanenuiakea [Kane in his encompassing aspect], and the divisions made by this or that man or family, it is only the names that are different. It was a single god, a single mana, a single god-spirit; the mana was a single mana within a single god and within a single spirit. So it was with Kunuiakea and Lononuiakea [Kū and Lono in their encompassing aspects]; they were combined within (*huipu ai iloko*) the one god and thus were regarded as sacred by the *po'e kahiko* [the people of old]."

are made. Forest birds whose feathers adorn warriors and chiefs' capes are again realizations of Kū. Kū: the term also means 'straight' or 'erect,' hence things high and straight in nature are manifestations of Kū's virility. The coconut tree is a *kino* of Kū; it is a man with his head in the ground and his testicles in the air.

Because these empirical judgments, these identifications of the god, are mediated by a distinct way of life, they cannot be determined from naive sensory perceptions, the way Obeyesekere would have liked the Hawaiians to evaluate Cook. Things are known by their relationships to a system of local knowledge, not simply as objective intuitions. For the same reason, the empirical cum language-game will seem arbitrary to us. Relying on our own sense of "reality," let alone our neurosensory equipment, we could hardly believe that someone could seriously take a sweet potato, or even an Englishman, as the manifestation of a god. "The sheer impossibility of thinking that!" In anticipation of his readers' incredulous reactions to the marvels he described on Cook's first voyage, Sir Joseph Banks quoted an old Joe Miller quip to the effect of: "Since you say so, I have to believe you; but I daresay if I had seen it myself, I would have doubted it exceedingly." But the point once more is that "objectivity" is culturally constituted. It is always a distinctive ontology. Nor is it then some sort of hypothesis or "belief" that is likely to be shaken by this or that person's skepticism or experimental attitude.[22] It is not a simple sensory epistemology but a total cultural cosmology that is precipitated in Hawaiian empirical judgments of divinity.

The relationships that can be established on strictly sensory grounds are, as such, humanly meaningless. For this reason, even the positivism of the Western philosophical empiricists in fact included a third term, or mediating condition, which related subject to object and organized the sensory perception of the latter by the former. I mean the condition of need and the project of satisfaction that constituted objectivity as utility. The practicality of Obeyesekere's "practical rationality" shows that the philosophy of Hobbes, Locke, Helvétius & Co. is still too much with us. On the other hand, the attachment of the condition of human utility to Western objectivity shows that the latter is not all that unique. From one perspective, it is simply a crabbed and impoverished notion of a cosmology, such as the Hawaiian, where the greater part of the universe is actually or potentially humanized, and accordingly everything finds some kind of "use" or another:

22. "We do not say that 'we believe,' precisely because we do not believe we believe: we are convinced we speak of things as they are. That is why it is only the unbeliever who believes the believer believes" (Pouillon 1993:26).

The acute faculties of this native folk noted with exactitude the generic characteristics of all species of terrestrial and marine life, and the subtlest variations of natural phenomena such as winds, light and colour, ruffling of water and variation in surf, and the currents of water and air. None of these observations, expressing a sense of significant relationship, were idle. One of the most notable things about the psychic (or subjective) relationship of our Ka-'u folk to external things is the fact that whatever is noted and distinguished as significant, psychically, has some real, specific and definite role in the business of living. It may be utilitarian, or aesthetic, or psychic. Breezes, colours, ruffling surfs, are noted and named because related to fishing and voyaging and because they enter into the symbolism of *mele* (chant), *hula* (dance), and naming. Every botanical, zoological or inorganic form that is known to have been named (and personalized) was *something* in some way *used*. (Handy and Pukui 1972:119)

"Nature apart from man is nothing for man"—this is a humanized cosmos. Lévi-Strauss speaks of a demand for intelligibility in this connection, in contrast to an interest in practical utility. Something more than a way of knowing, however, this Hawaiian schema is a total cultural system of human action. Hence the apparent violation of what seem to us to be purely phenomenal taxa. One wind is different from another, as likewise subtypes of food plants, fish, or colors are distinguished by their respective relations to human activity (as culturally constituted). This means that, in certain critical respects and contexts, one wind may be empirically more closely associated with sweet potatoes, as bodies of Lono or Kamapua'a, than it is like another wind. However, it does not mean that Hawaiians are thereby unable to recognize either that the Kona wind is a wind like others or that it has certain differentiating or individualizing properties. Indeed, many of the ways it is individually distinguished from other winds come precisely from its associations with different kinds of phenomena in human projects of determinate kind and organization. A Kona wind, with its winter rains and thunders, is a seasonal manifestation of Lono. Nor, again, is the idea that a distinctive individual form can be the particularization of another being really anything mystical, let alone nonempirical.[23] Or if it is mystical, still it is no more

23. The theory involved is broadly Polynesian. Commenting on the Maori concept of *atua* (cognate of Hawaiian *akua*), Johansen notes that it covers a "protean multiplicity," including flies, iron nails, guns, great chiefs, and Europeans, on up to the highest gods but also including demons—"all might be *atua*." Accordingly: "An *atua* need not distinguish himself by *mana, tapu*, immortality, nor any established determination" (Johansen 1958:5).

strange than the concept of descent, which is metaphysically the same (especially patrilineal descent, as it does not even have the empirical benefit of the metonymy of birth). In the same way that a wind or a person (such as Captain Cook) may be a manifestation of a specific god, so is any person, through the concept of a family line, an individual manifestation of a particular ancestral being. By this metaphysics called social relations, however, the person is no less an individual for being an instance of the ancestor, or vice versa. Ancestor worship and descent are two different practices of the same ontology—or at least of the same transcendental a priori—which is the same again as the doctrine of the god's many bodies. So it is not surprising that the great *akua* are also ancestors, or that their natural forms are sensible beings worthy of the sentiments of kinship. The most important 'ancestor' (*kupuna*) in Ka'u was Pele, the volcano goddess, according to Handy and Pukui (1972:29, 31), and the most important of her male relatives was Lonomakua.[24]

At every level of the social order, then, there is a potential interchange of being between humanity and divinity. In this respect, the 'ancestor deities' (*akua 'aumākua*) of families and craft professions replicate the character of the greater gods such as Kū, Kane, or Lono, to whom, besides, they are related. The *'aumākua* ancestors likewise have species bodies, or appear as individual animals, even as they are also manifest in human forms. They are manifest in anthropomorphic images, but they are also present in living persons whom they have sired directly or possessed. At a higher level, and in a more hierarchical form, we have already seen the same of the greater *akua*: they are realized in tabu chiefs, priests, prophets, and specific ritual figures (Kahoali'i) (above, 136–38). The metaphysics is just the opposite of Western distinctions of God, man, and nature, each occupying a separate kingdom of being. Empirically, then, never the three shall meet, or at least not until the last judgment; whereas, for Hawaiians, the appearance of Lonomakua at the Makahiki of 1778–79 could be substantiated by perceptual evidence.

God of human wealth and health, Lono was particularly associated with the rainfall agriculture of Kona, Hawai'i (where Cook landed). The month of 'Ikuwa (on Hawai'i island) is a Lono-form: *'ikuwa* means 'noisy' or 'clamorous'—*lono* as a common noun has a meaning of 'report,' spreading news—and this is the month of rough seas, high winds, thunder and lightning. It is

---

24. "It was Lono-makua to whom offerings of food and other products of the land were presented in the annual Makahiki festival. . . . Captain James Cook was led to put in at Kealakekua Bay to provision his ship at the season of Lono's festival. He was received and worshipped as Lono-makua" (Handy and Pukui 1972:31–32, see also p. 123).

the bad weather that prepares the planting of sweet potato, another form of Lono, in dry areas. Dark rain clouds, thunder, black, Kona winds, leeward, the Pleiades (of the rainy season) are all *kino* of Lono. The terrestrial counterparts of lightning and dark clouds, fire and smoke, are again associated with Lono in the form of the volcano god, Lonopele (a.k.a. Lonomakua). The pig, Kamapua'a, as a particularization of Lono, also has its own manifestations, including certain grasses and ferns, the *kukui* tree, young taro leaves, certain varieties of banana, some fishes, and various other things that are foods of pigs, have the color of pigs, the oiliness of pig fat, or otherwise remind Hawaiians of pigs by their shape, name, mode of action, habitat or habits (Handy and Pukui 1972:31–32, 40–41; Handy 1972:23, 137–38, 329f.; Valeri 1985:14–18).

The British, recall, had some obsession with pigs, and Hawaiians never tired of providing them, often ceremoniously. But we need not speculate about Hawaiian empirical judgments of the advent of Cook as a visitation of Lono. Certain of their observations are recorded in the Cook chronicles; more of the same appear in later Hawaiian reminiscences. True, the empirical arguments are not self-evident. Singling out salient resemblances to the apparent neglect of equally perceptible differences, the Hawaiian arguments have the quality of not seeming necessary for us yet being sufficient for them. Such is the empirical logic of another cosmology.

Hawaiians also paid great respect to the astronomical instruments set up by Cook's people in the precincts of Hikiau temple, where the celestial ceremonies of the Haole were protected by the tabus of Lono priests. The islanders called the clocks and watches 'gods,' *akua*. Fornander commented on this attribution, in connection with the reception of Cook "as a god, an 'Akua'"—a comment that reflects very well the difference between the otherworldly existence of the Judeo-Christian God and the this-worldly presence of "heathen" divinity:

It should be borne in mind that to the heathen Hawaiian the word *Akua* did not convey the same lofty idea as the word God or Deity does to the Christian. To the Hawaiians the word *Akua* expressed the idea of any supernatural being, the object of fear or of worship. This term was also, as Judge Andrews says in his [1865] Hawaiian Dictionary, "applied to artificial objects, the nature and properties of which Hawaiians did not understand, as the movement of a watch, a compass, the self-striking of a clock, etc. (Fornander 1969, 2:179n)

Indeed, the designation of such European novelties and potencies as *akua* (or in Fiji, *kalou*)—not *mana*, as Lévi-Strauss supposed—has been commonly reported in Polynesia (e.g. Best 1976:136; Sahlins 1994; cf. Lévi-Strauss 1966b: xli–xlvi). We shall see that in early times the term could also refer to the European masters of such contrivances. (Nowhere in Polynesia was the term *atua* or *akua* necessarily restricted to agreeable things.) For their part, the Cook people at the observatory probably did not disabuse the Hawaiians by telling them, when they wished not to be disturbed, that they were looking at the sun (Beaglehole 1967:520).

On the contrary, there are interesting suggestions in the Cook journals of a considerable Hawaiian scheme of interpretation linking the British with the heavens, and notably with celestial and terrestrial (volcanic) fires. Naturally the scheme was empirically informed, a concrete perceptual logic. Ledyard (1963:112) tells how the Hawaiians were fascinated by the astronomers' quadrants, "about which they made endless enquiries, and would have Idolized if one might judge from their extravagant exclamations and gestures." He relates that when the instruments were set up, Cook's company spent a great deal of time trying to inform the islanders of "our knowledge." From this Hawaiians took away the conclusion, "that as we had so much to do with the sun and the rest of the planets whose motions we were constantly watching by day and night, and which we informed them we were guided by on the ocean, we must either have come from thence, or by some other way [be] particularly connected with these objects" (ibid.). Moreover, the Hawaiians presented this conclusion as an empirical inference. So Ledyard continues, regarding the foreigners' heavenly status:

> to strengthen this inference they observed that the colour of our skins partook of the red from the sun, and the white from the moon and stars, besides, they said we dealt much with fire that we could kill others with it, but that it would not hurt us though we were close by it, and that we rendered it in all things intirely subservient to us. (Ibid., 112–13)

When Obeyesekere says that the Cook journals, with rare and suspect exceptions, do not indicate that the Hawaiians recognized any divinity to the Haole, it is partly because, as in this instance, he does not lend an ear to Hawaiian ethnography. On the contrary, he again takes the words from the Hawaiians' mouths and gives them to the Haole. Ledyard was lying when he attributed these statements to Hawaiians: "This account seems

to be a combination of information, hearsay, and gossip on board ship"
(Ob. 215n.78). True, Ledyard was stationed on shore and had the opportunity to make such observations, "but it is unlikely that Ledyard could undertake any complex conversation in Hawaiian" (ibid.). This should have been
disqualifying also for Obeyesekere's thesis that Cook was done in because
he took off the palings of Hikiau temple for firewood, since the argument
depends critically on Ledyard's assertion that the Hawaiians were deeply
offended by the supposed sacrilege. In this case, however, Ledyard's understanding of the Hawaiian language is perfectly sufficient—for Obeyesekere's
purposes (see appendix 14). So far as the Haole coming from the sun, Ledyard was perhaps inspired by Lieutenant Rickman's account (Ob. 215n.78;
cf. Beaglehole 1967:ccix). And Rickman is another one who cannot be
trusted, except for the vital and exclusive political information he supplies,
while at Kealakekua, about what the king was doing at Maui (Ob. 81). However, Rickman was also rehearsing shipboard gossip when he said that at
Kealakekua the king made Cook "the great E-a-thu ah-nu-eh" (*akua nui*), the
'great god' (Rickman 1966:305).[25] Neither is Rickman to be believed, according to Obeyesekere, when he reports the speech of a Ni'ihau chief several weeks later, claiming that the latter,

> expressed a desire to accompany us in our voyage, when, being told
> that we were never more to return to that island, he lamented the
> opportunity he had lost when we were here before; and pointing to
> the sun, seemed to suppose that we should visit that luminary in our
> course, and that the thunder and lightning of our guns [n.b.: both
> thunder and lightning are modes of Lono], and that which came from
> the heavens were both derived from the same source. (ibid., 332)

Obeyesekere correctly chides me for misreading the chief as saying the British had visited the sun between their first and second visits to Hawaii. This
leaves him only with the task of explaining how Rickman misread the chief
in saying the British would visit the sun after their second visit. No problem:
a critical reading indicates the Ni'ihau notable was frightened by the fact
that the British had just killed some people, which was the context of the
reputed discussion with Rickman. So the chief was merely pointing at the

25. Citing John Charlot, Obeyesekere wants to translate *akua nui* as 'large god,' which is
clearly incorrect for this context. The term refers to Lono in a high or encompassing capacity,
on the model of a 'great chief' (*ali'i nui*). We also have an attestation of 'Great Lono' (*Lono nui*)
from 1788, referring to the priest in charge of the Makahiki image at O'ahu and to Captain
Cook (above, 90–91).

sun, a metaphoric reference to the British guns made in fright, from which gesture Rickman concocted the business of "visiting that luminary." However, Obeyesekere does not quote the preceding phrase about the chief wanting "to accompany us" and lamenting he had earlier missed his chance. Presumably Rickman must have made that one up too, since it would surely violate a certain common sense to suppose the man was eager to accompany the Haole because they had frightened him. In any event, neither Rickman's log nor his published account indicates the supposed "conversation of gestures" was coincident with the killing of a man at Kaua'i (on coming in to Waimea, 1 March 1779), as Obeyesekere claims. On the contrary, the chief's words are reported after Rickman's notice that peace had been made, presents exchanged, and the ships had taken on water (Rickman 1966: 331–32).

But this is not the best example of how Obeyesekere can turn Hawaiian speech into European myth. More entertaining is his discussion of S. M. Kamakau's version of the Cook events.

Obeyesekere wishes to use Kamakau's text about the arrival of Captain Cook, written in 1866 and published the next year, to get at the idea of "stereotypic reproduction"—which he mistakenly supposes is entailed in the use of cultural logics to interpret historical events. Kamakau's description demonstrates that Hawaiian views of Cook were much more open, contested, and flexible. What this text shows, according to Obeyesekere, is a "pragmatics of common sense," marked by vigorous debate over whether Cook was a god or a man. Yet it also shows priests, chiefs, and others invoking mythical allusions of every shape and form in support of their empirical positions (including dubious legends of pre-Cook White men which Obeyesekere uncritically accepts as aboriginal tales; cf. Sahlins 1994: 80). Obeyesekere seems to forget he is using Kamakau to make a case against any mytho-praxis and for a Hawaiian sense of empirical reason. Hawaiians are not supposed to know percepts by their knowledge of myths but to reject myths by their knowledge of percepts. Worse yet, the Hawaiian mytho-praxis cited by Kamakau consistently contradicts the "commonsense" notion that Cook was too strange in empirical reality to be mistaken for a Hawaiian god. In both Kamakau and the earlier *Mooolelo Hawaii*, on which his account is based, the weirdness of the foreigners' looks and speech were no arguments against their divinity—on the contrary:

> Hikiau was the name of Lono's heiau at Kealakekua. . . . The kahunas
> [priests] of the heiau were among the first, together with those who

A.15
**The Language
Problem**

fed the god [a probable reference to the *hānaipū*], to adopt the error of the rest of the people [i.e., that Cook was Lono]. The men hurried to the ship to see the god with their own eyes. There they saw a fair man with bright eyes, a high-bridged nose, light hair, and handsome features. *Good-looking gods they were!* They spoke rapidly. Red was the mouth of the god. When they saw the strangers letting out ropes the natives called them Ku-of-the-tree-fern (Ku-pulupulu) and Coverer-of-the-island (Moku-hali'i). These were gods of the canoe builders in the forest. (Kamakau 1961:99; emphasis added)

In a previous passage a certain Moho (alias Kau-a-ka-piki) transmits the news of Cook's sojourn at Kaua'i in 1778 to Kalani'ōpu'u and his Hawaiian warriors at Maui.[26] When asked what the foreigners' speech was like, Moho produces a string of nonsense syllables. Their ship was like a temple, he added, and in appearance, "they were fair with angular heads, their clothes were fastened to their skin and had openings on the sides over each thigh and in front; they had narrow foot coverings, and fire at the mouth from which smoke issued like Pele's fires" (ibid., 96).[27] The sequitur to the incomprehensible and peculiar characteristics of the strangers is *precisely that Cook was Lono, returned from Kahiki:*

Ka-lani-'opu'u was in Ko'olau, Maui, fighting against Ka-hekili, the chief of Maui. When Moho told him and the other chiefs of Hawaii the story about Captain Cook and described his ship they exclaimed, "That was surely Lono! He has come back from Kahiki." (Kamakau 1961:97)

In sum, Obeyesekere puts Kamakau forward to illustrate the way Hawaiians disputed Cook's divine status, if only on the condition that we ignore the content of the debate, and above all the conclusion by Hawaiian lights that Cook was Lono, on grounds that the text is riddled with anachronisms

26. This story is clear only in the *Mooolelo* (Kahananui 1984:169–70); Kamakau (1961:96–97) adopts it and attributes what Moho said in the earlier story to a certain Kau-a-ka-piki. He then forgets himself and introduces Moho (without identification) as the one who told the news of Cook to Kalani'opū'u.

27. Kamakau has toned down Moho's fabulous description as it was set down in the *Mooolelo Hawai'i*: "The [Hawaiians at Maui under Kalani'opu'u] asked what the people on the vessel looked like. He told them the people were white, had loose skin, angular heads, . . . they were gods [*He akua lākou*]; they were volcanoes because fire burned in their mouth. There was a treasure hole [pockets] in their side which extended far into the body. And into this hole they thrust their hands and brought forth cutlery, trinkets, iron and beads; fabrics and nails, and many other things" (Kahananui 1984:169–70, 13–14).

and infected with the Hawaiian historian's intense Christianity. All the stuff Kamakau says about Cook as Lono can thus be written off as the usual indictment of Cook by the American missionaries. So Obeyesekere presents the case.

Now, it is true that Kamakau was devout and influenced by Christian conceptions; and it is also true that his 1867 newspaper articles amounted to a diatribe against Cook from that pious perspective. Hence the most general irony of Obeyesekere's reading: it is Kamakau's Christianity that accounts for the debate among Hawaiians he freely interpolated in an older text, and which turns on a radical distinction not found in the latter—that men are not gods. Comparison with the earlier versions of the *Mooolelo*, from 1838 and 1858, shows that this Western ontological hang-up was not a problem in the stories of Cook taken from the old folks by the students of Lahainaluna. A running debate about whether Cook was man or god does not occur in the originals of Kamakau's text (Kahananui 1984:167–75; Pogue 1978:69–76). The whole dispute that for Obeyesekere represents the flexibility of old-time Hawaiian thought was introduced by Kamakau to make a Christian point about the radical difference between the earthly and the heavenly cities; between a corrupt humanity and a perfect Divinity. The Christian tradition that has truly bollixed up the historiography of Captain Cook is not that he allowed himself to be taken for a god, but that he could not possibly have been one.

A.16
Kamakau's Gods

Foreign Spirits: Including Anthropologists

Hawaiians were not the only Polynesian people to interpret the advent of Captain Cook or other early Europeans as a spiritual visitation. The phenomenon is still less unusual if one considers other Pacific island peoples, notably New Guineans, of whom the like is well documented due to the recency in some areas of "first contact." Indeed, some of the latest avatars of local ancestors are anthropologists. Of course, there is no uniformity to the spiritual status of the Europeans in these early encounters, if only because the local concepts of divinity vary, as would the relevant historical circumstances. For similar reasons, the status of the Europeans is not fully defined by the reports that speak of them as "ghosts," "ancestors," "demons," "goblins," "nonhuman spirits," "culture heroes," "mythical beings" or "gods"—all of which and other designations, including the indigenous terms, are found in an extensive literature ranging from first-hand accounts through personal recollections to long-standing oral traditions. Like Cook in Hawaii, the foreigner may be identified with a particular spiritual being. In this respect there is nothing particularly aberrant or unusual about the reception of Cook as Lono—not even his death, apparently.[28] Also as in Hawaii, the spiritual identifications of Cook and other foreigners are reported from local speech.

Obeyesekere does not consider any of the Australian, Melanesian, or Micronesian deifications of Europeans, while denying anything of the sort occurred in Polynesia. Of "the apotheosis of Cook," he says that "if it indeed did occur," it would be "uniquely Hawaiian because no other Polynesian society seemed to have thought that he was a divinity" (Ob. 87). Even if this were true, it could only be evidence against the thesis that Cook's deification is a European myth, "created in the European imagination of the eighteenth century," and based on an even older myth model of "the redoubtable explorer cum civilizer who is a god to the 'natives'" (Ob. 3). For, how is it, then, that the Europeans did not lay it on the Polynesian "natives" everywhere? Obeyesekere wants to conclude that the absence of assertions in the British accounts that the people took them for gods proves that the people did not take them for gods. However, all it proves is that the Cook journalists were not disposed to that supposition. Actually, the surviving Polynesian testimonies on this issue are mixed. Some did categorize Cook or other early foreigners as manifestations of transcendent beings—as gods (*atua*), as particular figures of the local pantheon, or as other spirit forms (usually *tupua*)—and some did not.

Tongans evidently did not, if others such as Hawaiians and Marquesans did. When Mariner contrasted the Tongan attitude toward Cook with the Hawaiian veneration of him, the latter corroborated by Hawaiians at Tonga and involving ritual details of Lono of the Makahiki, the report is the credible result of an investigation (see above, 97–98). Nor is there reason to doubt that the Marquesans knew early Europeans as *atua*, a term generally applied to foreigners, according to the missionary William Pascoe Crook whose residence dates to 1797 (Crook 1800:30; cf. Robarts 1974:74n). In the Marquesas (as in other Polynesian islands), the designation could apply to a wide range of transcendent beings and to their human manifestations,

28. There are parallels to Cook's fall in the death of Reverend John Williams at Eromanga in 1839. For details of his death, see Turner 1861:490; Robertson 1902:56–57; Prout 1843: 388f.; Murray 1862:179, 195–96, 206–8; and Shineberg 1967:205–7. Among the parallels, was the missionary's reported intrusion in the great annual feast, a solstitial event marked by the interdiction of war and sham battles (Humphreys 1926:180–81). Like other Europeans, Williams was locally categorized as *Nobu*, the name of the lost creator-god at Eromanga (see Capell 1938:72–73).

such as certain inspirational priests. Some of the latter *atua*, according to Crook, were "superior to all the rest," as they were dispensers of agricultural fertility (Crook 1800:35; Thomas 1990:35).

In New Zealand, certain memories and traditions of the first Europeans, including Cook, recall them as manifest forms of spirit, most commonly *tupua* or alternatively *atua*. Salmond (1991:88) defines *tupua* in this connection as "visible beings of supernatural origin, regarded with a mixture of terror and awe and placated with *karakia* (ritual chants) or offerings." Speaking also of *tupua* (or *tipua*) as used for Europeans, Best (1972:557) noted that the expression "is applied to anything extraordinary, especially if it be credited with supernatural powers." The combination of observations is worth remarking for its implication of the Polynesian epistemological disposition when confronted with such an extraordinary experience: which is, once again, not simply to revert to an unmediated sensory contemplation of the object, but to cover the gap between its unprecedented attributes and its evident significance by intimations of divinity (cf. Lévi-Strauss 1966b). The disposition can be logically motivated, moreover, by the associations between the foreign or foreign lands and the home of gods and ancestors. So Best (1972:558, 554) says that "*atua* (god, demon, supernatural being) was also applied to Europeans in early days," and refers to a tradition of such at Poverty Bay. This is a counterpart to other recollections of Cook and of the French explorer Surville as *tupua*, recorded from elders who were children at the time (Salmond 1991:87–88, 340). Likewise, the early ships, including the *Endeavour*, were alternately *tupua* and *atua* (ibid.; Best 1972:553). In sum, nothing foreign was simply human to them.

Hence the critical ways that Polynesian concepts of divinity differ from the standard, average bourgeois realism. Such concepts apply precisely to strange appearances—of living men as well as their objects. In just those situations where empirical perceptions violate received categories, Polynesians, instead of slipping into a "practical rationality," invoke the manifestations and effects of transcendent beings. Epistemologies vary in accord with worldviews (cultural ontologies).

The Melanesian literature on "first contacts," often richer than the Polynesian because the events were more recent, confirms this disposition to interpret the intrusive coming of Europeans in ways consistent with the people's own cosmological schemes—including even the failure to remember the first White men as such, since they were never men. Here we have unequivocal testimony, often by participants and eyewitnesses, of what the people thought of Europeans. And quite commonly they were thought of as

A.17

Atua in the Marquesas and Elsewhere

local spiritual beings, of one kind or another. Most often they were ancestral ghosts, sometimes greater deities, but in any case they were distinct from ordinary people. And if, as it is claimed, Hawaiians were too savvy to suppose that Cook and company were their own gods, what are we to conclude about the "rationality" of these Melanesian peoples? Were they dumber than Hawaiians?

Or were they not like the Hawaiians, inasmuch as what they concluded was supported by close empirical attention to the White men?[29] In ways reminiscent of the story of Cook in the *Mooolelo Hawaii,* direct reports of Melanesians show them scanning their traditional knowledge, notably their so-called myths, to find whatever parallels they could to the observed behavior of the White folks—and thus achieve a satisfactory interpretation. For the first "reality" was embedded in myth and ritual practice: what they already knew about being and the world. And what they therefore concluded about the Whites could indeed be startlingly like the Hawaiian, as in the following ethnographic notice from the eastern New Guinea Highlands:

> There was much speculation as to who these Europeans were and whence they came. It was said that since they came out of the sky, they must have come from the sky world [a footnote here indicates "There are myths relating to the sky world, and to the visits of sky people to the earth."]; they were red in colouring because they had been close to the sun; they had control of the lightning and of other natural elements: and they were powerful spirits. On the other hand, it was said they were spirits who had come from Anabaga, the Land of the Dead, or their own ancestors revivified and sent by the great Creative Fertility Spirits, Jugumishanta and Mɔrofɔ:nu These beliefs relating to the origins of Europeans are still current. That is to say, a dead native would be reincarnated as a European. . . . This was, in some cases, regarded as two-way process, deceased Europeans returning as natives. Such a belief reduced in some degree their feelings of awe in relation to the newcomers; but it did not eradicate fear, or the idea some harm would accrue from their presence. Examining contem-

29. Melanesian myths themselves may involve such empirical investigation. F. E. Williams collected a myth from Lake Kutuba about a group of men sitting around a long house debating the gender of the sun and the moon. One man disagreed with the general opinion they were the same person, arguing the sun was a woman and the moon a man. The others lost their tempers with him and drove him away. He undertook an epic journey to these heavenly bodies, and proved he was right (Williams 1941:149–51).

porary attitudes concerning this initial period of indirect contact, we are told . . . that the natives regarded Europeans in a patronizing manner—"we understood all about their coming," they claim, "but you (Europeans) did not. We have a wider comprehension than you." It was not long before they came to regard the European as a potential source of wealth. (Berndt, 1952–53:51–52)

Notice that, contrary to a certain Western commonsense understanding, the interpretation of Europeans as known spiritual beings does not testify to an abject attitude. On the contrary, it may reduce "awe," not simply by virtue of familiarity, but potentially by bringing Whites under familiar modes of control: that is, ritual and exchange.

We will return to the New Guinea Highlands, but after a look at an episode on the North Coast that was again reminiscent of Hawaiian considerations of Captain Cook. It concerns the famous Russian ethnographer Nikolai Nikolaevich Mikloucho-Maclay, who lived for some three years in all on the shores of Astrolabe Bay in the 1870s. By his own and other accounts, Maclay "was called and believed to be a 'deity'" (*tibud* in the coastal language; Lawrence 1984:21). Indeed, according to Peter Lawrence, the name "Maclay" became a common noun for 'deity' among the peoples thereabouts, that is, in the neo-Melanesian (pidgin) form, *masalai*. Lawrence reported that the inland Garia used "Magarai" (Maclay) as a synonym of their own term for 'deity,' *oite'u*. So the Garia called the first foreigners they encountered *magarai*, beginning probably with German patrols in the 1890s and including the labor recruiters who came into their area during World War I. The Garia had concluded "their visitors were deities (*oite'u/magarai*)" (ibid.). The pidgin they heard was initially "the language of the gods." They called European goods that were red, "goods from spirits of men killed by violence," and European goods of other colors, "goods from spirits of men who had died naturally." By 1949, Lawrence reported, these phrases had become figures of speech; but *magarai* still meant 'deity' (ibid., 22).

During his own time, the people around Astrolabe Bay had formed a comparable opinion of Maclay (Mikloucho-Maclay 1975; Putilov 1982; Webster 1984). He was "a man from the moon" (Mikloucho-Maclay 1975: 173). This was not a supposition they left uninvestigated:

They questioned me about Russia, about the houses, pigs, villages and so on. Then they turned to the moon which they obviously confused with the idea of Russia and wanted to know if there were women on

> the moon, how many wives I have there; they asked me about the stars
> and tried to find out on which I had been, etc. (Ibid., 171; see also
> pp. 203, 217, 257, 287) [30]

When the New Guineans added Maclay's feats of shooting, together with
the water (mixed with alcohol) he set on fire, to his lunar provenance, "it
became clear to me that here they considered me an absolutely extraordinary being" (ibid., 176).

Maclay had a very good understanding of the relevant pensée sauvage:
the way the New Guinea people were elaborating their spiritual concepts of
him by the use of empirical evidence:

> "Once they had elevated me to the position of *kaaram tamo* (the man
> from the moon) and had become sure of my unearthly origin, seen in
> this light, my every word, and my every deed apparently served to
> confirm this opinion in them. . . . The Papuans believed that the intent
> look of the *kaaram tamo* was sufficient to harm the healthy and cure the
> sick." (Putilov 1982 : 86)

Moreover, once this empirical verification got under way, it was not easily
derailed by negative evidence. Maclay tells how the Gorendu people "seriously asked me to stop the rain," and when he answered he could not do so,
they concluded he did not want to (Mikloucho-Maclay 1975 : 167). But also
as in the instance of Lono cum Cook, the respect of the New Guineans for
Maclay's extra-terrestrial nature did not prevent them from appreciating
his sublunar individuality, his "ordinary human qualities," as his biographer
B. N. Putilov says. "'The man from the moon' and 'a good man' formed an
almost indivisible whole in the minds of the Papuans" (Putilov 1982 : 87).

From the other side, as the personal recollections of New Guinean
Highlands people, the same kind of stories are told about first encounters
with the Leahy brothers and their companions in the early 1930s. In a famous series of prospecting expeditions, the Leahys—sometimes accompanied by other Australians and always by a working complement of coastal
New Guineans—"opened" the densely populated Highlands to an unsus-
pecting European world. The local people were at least as amazed, but they
generally knew how to include the strangers in their own cosmology. In
their remarkable book *First Contact,* integrating the archival record with in-

30. Notice that Hawaiians had asked Cook the same sorts of questions about life in his
homeland, from which Obeyesekere incorrectly concluded they conceived him to be an ordinary man from another earthly land, "Brittanee."

terviews of the survivors, Connolly and Anderson (1987) indicate that for New Guinea people it was a matter of assimilating the strangers within their own categories of being. First impressions could be variable and hesitant, but extraordinary as the Leahys were, they were perceived as an extension of local society, placed in an already familiar spiritual dimension. Recollecting the event, "virtually all" of the people interviewed by Connolly and Anderson "used the word spirit to describe the strangers and their sudden arrival" (ibid., 34).

The specific spiritual determinations differed. *First Contact* is a compendium of reminiscences of old-timers from many different language groups. For some, the Leahys were incarnations of significant deities; others thought they were "sky people" (Connolly and Anderson 1987: 38–39). Sooner or later most people settled into the idea that their visitors were their own ancestral dead, returned now for better or for worse. As a Gama man explained, "we had experienced the presence of dead people before." The dead had already been heard to whistle and sing. It was just that "we'd never actually seen them in physical form" (ibid., 35). And the recounting of experience after experience of this sort in *First Contact* makes it impossible to suppose we are dealing with anything but indigenous conceptions. The spiritual status of the Europeans, their companions, and their equally remarkable paraphernalia were not the myths of the Leahys or any other White man.

Extraordinarily emotional scenes sometimes attended the Leahys' coming. Descriptions of the excitement they occasioned are like nothing so much as the chronicles of Cook's arrival at Kealakekua. From the first day in the Highlands: "There were smiles and tears, hugging and stroking, wonderment. Some blew eerie notes of welcome from high-pitched bamboo flutes" (ibid., 25). In Chimbu country there were "thousands of people following us, yelling and shouting and screaming and singing out" (ibid., 90). Or again, the following reminiscence of the wonderment provoked by the strangers' clothing, which is worthy of the analogous recollections of the *Mooolelo Hawaii:*

"We wondered what type of people are these strangers? We heard that the face was like a human's, but the body kept changing its skin. The skin had holes in it, which they could put things in, and then take them out again. They could put things inside their neck at the front and then take them out again." (Ibid., 110; see above, 176n.27, on old Hawaiians' descriptions of Cook *mā*)

Many of the strangers' material things were beyond comprehension—except as values of extraordinary power. When the Leahys broke camp, the local people rushed the ground to collect every scrap of rubbish left behind. The smoke from pieces of toilet paper burnt with pigs' blood strengthened the hands and weapons of Chimbu warriors (ibid., 55). In the recollection of a Wahgi Valley man:

> "Our old men believed that these were lightning beings from the sky, with special powers, and so they advised us to collect everything they had left behind. We swept the place and collected everything, tea leaves, matches, tin cans. And we went to the place where he had made his toilet and collected the excreta as well." (Ibid.)

Like the Hawaiians with Cook or the Gorendu with Maclay, the Highland people realized their understandings of the Leahy crowd by means of an empirical logic of the concrete. In numerous documented cases, they perceived the traces of particular ancestors in the lineaments or actions of one or another of the strangers. For instance,

> Kize Kize Obaneso of Asariufa Village near Goroka remembers that "after they had built their tents one of them took an axe and went across to an old dead, dry tree that had been planted long ago by a man who had since died. We thought this old man, whose name was Vojavona, had come back from the dead to cut down his own tree for firewood. We were very pleased he knew his own tree." (Ibid., 38)

When the foreigners gestured to their own bodies, they were telling of the wounds that killed them. When they washed the river gravels (looking for gold), they were searching for their own bones which had been thrown there. What to Western common sense might seem an empirical contradiction could be as easily accommodated. If the dead looked away from their relatives, it was because they did not wish to be recognized: the dead, "after all, did not always have the best interests of the living at heart" (ibid.).

Reflecting again from these events to the issue of Cook at Hawaii, it becomes clear that a main problem in Obeyesekere's notion of an objective discrepancy between the appearance of the British and Hawaiian conceptions of divinity is his implicit assumption of the inflexibility of so-called mythical thinking. But as the New Guinean said, "We could never really understand spirits, or explain them" (ibid., 258). With this sort of conception, and a sufficiently adroit mentality, almost anything and its opposite could be the empirical induction of a cosmic conclusion. As in Hawaii, a kind of Peircean interpretant, which was nothing less than a world order, connected the meaning to the sensible sign (the strangers' behavior).

The spiritual career of Europeans in the New Guinea Highlands also had a sociology and a destiny something like Hawaiian secularizations of the Haole. There were indeed skeptical attempts at investigation. Connolly and Anderson tell of how two Asaro Valley warriors went to great lengths to observe that the strangers' bodies did not turn into skeletons at night, as myth had it. The warriors concluded, "we should stop this belief that they were dead people" (ibid., 43). But the suggestion did not get very far as collective representation or social memory. From the Asaro as far as Chimbu, people retained the notion that the White men turned into skeletons at night (ibid.). Lacking a centralized or hierarchical order, it would be difficult to spread such skepticism, especially in the face of rapidly diffusing conceptions of a spiritual advent that could be accepted a priori. For similar reasons, the imagination of the strangers' divinity seems to have been inversely proportionate to intimacy. In the Highlands, again as in Hawaii, it was women who effectively took the lead in demystifying the foreigners, beginning with the New Guinea carriers. "We had sex together and then we knew they were men" (Connolly and Anderson 1987:140).

Yet, most people did not know the White men on such terms. And, although there were local and phased changes in the spiritual estimation of Europeans, it does not seem to have been a simple epistemological process dependent merely on observation. Nor an altogether complete one. Richard Salisbury, ethnographer of the Siane, said that when the things they acquired from the Leahys in 1933 failed to turn into indigenous shell valuables, as they had expected, they began to appreciate their visitors as men rather than spirits. On the basis of his own experience with Hageners and other Highland peoples, however, Andrew Strathern is inclined to be dubious. "One may wonder a little about this, since in Hagen and Pangaia the idea that the Europeans may be spirits continues to be entertained along with the normal working assumption that they are probably people" (Strathern 1984: 108). Indeed, Salisbury noted that, just as the Leahys were called *Makana*, meaning "spirits [who] had returned from the dead," in the late 1950s, when he did his fieldwork, old men "still call[ed] Europeans *Makana we* or 'Makana men'" (Salisbury 1962:114). The point here is that personal experiences, opinions, and memories should be distinguished from collective representations. In the Southern Highlands, the Hides patrol of 1935, which made a passage similar to the Leahys' and was likewise generally received as a spiritual visitation, did not for all that pass into social memory. In Schieffin and Crittenden's excellent study of this "first contact" they observe that while people can recount their personal experience of the Hides patrol in detail, the story is not generally known to the younger generation. It has not become part of the peoples' history.[31] Or else—we will have examples in a moment—the event does not turn up in social consciousness as a "first contact" with White men because the latter were not "men" at all. They were spirits. So far as Europeans have been secularized, then, this has not come about as a simple recognition of their humanity by virtue of experience. What Melanesian history shows is that the humanization of "White men"— a determination of being, incidentally, which is no more self-evident than the local concepts of "spirit"—has come about as a social process. And more significant to the process than this or that individual experience has been the wholesale assault of European power, including its Christian poetics, on the indigenous cosmologies.

A number of ethnographers have been able to record memories similar to those elicited of the Leahys by Connolly and Anderson. So the early Whites were "sky people" for Raiapu Enga. Created by the sun and the moon, sky people live in a demi-paradise of plenty; they gave rise to the major social groups (phratries) of the Raiapu (Feachem 1973:63; see also Salisbury 1962:114; Strathern 1984:43, 107–8; Nilles 1953). Outside the central Highlands, similar notices of the spiritual nature of early contacts have been made of the Orokaiva and nearby peoples (Williams 1976:342– 44), of Telefomin (Craig 1990:125), and of Mundugumor (McDowell 1991:79), among many others. Using information supplied by ethnographers, Schiefflin and Crittenden's study of the Hides-O'Malley patrol shows the like in group after group in the Southern Highlands. Local congeries of the Onobasulu, Wola, Nembi, Kewa, and Huli peoples all perceived the strangers as spiritual beings. Most commonly the strangers were ancestral ghosts, but sometimes they were never-human spirits from the original time (Schiefflin and Crittendon 1991; see also Stilltoe 1979:16n). As for the Etoro, they do not remember the whole affair, nor do they in any way associate the Hides patrol with the first government patrol they do recall, in 1964—perhaps for interesting reasons:

31. "As a matter of fact, it is our impression that stories of the [Hides] patrol were not often told by the people amongst themselves and were not particularly well known to the younger generation. Most of what informants have to say in this book was gathered through interviews initiated by the ethnographer's request for information. Given informants' enthusiasm for telling these stories once they were requested, however, it seems unlikely they were being deliberately withheld" (Schieffelin and Crittenden 1991:9).

Inquiries which I made in the field failed to turn up a single Etoro who recalled Hides's expedition, all informants dating first contact with Australians to a 1964 patrol. In retrospect, I believe this was due to the fact that Hides and O'Malley were thought to be witches and have been mythologized as witch-spirits distinct from the *barigei*, or light-skinned men, of thirty years later. Schiefflin (personal communication, 1972) reports that the Kaluli say the Etoro wept upon first seeing steel tools because the chips they made were like those left by the "big witches" of the past. Moreover, the southern Etoro communities that Hides contacted were all extinct long before 1964, and it is quite possible that no one witnessed both contact patrols and hence no association between them was drawn. Also no Etoro saw Hides at close range, or at least none who lived to tell of it. (Kelly 1977:26)

What Kelly here suspects, that the initial passage of Europeans has been wholly resolved into indigenous concepts of spirit, was verified in an analogous case by Chris Ballard, working with central Huli people (Ballard 1992).

In 1934, two gold prospectors, the brothers Jack and Tom Fox, made a terrible crossing of the densely populated Huli area killing more than forty-five people and wounding at least another twenty. More than fifty years later, Ballard interviewed some eighty eyewitnesses of the events, thus amassing "a remarkably detailed local account of first contact with the Fox brothers." Except that it was not "first contact" and not "the Fox brothers." From that time until today, for the great majority of Huli it was an encounter with *dama*. "*Dama*," Ballard explains, "is a generic term for spirits, referring equally to the 'deities' of origin myths, the more accessible and potentially benevolent ancestral spirits, and to a more recent cohort of malevolent beings who required continual supplication to be kept at bay." So, despite that the carnage wreaked by the Fox brothers far exceeded anything known in local battles, the episode did not enter into memory in the usual form of war narratives. Indeed, it did not much enter social memory at all, being of consequence only to the eyewitnesses and those who had lost kinsmen. On the other hand, if it survived in their recollections as a visitation of *dama*, it was because for Huli the Foxes fit into a tradition of cosmic entropy: of a universe in decline, which will continue to do so unless proper exchange relationships are established with *dama* spirits. This clearly did not happen with the Fox brothers. So "the Foxes were not recognized either then, or since, as human." If you will, the Foxes were a historical metaphor of a mythical reality.

Other conclusions are also possible. For one, that there are evident differences between these Melanesian histories and our own category of "first contact." Quite different cultural values are being attached to the same events. What seems to us a fateful world-historical irruption into their "traditional" existence is for many Melanesian peoples not historically or socially remarked as such. The seeming amnesia may be contrasted to the memories of later government patrols, as among the Huli or Etoro. Probably because they introduced a previously unknown political control, the later patrols were the operative "first contacts" with Europeans. I believe this sort of historic divide is common. From the perspective of many colonized peoples, it is the moment of domination and transformation, the assumption of subaltern status, that is marked in historical consciousness rather than the period of early contacts that preceded it (perhaps for decades). For Europeans, of course, the great rupture in the history of the rest of the world is initiated by their own appearance there: an epiphany that they suppose produced a change in the quality of indigenous life and historical time—though it need not have done either. Nor did the "violence" of the European intrusion always mean what we (by common sense) think. Huli history reminds us that such violence has neither self-evident meaning nor patent historical significance. The Huli did not lay their deaths on White men because the killers were not White men. So nothing can be taken for granted or deduced a priori, even from The Horror. Not without the indigenous understandings of what happened, why, and who was concerned—which may well turn out to be cosmic questions. Nothing here could have been deduced directly or transparently from our own moral sentiments.

Finally, let us mention the latest incarnations of Melanesian spirits: the anthropologists. More than one has been apotheosized, even within the past decade. Maria Lepowsky (1992) tells how it happened to her when living with Vanatinai people of the Louisade archipelago. Older Vanatinai believe that the spirits of the dead turn white and go to America. When Lepowsky turned up, she was understood to be the spirit of a deceased "big woman" on whose ground she was living. Her strenuous denials produced only mixed results. There were too many continuities here with "cargoistic beliefs," Lepowsky noted. "To this day when Vanatinai people see the rare European freighter outside the lagoon moving eastward in the hazy distance, they call it a 'spirit boat.'" In this connection, Lepowsky goes on to mention Obeyesekere's skepticism about Captain Cook at Hawaii; she can sympathize with his suspicions about the European imperialistic conceits. She continues:

It is politically uncomfortable for me to talk publicly about being taken for a supernatural being. But it happened to me, and it has happened to a number of other living European scholars who have worked in Melanesia. So Cook as god/ancestor spirit/exchange partner seems completely plausible to me. (Lepowsky, 1992; quoted with permission)

One may suppose that the people who considered Lepowsky "a supernatural being" did so on the basis of empirical observation and investigation. Certainly this is what happened to Don Kulick in New Guinea:

About a month after my arrival in Gapun, I was solemnly informed I was a ghost. The villagers had been watching me, I was told, observing me closely as I copied down genealogies, politely tried to force down foul-tasting pink globs of sago jelly during meals with them, attempted to mouth phrases in their vernacular language. They were unsure when I first came into the village; initially they were confounded. But now, after a month, the villagers were convinced. I was a ghost. (Kulick 1992:ix)

Historiography, or
Symbolic Violence

Obeyesekere considers that his scholarship is worthy of approbation, as it is distinguished, like John Charlot's work, by its scrupulous respect for evidence:

> I found it fascinating that Charlot, a meticulous cultural historian with an eye for detail, and I, an inveterate interpretive anthropologist, could agree on the general lines of interpretation spelled out in this book pertaining to the events following Cook's arrival in Hawai'i, his apotheosis, death, and subsequent "return." The reason is, I think, that both of us, in our different ways, feel that ethnography is an empirical discipline that cannot afford to turn its back on *evidence*. (Ob. xv; emphasis in original)

The preceding pages, however, would seem to suggest that *The Apotheosis of Captain Cook* does not merit such self-regard, whether in respect to the primary sources on Hawaiian history, the words of Hawaiians recorded there and elsewhere, or the writings of others it attacks. On the contrary, the book is a veritable manual of sophistical and historiographical fallacies. How, and why, did all these distortions, misrepresentations, fictions and false accusations happen?

Obeyesekere's reminiscences of how he was engaged by the problem of Captain Cook in Hawaii suggest an alternative description of his historical project. By his own account, the method was nothing like a reasoned induction from the documentary evidence. On the contrary, it began with the "ire" provoked by a lecture I gave at Princeton (in 1982 not 1987) and his a priori intuition, based on his personal experience as a Sri Lankan, that the argument of the lecture about the apotheosis of Captain Cook was wrong, not to say a slur on the "natives'" mentality. I think this is how it really began and a major reason why his counter-thesis has such an ad hoc quality. One gains the sense of helter-skelter attempts to shore up a continuously floundering parti pris. Different arguments are tried at different times without too much regard for consistency, so as to produce in the end a stratified palimpsest of confusion and self-contradiction. At some point Obeyesekere must have decided that he could finesse all the apparent god-stuff about Cook by adopting Sir Peter Buck's idea of a postmortem (only) deification, which he did with such enthusiasm that he forgot that the deification of Europeans was supposed to be a Haole myth. In the same way he tried to force a Hawaiian distinction between a tabu chief and a god, forgetting that he would still have to allow Cook (as a "sacred chief") the "divine qualities" of persons of godly blood (*waiakua*)—and thus again, that such glorifications of White men were supposed to be European conceits. In any case, Cook was supposed to be too far off, empirically speaking, to be taken for a Hawaiian god, presumably dead as well as alive. Still, making him a dead god would have the virtue of allowing Obeyesekere to deal with all the documentary testimony of Hawaiian expectations that Cook/Lono would return to them, or indeed that he did so annually. It could mean that he returned by a kind of soul transfer, like a certain Welshman in Honolulu, who was taken to be the spirit of a dead Hawaiian who had gone to Kahiki (or England) and come back in that form. All one can say about this is, that's funny: he didn't look Hawaiian.

Clearly the article, "Captain Cook at Hawaii" (Sahlins 1989) bothered Obeyesekere, since it contained a lot of evidence of the kind that an empirical anthropology "cannot afford to turn its back on." He seldom refers to it. But he makes a number of cryptic dismissals of it (without citations) and then fails to erase from his own work the arguments against Cook's deification it refutes. At some earlier point, for example, Obeyesekere must have thought he had something when he came across accounts of the man who struck Cook declaring that since the stranger bleeds, or since he fell, he is not a god. As was noted in the 1989 article, however, this implies that up to that moment, while Cook was still alive, he was believed to be a god. So Obeyesekere declares, in reference to Ellis's rehearsal of the story, that this episode is mythological (Ob. 158). He ignores, or forgets to delete, his passage of some pages before, where he treated the same episode as believable—in order to draw the incorrect inference that Cook's deification must have been post mortem (Ob. 147).

In sum, for all the blustering and blundering character of Obeyesekere's work, together with the evasions and distortions of the texts, it is hard to credit the self-congratulatory assertion that at least his interpretations reflect a proper respect for the evidence. On the contrary, this combination of prosaic error and high righteousness can only come from moral conviction. The truth lies in Obeyesekere's cause.

A critique of Captain Cook and Marshall Sahlins, Obeyesekere's book, as he explains, is written against "the culture of violence" enveloping the world and particularly his native Sri Lanka. A preface tells the tragic story of Wijedasa, to whom the work is dedicated. A gentle and dignified man who for years drove Obeyesekere around Columbo in his taxi, Wijedasa was killed protecting his son, whom "they" accused of being a terrorist. Obeyesekere hopes that "a memorial to Wijedasa might serve as an encouragement to those who, back home, record such events, refusing to keep silent" (Ob. xvii). The criticism of Cook and Sahlins, the former for his own violence and the latter for creating new versions of the ideology that sustains such cruelties, might somehow rectify the moral failings of a "traditional social science" that "simply bypasses the terror in explaining it" (Ob. xvi).

I could not even guess at the deeper motivation for making Cook and me somehow responsible for the tragedy of Obeyesekere's friend. It seems an odd way to end the violence, by thus wildly displacing it. Anyhow, for Obeyesekere, the ostensible connection between the Sri Lankan terror and the remote events of Captain Cook's death at Hawaii runs along the "myth" that Cook was received as the Makahiki god. In itself an arrogant put-down of the "natives'" practical rationality, the myth would at the same time serve as a cover for Cook's irrational violence—which was in fact what did him in. The myth of Cook as a Hawaiian god would thus mystify as "civilization" a culture whose truth has been cruelty and domination. By undermining the supposed apotheosis of Captain Cook, Obeyesekere reveals the imperialist truth and defends those oppressed by it. Combating the historian's assertion that "Captain Cook was the god Lono," Obeyesekere writes:

> I question this "fact," which I show was created in the European imagination of the eighteenth century and after and was based on antecedent "myth models" pertaining to the redoubtable explorer cum civilizer who is a god to the "natives." To put it bluntly, I doubt that the natives created their European god; the Europeans created him for them. This "European god" is a myth of conquest, imperialism, and civilization—a triad that cannot be easily separated. (Ob. 3)

In contrast to this European "myth of conquest," Obeyesekere goes on to show that Hawaiians inclined before Cook as a chief of "divine attributes" and, within a month of his appearance, deified him as a royal ancestral god in order to appropriate his powers.

Sahlins, on the other hand, proves himself the ideologue of imperialism by arguing that Cook was apotheosized by Hawaiians as a form of their ancestral god—which is also to say that Cook was culturally appropriated by them on their own terms. True that this act of bad faith on my part might not seem so, given the marginal differences with Obeyesekere's irreproach-able version. Its true moral character, however, comes out in another com-parison: with Todorov's (1984) analogous work on Cortés and the Aztecs. For, "Todorov, in contrast to Sahlins, is informed by a deep ethical concern, namely his sympathy for the Aztecs and his unequivocal condemnation of the brutality of the conquest" (Ob. 16). Obeyesekere thus proves that ter-rorism does indeed take many forms, including writing. Yet like so many of his textual readings, this unworthy comment is as irrelevant as it is symboli-cally violent, since Todorov's sympathy for the Aztecs did not prevent him from concluding that the Aztecs took the Spanish for gods. Even worse, the Aztecs by Todorov's account fell dupes to Cortés's masterful manipulation of signs—rather the opposite of what I said of Cook's victimization by Hawai-ian signs.

Having thus occupied the moral high ground of anti-imperialism, Ob-eyesekere cannot refrain from pressing the attack to the absurdity of its logi-cal conclusion: which is that (all) "natives" are alike, in thought and reaction to Europeans. Hence in contrast to (Western) anthropologists, he as a Sri Lankan "native" has a privileged understanding of what Hawaiians must have made of Captain Cook:

> The assumption of a lack of discrimination in cosmologically bound natives is endemic to Polynesian ethnography. Thus, when Cook ar-rived in Hawai'i, some anthropologists thought that for Hawaiians he was the god Lono arrived in person [sic]. . . . But real-life natives, I think, make a variety of *discriminations* about the nature of divinity. In South Asia, the king is considered an embodiment of Śiva; yet, as a native, I know that this form of Śiva is different from someone like Sai Baba, who claims he is the *avatar* of Śiva; or from the possessed person I consult who becomes a vehicle of that god; or from Śiva worshipped in his phallic representation (*lingam*) in my temple; or from Śiva or-

nately dressed in full regalia when the priest opens the curtains of the temple; or from my friend whose name is Śiva, whom I meet in the cafeteria; and so on. But the anthropologist's version of the native cannot make these discriminations regarding the varying refractions of the essence of the one god. Thus, for Marshall Sahlins, there is not all that much difference between King Kalani'opu'u of Hawai'i, who is the embodiment of the god Kū, and the god Kū who is worshipped in the temple and brings success in war. We (we assume) can make these discriminations but we should not be ethnocentric and foolishly assume natives can. I think the reverse is true: the native can make all sorts of subtle discriminations in his field of beliefs; the outsider-anthropologist practicing a form of reverse discrimination cannot. Needless to say, my reified "anthropologist" is the one who has reified the whole idea of a symbolic or cosmological order that exists super-organically outside the consciousness of human beings. (Ob. 21–22)

As a "real-life native" able to discriminate between spiritual concepts and the worldly realities to which they refer, Obeyesekere has insights into Hawaiian practices of the same kind. Such insights are denied to the Western anthropologist, who is in thrall to the ethnocentric notion that the "natives" are prescriptively governed by superorganic cosmological codes. The intellectual chutzpah here—*car nous aussi, nous avons nos aïeux!*—the chutzpah is worth some reflection. Obeyesekere is "a real-life native" as distinct from an anthropologist; Sahlins is a Western anthropologist but not a "native." A Sri Lankan is the same as a Hawaiian in the capacity of being a "native," thus an insider in these matters of belief, as opposed to the "outsider anthropologist" who projects his Western ethnocentric beliefs onto the "natives." From this it follows that Obeyesekere can explicate Hawaiian concepts from Sri Lankan ones, most particularly what Hawaiians really understood by according spiritual dignities to intruding White men. Unlike the self-mystified Western anthropologist, the "natives" knew the difference between a real god and real White man.

Notice that the substantive issue of Hawaiian doctrine, the question of divine embodiments, has been displaced onto a nonissue of epistemology. Whether Cook was a manifestation of Lono is turned into the question of whether Hawaiians recognized any difference between them. But for the nth time, the latter is not in question. Neither the outsider-anthropological texts nor the native Hawaiian doctrines suppose the fatuous sense of Cook's identity that Obeyesekere is tilting against. The Hawaiians did not "mistake" Cook for the god. The person of Cook was not Lono "in person." Being transcendent, the god could not be completely or, as such, translated into any particular embodiment; as, conversely, being a specific manifestation of Lono, the Makahiki form Lonomakua, would not make Cook any less the person Cook. After all, the notion that the spiritual god is not the material man, that the two are mutually exclusive by nature, is the Judeo-Christian ontology (with one notable exception). We have seen that it is not Hawaiian.[1]

Curiously enough, as Obeyesekere proceeds to explicate early Hawaiian concepts of White men by Sri Lankan beliefs and his own experience, he gets farther and farther from the Hawaiian and closer and closer to the native Western folklore of divine vs. human, spiritual vs. material. This, again, because he dissolves the issue of whether men could be forms of god into whether the "natives" can discriminate between them. For, by the Western positivist syllogism that guides him (as it seems) unawares, if one thing is differentiated empirically from another, the man from the god, the two cannot have the same nature—since all we know, as Locke said, is what we

---

1. I am not making this point for the first time—however often Obeyesekere caricatures it as "Sahlins's position" that "Cook was Lono in person." I have repeatedly invoked a principle of manifestation in discussing the royal Hawaiian predecessors of Cook who were likewise worldly instances of Lono. *Historical Metaphors*, for example, spoke of them as "chiefly figurations of Lono"—

> The chiefly figurations of Lono, predecessors of Cook in this role, were all descendants of women of relatively indigenous or early lines. They were likewise married to sacred women, but all lost their wives and chiefdoms to upstart rulers. Hence like the Makahiki god Lono, theirs was the original power over the fertility of the land. (Sahlins 1981: 12; see also 1985b:206–9; 1989:371, 384–385)

The same text discusses Cook's status as a "historical representation or incarnation" of Lono, in the context of the doctrine of the god's bodies:

> Indeed the logic of divine classification works on the same principle of genus and species as the concept of descent, providing motivation for the principle of historical representation or incarnation even in the absence of demonstrable genealogical connection. Or rather, the functional similarity between gods and men then becomes the basis of a genealogical supposition, as in the instance of Captain Cook. The great multitude of Hawaiian male gods, almost without exception, are classified as individual forms of the four major classes whose "heads" are the generic gods, Kū, Lono, Kane and Kanaloa. God names therefore are typically binomials, with a stem composed of one of the four great names and a particularizing attribute (Valeri [1985]). The Lono image of the Makahiki festival is, by most accounts, Lonomakua (Father-Lono) or Lonoikamakahiki (Lono-of-the-Makahiki), names also associated with Cook. (Ibid., 16–17)

know by experience. Actually, Obeyesekere does not start off badly. The initial analogy between Hindu and Hawaiian was not wild: the king as an "embodiment of Śiva," Sai Baba as "an avatar of Śiva." But he soon loses the track: "We noted earlier that no Hindu would mistake the king who is, let us say, an embodiment of Śiva for the same Śiva whom they worship in the temple" (Ob. 91). Fair enough, but the relevant question is whether the king (or the temple image) is an embodiment of the same Śiva, not whether one could be mistaken for the other.

Having stumbled on this logical hurdle, Obeyesekere's further explications of Hawaiian concepts of Cook by the (supposed) South Asian grip on reality progressively trivializes "native" thought. As kids growing up in Columbo, we did not really believe the choo-choo train was an "iron demon" (Ob. 173–74). And it all turns out to be innocent metaphor: the way, in Sri Lanka, chiefs are occasionally addressed as "deiyo" (god), "even though everyone knows that chiefs are not gods. Such metaphors are very common . . ." (Ob. 197). But if one ends up in the good Western positivist tradition, by thus contrasting metaphor and reality, is it not because the argument began with such ideological relics of Western imperialism as the blanket distinction of "natives" and "Europeans?" The only significant difference between Obeyesekere's position and the garden variety of European imperialist ideology is not that he eschews the opposition between the West and the Rest but that he reverses their values. He would give the "natives" all that "rationality" Western people take to be the highest form of thought, while endowing the Europeans, including the outsider-anthropologists, with the kind of mindless repetition of myth they have always despised—that is, as "native." Which is also to say that this self-proclaimed defense of "preliterate people who cannot speak for themselves" is imperialist hegemony masquerading as subaltern resistance.

The ultimate victims, then, are Hawaiian people. Western empirical good sense replaces their own view of things, leaving them with a fictional history and a pidgin ethnography. The herald who proclaims the public advent of Lono becomes a protocol officer for guiding Cook through temple ceremonies. The English officers fed as image-bearers of Cook/Lono (in the *hānaipū* rite) are thereby "reborn as children of the Hawaiian gods" in a ceremony that "had the effect of imbuing Cook with the mana of the war god Kū" and "converting" all these gentlemen into "Hawaiian chiefs" (Ob. 62). Traditional rituals are thus dissolved; social cleavages on which Hawaiian history turned—as between priests and chiefs, women and men—are ef-

faced; genealogy is invented and theology ignored; cosmography is miscon-
strued and cosmology traduced. And then, when Hawaiians explain otherwise, their words are attributed instead to the Haole who wrote them down
or the missionary who taught them to speak thus. Hawaiian people appear
on stage as the dupes of European ideology. Deprived thus of agency and
culture, their history is reduced to a classic meaninglessness: they lived and
they suffered—and then they died.

What the Sailors Knew

In the passage quoted on page 19, Obeyesekere says that none of Cook's people could determine from Hawaiians that the captain was the god Lono, but elsewhere this statement is qualified in various forms and degrees. So, he also says that none of the major journal keepers supposed Cook was deified, thereby excepting Lieutenant Rickman and Heinrich Zimmermann, who did so (Ob. 75–76, 122–23). Again, he says, of the officers, only Lieutenant Rickman tied Cook to the god, thus excepting the ordinary seamen, who did so—on the basis of an a priori Haole tradition that "natives" take them for gods (Ob. 123). The officers did not come to this conclusion because "their empirical observations did not warrant it" (Ob. 124). Alternatively, Obeyesekere writes that the officers knew about the old tradition of European-as-native-god, "and were therefore cautious in accepting the popular shipboard equation that Cook was a god for Hawaiians" (Ob. 123). This must mean that the sophisticated officers refrained because they knew the seamen's notions were folkloric. All the same, and despite the (hypothetical) empirical evidence to the contrary, Lieutenant King on his return to England wrote of the "religious adoration" of Cook and made other intimations of his divinity—enough to convince the poet William Cowper that God had struck down Cook for playing god (Ob. 125–26). Likewise, according to Obeyesekere, Midshipman Trevenan spoke of Cook as an "idolized man" in the marginal notes he made in his copy of King's official account (Ob. 125). Mr. King, says Obeyesekere, was clearly influenced by London debates about Cook's death and the earlier publications of Rickman and Zimmermann (as if the confused narratives of these two could persuade a person of King's observational talents). In sum, if one assumes the hypothesis that the deification of Cook was a European myth, then makes the ad hoc assumption that any report of Cook's divinity in Hawaii must be due to the influence of that myth, and for good measure throws in the assumption that if people did not say Cook was a god they must have evidence he was not a god, it can be reasonably concluded that the deification of Cook was a European myth.

On the other hand, Obeyesekere may have sensed that this one type of negative evidence—the failure of the British to report that Cook was received by Hawaiians as a god—would be evidence against his own thesis, which is that Haole are predisposed to say just that. Perhaps the sense of contradiction accounts for his curious speculation that, although the common seamen were inclined to this conceit, the officers were inhibited by their consciousness of the tradition. But this also suggests Obeyesekere's sensitivity to the ambiguity of many British chroniclers about the respects Hawaiians paid to "the Orono": their reports are marked by a distinct reticence in equating Cook and the god rather than by any eagerness to do so. Reviewing the Cook documents, John F. G. Stokes, a well-known scholar of things Hawaiian, spoke of the colossal ignorance of the British in not recognizing that Hawaiians were identifying Cook with Lono in so many words (1931:92–93). But was it ignorance—or delicacy?

European views about the propriety of such allegations of their divinity were hardly monolithic. Obeyesekere speaks of this conceit as a structure of the long run in Western ideology. But the sin of playing god is surely a structure of the longer and stronger run, it being in fact the Original—"ye shall be as God," said the serpent, "knowing good and evil" (Gen. 3:5). People such as Lieutenant King and David Samwell, who were very sympathetic to Hawaiians, especially to the priests, speak only obliquely of the islanders' disposition to cross the great Western ontological divide between god and man; of course, they are even less direct in speaking of Captain Cook's role in the affair, which they must have known would be a scandal to many of his compatriots. In an oft-quoted footnote to the official account, King puzzles over what precisely this designation of Cook as Lono meant. He says the Hawaiians sometimes applied it to an invisible being who lived in the heavens. Referring to Omeah, a high priest of Lono who analogously bore the god's name, King writes that this personage "resembles pretty much the Delai Lama of the Tartars, and the ecclesiastical emperor of Japan" (Cook and King 1784, 3:5n). Yet, it had been well-known in Europe for at least a century that the Dalai Lama and the Japanese emperor were incarnate gods (see above, 135–36). This passage is pure circumspection all the way around. The kind of criticism of Cook's divine career penned by Cowper—on the basis of Mr. King's narrative—is testimony to the complexity of the ideological pressures surrounding the issue. Expressing these pressures as ambiguity, a text such as King's is neither arrogant nor ignorant—just reticent.

Obeyesekere, however, thinks Mr. King exaggerated Cook's supposed godliness in the published version of the voyage by comparison with his private journals. As was said, this presumes King was swayed by Rickman and Zimmermann (thus that he read German), and by debates in England over Cook's death. The evidence of exaggeration is that, in the published account, King described the ceremony of the first day at Kealakekua in which Cook was formally offered a pig on board the *Resolution* as, "a sort of religious adoration," and says it was "frequently repeated during our stay at Owhyhee"; whereas, the private journal, according to Obeyesekere, does not contain a reference to "religious adoration" (Ob. 125). Again, regarding such offerings to Cook, where the official account says they were made, "with a regularity, more like a discharge of religous duty than the effect of mere liberality," the unofficial journal (merely) says: "All this seemed to be done as a duty . . . either as a peace offering or to a mortal much their superior" (ibid.). But here Obeyesekere's literalness misrepresents Lieutenant King's private journal, both with regard to its wording and its tenor.

By the second day of the British sojourn at Kealakeku, Mr. King *in his private journal* was describing the ritual respects the Lono priests paid to Cook as approaching "adoration." In fact the ceremony of that day was the *hānaipū*, the formal greeting of Lono at the Makahiki (see above, 55–59). Writing of "the remarkable homage they pay to Capt" Cook & also to Captain Clerke," King says:

> This [homage] on the first visit of Capt" Cook to their [the Lono priests'] houses seemd to approach to Adoration, he was placed at the foot of a wooden image [of Lono] at the Entrance of a hut [a Hale o Lono or 'House of Lono' temple], to which [image] from the remnants of Cloth round the trunk, & the remains of Offerings on the Whatta [altar], they seem to pay more than ordinary devotion; I was here again made to support the Captains Arms. (Beaglehole 1967:509–10)

The support of Cook's outstretched arms would make him an image of the cross-piece Makahiki image, Lonomakua, the one received thus during the New Year festival. But Mr. King had been impressed with the unusual Hawaiian reactions to the British from the time of the first visit to Kaua'i, exactly a year earlier. He wrote of some Kaua'i people who had come aboard the *Resolution*:

In their behaviour they were very fearful of giving offense, asking if they should sit down, & spit on the decks, etc. & in all their conduct seemd to regard us as superior beings. (King Log, 20 Jan 1778)

Again, in summing up the British experience at Hawai'i, King wrote:

As they certainly regarded us as a Superior race of people to themselves, they would often say, that the great Eatooa [*Akua*, 'god'] liv'd with us. The little Image which we have mention'd as being the center one in the Morai [Hikiau temple] they calld Koonooe aikai'a [Kūnuiakea, an encompassing form of the royal god, Kū] & said it was [King] Terreeoboos God, & that he also livd with us, which proves that they only regard these Images as types or resemblances of their Deitys. (Beaglehole 1967:621)

We shall see that Obeyesekere misquotes the version of this passage in the published *Voyage*, which reads that the great god "dwelled in our country" and the king's God "resided amongst us," as saying that the latter "resided *in* us" (Cook and King 1784, 3:159–60; Ob. 86, emphasis added). For the amusement of his readers (who have checked the originals), he then makes this Hawaiian (mis-)statement, that the Hawaiian god lived in Englishmen, part of his argument against the idea that Englishmen were received as Hawaiian gods, this being a purely European invention (see above, 62–63).

Literalism and Culture

M any of Obeyesekere's criticisms are marked by a curiously flat literalism, as in this issue of the Makahiki god appearing in human
form rather than the traditional wooden image:

> Sahlins seems to assume that the arrival of Lono-Cook at Makahiki
> time was right on ritual schedule. But in fact this is a totally *unprece-
> dented* event, for no Hawaiian god is supposed to arrive as a physical
> person during these ritual festivals. As in other societies, the gods are
> invoked in chants and prayers to be "present" in the ceremony; they
> may also appear in various forms, as for example, a wind. Thus, the
> arrival of the god Lono in person would have upset their ritual sched-
> ule, compelling them to make readjustments and alterations to deal
> with this unprecedented and unexpected event. (Ob. 64–65)

As Obeyesekere is well known for his imaginative symbolic interpretations of a psychoanalytic kind, it may be worthwhile to reflect (method-
ologically) on the repeated recourse to such banal realism in *The Apotheosis of
Captain Cook*. The disputational strategy is fairly evident. By means of his
own new-found literalism, Obeyesekere opens a space of commonsense in-
credulity that can be filled by Hawaiians' hard-headed objectivity. It helps
not to mention here that the god is represented at the Makahiki by a cross-
piece image with an anthropomorphic figure or head at the top (Malo 1951:
143–44; Ii 1959:71), or that Cook was made to assume the form of this
image the day he landed at Kealakekua (Sahlins 1989:400). The rhetoric of
an unprecedented arrival of Lono "in person" also fails to consider that a
physical person, every bit as much as an image or a wind, would be a *representation* of the god. But, most important, the form of the literalist argument,
by denying that Hawaiians were able to motivate a substantial relationship

between Cook and Lono on logical and perceptual grounds, has the effect of confining them to a mindless repetition of their preexisting cultural forms. Of course, I am repeatedly accused by Obeyesekere of advancing just such ideas of "stereotypic reproduction"—a phrase and concept I have been explicitly criticizing since 1977 (see appendix 11). Indeed, my own argument is that Cook was creatively and flexibly assimilated by Hawaiians to their Makahiki tradition, since as Obeyesekere says that tradition did not prescribe the advent of Lono as a "physical person." But in the realist theoretical practice adopted by Obeyesekere, in order for cultural schemata to function in practice, in order for people to successfully use their understandings of the world, the world will have to consistently and objectively correspond to the ideas by which they know it. If not, their minds turn into Lockean blank sheets of paper, and the biological capacity for realism takes over. Indeed, a utopian Lockean world of empirical truth would be the pan-human fate, since, sooner or later, usually sooner, reality proves a disappointment to all peoples' categories.

> . . . peace . . . how peaceful . . . how quiet. Now we have won. Much better. All those voices . . . stilled. What were those endless arguments about? We can hardly remember. Now everyone agrees; everyone knows the truth. Which is . . . we can hardly remember. It doesn't matter anymore. Nothing seems to matter much anymore. So quiet. Nobody talks—what is there to talk about? Nobody writes—who for? what for? We all agree, we see. We just live our lives and doze and die. And that at least, we all agree, is REAL. (Ashmore, Edwards, and Potter 1994:11)

In the face of empirical discrepancies to received ideas, Hawaiians, like everyone else, will be reduced to their senses alone and a built-in capacity for "practical rationality." They will forget everything. They will interpret experience for what it really is. If circumstances do not conform to their cultural order, they (or it) are so inflexible they have no other recourse except to give it up.

The reason this theoretical practice is unworkable is that every situation to which a people refer a given category is empirically unique, distinct from every other to which the same notion may be applied. One never steps into the same river twice—which never stopped anyone from calling it by the same name. To paraphrase John Barth, reality is a nice place to visit (philosophically), but no one ever lived there. Unless experiences were selectively perceived, classified, and valued by socially communicable criteria, there would be neither society nor intelligibility, let alone sanity. Not to say that the interpretive categories are *culturally prescribed*—as if there were no improvisation or innovation—*only that events are culturally described*. The great irony in all this is that the word that Polynesians most commonly use to designate unprecedented yet clearly significant phenomena, including persons, is *akua* or its equivalent (Fijian, *kalou*), indicating divine power and godly nature (see above, 178–79).

The passage from Obeyesekere cited at the head of this note has several errors. I have never assumed, or seemed to assume, that the arrival of Cook at the Makahiki "was right on ritual schedule" (see Sahlins 1989). Cook began the circuit of Hawai'i island two weeks in advance of the Makahiki god and arrived at Kealakekua nearly two weeks after its scheduled arrival (see ibid.). It is also incorrect that no Hawaiian god normally appears as a physical person during those ceremonies. Kahoali'i, a physical person who is the king's 'god' (*akua*) and plays an important role in human sacrifices, has an analogous function in the dismantling of the Lono image at the Makahiki (Vancouver 1801, 5:37; Sahlins 1985a:119–20). Nor is it unknown for such gods to appear ceremonially "in other societies"—consider the Aztecs, among numerous others. Finally, that Cook's arrival did create discrepancies in the Hawaiians' ritual schedule to which they did adjust is a point I have made in detail: the suspension of the tabu on putting to sea during Lono's procession, since Cook's circuit was by ship; the improvised re-offering of an already sacrificed pig at Hikiau temple, reflecting a thirteen-day difference between Lono's scheduled entrance to the temple and Cook's; the performance of the *hānaipū* ceremony for welcoming Lono outside the 23-day period of the Lono procession; the transposition of sham fighting in the several districts of the island presided over by the "god of sport" forms of Lono to the boxing entertainments provided for Cook's people, likewise marked by the appearance of Makahiki images: see Sahlins (1989) for these and other such improvisations.

On the Kāliʻi Rite

In effort to deny the analogy between the historical death of Cook, killed on the shore of Kealakekua Bay by a crowd of armed men defending their king against him, and the kāliʻi ritual of the Makahiki that pits the king against the party of Lono, Obeyesekere asserts that it is "doubtful whether the ritual of Kāliʻi could be seen as a grand conflict between the king (as the god Kū) and those who ritually oppose him (Lono)" (Ob. 198). The assertion is partly contingent on a preceding argument—a reading based on his Sri Lankan concepts of divinity and a misreading of the Marquesan practice of designating foreigners as akua 'gods' (see appendix 17)—that the king does not represent the god Kū. But of course, the king is, in his warrior aspect, directly representative of Kū, especially the mobile war form, Kū-kailimoku ('Ku-Snatcher-of-the-Island'); and the kāliʻi marks the turning point in the year when the ceremonial presence of Lono is superseded by the temple rites centered on Kū (Valeri 1985). Obeyesekere apparently believes that if he obscures the affinity of the king and Kū, it will nullify the opposition between the king and Lono at the kāliʻi, and a fortiori the parallels to Cook's death. So, in testimony to the above statement doubting that the kāliʻi "could be seen as a grand conflict between the king (as the god Kū) and those who ritually oppose him (Lono)," Obeyesekere quotes the significant text of Kelou Kamakau—who nevertheless described the ritual of kāliʻi in the explicit terms of the conflict of the king and the god (Lono):

> The king came in from the sea, and when he was near the lower side of the temple towards the sea he saw a great number of people with the deity. A very large number of men ran in front of the image [of Lono], holding spears in their hands. One of them had several spears in his hands which he intended to throw at one of the men who landed

with the king from the canoe. The king and his companion landed, and when the man who held the several spears saw them he ran forward quickly and threw a spear at the king's companion. He parried it with something that he held in his hand, leaping upwards. The people then shouted at the man's skill. The man then touched the king with a second spear thus freeing him from restrictions. Then there was a general sham fight among the people. (K. Kamakau 1919–20:42–45)

In sum, the king and Lono came into conflict at the Makahiki, as did King Kalani'ōpu'u and "Lono" (as Hawaiians knew Cook) on the 14th of February 1779. In both instances, Lono was ultimately dismembered and the king ritually absorbed the benefits of his passage.

Historiography
of the Makahiki

part from the accounts of the Cook voyage, there are essentially two sorts of primary documents on the Hawaiian Makahiki festival: early-nineteenth-century descriptions of the ceremonies written by Hawaiians, and notices by various European observers before 1819, when the Makahiki was formally abolished. Obeyesekere relies on the two main Hawaiian sources (K. Kamakau 1919–20; Malo 1951), and for the most part ignores the European sources. He is thus able to give the impression that a correlation of nineteenth-century Hawaiian descriptions with incidents of the Cook voyage would be a leap of historic faith—faith in the continuity of the ceremonies—across an evidential void of several decades. This gives him the liberty to accuse me of the supposition that the ceremonies were unchanged all that time, Hawaiians merely repeating their fixed traditions, and to doubt it himself. He hopes to render dubious also—doubt being his main rhetorical objective—the possibility of Cook being identified with the Lono hero of the Makahiki. The Makahiki of Cook's time would be unknown. The formal Makahiki we do know can then be sucked up in the great black hole of Hawaiian historiography: the undocumented innovations attributed to the later conqueror of the archipelago and founder of the Hawaiian kingdom, Kamehameha (r. 1795–1819).

The principal Hawaiian texts on the Makahiki are those of Kelou Kamakau (1919–20:34–45) and David Malo (1951:141–59). They are complemented by partial notices in the works of Kepelino (Beckwith 1932; Kirtley and Mookini 1979; Kepelino HEN), John Papa 'I'i (1959), and an anonymous chronicler from Kohala, Hawai'i (Anonymous of Kohala 1919–20). Malo's account is the most comprehensive. Born in 1793 or 1795 not far from Kealakekua, Malo reached manhood under the old regime and no doubt participated in Makahiki festivities. Kelou Kamakau of Ka'awaloa (where Cook was killed) wrote a description similar in content to Malo's, though different in style and detail; unfortunately, it breaks off not long after the return of Lono from the circuit, the remainder of the manuscript having been lost. Obeyesekere observes that the Makahiki text of Kamakau, "who might have actually witnessed Lono rituals as a boy," makes "no reference either to Cook or his deification" (Ob. 49). In fact, as Kamakau was about fifty years old when Rev. William Ellis met him in 1823, four years after the Makahiki was abolished, he had long and often witnessed the Lono rituals as a mature man—he could have witnessed Cook's death as a boy (Ellis 1833, 4:57). That his unfinished ritual text does not mention Cook means nothing. On the other hand, as Kamakau was the headman of Ka'awaloa and one of Ellis's principal sources of information, he may well be responsible for the local lore of Cook as Lono recorded by the English missionary. Ellis, who had substantial conversations with Kamakau and praised his intelligence, relates that several Ka'awaloa people were among his authorities on Cook's fate. In addition to other things, they told Ellis, "We thought he [Cook] was the god Rono [Lono], worshipped him as such, and after his death reverenced his bones" (Ellis 1833, 4:103).

John Papa 'I'i was born in O'ahu around 1800 and at age ten became an attendant of the future Kamehameha II, Liholiho. His reminiscences of the Makahiki include childhood memories of its sham battles.

Kepelino's references to the Makahiki, however, were second hand, as he was born about 1830. A member of a priestly line and an informant of Jules Remy, Kepelino was a man of considerable intellectual talents whose notices on the Makahiki share a virtue with the other Hawaiian accounts: none of them seriously contradicts the others or is in any way aberrant. They are all speaking of the same Makahiki.

There is every reason to believe that the extant Hawaiian descriptions of the Makahiki represent a canonical tradition of some antiquity— including the fact, as we shall see, that *most known or alleged innovations of Kamehameha I do not appear in them.* Before referring to historical evidence from the late nineteenth century to the same effect, we should consider Obeyesekere's objections to the attempt to correlate these descriptions with episodes recorded in the Cook journals. He objects that Kamehameha imposed a formalized Makahiki festival throughout the islands after he had conquered them, presumably as an instrument of his rule. The classic descriptions, then, refer to this state cultus of the early nineteenth century. Before that, according to Obeyesekere, each of the island chiefdoms would have its own distinctive ceremonies, at its own time. So there is no reason to suppose that a Makahiki was in progress at Kaua'i and Ni'ihau in January–February 1778, when Cook first visited the Hawaiian Islands. Nor would the festival at Hawai'i island in 1778–79, during Cook's second visit, necessarily be the one described by Malo *mā* (Malo and company) in the nineteenth century. Obeysekere places great significance on the pre-Kamehameha inter-island variations, repeating the argument several times: a significance based on the dual misconception that I insist there were no such differences, and that the absence of the ceremonies at Kaua'i in January 1778 is somehow evidence that Cook was not caught up in the Makahiki festival of Hawai'i island a year later (Ob. 59, 95, 99). He objects, further, that the very attempt to correlate the Cook voyage and the Makahiki notices of Malo et al. ignores the political flexibility of calendrical reckonings and ritual performances. He says I am asserting that Hawaiians merely mechanically reproduced their customary ceremonies (see also appendix 5).

Here are a couple of extended samples of Obeyesekere's historiographical objections:

> The extant descriptions of the Makahiki come from the nineteenth century, after the tabu system was abolished in 1819; the ceremony itself was systematized and formalized by the great Kamehameha. Yet, on the basis of these formalized accounts, Sahlins calculates the exact time period for the Makahiki, in 1778 and 1779, and then further argues that this festival was held on all the major islands at the same time [*sic*]. . . . But this function of the theory ignores the reality that the formalization of this ceremony was a nineteenth-century phenomenon, and that the empirical evidence gathered by [S. M.] Kamakau [not Kelou Kamakau] shows that not only did the timing of the Makahiki vary from one island to another but it might well vary in the same island. (Ob. 59)

Again, referring to the argument of Bergendorff et al. (1989) that the Makahiki was a minor festival later refashioned by Kamehameha into a state cult, Obeyesekere writes:

> Sahlins replies vigorously that, although Kamehameha formalized the cult, Makahiki was an ancient and continuing ritual of fertility [footnote reference here to Sahlins 1989, but no page noted]. But Sahlins cannot show how the formalized Makahiki calendars of Kamehameha's time can be retrospectively used to reconstruct the timing of the

Makahiki festival in the period of Cook's arrival in Kaua'i and Hawai'i in the pre-Kamehamehan era, when the islands were under independent chiefdoms. I think it is virtually certain that there was no Makahiki festival during Cook's visit to Kaua'i in 1778. (Ob. 95)

First, to clear up Obeyesekere's routine misrepresentations of what is at issue. In reply to the speculations of the Danish scholars, I did not say that "although Kamehameha formalized the cult," the Makahiki was an ancient fertility ceremony. On the contrary, I said that the Danish scholars failed to specify any of the changes allegedly introduced by Kamehameha, let alone provide any evidence for them (Sahlins 1989: 386). Moreover, the reply in question consisted of a sustained examination of the parallels between the Malo *mā* texts and historical reports from Cook's time onward (Sahlins 1989; see also Sahlins MS). In other words, I offer an empirical documentation of what is, for Obeyesekere, an a priori impossibility. (The major points of this comparison of the ethnographic and historical accounts are rehearsed in the present work.) Again, I have not insisted that the Makahiki was in progress *in Kaua'i* when Cook landed there in late January 1778. This remains an open question, about which I have been careful to note that the British accounts do not say Cook was "Lono" for the Kaua'i people (Sahlins 1981: 17, 18). "Careful," because as we shall see, Cook was so identified in later Hawaiian traditions about his coming to Kaua'i; and also, by local traditions, there *was* a Makahiki festival with classic features in Kaua'i during pre-Kamehameha times. But the question does not directly concern Kaua'i. It was Hawai'i island people who knew him as "Lono" and it was *their* Makahiki that was relevant to his fate. All that is necessary to the argument is that *from the Hawai'i island perspective*, by *their* calendar, Cook arrived at successive Makahiki periods (Sahlins 1985a: 93; cf. Sahlins 1981: 73n). And this is pertinent because when Cook's ships came off Maui in late November 1778, they met a Hawai'i island war party there, one of whom, a chief, came out to the *Discovery* and promptly asked the whereabouts of Lono. But then, according to traditions collected around 1833 or 1834,

Cook was already known as "Lono" to Kalani'ōpu'u's party encamped at Maui when the British arrived there in late November, 1778 (Kahananui 1984: 12). Cook, of course, had been at Kaua'i earlier in the year: in late January, 1778—which is to say in the previous Makahiki season. Moreover, there was at least one man at Maui who had seen Cook at Kaua'i. (Clerke's log entry for November 26, 1778, reads:

"The first man on board told me he knew the ship very well, & had been on board her at A tou I [Kaua'i] & related some anecdotes which convinc'd me of his veracity" [see also King in Beaglehole 1967 : 497]). Probably, then, Cook's appearance at Maui in November was Lono's second coming. In any event, on . . . November 30 . . . a large sailing canoe bearing a man wearing a red feather cloak . . . came out to the *Discovery.* This notable, according to the journal of the master Thomas Edgar, "Ask'd for our Aronna [O Lono] or Chief." (Sahlins 1989 : 403–4; see Edgar Log, 1 Dec 1778)

The point is that Hawai'i islanders knew Cook as "Lono" before they set eyes on him. Evidently the people who came out to the *Resolution* as it circled Hawai'i, before Cook anchored at Kealakekua, likewise named him "Lono" (Cook and King 1784, 3 : 5n). Written history is thus in accord with oral history *(Ka Mooolelo Hawaii)* in ascribing Cook's status as Lono at Hawai'i to already settled opinions of his earlier sojourn at Kaua'i.

We return, then, to the historical record and to Obeyesekere's assertion that "the formalization of this ceremony [the Makahiki] was a nineteenth-century phenomenon," a politics of religion sponsored by Kamehameha. This means that the descriptions of the rituals by Kelou Kamakau and David Malo in particular reflect a formalized nineteenth-century Makahiki and cannot be used to interpret the events of Cook's visit. The argument dispenses Obeyesekere from considering the historical notices of the Makahiki in the eighteenth century (or in Kaua'i before 1810 when the island was surrendered to Kamehameha). A manuscript summary of such notices has been publicly available since 1989 (Sahlins MS); I have also published specific details of the pre-Kamehameha Makahiki in O'ahu, about which Obeyesekere refrains from comment (Sahlins 1989, 1991). The eighteenth-century accounts conform to the ritual rules and calendar of the Makahiki set forth by K. Kamakau and Malo. On the other hand, the documentable changes introduced thereafter by Kamehameha do *not* appear in these standard accounts—with one exception which indicates that Kamehameha simplified rather than formalized the ancient ceremonies.

There are no records of European contacts with Hawaii from the departure of Cook's ships in 1779 until the Northwest Coast fur traders began to stop in 1786. The observations of rituals by the first of these traders, Portlock and Dixon, are too fragmentary to make a definitive call, but they do correspond to the character and dates of specific Makahiki ceremonies:

certain temple rituals in December 1786 at O'ahu that fall on the appropriate lunar dates of the construction of a temporary booth for the royal purification, and a tribute ceremony in Kaua'i, 1 January 1787, which was the correct lunar date of the final small tribute of the Makahiki, the "heap of Kuapola" (Portlock 1789:164–65, 170–79; Dixon 1789:109; cf. Sahlins MS, Notes to Table II:1–4). For the next Makahiki, of 1787–88, we have unmistakable evidence from O'ahu of the appearance of a classic image of Lono, borne by a priest who is in this capacity appropriately called "Lono Nui" (Great Lono)—which is the same name, the fur traders learn, that was given to Captain Cook (Sahlins 1989:391–92; Sahlins 1991; Colnett Journal, 17 Jan 1788; Taylor Journals, 17 Jan 1788, two versions). Note that this cross-piece image was abroad at O'ahu, the domain of the Maui paramount Kahekili, in a time well before Kamehameha's conquest of that island, in 1795.

The evidence of the next year's Makahiki, 1788–89, comes from Kealakekua, Hawai'i, an area controlled by Kamehameha—though he was not as yet the uncontested ruler of Hawai'i, let alone the archipelago. William Douglas, master of the *Iphigenia*, was received by Kamehameha on 12 December 1788, with a ceremony that appears to correspond to the *hānaipū* rite for the reception of Lono. Douglas was one of the first Haole to visit Kealakekua since Cook—the first to do so at Makahiki time—and, like Cook, Douglas was twice more honored in the same way (Meares 1790:338). Moreover, the tabu on pork specific to the Makahiki was in effect at this time: "at this season of the year even the chiefs are forbidden to eat hogs and fowls, from the King down to the lowest Eres [*ali'i*, 'chiefs']" (ibid., 339).

The first full notices of the scope of the Makahiki come from the accounts of the successive visits of the Vancouver squadron to Hawai'i in 1793 and 1794. Arriving at Hilo on 9 January 1794, the British found Kamehameha there celebrating the Makahiki, but for that reason unable to proceed to Kealakekua, as Vancouver desired. "The tabu appertaining to the new year," Vancouver explained, "demanded his continuance for a certain period, within the limits of the district in which these ceremonies commenced" (Vancouver 1801, 5:8). Hence, the ceremonies were not over at this time, as the clerk, Edward Bell, had supposed in speaking of "a kind of festival that is held annually at this Island about the months of October and November. . . . It generally lasts about 6 weeks, or two months, and draws together the principal chiefs, and a vast concourse of Islanders" (Bell 1929–30, 2(1):81). Clearly, what had finished by early January was the "Makahiki" in the unmarked sense, the central tabu and procession of the god—a reckoning that may be confirmed by notices of the Makahiki of the previous year. I have elsewhere detailed these references to the ceremonies in the Vancouver journals (Sahlins 1989:389–91; Sahlins MS, Notes to Table II: 11–28). Here I summarize some of the other classic Makahiki practices witnessed by the Vancouver people:

- The termination rituals during the full moon of the last month, 12 or 13–14 Kā'elo, allowing the king to eat pork (Malo 1951:152; Vancouver 1801, 5:36–39). Delayed a month when Vancouver forced Kamehameha to accompany him to Kealakekua, these ceremonies were actually witnessed by Vancouver at Hikiau temple from 12 to 15 February 1794, which corresponds to the correct lunar phase. Vancouver noted that the purpose was to permit the king to eat pork and that, as in Malo's text, the rituals were marked by the presence of Kahoali'i, the human "god of Kamehameha." Vancouver does not say, however, that Kahoali'i ate the eye of a human sacrificial victim together with the eye of a bonito.

- The bonito tabu presents an interesting discrepancy between the historical and ritual texts. The consumption of the eye of the fish is supposed to mark the end of the tabu on taking it, the inauguration of the bonito season. The Vancouver documents testify to the association of this rite with the end of the Makahiki. But in addition to showing that Kamehameha abridged the preliminary ten-day tabu on the water associated with the bonito rite, these documents indicate that in 1793 and 1794 the bonito ceremonies occurred an *anahulu* or ten-day ritual period earlier than in the Malo description (Vancouver 1801, 3:183–89, 282; Bell 1929–30, 1(5):59–62; Manby 1929, 1(2):38–39; Menzies Journal, 13–15 Feb 1793; Puget Log, 12–15 Feb 1793). This means that if Malo's description of the Makahiki represents nineteenth-century practice, the ceremonies had actually been simplified by then.

- Note in this connection that the early historical accounts are more complex than the latter ethnographic descriptions, which do not document the ten-day bonito tabu or the rule immobilizing the king. The proscription on the king's movement, probably lasting through the purification following the dismemberment of the Lono image, is not only a ritual replication of a royal succession to Lono's dominion, including the ten-day seclusion of the heir after his predecessor's death, but it is precisely paralleled in cognate New Year rituals in Polynesia (Williams LMS; Kennedy 1931:314–16).

Taken in combination with earlier reports, the Vancouver documents provide determinate evidence of a complex, four-month Makahiki cycle, as well as specific ritual practices of the New Year as recorded by Malo and Kelou Kamakau. All this was in place before the supposed "formalization" of the ceremonies sponsored by Kamehameha in the nineteenth century in interests of state. Indeed, in Vancouver's time, Kahekili of Maui was the dominant chief of most of the group, all the way to Kaua'i. Kamehameha had barely secured the rule of Hawai'i island, having sacrificed his last great rival, Keoua Kuahu'ula, only a year or two earlier.

By 1795, however, Kamehameha had taken Maui and O'ahu, and in 1810 the Kaua'i ruling chief acknowledged his supremacy. Reports of Kamehameha's innovations in the Makahiki ceremonies refer to this conquest period. But most of these reports were written substantially later than Malo's or Kelou Kamakau's, or were written by people substantially younger; nor do the changes of which they speak appear in the standard texts of the old-timers who had seen these things themselves.

Some of these changes were not radical. Famous warrior and conqueror, Kamehameha was well known for parrying the spears himself in the king-making *kāli'i* rite, thus doing away with the expert defender of the classic accounts. Historical testimony of this derring-do begins in 1796, and the documents even suggest that the ritual could be performed more than once during the Makahiki (Péron 1824 : 162; Sahlins 1989 : 393–94). More directly political, however, and more significant economically, were the innovations Kamehameha appears to have introduced in the Lono circuit. The most accessible statement of these changes (the one on which Obeyesekere relies) was written by S. M. Kamakau in 1870:

> The way in which the Makahiki was observed in the time of Kamehameha I was in some ways different in the ancient days. For one thing, the months of the year of the people of ancient times were not the same as when he ruled; they were changed to be according to the counting of the Hawaii island people perhaps. . . . Also, the Makahiki gods made a circuit of the island to ask for and to seize the wealth of the people. These were new practices and were not observed by *ka po'e kahiko* ['the people of old']. Some of the gods of Kamehameha I who made the Makahiki circuit were new gods who had been created (*ho'oakua*). Lonoikamakahiki had been a real man of Hawaii, and Kihawahine had been a chiefess of Maui; the man-god (*akua kanaka maoli*) Kaho'ali'i of Kamehameha had been made a god, perhaps because the

spirit of an ancient god by the name of Kaho'ali'i possessed him (*noho pu ana*). These were the Makahiki gods who went about the land. (Kamakau 1964: 19–20)

Before Kamehameha's conquest, the names of months and seasons differed in the several island calendars (Malo 1951: 33–36). Whether this means the timing of their Makahiki ceremonies also differed, as Obeyesekere supposes, is not known. It is possible that, as in analogous annual festivals in the Trobriands, Samoa, and other Austronesian societies, the central ritual, involving the circuit of the god, occurred successively over four months on the four major Hawaiian islands: Kaua'i, O'ahu, Maui, and Hawai'i. Be that as it may, we have some interesting testimony of the pre-Kamehameha Makahiki in Kaua'i in the records of an 1854 boundary dispute between the districts (*ahupua'a*) of Lumahai and Wainiha (LC/FT 10: 393–400).

The context is already symptomatic of the significance of the Makahiki. For, the boundaries of the ancient land divisions called *ahupua'a*, 'pig altar,' were marked by a stone shrine where the Makahiki god stopped and received the offering or tribute of the land. (The term *ahupua'a*, 'pig altar,' is usually explicated as a reference to Lono, the pig being one of the principal 'bodies' [*kino*] of that god.) So, in this case, certain witnesses attempted to verify the boundaries by reference to the place the Makahiki god stopped during its circuit of Kaua'i. These witnesses were invoking events before the control of Kaua'i by Kamehameha, referring to the rule of the Kaua'i ruling chief Kaumuali'i or of his predecessor Ka'eo. For Kaumuali'i gave up nominal sovereignty of Kaua'i to Kamehameha only in 1810, though he remained the actual ruling chief until after Kamehameha's death in 1819, annually paying tribute to the latter. Indeed, two of the witnesses were formerly priests of Kamehameha's conquering god, Kukailimoku, who came after 1810 to perform ceremonies in Kaua'i temples, including the *heiau* (temple) at Wainiha. The other witnesses were local old-timers. For example, one Koha:

> I was born at Hanamaulu in the time of Kaumualii; and when I was grown we went with the makahiki god, and [swears] that once I saw in the circuiting of the makahiki god that he stood at Kaunupepeiao. I was a stranger, going on the circuit of the island with the makahiki god. . . . That is my knowledge in the time of Kaumualii.

Even more interesting is the succeeding witness, Kamoolehua:

I was born at the time Kaeo was chief of Kauai [Kaeo was Kaumuali'i's
father; the time in question would be between 1779 and 1795]. Lumahai is the place of my birth, and I grew up there with my father
Upepe, the Konohiki [headman] of Lumahai. When he died, the
Konohiki-ship descended to me. The boundary that separates Lumahai and Wainiha . . . comes to . . . Keakuakahea, a noted place, [be-
cause] when a certain man of Lumahai, whose name was Kuli, was
offering to the makahiki god at Lumahai, the god called out to him,
"E Kuli, do not bring your offering of fish here to Wainiha," and he
fetched the fish and took it back to Lumahai. This is what I heard from
my grandfather. At the time I was living with my parents, the time
when the makahiki god came on its circuit, those of Lumahai took
[their offering] to the altar called Kahalahala, and when the god came
to Kalukakae a noted place on the ridge there the people of Wainiha
paid their tribute. . . . I have always known these boundaries, from the
time I was born. (Ibid.)

By these testimonies, then, the classic centerpiece of the Makahiki festival, the god's annual circuit of the island, collecting offerings in each *ahupua'a*, was a tradition in Kaua'i before Kamehameha's rule. The Kaua'i reminiscences of the Makahiki god are notable, moreover, in mentioning only
offerings of food: fish in the text just cited, and in another, *ai*, a term for
'food' that usually means 'taro' when unmarked. This helps us understand
what was new in S. M. Kamakau's discussion of the Kamehameha reforms:
"The Makahiki gods made a circuit of the island to go and seize the wealth
[*waiwai*] of the people." There is good reason to believe that Kamehameha
put a considerable number of his personal gods into the Makahiki progress
of Lono, and that he thus turned the occasion into a centralized collection
of tributary wealth.

Or, to put it even more generally, Kamehameha made the Makahiki
into a ritual of state power, at the expense of his own chiefs as well as those
he had conquered. In a remarkable document published in 1906 but based
on older sources, Mokuoha'i Poepoe (1852–1913) tells how Kamehameha,
after achieving hegemony in Hawai'i, installed his living god, Kahoali'i, as
"the travelling god of the Makahiki." The honors accorded to Kahoali'i included the prostration tabu: "who does not prostrate himself before the procession of Kahoalii is a rebel." But the powers were even more significant, as
they amounted to a reservation to the king of the right to use force, which
is to say, the institution of state. For, Kahoali'i and the priests (*ka papa ka-*

huna) were constituted judges in all matters concerning injuries to the chiefs, who were thereby prohibited from taking life or using force in their own cause (Poepoe 1905–6:294–96).

In 1821, the British traveler Gilbert Mathison was apparently sold a bill of goods along with what appears to be the emblem *(lepa)* of Kaho'ali'i, which was represented as preceding the image of Captain Cook in processions around Hawai'i. This emblem was meant to clear the way for *"the Wandering God,"* Cook, as Mathison believed, and anyone who was touched by it was put to death (Mathison 1825:431–32). Rather than Cook-Lono, Mathison's description better fits the appearance and disposition assigned to Kahoali'i in the Makahiki.

Nor was Kahoali'i the only god of Kamehameha to appear in the Makahiki procession. Relating what seems to be a well-established tradition, Kepelino and S. M. Kamakau list a number of others, all of them notoriously associated with the protection of Kamehameha's rule: the poison god Kālaipāhoa, described by Kepelino as "the god who executes the law"; Kukama'ilimoku, "the god who takes the government by force"; Kihawahine, a deified chiefly woman of Maui, become a lizard goddess who protected Kamehameha's kingdom with the tenacity of a lizard's purchase; Kāpala'alaea, "the god of tribute"; and Lonoikamakahiki, the former ruling chief of Hawai'i and manifestation of Lono—whose bundled remains *(ka'ai)*, I believe, were indiscriminately considered those of Lono-Cook in the popular imagination (Kepelino HEN 1:113–25; Kirtley and Mookini 1977:50; Beckwith 1970: 125–26; S. Kamakau 1964:20; Sahlins 1989:384). In addition to "the god of tribute" (Kāpala'alaea), Kepelino also describes the Lono image or long god *(akua loa)* as the collector of tributes in men's loincloths *(malo)* and the short god *(akua poko)* as the collector of women's skirts *(pā'ū)*, thus reinforcing the sense of a Makahiki turned to the function of provisioning the kingship of Kamehameha.

The older descriptions of Malo and Kelou Kamakau depict a different, more decentralized Makahiki economics. Just prior to the procession of Lono, a large collection of offerings in food and goods was redistributed by the king, at least to the chiefs and their fighting men (K. Kamakau 1919–20:38–41; Malo 1951:142–43). But just as the powers of the ruling chiefs were undermined by Kamehameha's sovereignty, it appears that the redistributive economy in which they shared was superceded or eclipsed by the centralized accumulation of tributes rendered to the coterie of Kamehameha's gods joined to the Lono circuit. This explains S. Kamakau's (1964:20) complaints about the new practices of the Makahiki gods seizing the wealth of the people. John Papa 'I'i describes the storehouses of Kamehameha at Hawai'i island piled with bundles of tapa, skirts, and loincloths. These goods, he says, "had been given to the chiefs as *makahiki* taxes that were presented to the gods when they made their circuit of the island every twelfth month" (1959:121; see also Gast and Conrad 1973:200, 209, and Sahlins 1992:50–51, on the collection of royal tributes at Makahiki time). Malo mentions the collection of taxes during the Lono progress, but says nothing about their disposition.

Contrary to the assertion that the canonical Makahiki texts reflect the "formalization" of the ceremonies sponsored by Kamehameha, the detailed descriptions of Malo and Kelou Kamakau at best elide the innovations that are traditionally ascribed to the conqueror and, for the most part, ignore them altogether. By all evidence, Kamehameha used the Makahiki to sustain his conquest kingdom, politically and economically. He introduced his own gods of order and tribute into the Lono procession, and transformed the occasion into a centralized payment of taxes (*'auhau*). But Malo and K. Kamakau—the latter especially a witness to the old ceremonies—do not speak of these new gods and hardly or not at all of thesaurized royal levies. Their interest is in the archaic forms. One could even say their accounts are archaizing. Hence the possibility of the empirical findings indicated in the present and previous works: that Makahiki practices depicted in the Hawaiian ethnographic texts are paralleled in incidents of Cook's visit of 1778–79.

Calendrical Politics

Obeyesekere misunderstands the issues in the alternative possibilities for correlating Makahiki dates with the Gregorian calendar for 1778–79 (Sahlins 1989:404f.). He mistakenly represents these issues as follows:

> Sahlins never gave up the idea that Cook visited Kaua'i also in the time of Makahiki [another misrepresentation], but he is forced to recognize in his later work that the empirical evidence does not warrant a single Makahiki calendar. Thus he has recently come up with two standardized Makahiki calendars for the period of Cook's visits, which I reproduce in Figure 6 [table 1.1 in the present work]. The new flexibility is more apparent than real. The two optional calendars are also based on information available from Kamehameha's time, such that instead of a single formalized calendar we now have two! Although this might suggest that a Makahiki festival was going on in *Hawai'i* during the period 1778–79 [why?], it renders even more remote the idea that other islands, independent of and hostile to Hawai'i, were going to practice these same calendars. The existence of *two* calendars for the Kamehameha period may well indicate the existence of multiple calendars in other islands during the pre-Kamehameha period. (Ob. 99)

The question of inter-island variation in the Makahiki is of course a non sequitur to the already mistaken notion of "the existence of two calendars for the Kamehameha period [sic]." Once again the issue is not two Makahiki calendars but how to correlate the lunar dates of the Hawaiian rites with the Gregorian dates of Cook's visit, as the former would have two possible realizations in the terms of the latter, the November and December concordances. The issue of the political manipulation of Makahiki celebrations is also discussed in detail in the article laying out the calendrical options as well as in public archival materials (Sahlins 1989; Sahlins MS, Historic Dates of the Makahiki and Notes to Table II). The *Journal of the Polynesian Society* article documents Kamehameha's alteration of the dates of the Makahiki in 1793 and 1794 for the benefit of his relations to Vancouver (Sahlins 1989:389–91). On the first occasion, there was an abridgment of the bonito fishing ritual that interdicted movement on the sea. Indeed, the Vancouver documents "indicate that the termination rites [including the bonito fishing] were more complicated in ancient times than represented by Malo *ma*" (ibid., 389)—not less formalized, as Obeyesekere and others have said. Again in 1794, Kamehameha evidently postponed the final Makahiki rituals for one lunar month, when Vancouver obliged him to move from Hilo to Kealakekua. Obeyesekere pretends I never said any of this, and cites Valeri's observation of the 1794 alteration—also cited in Sahlins (1989:390)—as an argument against my supposed theory of the inflexibility of Makahiki calendars (Ob. 59). (In the manuscript work on Makahiki calendars publicly available since 1989, I proposed that Hawaiian intercalation practice was not regular, as in the ancient Greek or Chinese systems; rather, "the rectification of the calendar was a priestly function, and appears to have responded to pragmatic considerations, if averaging out over the long run near the appropriate three lunar-month intercalations every eight years" [p. 46B].)

The *Polynesian Society* piece again raises the possibility of political manipulation of the Makahiki calendar in connection with Cook's visit of 1778–79. Indeed, the section dealing with details of Cook's visit is prefaced by a Samoan proverb to just this effect: "With chiefs one does not count [i.e., argue about] phases of the moon" (Sahlins 1989:397). The problem arose particularly in the discussion of the alternative November and December Makahikis:

> We shall see that the coincidences between events recorded in the Cook annals and rites described in Makahiki annals (of Malo *mā*) definitely favor the December Makahiki, which is the one I have adopted in previous works (1981, 1985a). However, insofar as by either concordance Cook's course would intersect the god's progress, we should reserve the possibility that the Hawaiians then intercalated a month or otherwise improvised on the ritual sequence to accord with Cook's own movements. One does not argue with chiefs about phases of the

moon: we know this was done during Vancouver's visit of 1794. For that matter, the appearance of the Makahiki gods of sport (*akua pā'ani*) on the eve of Cook's departure in early February could have no justification in the traditional calendar—except by the logic that these gods and activities do indeed preside at Lono's passing on [from one district to the next]. In the same vein, we shall see in a moment, the Hawaiians would also have to compromise Makahiki rules by coming off to Cook's ships; on the other hand, the distinctive pattern of trade that ensued, as well as the activities and movements of King Kalani'ōpu'u and many other transactions recorded in the chronicles of the voyage, as I say, closely fit the classical Makahiki, assuming the December dating was in effect. (Sahlins 1989:405–6)

Cook Wrapped

Obeyesekere attempts to write off the significance attributed by Lieutenant King to Koah's actions in wrapping Cook in red tapa cloth and offering a small pig by the contention that Reverend Ellis's recording of the same from old Hawaiians is tautological. Regarding Ellis's report that "the priests clothed him [Cook] with the sacred cloth worn only by the god," Obeyesekere says there is "not a trace of evidence" for this, "except on the assumption that because Cook was Lono, and because he was draped in a red cloth by the priest, that cloth must be the god's own vestment" (Ob. 158). This argument is part of a now familiar historiographical enterprise involving the transfer of all information cited on the authority of Hawaiians that identifies Cook with Lono to the missionary who reports it. A footnote appended to it says the ship's officers "were clear that it was not Lono but Kū who was covered in (probably red) cloth" [Ob. 230n.15]; this is not true, if only because the principal image standing before the temple of *Lono* was described and drawn as so covered. In the same connection, Obeyesekere ignores Valeri's observations on the ritual wrapping of persons and things:

> In the course of the temple ritual several objects regarded as manifestations of the gods, such as plants and statues, are consecrated by being wrapped in bark cloths [a footnote here cites illustrative references of "innumerable examples of the consecration of idols, temple houses, and bones by wrapping them"]. . . . Why does wrapping have this effect? In the first place, this happens by convention; wrapping is the collectively accepted sign of the god's presence. But the relation of this sign to the belief in the god's invisible presence is not purely arbitrary (in the Saussurean sense). Indeed, the act of *removing* the object

from sight, of making it invisible, favors the implantation of a belief in the god's invisible presence because it creates the experience of a passage from a concrete reality to an invisible one, from a thing of perception to a thing of the mind, and therefore from an individual object to a general concept. . . . [W]hat is valid for the natural or artificial manifestations of the gods is no less valid for their human manifestations, that is, the high-ranking ali'i [chiefs], who come fully to embody the divine only by passing from the visible to the invisible and vice versa. This passage is often made possible by wrapping and unwrapping with bark cloth, feather mantles, and so on. (Valeri 1985: 300–301)

Of course, this was not the level of British understanding of what was happening at Kealakekua when they described the wrapping of images or of Captain Cook. But the notices confirm Lieutenant King's insight that Cook and the gods were thus accorded the same respect. The two images at the entrance of Hikiau temple were wrapped in red cloth at the beginning of Cook's stay, as were also the central image of Kū and the feather gods in the priests' canoe at the formal welcoming of Cook (Cook and King 1784, 3:6, 7–8, 160; Beaglehole 1967:513–14). One of the images wrapped in tapa at Hikiau was specifically identified by Ellis as Lono; also, the principal image in front of the Lono temple was wrapped in a red tapa cloth or red covered with white (Ellis 1782, 2:180, cf. 181; Murray-Oliver 1975:112–13). Again, after Cook's death, in a ceremony at Hikiau "the carved Images on the Morai were covered with red cloth" (Anonymous of NLA Account, 18). Captain Cook was repeatedly honored with the same treatment: wrapped in red cloth for the second time on 17 January in a ceremony at Hikiau, again the next day in a ceremony at the House of Lono (Hale o Lono), once more at the "occasion of state" by the Lono priest Ka'ō'ō, not to forget the red cloth "presented" to him before the king's house on the fatal 14 February (Cook and King 1784, 3:7, 13, 18; Samwell 1957:14). On one occasion, too, Captain Clerke was so draped in red tapa when he came ashore, and Samwell in white (Beaglehole 1967:1165).

Lono at Hikiau

It would be more precise to say the British recognized Cook's *status* as "Lono" (rather than his appellation as such), since for the most part the chroniclers refer to his Hawaiian identity as "*the* Orono." This indication of an abstract status is worth noting also because of Obeyesekere's contention that the ceremonies which followed at Hikiau saw the installation of Cook as a Hawaiian chief by the proper name of "Lono"—who was by no means the god of that name. Getting Cook to Hikiau under a chiefly name allows Obeyesekere to raise the distraction, which he must know is erroneous, that if Cook were the manifestation of the Makahiki god, he should not have entered this sacrificial temple (of the *luakini* type):

> It is clear that Cook is being introduced to the Hawaiian deities, but not as the god Lono. This particular temple [Hikiau] was the shrine of the king and sacred to the war god Kū, and as Sahlins says, "It was a temple of human sacrifice, specially forbidden in the peaceful rites of Lono." It is strange that if Cook was considered to be the god Lono himself he would have been invited to this place antithetic to his persona. (Ob. 83)

It is human sacrifice which is forbidden in Lono rites, not the god that is forbidden this temple. Obeyesekere must know his objection is erroneous because Hikiau was the center of the Makahiki rite, the place from which the god departed on his circuit of the island and to which he returned. Indeed, as Malo and Kelou Kamakau clearly state, it is at the *luakini* (or temple of the Hikiau type) that the king ritually met Lonomakua after the sham battle (*kāliʻi*) between them that reinstated the earthly ruler. The ritual of welcome, remark for future use, includes a royal sacrifice of a pig to Lono (K. Kamakau 1919–20:44–45; Malo 1951:150). So, if on landing for the first time at Kealakekua, having made a near circuit of Hawai'i island, Cook is directly escorted to Hikiau temple, this can hardly be taken in evidence against his status as Lonomakua—au contraire. And if Obeyesekere had forgotten the relevant passages in Malo *mā*, there is the explication in the article under (sometimes) discussion, in rejoinder to essentially the same criticism as penned by Bergendorff *mā*. The Bergendorff folks' arguments about Cook at Hikiau, I suggested, were based on simple misunderstandings of the ethnography (Sahlins 1989:397–98):

> For instance, their mistaken idea that, because the normal *haipule* ceremonies are suspended during the Makahiki, the royal *luakini* temples are not used during this season—hence that Cook was received in the *luakini* temple (Hikiau) at Kealakekua in 1779 indicates there was no Makahiki going on. Or again, their argument that, as Kū was the major god of the temple, Lono was not worshipped there, so how could Cook be? Even Malo's text is clear on these points, since the term *luakini* remains untranslated in his description of the Makahiki: "It was on the same evening that the Makahiki god was brought back to the *luakini*" (1951:150; Emerson's footnote to this sentence explains: "A *heiau* [temple] of the highest class, a war temple, in which human sacrifices were offered"). Or, if the Danish scholars had consulted the neglected text of K. Kamakau on the ritual events of the evening to which Malo here refers, they would find that the king enters the temple—again *luakini*, as this is a bilingual text—to sacrifice a pig to Lono: "calling upon the deity: 'O Lononuiakea [All-embracing-Lono], here is your pig'" (K. Kamakau 1919–20:44–45). The image of Lono in the forecourt of Hikiau temple is noted in the Cook documents. (Ellis 1782 2:180; cf. Valeri 1985:184)

Clark Gable for Cook?

Having effaced the major cleavage in Hawaiian society between the ruling chiefs and Lono priests (in the interest of ignoring their differential relations to Captain Cook), Obeyesekere claims to uniquely take account of the play of structural differences among Hawaiians in the determination of Cook's fate (cf. Sahlins 1981 : 33ff., 1985a : 122–25). This in contrast to essentialist views of "stereotypic reproduction" which presume that Hawaiians monolithically responded to the arrival of the foreigners by prescriptively acting out a preexisting cultural scheme:

> On the analytical level, the strategy employed here refutes the idea that Hawaiians (and other preliterate people) are given to a form of "stereotypical reproduction," as if they were acting out a cultural schema without reflection. By contrast I have shown how the pragmatics of common sense, practical rationality, and improvisational creativity result in the choice of a cultural scenario from a variety of possible ones. Yet it can be argued that, although I introduce some flexibility into the analysis, I have nevertheless attributed to Hawaiians a single scenario, one that reflects the political motivations of Kalani'opu'u and perhaps the ruling class of Hawai'i. Following my stated assumption that there are multiple structures being manipulated in terms of rational pragmatics, I shall show that such structures and motivations are by no means confined to the political life. Cook's arrival was a powerfully unsettling experience and people must have reacted to it in a variety of ways. It is, for example, difficult to believe that the women and lower classes shared the chiefly interpretations; but even if they did, owing to the power of the establishment and its

priests, they must have had other ideas about Cook and his crew. (Ob. 91)

This must be an example of what Obeyesekere, in a fit of grave humor, refers to as marshalling the evidence (Ob. 100), since he repeatedly taxes me with a view of Hawaiian history as "stereotypic reproduction." For a number of reasons, however, including that I have been explicitly criticizing this disposition of structuralist history since the 1970s—for which critical purpose I brought the phrase (of Godelier's) into discussion—one might better characterize Obeyesekere's objections as "de-sahlinization" (see appendix 11). The simple fact about social variations among Hawaiians in response to Cook is that, while Obeyesekere claims to take such differences seriously whereas I do not, the opposite is true. What he says about women and lower classes is a self-serving and unacknowledged copy of what I have written (e.g., Sahlins 1985a: 121–25). It plays no particular role in his analysis. On the other hand, he makes the critical conflicts of chiefs and priests disappear—indeed he makes the Lono priests disappear altogether—since these differences would implicate Cook's connection to the god, not to mention their role in the motivation of Cook's death.

A related historiographical issue may be introduced by a citation from the Frazer lecture (Sahlins 1985a):

Death of Cook: death of Lono. The event was absolutely unique, and it was repeated every year. For the event (any event) unfolds simultaneously on two levels: as individual action and as collective representation; or better, as the *relation* between certain life histories and a history that is, over and above these, the existence of societies. To paraphrase Clifford Geertz [1961: 153–54], the event is a unique actualization of a general phenomenon. (Sahlins 1985a: 108)

The passage is apropos of Obeyesekere's presentation of my position as unconcerned with individuality in general and with the individuality of Cook in particular. The same text—which had already made the point that Cook would not have been killed had he known how to swim—ends with a discussion of the significant role of Cook's temperament, specifically of his hubris, in his death (Sahlins 1985a: 131, 134–35). Besides, the whole point of the Frazer lecture was that Cook died because he did not conform to the cultural categories and scenarios by which Hawaiians understood him. According to Obeyesekere, however, in my view,

Cook was Lono. The individual Cook is irrelevant; Clark Gable could as easily have taken his place. Sahlins does not tell us what would have happened if Cook's actions did *not* fit the cultural scenario. (Ob. 56)

I have to disagree with this reading. Clark Gable for Cook? No, no: Clark Gable for Mr. Christian. Gary Cooper for Cook.

Blurred Images

Obeyesekere sows considerable confusion about the Makahiki im-age—about what it looked like and represented, let alone its direct observation by the British or that Cook was obliged to imitate it. By Obeyesekere's telling, the Makahiki images illustrated in Malo's book (our fig. 1.1) and by Webber in 1779 (fig. 1.3) are supposed to represent, not a figuration of Lonomakua, but the mast and canoe of Lono. "Did Ha-waiians really believe," he asks, "that Cook's two enormous ships showed even a remote resemblance to Lono's mast and canoe, represented by Malo and Webber (see Figures 2, 3, and 4)" (Ob. 61). But then, the "Figure 2" to which Obeyesekere refers is captioned "Lono, Represented as a Crosspiece Icon"; it is from Malo's *Hawaiian Antiquities* (1951 : 144). On the other hand, his "Figure 3" is a drawing of a canoe with a basketwork food container attached to its outrigger, rendered according to the description contributed by Malo's editor, N. B. Emerson—being Emerson's version of the canoe by which Lono returns to Kahiki. Finally, "Figure 4" is a drawing of *H.M.S. Reso-lution* by Webber. A clue to this mishmash of representations—the Makahiki icon, the so-called canoe of Lono, and Cook's ship—seems to lie in the question, "did Hawaiians really believe" all these were alike? The confusion is apparently motivated by Obeyesekere's haste to demonstrate the Hawai-ians' empirical rationality (as usual by an appeal to our own), here rendered irrefutable by a kooky congeries of images. What it actually turns into is an example of how Hawaiian ethnography and testimony can be dissolved in the acid bath of Western commonsense realism. For, if one rephrased Obe-yesekere's question in a more pertinent form, namely, could Hawaiians really believe that the image of Lono could resemble the sails of Cook's ships? the answer would be yes. Discussing the Lonomakua cross-piece with its pendant tapa cloth, Malo (1951:145) said just that: "Captain Cook was named Lono after this god, because of the resemblance the sails of his ship bore to the *tapa* of the god." As for his ship, tradition speaks of it as a temple (*heiau*) or a floating island (this from Kahiki). Hawaiian thought is not the pensée bourgeoise—although it is just as given to empirical speculations.

Cookamamie

The narrative of Cook's death presented here closely follows an earlier discussion (Sahlins 1985a:105–7, 129) in order to consider Obeyesekere's objections to it (Ob. 177ff.). These objections include a denial (of the familiar literalist kind) of the whole framework:

> One of the serious problems that Sahlins faces in his mythic interpretation of Cook's death is that there is nothing in Hawaiian culture that recognizes a Kāli'i in reverse. At best one might say that in the Kāli'i the king is symbolically killed, never the god. (Ob. 182)

Of course, the point is that, in reverse, everything is reversed: the god comes ashore to be killed by partisans of the king. A radical historical contradiction set off a series of motivated categorical negations. But the premise of Obeyesekere's objection is that Hawaiians can only stereotypically reproduce their prescribed cultural schemes (the *kāli'i*), or else all such cultural schemes are off. As previously noticed, this demand of cultural inflexibility is not an ad hoc disputational tactic on Obeyesekere's part but an aporia of his theory of "practical rationality"—which also accounts for the literalism of the critique. So, for Obeyesekere, the scene was no *kāli'i* in reverse because Cook did not wade ashore to confront the king, but came in one of the ship's boats, and went inland to the house where the king was staying. (In fact, judging from the problem the survivors had reaching the boats an hour later, the tide was out; according to information from land records and visible remains, Keaweaheulu's house where the king was staying was up the main path at Ka'awaloa about 100 yards from the shore.) Moreover, it was on Cook's way back to the shore with the king literally in hand that the conflict broke out. Obeyesekere makes out that I am concealing all this because it would falsify the notion of the *kāli'i* in reverse (Ob. 181). But obviously the literal differences do not contradict the inversion of the *kāliʻi* struc-tures. Cook waded ashore with his marines to confront the king, to take him hostage; everyone knows that. The king's wife, Kaneikapolei interposed herself between them. Cook was defended by a second (Lieutenant Phillips) and killed by a warrior henchman of the king. All this is the *kāliʻi* in reverse. But in the event, the denouement was the same: the god fell and was sacri-ficed by the king. Cook's body was offered at the temple by Kalaniʻōpuʻu.

Alternatively, consider the structural implications of Obeyesekere's theoretical practice. Unless the historical circumstances afford or permit a literal implementation of a people's cultural categories—if instead, there are perceptible contradictions—then they will forthwith abandon such re-ceived cultural understandings and rely on a universal natural realism.

Paradoxically, this literal realism leads again and again to critical exag-gerations. With regard to the details of Cook's death, Obeyesekere poses an extraordinary farrago of inaccurate charges against my narration, marked as often by misrepresentation of the historical texts as by distortions of mine. Some of these arguments are so tortuous they get tangled in their own traces and wind up non sequiturs. Some others have no apparent relevance to Cook's apotheosis. Still, the general intention seems to be something else: to show that my presentation of the historical evidence cannot be trusted—and if not in these details, then presumably even less on the big issues. Hence I am accused of a variety of scholarly misdemeanors, including subtle—and sometimes not so subtle—"rephrasing" of the documentary re-ports (Ob. 177), and also of inventing pieces of the story of Cook's death without any textual warrant (Ob. 178, 179, 182). What is most extraordi-nary about all this calumny is that it is false: plainly and simply untrue.

The main items of this cookamamie critique are the following:

1. Obeyesekere supposes that I have falsified the tone and character of Cook's death scene by inserting a Shakespearean allusion of which I (and readers) are presumably unaware—though it was of course purposive. It is where I say Kalaniʻōpuʻu's wife (Kaneikapolei) and two chiefs told the king "such *stories of the death of kings* as to force him to *sit upon the ground*" (Ob. 178). The italics, which are Obeyesekere's, indicate that he is onto my game, which he proceeds to prove by quoting from *Richard II,* act III, scene 2. This discovery shows how I make a Frazerian divine king myth out of Cook's death. Besides, the dramatic allusion is untrue to the event:

Because there were no contemporary Hawaiian accounts of these events, one must rely on the British ones. Not one British account even remotely indicates that Kalaniʻōpuʻu's wife and the two chiefs told the king "stories of the death of kings." Quite the contrary, this was a tense and moving scene and no time for story telling. (Ob. 178)

Well, for starts, here is the text of Samwell's journal (a source Obeyesekere cites often enough):

> The Indians [Hawaiians] opened and made a Lane for the marines to pass and did not offer to molest them. Captain Cook followed them having hold of Kariopoo's [Kalaniʻōpuʻu's] Hand who came with him very willingly, leaning on two of his people and accompanyed by his two Sons, the younger of whom (Ke-owa) went directly into the Pinnace expecting his father to follow. The old Priest still attended them making the same savage Noise. When they had come near the Beach an old Woman came crying to the King & throwing her arms round his neck, with the assistance of two of the Chiefs attending him made him sit down by the side of a double Canoe hauled on the Rocks. They wou'd not suffer him to go any further, *telling him that if he went on board the Ship he would be killed.* Kariopoo on this hung down his head & looked disconsolate as if expecting some disagreeable Consequences would ensue which it was not in his power to prevent. (Beaglehole 1967:1196; my emphasis)

Samwell's statement is consistent with other British accounts that (not at all remotely) indicate the Hawaiians gathered at Kaʻawaloa were apprehensive of Cook's "designs," including the explicit fears he meant to kill the king (Anonymous of Mitchell 1781; Ellis 1782, 2:107; Gilbert 1982:106; Rickman 1966:319).

2. Notice Samwell's remark about Kaneikapolei, the king's wife: "an old Woman came crying to the King & throwing her arms round his neck, with the assistance of two of the Chiefs attending him made him sit down." Obeyesekere refuses to see this as an analogy to the cosmogonic triad of the Kumulipo—the struggle of man and god decided by the woman's choice— because I deliberately eliminated the two chiefs who, according to him, played the decisive role (Ob. 181–82; but see Sahlins 1985a:106 on the two chiefs). He also thinks I misunderstood the relevant passages of the cosmogonic chant, and that I got the idea of a triad from Christianity. He is wrong about the Kumulipo (see above, 22–25). Nor is there any analogy to the Christian Trinity in the cosmic contest of the original personages, Kane the god and Kiʻi the man, over the first-born woman, Laʻilaʻi. As for the initiative taken by Kaneikapolei "with the assistance" of two unnamed chiefs,

Samwell was hardly the only one to so report it. The master's mate William Harvey said the king had consented to go to the boats when "his wife fell aweeping and urged him not" (Log, 14 Feb 1779). Henry Roberts wrote likewise that Kalani'ōpu'u would have willingly come off "but was hindered by his wife and those about him" (Log, 14 Feb 1779). Another account has it: "as they drew near the water side Kerreboo was stoped by a Woman who was crying and two Chiefs, the Woman and a Chief forced him to sit down, the Old King then seemed dejected and frightened" (Anonymous of NLA Account, 14). In Bayly's description, Cook and the king had stopped at the water's edge and were talking "when an elderly woman (of some note) came & threw her arms around the King's neck & begun to cry, & the Chiefs encircled him & made him sit down—they moreover said he should not go on board" (cited in Gould 1928:315). In the official version published by Lieutenant King:

> Things were in this prosperous train, the two boys being already in the pinnace, and the rest of the party having advanced near the waterside, when an elderly woman called Kaneekabareea, the mother of the boys, and one of the king's favourite wives, came after him, and with many tears, and entreaties, besought him not to go on board. At the same time, two Chiefs, who came along with her, laid hold of him, and insisting, that he should go no farther, forced him to sit down. (Cook and King 1784, 3:43)

Shifting the decisive role to the two chiefs, as Obeyesekere does, would seem not to meet the criticism about anthropological treatments of the pivotal action of the woman in this affair recently articulated by John Charlot:

> Curiously—although, in the most studied, discussed, and disputed episode in Hawaiian history, a woman is at the very pivot of the action, changing the direction of a crowd of warriors against the wishes of her husband—no anthropologist has analysed the role of Kalola, the wife of Kalani'ōpu'u in the events surrounding the death of Captain Cook. (Charlot 1991:147)

Charlot is literally correct about the failure of any anthropologist to analyze the role of Kalola, another of the King's wives, since she was still in Maui at the time, as the British learned (Beaglehole 1967:616). They also knew that the woman concerned was Kaneikapolei, as documented by Mr. King's notice (see also Beaglehole 1967:513n, 535, 616, 1168). With regard to Kaneikapolei, it would be incorrect to say that no anthropologist has analyzed her role in the events, i.e., "at the very pivot of the action, changing the direction of a crowd of warriors against the wishes of her husband"; see Sahlins 1985a: 106, 129. Otherwise, Charlot's point about the pivotal role of the king's wife is well taken (if not heeded by Obeyesekere).

3. Obeyesekere offers an involuted criticism of my representation of what went on when Cook initially set out to find the king. In the end, Cook had no more success than Obeyesekere, who along the way somehow loses the thread (Ob. 177–78). The argument concerns the sentence (in Sahlins 1985a: 106): "In the beginning, as he [Cook] went 'to find the king,' pigs were pressed upon him; and as he waited for Kalaniopu'u to waken, more offerings of red tapa cloth—proving that the English captain was still the image of the Hawaiian god." The statement contains an allusion to Mr. King's observation that Cook was often so wrapped in red tapa cloth, in the same way as Hawaiian temple images.

Obeyesekere devotes two paragraphs to an attempt to deconstruct this sentence. Failing to disprove it, he ends by misrepresenting it, offering his own rephrasing as an example of my tinkering with the texts. First comes the null evidence that Lieutenant Phillips's account, as transmitted by Captain Clerke, does not mention pigs or tapa cloth offerings—and Phillips was an eyewitness. Note again, however, that a nonmention is not the same as a mention of nonexistence, and that Phillips and other eye-witnesses contributed anonymously to the descriptions of the event penned by other journalists.

In the same vein, Obeyesekere goes on to say that neither did Mr. King mention the pigs or tapa cloth in his private journal. However, in the next paragraph it is acknowledged that in the published *Voyage,* King spoke of the "accustomed offerings of small hogs" being presented to Cook as he made his way to the king's house. To offset this, Obeyesekere now relates that on the evening before, as King's own journal reports, the Hawaiians were becoming "insolent," that they recoiled and then laughed when Cook had the marines threaten them with muskets, and that they led Cook on a wild goose chase when he tried to intervene in the altercation between Palea (the king's man) and Midshipmen Edgar and Vancouver. Inserted by Obeyesekere to show that Captain Cook was hardly being treated as a god, these incidents could only demonstrate such by our standards of divinity. The argument ignores the specificity of the status of Cook-Lono as a royal adversary at this moment and the ambivalent dispositions of the chiefs. Indeed Maui-the-trickster is a paradigmatic Hawaiian figure of defiance of the god in favor of humanity. Nothing is known, incidentally, about prostration and other deferences that may have been involved in the Hawaiians' stratagems.

Obeyesekere's argument now goes back on itself by acknowledging that Samwell does say Cook was accorded the usual prostration and asked if he wanted hogs while on the way to find the king; and when Cook got to the house he was presented with red tapa cloth. However, Obeyesekere observes, Samwell was not there. On the other hand, still, "there is nothing inherently improbable in this account" (Ob. 178). But then, says Obeyesekere, Lieutenant King converted Samwell's report about asking if Cook wanted pigs into "the accustomed offerings." This is hardly relevant, since I conservatively adopted a Samwellian phrasing—"pigs were pressed upon him"—because the usual ceremonies of offering apparently were not achieved, Cook brushing the prestations aside. Yet certainly King was correct: such were customary offerings to Cook. They had invariably been made to him with ritual orations. King's wording is paralleled in other accounts, such as Burney's: "When Captain Cook with his party landed, the Indians made a Lane and some of them brought Hogs which they offered him" (MSb, 14 Feb 1779).

So now where are we? Exactly where we began, with Sahlins's description of the prestations, now reconfirmed: "In the beginning, as he [Cook] went 'to find the king,' pigs were pressed upon him; and as he waited for Kalaniopu'u to waken, more offerings of red tapa cloth—proving that the English captain was still the image of the Hawaiian god" (Sahlins 1985a: 106). And what, then, is Obeyesekere's objection? It is that "These two references are compressed into a single event: Cook, as a divinity, is given pigs and offerings of red tapa cloth" (Ob. 178). A single event? You figure it. Lono (Cook) was prostrated to as usual and offered pigs as usual on the way to the house; and he was given red tapa cloth, also as usual, while waiting for the king in front of the house.

It only needs to be added that Obeyesekere presents this disputation as the leading example of his superior attention to language use in the historic documents, in contrast to Sahlins's dubious rephrasings thereof (Ob. 177).

4. Here is another such example: "Sahlins says that over a hundred Hawaiians participated in Cook's death. Aside from the fact that this numerical indicator is entirely Sahlins's invention, is there any resemblance here to Kāli'i? 'Ritual murder' is *ritual* and never murder" (Ob. 182).

Obeyesekere is doubly reckless in these comments. Certainly he was careless in making the false charge that "the numerical indicator is entirely Sahlins's invention." A very accessible journal, Mr. King's, reads: "the Indians set up a Great Shout & hundreds surrounded the body to dispatch him [Cook], with daggers & Clubs" (Beaglehole 1967:557). This is also to be found in Admiralty Log 55/123, attributed to Trevenan, which states that when Cook fell the Hawaiians set up a great shout "& pressed on him by hundreds to dispatch him" (Trevenan Log, 14 Feb 1779). It is also reckless to say that "'ritual murder' is *ritual* and never murder" in hierarchical orders that symbolically synthesize regicide, deicide, human sacrifice, and royal succession (see, for example, Adler 1982; Heusch 1982, 1985). Note that in Hawaii, *kauwā*, who are despised transgressors of the king's authority or enemies destined for sacrifice, are in that respect also *akua*, 'gods' (Malo 1951: 70). In any event, in Hawaii, where the new ruler is generally responsible for the death of his predecessor, either in battle or by sorcery, Obeyesekere's dictum is better reversed: the king is always murdered, and the murder is ritual—by sacrifice or as sorcery (Valeri 1985). Nor should it be forgotten that the king's sovereignty is achieved in the Makahiki at the expense or by the inclusion of the god; hence the fears of a takeover expressed at the British return to Kealakekua.

5. Another species of criticism combines the accusations of fabrication of evidence with the involuted self-deconstruction. The occasion is my citation of Lieutenant King as saying that when the report came to Ka'awaloa that the British blockading party had killed a chief, the king was still on the ground "with the strongest marks of terror on his countenance"; whereas, according to Obeyesekere, Mr. King had actually said "terror and dejection," which anyhow King borrowed from Phillips's "dejected and frightened." I also fail to mention that Phillips said so in reference to the moment the chiefs forced the king down, while Lieutenant King "has this experience much later." These accusations of playing fast and loose with the documents are trumped by the assertion that I made up the story that in the sequel the king "soon disappears from the scene" (from Sahlins 1985a:107). Says Obeyesekere:

> Not one account confirms this. Rather, the king's exit is required by the dramaturgical view of these events that is at the heart of Sahlins's thesis. Consequently, like a character in a play, Kalani'ōpu'u "disappears from the scene." (Ob. 179)

Obeyesekere frequently dismisses Lieutenant King's official account of the voyage when it conflicts with his own theories simply by alleging without further warrant that it must have been cribbed from Samwell, Phillips, or whomever, since nothing is said about the issue in King's personal journal.

In any event, I had already cited Phillips's "frightened and dejected" on the same page (Sahlins 1985a: 107). Nor are King's descriptions of Kalani'ōpu'u's state out of line. Others say the old king "appeared much distressed" (Samwell 1957: 17) or "looked disconsolate" (Samwell in Beaglehole 1967: 1196), "irresolute and frightened" (Burney MSb, 14 Feb 1779), and again "dejected and frightened" (Anonymous of NLA, 4 [14 Feb 1779]). If Obeyesekere is attempting to deny that the king was made to perceive Cook as a threat—or indeed a mortal threat as Samwell and certain other journalists said—the attempt is again quixotic. Nor is it true that Lieutenant King's mention of Kalani'ōpu'u's terror refers to a moment much later than the time he was forced to sit upon the ground (by sad stories of the death of kings). Lieutenant King merely said it was a continuing apprehension from that moment: "All this time, the old king remained on the ground, with the strongest marks of terror and dejection in his countenance" (Cook and King 1784, 3:44). As for the insinuation that I fabricated the notion that the king soon left the scene, that he did so is remarked by Hawaiian as well as British sources. In Lieutenant Burney's account "gathered from those who were on the spot," Cook let Kalani'ōpu'u go just after the intercession of Kaneikapolei and the two chiefs, when the people began to arm themselves. At that time, before overt hostilities began, "the Old Chief was immediately taken away and no more seen" (Burney MSb, 14 Feb 1779; also in Manwaring 1931: 135). (Note that he is also not seen in Webber's famous painting of Cook's death.) Although S. M. Kamakau mistakenly presumed that the royal wife at the scene was Kalola rather than Kaneikapolei—which at least indicates his description does not come from Lieutenant King's official account (see Cook and King 1784, 3:43)—he likewise places the king's disappearance from the scene at the same moment as Burney, that is, as sequitur to Kaneikapolei's pleading:

> When Ka-lola heard that Ka-lima was dead, shot by the strangers [Rickman's party on the southern side of the bay], she ran out of the sleeping house, threw her arms about the shoulders of Ka-lani-'opu'u and said, "O heavenly one! let us go back!" Ka-lani-'opu'u turned to go back. Captain Cook tried to grasp him by the hand, but Ka-lani-mano-ok-a-ho'owaha stuck his club in the way, and Ka-lani-'opu'u was borne away by his chiefs and warriors to Maunaloia, and the fight began. (Kamakau 1961: 102–3)

So goes Obeyesekere's critique of the narrative of Cook's death, a mixture of slander and error, careless or unaware of the documentary sources and too quick to make charges of disreputable scholarly conduct against others.

The reader is invited to make a serious investigation of the rest of this narrative, mainly concerning who in particular stabbed Captain Cook, which is not directly pertinent here. I argue it was the warrior Nuha (or Kanuha) of Ka'awaloa, a henchman of the king (and father of Kelou Kamakau). The identification is supported by the explicit testimony of Edgar (Log, 14 Feb 1779), the astronomer Bayly (citing "natives," MSb, 21 Feb 1779) and Samwell (on the authority of the Lono priest, "honest Keli'ikea"; Beaglehole 1967:1202; Samwell 1957:23–24). The *Mooolelo Hawaii*, it should be said, identifies the man who wielded the dagger as Kālaimanōkaho'owaha, also a king's man; Samwell (on the priest's information) identifies this person rather as the one who first struck Cook with a club, which was not a fatal blow (Kahananui 1984:174).

Priests' Sorrows, Women's Joys, and Stereotypic Reproduction

It has been noticed how Obeyesekere claims to uniquely take into account the socially differentiated responses of Hawaiians to Captain Cook, as between women and men, commoners and chiefs, while accusing the anthropologists of monolithically overriding these differences. "Essentializing" is the current word for it. It has also been noticed that the reverse is true: Obeyesekere ignores the documented differences, as between Ka'awaloa chiefs and Lono priests, that others have remarked in detail as being critical to Cook's downfall. In the name of a superior attention to the historical texts, this critical gambit continues with regard to the events following Cook's death, especially as it concerns the Lono priests and Hawaiian women aboard the British ships.

Of the "tabu man" and the other Lono priest who asked the famous singular question, when would Cook come back to us? Obeyesekere writes: "It is very clear that their feelings were not of 'great sorrow,' as Sahlins says, but fear of Cook's 'ghost' or his return as an avenging deity" (Ob. 138). Let us leave aside the "ghost" and "avenging deity" except to note again the contradictions to Obeyesekere's arguments about Hawaiians' pragmatic realism (= ghosts?) and the European origin of the idea that Cook was a deity. Actually, Obeyesekere is correct with regard to the last: they did fear Cook would be an "avenging deity," namely Lono, as the descriptions of this incident and later reports confirm (see pp. 91–93). What remains unclear is why Obeyesekere denies that the priests expressed "great sorrow," alleging instead that it was Sahlins's idea, were it not that this move is part of a larger project of stonewalling the connections between the Lono priests and Cook. For, Lieutenant King's remarks about the tabu man "lamenting with abundance of tears, the loss of the *Orono*" (Cook and King 1784, 3:68) is not the only observation of the priests' attitude and their solidarity with the British on this occasion. The two men, according to another close account, had been "sent by our friend Kerrikae [Keli'ikea, the Lono priest] with a piece of the Capt.ʼ flesh, this they told us was his share and knowing that we were desirous of recovering the remains of the Body he had sent it as a testimony and grief for our loss" (Anonymous of NLA Account, 13–14).

Mr. King's personal journal adds specifications of the incident, including another testimony to the split between the Lono priests and Kalani'ōpu'u *mā* (Kalani'ōpu'u 'folks') at Ka'awaloa. It indicates that,

> the flesh before us had been sent to Kao [Ka'ō'ō, the old head priest of Lono, the "bishop," uncle or grandfather to Keli'ikea] (to perform with it as we suppose some religious ceremony), but that he had sent it to us, as we had desir'd so ardently the body. He [the "tabu man," now on board the *Resolution* with the flesh] told us that if it should come to the Knowledge of the King they would be all kill'd, which was the reason of his bringing it in the dark, nor could our perswasions make him stay all Night, he asking us if we wishd him taken & killd; he told us that Koah (Brittanee) was not to be trusted, that Terreeoboo [Kalani'ōpu'u] & all the people were our Mortal enemies, & were mad with revenge: he by all means advis'd me not to go on shore, for that above all they wishd to kill me (as the supposed Chief) & in fact that they wishd for nothing more than to fight us. (Beaglehole 1967:560)

Perhaps nothing so well epitomizes the state of opposition between these priests of Kealakekua and the Ka'awaloa people of the king, or their contrasting relations to the British, than the distinct character of the contacts between the two Hawaiian parties and Cook's ships on the following morning, the 16th of February. At nearly the same time, two young men swam out to the *Discovery* from Hikiau temple at Kealakekua and a canoe with three men approached the *Resolution* from Ka'awaloa. Samwell recorded the remarkable differences in their behavior:

> two Boys swam from Oheekeeaw [Hikiau] to the Discovery, each with a Spear in his hand; they came to the stern of the Ship and sung together in a solemn Manner, concerning the late accident as we guessed, by their naming Orono (Capt. Cook) & pointing to the Town where he was killed & sometimes to the opposite shore. They remained in the water about 10 or 15 minutes singing all the time, at last we told them to come on board, which they immediately did and presented their Spears to us, which we returned to them when they went

ashore, which they did in a short time tho' they wanted to stay with us; it is difficult to guess what could induce these Boys to put such confidence in us as to venture on board at this time at the hazard of their Lives. (Beaglehole 1967:1210)

Samwell goes on, without a break:

Much about the same time a Canoe came to the Resolution from the Town of Kavaroa [Ka'awaloa] in which were three men, they came almost within pistol shot of the Ship, then one of them stood up with Capt" Cook's Hat on his head, he threw Stones at us, smacked his backside in Contempt of us, shewed us the Hat & in an insulting manner waved it over his head; we fired several muskets at him but they all got ashore unhurt.

Although Obeyesekere claims to alone recognize such diversity in Hawaiian responses to Cook *mā*, including the relevant contrasts between women and men, he manages to obscure the latter distinction as well. This was for the purpose of denying an interesting distinction in women's behavior I had pointed out—though he also denies I make any such distinctions (Ob. 91). Indeed, he offers my observation of the women's distinctive behavior as "Example 1: Uncritical Reading of Texts" (Ob. 67). As the example turns out to be spurious, the caption is a fair commentary on Obeyesekere's historiographical and disputational methods. The event in question occurred on February 17, when the British (in Obeyesekere's words) "set fire to the village [of Kealakekua], including the royal temple and the residences of priests" (Ob. 67). Parenthetically, the royal temple of Hikiau was not consumed on this occasion, nor did the British ever burn it down. Hawaiians had partially done so nearly two weeks before, apparently accidentally—a critical reading hardly worth mentioning were it not that Obeyesekere uses this mistaken supposition of vandalism in the psychological cocktail he later serves up as an explanation of Cook's fatal behavior (see below, appendix 14). However, the significant detail at stake is whether, as Lieutenant King said, some women on board the British ships cried out 'good' [*maita'i*] on seeing the flames of the burning town on February 17—or more exactly whether *some* did, as Mr. King reported, or only *one* did, as Samwell said. Since I used King's statement (of "some women") as an evidence of certain gender cleavages in Hawaiian society, this shows how untrustworthy I am with the texts. Also J. C. Beaglehole, who made the same error (Ob. 68).

First, Lieutenant King's remark, which both Obeyesekere and I quote:

It is very extraordinary, that, amidst all these disturbances, the women of the island, who were on board, never offered to leave us, nor discovered the smallest apprehensions either for themselves or their friends ashore. So entirely unconcerned did they appear, that some of them, who were on deck when the town was in flames, seemed to admire the sight [my edition looks like 18th-century 'fight' because the i is undotted; I will accept Obeyesekere's 'sight,' however], and frequently cried out, that it was *maitai,* or very fine. (Cook and King 1784, 3:77)

To this I had appended the comment that Samwell "heard the same on the *Discovery*" even as he reported that "we could see the Indians flying from their homes all round the Bay, and carrying their canoes and household goods on their backs up the country" (Sahlins 1981:51).

According to Obeyesekere, the error of Beaglehole and myself comes from trusting Mr. King's published account, which was edited by Reverend Douglas and "used all sorts of other sources" (Ob. 68) in describing Cook's death (three days before what we are talking about here). Now, since only Samwell mentions the *maita'i,* King must have got it from him. And Samwell had said *only one* woman cried "maitai": "We had two or three Girls on board all this Day, one of them looking on the Town burning said it was maitai or very fine" (Beaglehole 1967:1213). So this is the accusation:

Sahlins uncritically accepts the line of prejudice coming from King through Beaglehole and inadvertently omits the crucial sentence that precedes the Samwell quotation he uses. In any case it is naive to unambiguously state that expressions like "very fine," be it in Polynesian or English, can be divorced from the context of utterance and given a literal interpretation. One must heed what Bakhtin calls their "expressive intonation." From reading Sahlins, one gets the impression that the decks of the ships were crowded with women gleefully shouting, "Very fine" as the houses of their priests and fellow countrymen were being consumed by flames. (Ob. 68)

Yes, and for a heterology, one must heed what Certeau considers the cultural "lapsus" of the voyaging account: the episodes that "resist Occidental specification." But first, to note the obvious: Lieutenant King was on the *Resolution,* whereas Samwell was on the *Discovery.* King seems to be referring to his own ship, as Samwell was, and the fact that the former published a remark that was not in his private journal proves neither that it did not happen in his presence nor that he cribbed it from someone else. As for the disengagement of ordinary women from the interests of the high chiefs and priests, the women had been violating the dictates of the powers-that-be well before these events, notably by going off to the ships and eating prohibited foods in defiance of proclaimed tabus. And they would repeatedly be doing the same for decades to come (Sahlins 1981:46–51). After Cook's death on the 14th of February, Hawaiian women continued to maintain their liaisons with British seamen, despite the ongoing hostilities with their own countrymen, by swimming off to the ships at night. "Notwithstanding our state of hostility," wrote Mr. Trevenan, "the women swam off to the Ships every night" (Trevenan, Marginal Notes; see Cook and King 1784, 3:65). Hawaiian men were not allowed on board at this time, and, according to Edgar's surmise, in at least one case those who were turned away were trying to take the women back to shore (Edgar Log, 16 Feb 1779; cf. Ellis 1792, 2: 115–16). Moreover, there is explicit evidence to the contrary of Obeyesekere's appeal to common sense, his assertion that the women could hardly express admiration when the houses of their priests and countrymen were going up in flames. The well-informed letter of the Anonymous of Mitchell to Mrs. Strachan dated 23 January 1781, penned by someone on board the *Discovery*, speaks of the behavior of the women the day of Cook's death, when a number of Hawaiians were also killed:

> you may think it strange to tell our Ships were at this time full of women no body bid them go and they thought proper to stay though we were all in such a bustle the ladies were securely inquired after and they seemed to be little affected by anything they had seen and yet it was not possible but that many of them must have lost their Relations.

Obeyesekere's arguments about the priests' sorrows and the women's approbations are as groundless as they are trivial. Their only interest here is the way they suppress the variety of Hawaiian relationships to Cook's people that he claims to uniquely take into account.

But then, repeatedly and inflexibly, Obeyesekere characterizes my views on Hawaiian history as "stereotypic reproduction." This is the absurd idea that people will prescriptively and unthinkingly reproduce their existing cultural categories in all circumstances and notably to the neglect of evident differences between the old concepts and new objects. But Obeyesekere will rescue Hawaiians from this fate. His own emphasis on the people's contested and differentiated responses to the Haole "refutes the idea that Hawaiians (and other preliterate peoples) were given to a form of 'stereotypical reproduction,' as if they were acting out a cultural scheme without reflection" (Ob. 91).

Obeyesekere is apparently unaware that I introduced this phrase (coined by Maurice Godelier) into the discussion of Hawaiian history in order to repudiate it as an appropriate description of cultural-historical practice. Or at least, he gives the opposite impression:

> Cultural categories (structures) are pregiven: Events (what one might call the world's messiness) are fitted into these pregiven categories. There are no perceptions that are pan-human, no "immaculate perceptions"; they are ipso facto fused into cultural conceptions. Insofar as these cultural conceptions are finite [?] and pregiven, they are, following Braudel, "structures of the long run." Hawaiian culture is especially amenable to this form of structural analysis, says Sahlins, because it is given to "stereotypic reproduction," a term Sahlins borrows from Maurice Godelier. Stereotypic reproduction is the propensity of a society to replicate its structures continually, such that for example, the theme of a god who returns from beyond the sky [sic] can be replicated in a large number of myths that, while sharing substantive differences [what can that mean?], embody a single structural theme. (Ob. 55; see also the "stereotypic reproductions" of Ob. 58, 59, 98 and 168)

Obeyesekere's rehearsals of the allegation of "stereotypic reproduction" are part of a sustained misrepresentation of the historical perspective I have tried to develop for the study of Hawaii and other Polynesian societies. Without going into all of the details, a rectification of Obeyesekere's description of this perspective may give some appreciation of its main principles.

Since 1977, I have repeatedly adopted the phrase "stereotypic reproduction" as a *negative characterization* of the ahistorical disposition of a certain structuralism. With one partial exception (to be considered presently), "stereotypic reproduction" has long been cited by me as a *defect* of classical structuralist theory—if only because such reproduction does not occur in historical practice:

> if a cultural theory of history is necessary, modern structuralism, as is often remarked, seems unprepared to provide it. On the contrary, a radical distinction between system and event has been taken as a condition of the possibility of structuralist knowledge. The usual effect

has been to devalue action to the role of "execution" (in Bourdieu's term), the simple projection of an existing system, thus collapsing message into code, *parole* into *langue*, pragmatics into semantics. Structuralism would then be innocent of any temporal knowledge save that of "stereotypic reproduction" (Godelier 1972). . . . *As for stereotypic reproduction, strictly speaking, it does not occur.* Proceeding by the metaphorical association of the new to the old, so making differences at the same time it generates analogies, the process is as much reconstruction as reproduction, necessarily creating changes in the relative functional values of pre-existing categories and oppositions. (Sahlins 1977:22–23; emphasis added)

Obeyesekere apparently missed this discussion, as he does not mention it. However, the equivalent is presented in the opening pages of *Historical Metaphors*, where "stereotypic reproduction" is again criticized as a "nonhistorical appropriation of action" (Sahlins 1981:6). As an antidote, I adopted Pouillon's inversion of the common structuralist incantation, "plus c'est la même chose, plus ça change" (see Pouillon 1993:79ff.). The point made there and in several subsequent works on Polynesian histories is that continuity and change are false alternatives, since they always go together in the dialectics of practice. In practice, there is cultural continuity even in novelty, inasmuch as the knowledge and communication of what is new has to be related to what people already know. But at the same time, what is known, the received understanding of things, has been risked. So again from *Historical Metaphors*:

Nothing guarantees that the situations encountered in practice will stereotypically follow from the cultural categories by which the circumstances are interpreted and acted upon. Practice, rather, has its own dynamics—a "structure of the conjuncture"—which meaningfully defines the persons and objects that are parties to it, and these contextual values, if unlike the definitions culturally presupposed, have the capacity then of working back on the conventional values. Entailing unprecedented relations between the acting subjects, mutually and by relation to objects, practice entails unprecedented objectifications of categories. (Sahlins 1981:35)

The cultural schemes that actors bring to the ordering of practice are always at risk. They are risked "objectively," that is, by the behavior of the persons or things referred to, who or which are "under no inevitable obligation to conform to the categories by which certain people perceive them" (Sahlins 1981:67). In the *event*, the conventional understandings people bring into action may be more or less radically changed:

> The god Lono would no longer be the same concept once Captain Cook was referred to it; nor could the ideas of foreign lands, tabus, or the divine in general be sustained in the way they were. And as the given category is revalued in the course of historic reference, so must the relationships between categories change. . . . What Marc Bloch [1966:90] observed of fifteenth-century Europe happened even more dramatically in Hawaii: "although men were not fully aware of the change, the old names which were still on everyone's lips had slowly acquired connotations far removed from their original meaning." (Sahlins 1985a:31)

But the received understandings of a society are also risked subjectively in action, by the intentions and inventions of interested actors. Here the risk is not only a posteriori, by the "improper" conduct of what has been conventionally represented. The risk unfolds in the act of representation itself. "For even as the world can easily escape the interpretive schemes of some given group of mankind, *nothing guarantees either that intelligent and intentional subjects, with their several social interests and biographies, will use the existing categories in prescribed ways*" (Sahlins 1985a:145; emphasis added). That the response to circumstance thus varies with the social subject is argued (in several works) by means of a distinction between the sense of signs, or their meanings in the community, and their differentiated values to interested persons. The details need not be rehearsed here. What they imply is, first, "a world on which people act differentially and according to their respective situations as social beings" (Sahlins 1981:vii). Hence,

> Captain Cook appears as an ancestral god to Hawaiian priests, more like a divine warrior to the chiefs, and evidently something else and less to ordinary men and women. Acting from different perspectives, and with different social powers of objectifying their respective interpretations, people come to different conclusions and societies work out different consensuses. (Sahlins 1985a:x)

Secondly, then, the subjective manipulation of understandings may give rise to an unprecedented definition of the practical situation. The responses are not prescribed in content—however they may be limited by a system of intelligibility, to the logic of which all effective novelty must minimally conform. I made this point in response to Jonathan Friedman's challenge of "cultural determinism," which was much like Obeyesekere's charge of "stereotypic reproduction" (Sahlins 1988). Obeyesekere does not refer to this debate, which concerns Hawaiian appropriations of "empirical realities" in cultural classes:

> The meanings may or may not have been known before; moreover, as selective valuations of experience they can only imperfectly notice the "objective properties". . . . Nonetheless, worldly experiences are socialized as referential tokens of cultural types, of concepts that can be conceivably motivated in the existing scheme. Notice that just because there is a culture this does not mean there is no invention or novel response to material realities—albeit *by the same token*, the realities will then have effects of a distinct cultural type. (Sahlins 1988 : 45)

Common ways of thought persist even in social change, even when they are ways of thinking no one has ever thought. Or even when they refer to things no one has ever seen. True, the perceptual capacities involved in reference are universal. But however universal, no perception can be described, let alone communicated, without particular conceptions. Again, empirical contradictions of categorical expectations do not simply remove all the cultural traces of their lives from people's minds, restoring them to neonatal specimens now ready to become Lockean sensationalist philosophers. Which is why there is history, and not the dead hand of "reality."

Just so, what is argued from all this is different historicities: different possibilities of continuity and change. And it is with this purport that I made the statement which Obeyesekere—not without a significant alteration— uses to epitomize my approach to structure and history, reducing it all to a mindless sense of "stereotypic reproduction." "Polynesian cosmology," I wrote at one point, "may lend itself in a specially powerful way to stereotypic reproduction" (1981 : 13). In undocumented allusions to this passage, Obeyesekere says I argue that "Hawaiian culture is specially conducive to 'stereotypic reproduction'" (Ob. 58, see also 55). The substitution of "Hawaiian" for "Polynesian" here is abusive because what follows in the original text is a comparison of Hawaiian with Maori modes of historical action, the advantage in flexibility going to the Hawaiian. New Zealand is the homeland, the archetype of the structuration of experience by mythical categories; by comparison Hawaiian society was more responsive to the immediately pragmatic and political. Yet even Maori historicity involves the interested selection of cosmological precedents:

Clearly, Maori are cunning mythologists, who are able to select from the supple body of traditions those most appropriate to the satisfaction of their current interests, as they conceive them. The distinctiveness of their mytho-praxis is not the existence (or the absence) of such interests, but exactly that they are so conceived. The Maori, as Johansen says, "find themselves in history." (Sahlins 1983:526; Sahlins 1985:55)

As for the "performative" Hawaiian mode, compared to the ideally "prescriptive":

In the Hawaiian case, circumstantial happenings are often marked and valued for their differences, their departures from existing arrangements, as people may then act upon them to reconstruct their social conditions. . . . By comparison [to prescriptive systems], the Hawaiian order is more active historically, in a double way. Responding to the shifting conditions of its existence—as of, say, production, population, or power—the cultural order reproduces itself in and as change. Its stability is a volatile history of the changing fortunes of persons and groups. But then, it is more likely to change as it so reproduces itself. (Sahlins 1985a:xii–xiii)

So, if the Hawaiians received Cook as the Makahiki god—and the authorities reified such understanding of him—this does not mean that their conceptions of "Lono" were undifferentiated or unambiguous. The varied relations to Cook of *ali'i* and Lono priests, women and men, elites and ordinary people have all been noted elsewhere. Reference has also been made to the apparently secular and unique inquiries of one chief, singled out by Lieutenant King for his curiosity and acumen. In the official published account this notable is identified as Kanaina of Hawai'i island, one of the king's men; but Mr. King's own journal, which would be the preferred source in such a case, attributes the same remarks to a different person altogether, Kā'eokalani, husband of the ruling woman of Kaua'i. Both he and his wife, according to King, wished very much to see "Brittanee." Moreover, Kā'eo was

very inquisitive about our Manners & Customs; the Questions that he ask'd would alone be proof that these people have a great Variety of Ideas, he ask'd after our King, our Numbers, how our Shipping was built, & our houses, the Produce of the Country, if we ever fought, Who was our God, & such like. (Beaglehole 1967:625; cf. Cook and King 1784, 3:131)

Insofar as "Brittanee" is encompassed in the Hawaiian conception of Kahiki, the overseas sources of the gods, the meaning of these inquiries is not self-evident. We shall see New Guineans asking Mikloucho-Maclay analogous questions about the place he came from, "Russia," seeking to determine from this "absolutely extraordinary being" what villages, houses, and pigs actually were like on the moon. To cite in full a passage previously discussed, Lieutenant King, in his private journal, records in quite similar terms the common Hawaiian surmise about the gods living with the British:

> As they certainly regarded us as a Superior race of people to themselves, they would often say, that the great Eatooa ['god'] liv'd with us. The little Image which we have mention'd as being the center one in Morai they calld Koonooee aikai'a [Kūnuiakea] & said it was Terreeoboos [Kalani'ōpu'u's] God, & that he also livd with us, which proves that they only regard these Images as types or resemblances of their Deitys. (Beaglehole 1967:621)

It is worth underscoring a general implication of the preceding for the place of cultural structures in historic events—which is that, while they invariably do find a place in the ordering of history, this does not mean that the order so effected is compulsory, prescribed in advance, or achieved without benefit of conscious subjects. The logic of any given response to a historical situation is never the only one possible and rarely the only one available. At the same time, different responses, including those altogether novel, will all entail specific understandings of the local cultural regime, predicable on its schemata and communicable in its terms. It follows that the event is culturally constructed, devised from a certain cultural logic and ontologic, although not by that quality unreflexively determined or superorganically imposed (Sahlins 1991). Once again, to say that an event is culturally described is not to say it is culturally prescribed. To conflate the cultural structuration of events with the necessity of one particular ordering is abusive, leaving the realist interpretation based on universal sensory capacities as the only analytic alternative. But then, if biology is invited in to rule intelligibility, we are truly in the kingdom of the prescribed and the essentialized. The resort to an empirical reason based on perceptual mechanisms leaves no place for differences—unless they be irrational.

Divine Chiefs
of Polynesia

Obeyesekere's blanket assertion of doubt about "the divinity of kings" in Polynesia does not do justice to the interest and complexity of the literature. There are several well-known compendia of observations, including observations from early days of European contact, on the "sanctity" and "divinity" of Polynesian ruling chiefs (Williamson 1924, chap. 31; Handy 1927:138–49; Koskinen 1960; Marcus 1989). A repeated theme of this literature, from all over Polynesia, is the direct descent of ruling chiefs from gods, which entitles the former to respects and privileges customarily given to the latter as forms of worship. Relative to other people, such chiefs are "divine" and "sacred." Not only are they accorded the ritual obeisances appropriate to the gods, they are considered to have the same kinds of "supernatural" powers. But persuasive as these observations are, there is reason to believe that the evidence of chiefly divinity underestimates its significance. It was and still is a scandal to Christianized Polynesian people, one of the worst forms of "idolatry" and reminders of their former "darkness," that chiefs could be gods. For a long time now it has not been an easy topic of discussion, let alone a cherished treasure of collective memory.

Edwin Burrows relates the story of Niuliki the Futuna king who in 1841 was involved in the assassination of the early Catholic missionary, Pierre Chanel. The king, said Burrows (1936:20), "had two principal means of maintaining his power—the belief that he was the tabernacle of the ancestral god, and force." The early missionaries "wrote repeatedly about the belief that Futunan gods were incarnated in the king, and spoke through him" (ibid., 110; see also Chanel 1960:224, 266, 297). But the missionaries, who had at first sought the king's protection, used it to teach that the belief in an ancestral god was false. When his own son was converted, Niuliki reached the limit of his religious toleration and resorted to his other source of power.

By its doubly pragmatic dimensions—decision by force, radical separation of chief and god—the story is a virtual parable of Western impositions on Polynesian world views. Still, some specific intimations of Niuliki's divine powers did become known.

Marc Bloch (1983:59) exaggerated when he complained that Sir James Frazer was forever trotting out the Tui Tonga as the sole Polynesian example of a divine king, something like an extra in the theater dressed as a soldier who circles endlessly around the same piece of scenery so as to give the impression of the movement of a great armed column. Perhaps also thinking of the Tongan ruler—or perhaps of Fijian chiefs, about whose divinity there is no cavil—Burrows saw the Futunan concepts of godly kings as a development on western Polynesian models:

> Emphasis on belief in the embodiment of ancestral gods in living chiefs and the divine character of the utterances of these "vessels of the gods" while the god is in them is to be expected from Futuna's geographical position in western Polynesia. But in Futuna this belief had an extreme specialization as a support of the power of the king. The gods regarded as most powerful were ancestors of the Tua kings. The most powerful of all, Fakavelikele, the founder of the royal line, was embodied in each successive king, and spoke through him. . . . The emphasis on Fakavelikele as the leading god overshadowed the worship of Tangaloa and whatever other primal gods the Futunans had known, and of the animal gods. . . . Ancestral gods spoke through their living oracles on all questions of supreme moment, and were quick to avenge any slight on their dignity. That is how they won and maintained their supremacy. (1936:112–13)

Such were the chiefs of whom Handy spoke as "actually believed to be the embodiment of divinity" (1927:140). Beyond western Polynesia, however, he was also referring to tabu chiefs of Hawaii and Tahiti, in whose presence the people prostrated (Hawaii) or stripped to the waist (Tahiti). In Hawaii, such a chief, as Malo said, was called *akua*, a 'god,' and the terminology was also known elsewhere in central and eastern Polynesia. The Mangareva king was a "god of the night, that is to say, a 'Great God'" (Laval 1938:224). Nobles and commoners allowed him so much authority over themselves "that they made him a being who was nearly supernatural—to whom indeed they gave the title of god during his lifetime" (Caillot 1914:147; see also Buck 1938:154).

Clearly there were different forms of chiefly divinity in the several Polynesian islands—not to mention that the concept of divinity could extend to beings and things that we would not include in such a category. On one axis, the chiefly appropriations of divine powers range between instituted and heroic forms: the godliness associated with descent, office and ritual function (the Tu'i Tonga, the Ra'iatea king, the Hawaiian *ali'i nui* and his ritual double Kahoali'i), in contrast to the divinity associated with actions that transcend the established order and expressed as claims to personate particular gods. Although regularly generated, the latter phenomenon appears as extrastructural, or even anti-structural when it represents an affront to the legitimacy of descent. This helps explain the seemingly idiosyncratic notices of the irruption of living gods one may find in the historical literature: the ruler of one Samoan district who at night became the god Moso, specifically one of the great land gods, as opposed to the supreme Tangaloa, god of the heavens (Turner 1884:36–37); or the children and grandchildren of the Marquesan tribal chief who, unusually for these islands, were regarded as *atua* (Williamson 1924, 3:85). A good example concerns a certain contrast in kingships in the Society Islands: between the established rulers of Ra'iatea and the Pomares of Tahiti.

Descended from the creator Ta'aroa, the rulers of Ra'iatea were probably the most famous of the ancient Polynesian "sacred kings." Their residence at Opoa was the site of the great temple of Tapu-tapu-atea, center of the cult of the great war god 'Oro and sanctuary where the kings were installed. By virtue of their descent, their ritual offices and the palladia they detained, the Ra'iatea kings were sources of royal legitimacy all over the Society Islands and beyond (see Oliver 1974:664–67, 891–93, and passim). In 1822 the LMS missionaries Tyerman and Bennet encountered the incumbent Tamatoa—that was the Ra'aitea king's title—and were properly scandalized to learn that he "had been enrolled among the gods . . . was worshipped, consulted as an oracle, and had sacrifices and prayers offered to him" (1832: 123). Not long after the missionaries visited "the metropolis of idolatry," the great 'Oro temple at Opoa. Again they spoke of the king:

> Opoa was also the residence of the kings of this island, who, beside the prerogatives of royalty, enjoyed divine honors, and were in fact living idols among the dead ones, being deified at the time of their accession to political supremacy here. In the latter character, we presume, it was, that these sovereigns (who always took the name of Tamatoa) were wont to receive presents from the kings and chiefs of adjacent and distant lands, whose gods were all considered tributary

to Oro of Raiatea, and their princes owing homage to its monarch, who was Oro's hereditary high priest, as well as an independent deity himself. (Ibid., 126–27; see also Ellis 1833 1:263, 3:75)

Now, contrast this notice with the information obtained (in 1788–91) by the *Bounty* man James Morrison, about the ambitious Tu chiefs (the Pomares) of Tahiti, then on a course that would take them from the rule of the Pare-Arue area to the sovereignty of the Society Islands:

The present Earee Nooi [*ari'i nui*] (or King) is the son of Matte or O' Too, his name is Toonooeayeteatooa which may be thus translated, 'Too, the great begotten of God,' and his title Eatoa Raa or Sacred God—which Sacraligous Name and title He obtained by His Mother declaring that the Deity (Taane) Cohabited with her in her Sleep and, proving Pregnant soon after, the Child was declared to be the Offspring of the Deity and is rever'd as something supernatural. (Morrison 1935:166)

Hawaiians also knew such royal demi-gods (Valeri 1985:144).

Priests and Genealogies

The two priesthood orders of Kū and Lono—respectively the orders of Nahulu (or Holoa'e) and Kuali'i (or Kauali'i)—are attested to in the standard Hawaiian-language sources as well as in archival documents. Their traditions are consistent with the contrasts in their sacerdotal character. The Lono priests can be traced to an early Kona chief, Ehukaimalino, and beyond that to the ancient aristocratic line of Nanaulu chiefs (AH/GB 3:13; 14:18; 15:12; BM/GB 10:8, 31, 44, 47; 46:49–50; cf. Sahlins 1992:23). The Nanaulu were original ruling chiefs. Still associated with Kaua'i and O'ahu, they were superseded by immigrant kings in Maui and Hawai'i. Several Lonos appear in the genealogies of this order of priests cum ancient kings, three at about the generation of Lono a.k.a. Omeah (namely, Lonoikahaupu, Lonoakai and Lonomauki). The Kū succession, by contrast, is linked to Pa'ao, the later priest from Kahiki. A famous legendary figure, Pa'ao is generally credited with the introduction of the reigning dynasty of Hawai'i island and the royal cult of human sacrifice (AH/GB 5). The opposition of priests thus parallels the functional diarchy or alternating modalities of Hawaiian kingship.

The various notices of the dual priesthood, together with certain traces in mid-nineteenth-century land records from Kealakekua, support the conclusion that the Ka'ō'ō *mā*, priests of Lono, were displaced early in Kamehameha's reign.

Malo's observations on the two orders are as follows:

> 2. There were two rituals which the king in his eminent station used in the worship of the gods; one was the ritual of Ku, the other that of Lono. The Ku ritual was very strict (*oolea*), the service most arduous (*ikaika*). The priests of this rite were distinct from others and

outranked them. They were priests of the order of Ku [*mo'o Kū*], because Ku was the highest god whom the king worshipped in following
their ritual. They were also called priests of the order of Kanalu, because that was the name of their first priestly ancestor. Those two
names were their titles of highest distinction.

3. The Lono ritual was milder, the service more comfortable. Its
priests were, however, of a separate order and of an inferior grade.
They were said to be of the order of Lono (*moo-Lono*), because Lono
was the chief object of the king's worship when he followed the ritual.
The priests of this order were also said to be of the order of Paliku.
(Malo 1951:159)

The succession of high priests in the Kū order is described as "the genealogy of Holoae" in an important archival document, commencing with
one Kanaluakea (= the Kanalu of Malo's account; AH/GB 5:188–89). The
succession list includes Holoa'e, his son Pailili (a.k.a. Pailiki), and the latter's
son Puou, who was the father of Kamehameha's so-called head priest Hewahewa. There is no trace of Ka'ō'ō in this record, nor of any other Lono
priest of Cook's time. (Paliku, the eponym of the Lono order in Malo's account, appears in the Kumulipo creation chant.)

The two orders of priesthood were also described by John Papa 'I'i:

If the *'aha* [service] was the Hulahula, it belonged to the Moo Ku
order, whose kahunas [priests] were of the class called Kanalu. Hewahewa and his fellow kahunas were of this order. If the Hoowilimoo
was the *'aha*, it belonged to the Moo Lono order. These *'aha* were used
in the *luakini* heiau [royal temples], whose *paehumu* enclosure and
house beams and posts were made of *'ohi'a* wood. (Ii 1959:39)

Another description of the two priestly groups was penned by S. M.
Kamakau:

Kamehameha I maintained two priesthood orders—the order of Holoa'e, which had come down from Pa'ao, and the order of Kuali'i.
Holoa'e had been the *kahuna nui*, high priest, in the hereditary line of
kahunas (*mo'o kahuna*) from Pa'ao, and Hewahewa became the *kahuna
nui* of the order of Holoa'e in Kamehameha's old age. The kapus, or
rituals, of these orders were very high; and there were two gods of
these orders. The ritual (kapu) for the order of Holoa'e was that of the
god Kunuiakea, the *kapu 'ohi'ako*. The visible symbols of Kunuiakea,
the great unseen god [n.b., the unperceived primary form] in the dark

clouds of heaven, were Kuka'ilimoku, Kuho'one'enu'u, Kukeolo'ewa, and Kukalani'ehu. Kuaiwa and Holoaialena were the kahunas of the order of Kuali'i and there were many chiefs who belonged to this order—Ulumaheihei Hoapili, Kuakahela *ma*, Lonomauki *ma*, and others. Their rituals were those of the god Lonoika'ouali'i, the *kapu lama* and the *kapu loulu*, which were heiau [temple] rituals. Lonoika'ouali'i was the visible symbol of the god Lononuiakea, and it was called Lonoikamakahiki. The real man Lonoikamakahiki was different from the god, but he too was covered *(uhi)* with bird feathers on the head and had a *ka'upu* bird for an ensign *(lepa)*, as a flag of privilege *(hae no ka lanakila)*. (Kamakau 1964:7; see also Kamakau 1961:187, 226, 227)

It might be noted that the recurrent reference to the Kū priesthood as the "order of Holoa'e" reflects a genealogical break in the succession of these priests from Pa'ao and a long line of predecessors. So far as can be determined from extant records (see below), the ancestors of Holoa'e were not Kū priests. They do not appear on the known lists thereof (AH/GB 5).

An account similar to Kamakau's but with interesting further details appears in the book of the genealogist E. K. Lilikalani, who functioned in this capacity for King Kalākaua:

> In the time of Kamehameha I there were two Kahuna classes [papa kahuna] that served in his reign: the Papa Kahuna of Holoae, the papa kahuna of Paao, in which arose Pailili, Puou, to Hewahewa and Kaauamoku [female] who lived with Kamakau Kelou of Kaawaloa; and the Papa Kahuna of Kualii. Hewahewa was the kahuna nui of the papa kahuna of Holoae, and the kahuna of Kamehameha's old age. Kuaiwa and Holoialena were the kahuna nui of the papa kahuna of Kualii, and there were many who belonged to this class. Ulumaheihei [Hoapili, friend of W. Richards], Kuakahela *ma*, Lono-a-Mauki *ma*—Lono-i-ka-ou-alii was their kapu—the Kapu lama. The loulu was the kapu of Kunuiakea, that is, the kapu ohi'a ko, which belonged to Holoae the kahuna nui of the mo'o kahuna of Paao, and Kukailimoku was the visible representation [*ka hoailona ike maka*] of Kunuiakea. (BM/GB 1: no pagination)

The identification of Kuaiwa and Holoialena as Lono priests is of some interest since, according to Kamakau—who also contradictorily speaks of them rather as "soldiers of the kahuna lines of Ka-uahi and Na-hulu"—these two were on the side of the rebel Kekuokalani, the chief who fell attempting to maintain the ancien régime when King Liholiho declared free-eating in 1819 (Kamakau 1961:225–26). As is well known, the head Kū priest, Hewahewa, sided with Liholiho and Ka'ahumanu. Hewahewa's motivation has always been an enigma, but the split in the priesthood, and more generally between the Lono *kahuna* and reigning dynasty, may help explain it.

A reflection on the two orders of priesthood, with a similar implication of the opposition of the Lono people to the Kū-linked royalty, was recorded in 1853 by Jules Remy. The information was taken from a venerable resident of South Kona, who claimed to have been in the service of Kalani'ōpu'u:

> Paao has always been considered as the first of the kahunas. For this reason his descendants, independently of the fact that they are regarded as *Moo kahuna*, that is, of the priesthood, are more like nobles in the eyes of the people and are respected by the chiefs themselves. Some Hawaiians claim that there exists another sacerdotal race besides that of Paao, more ancient even than that, whose priests belonged at the same time to a race of chiefs. This is the family of Maui, probably of Maui-hope, the last of the seven children of Hina, the same who captured the sea monster Piimoe. The origin of this race, to which Naihe of Kohala claims to belong, is fabulous. Since the reign of Kamehameha, the priests of the order of Maui have lost favor. (Remy 1859:13–14)

This is in fact a revelatory text. It helps identify the priests of the "order of Maui" who "have lost favor"—parallel to the other testimonies to such effect—as the Lono priesthood. The Naihe of Kohala mentioned by Remy was a big man of the middle nineteenth century, J. W. Naihe (not to be confused with the earlier Naihe of Ka'awaloa, Kona). He was a descendant (in the fifth generation) of Lonomauki of the Kualii (Lono) order (BM/GB 10:47; BM/GB 46:49–50; see also LC/NR 8:126). The text speaks to what must have been the most radical of the so-called reforms of Kamehameha, the elimination of the Ka'ō'ō *mā* of Kealekekua—a change, again, not confronted by the canonical Hawaiian sources (Malo *mā*).

The like is implied by documentary notices of Kepo'okulou, a priest of Ka'awaloa and a son of Kekuhaupi'o, the warrior who would be accorded Captain Cook's skull as his share of the victory over Lono. It will be recalled that, in 1822, Kepo'okulou told the American missionaries the story of Lono's exile, linking Cook to the return of the god. However, Kepo'okulou was

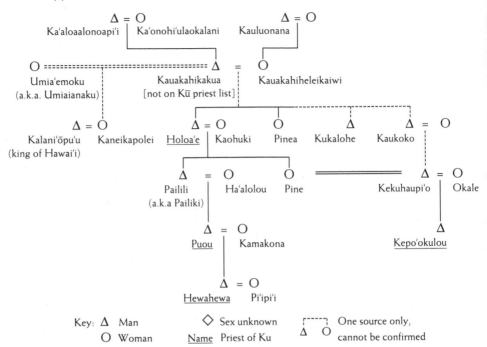

Fig. A.13.1 **Genealogy of the Holoa'e priests of Ka'awaloa.** Sources: Bridges/Kanahele Private Collection. *Aloha Aina:* 2 March 1907 (McKinzie 1986, 2:106). AH/GB 14:17, 30; 3:13, 15:12. MKP/GB 20, 65. *Ka Nupepa Nuhou:* 23 December 1873 (McKinzie 1986, 2:85). BM/GB 1.85, 174; 10:57-58; 13:42. *Ka Nupepa Kuokoa:* 24 March 1877 (McKinzie 1986, 2:86). *Ko Hawaii Pae Aina:* 8 June 1885.

a Kū priest, associated with the Holoa'e crowd of Ka'awaloa (indeed Holoa'e was a father-in-law of Kekuhaupi'o; AH/GB 14:37, 38; see fig. A.13.1). A notice in the newspaper *Kuokoa* (23 Feb 1865) relates:

> The feather god Ku'ka-ili-moku was worshipped at the heiau Hikiau, Punaluu, Wahaula, Kanoa, Mailekini and Puukohala. Hikiau was where the god was kept. The kahuna of this god were Hewahewa, Kepookulou, Puou, Kaleikuahulu.

Now, the same Kepo'okulou appears in the land records of the midnineteenth century as a donor of lands at Ka'awaloa in 1819 and 1834, and of a considerable tract *('ili 'aina)* at Kealakekua in 1819 (LC/NT 8:613–14, 586). This interesting information corresponds to the observation of Vancouver's that the land occupied by the Lono priests at Kealakekua in Cook's day was appropriated to Kamehameha in 1793. Until then, the Lono priests not only controlled the village of Kealakekua, including Hikiau heiau, but the large land district *(ahupua'a)* above it, explored by Cook's people under the protection and with provisioning provided by Ka'ō'ō. Hence the sacking of Ka'ō'ō *mā* by Kamehameha is again implied by Kepo'okulou's land deal-ings in Kealakekua. Indeed, at least one known priest of Lono, Kuakahela (son of Lonoakai), was in the service of Keoua, Kamehameha's rival for the rule of Hawai'i, when Keoua went to his death at Kawaihae in ca. 1792 (Kamakau 1961:157; AH/GB 5:110; BM/GB 10:347; BM/GB 49:38).

The basic genealogy of the Holoa'e priests of Ka'awaloa is well known, from multiple versions (fig. A.13.1). In no case are there any names that correspond to the priests of Lono in Cook's time (Ka'ō'ō *mā*), as in Obe-yesekere's hypothetical genealogical overlay (Ob. 93). One source (MKP/GB:20 from *Ka Hoku o Hawaii,* 4 Aug 1921) would make Holoa'e's father the sire also, by a different mother, of Kalani'ōpu'u's wife Kaneikapolei—the one who stopped the king from going on board Cook's ship on the fateful 14th of February 1779.

The genealogical records that mention a Ka'ō'ō of the appropriate time as the old Lono priest of Kealakekua are relatively rare and not always consistent with each other. The most intriguing depicts Ka'ō'ō as a junior offspring of a royal father-daughter marriage (fig. A.13.2). By this reckon-ing, the Lono priest is a half-brother to Kalaninui'Iamamao (a.k.a. Ka'I'imamao), who was himself a Lono figure (for whom the Kumulipo was

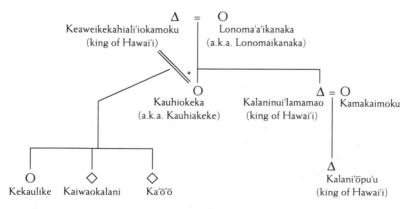

Fig. A.13.2 Genealogy showing descent of Ka'ō'ō. Source: AH/GB 8:22.
* = Father-daughter marriage

composed) and father to Kalani'ōpu'u. Another genealogy, appearing in the 1880s record of the Hawaiian Chiefs Genealogy Board (fig. A.13.3, from BM/GB 12) identifies Ka'ō'ō as "the prime minister of Kalaniopuu"; this genealogy includes certain of the same persons as in the royal one just mentioned The same figures appear on other genealogies, the most interesting of which apparently mentions another Lono priest of Kealakekua, Kanekoa (fig. A.13.4). The name would correspond to Clerke's "Car'na'care who I believe is son to the Bishop [Ka'ō'ō]," and who brought off the piece of Cook's flesh to the *Resolution* (Beaglehole 1967:543). (This person does not appear in Obeyesekere's conflation of the Ka'ō'ō and Holoa'e genealogies. "Son" as noted by Clerke could equally mean a sister's or brother's son, though from the correlation of extant genealogies, Kanekoa would most likely be mother's brother's son to Ka'ō'ō. By Clerke's description, he may have been the tabu man.)

If the paucity of genealogical records of the Ka'ō'ō *mā* reflects the decline of the Lono priesthood, it may still be said that their eclipse contrib-

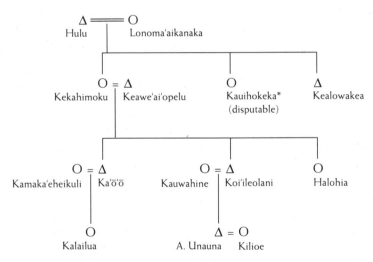

Fig. A.13.3 Alternative genealogy of Ka'ō'ō. Source: BM/GB 12, to which is appended the following note: "The Ka'ō'ō mentioned in this genealogy was the Prime Minister of Kalani-ōpu-u in his latter days. When he (Ka'ō'ō) died the Premiership fell on Keawe ma'uhili. The said Ka'ō'ō and Keawema'uhili were the Chiefs at the side of Kalani-opu-u who were meant to be taken by captain Cook on account of one of the vessel's boats being stolen by Palea and others. He is the grandparent of [Queen] Emma. . . ."

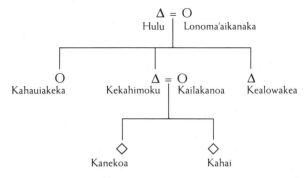

Fig. A.13.4 Genealogy of Kanekoa. Source: AH/GB 8.

uted finally to the heightened political value of their god. We have seen that
Kamehameha occupied the grounds of Ka'ō'ō *mā* at Kealakekua in the early
1790s. This substitution of the king for the priests of Lono continued in the
ensuing decades. While Kamehameha was established at Honolulu in ca.
1808–12, the Hale o Lono (House of Lono temple) was for most of each
month the ritual residence of the king's son and heir, Liholiho (Ii 1959:
56–58). The royal living arrangements at Waikiki during the period from
1804 to about 1808 are unknown. But after the move to Kona (Hawai'i),
from 1812 until Kamehameha's death in 1819, Liholiho regularly officiated
at Hikiau heiau and regularly resided in the Lono temple at Kailua (ibid.,
110, 123). The correspondence between the emphasis on the productive
and peaceful aspect of divinity, Lono, and the consolidation of Kamehameha's conquest state, has been analyzed masterfully and in detail by Valerio
Valeri (1991). The "transcendence of war," as he called it, the process by
which the kingship appropriated the cult of Lono and wrote finis to the
Lono priests, also transformed the character of Hawaiian royalty—precisely
in the direction of the god whose rituals the king had usurped. Hence the
growing significance of the Makahiki in relation to the Kū rites of human
sacrifice and the apparent use of the Lono procession for the stocking of the
royal storehouses with tributes of the land. Here also is a motive for the
recurrent historical references to a cult of Cook/Lono from the early 1790s
until well into the nineteenth century. Kamehameha turned Kalani'ōpu'u's
victory of 1779 into a system of state—which had the added, if also traditional, advantage of "linking our dynasty to Kahiki," i.e., to Beretania via
Lono.

On the Wrath of Cook

> "James Cook is a hard as well as an easy man to talk about,
> and character studies have an evil propensity
> to degenerate into hypothesis."
> —J. C. Beaglehole (1956:417)

Although not announced as part of the "alternative theory," a contrapuntal discussion of Cook's psychological state plays a significant role in Obeyesekere's explanation of his death. According to this explanation, Cook became increasingly wrathful and irritable during his stay at Hawaii. The problem had been building up throughout the voyage, but was exacerbated by a combination of an exalted self-esteem and the humiliation Cook had endured by prostrating before the image of Kū in Hikiau temple on the 17th of January, the day he landed at Kealakekua. Moreover, in the evening of 31 January or the next morning, the old seaman William Watman, to whom Cook had been long and closely attached, died on the *Resolution*. According to Obeyesekere, Cook's remorse at Watman's death provoked him into an act of desecration against Hikiau temple that would annul the chagrin and guilt he now felt for having inclined before the pagan god. In an explosion of anger, he had the wooden fence that surrounded the temple and the god images of the main altar carted away "by the marines" as firewood for the ships. There is the small detail that this event transpired before Watman died, perhaps as much as a day before. Obeyesekere finesses the problem, however, by noting that the old sailor lay dying when it happened. Moreover, the sacrilege against the heathen temple, thus cleared of its "idolatrous images," could then be compounded by defiantly burying Watman there: amidst "Hawaiian royalty," as the British (mistakenly) thought, but according to Christian rites. This was done on the afternoon of 1 February, Cook presiding. The temple was thereby "polluted." Hawaiians—notably including the priest Keli'ikea—resented it bitterly. Hence when Cook went to take the king hostage (on 14 February), it provided an opportunity for the people to vent their own murderous anger on this so-called Lono.

Thus Obeyesekere. I cannot comment on the psychological dispositions he attributes to Cook and the Hawaiians. But I can show that as far as these motives are alleged to explain the events leading to Cook's death, as history, they are groundless.

The unresolvable amphiboly in Lieutenant King's description of Cook's supposed abasement before the Kū image has already been remarked. Coming to this figure, the priest "prostrated himself, and afterwards kiss'd, and desired the Captain to do the same; who was quite passive, and suffered Koah to do with him as he chose" (Beaglehole 1967:505–6). It is difficult to see where Obeyesekere gets from this his contrary assertion that "Cook was made to prostrate, with some reluctance" (Ob. 46), except that it helps him make the point about Cook's humiliation and subsequent guilt. In any event, there is no way of disambiguating King's sentence: we don't know if Cook merely "kiss'd" the image, as Beaglehole and Valeri supposed, or also prostrated, as I too have thought. (Again, "kissed" means to touch noses or cheeks side by side while sniffing, not a "kiss" as Cook would know it.) In short, as history the presumed motivation of Cook's presumably wrathful act against Hikiau temple is hypothetical and nothing else.

Whether or not the removal of the wooden fence and god images from Hikiau was "sacrilege" has been investigated and disputed since the late eighteenth century, likewise without a definitive solution (see Sahlins 1985: 126; Beaglehole 1967:cxlvi). However, Obeyesekere's attempt to make it sacrilege takes the liberty of adding incorrect historical assertions to the existing uncertainties. To begin with, he would render Cook's act arbitrary by denying the British had any true need for firewood. "Firewood," he says, "was hardly a scarce item and presumably the ships had a regular supply" (Ob. 115). In fact, the ships had not had a regular supply of wood since leaving Northwest America more than three months earlier. They could neither resupply in their running circuit around Hawai'i island nor do so easily at Kealakekua Bay, where they finally anchored. Obeyesekere is no better on this aspect of the local ecology than on the food supply, as he evidently does not realize that Kealakekua is at the foot of a rising, virtually treeless lava plain. At some two to three miles inland and upland, useful breadfruit and candlenut trees are found. But as Thomas Edgar reported—he had made an excursion inland—firewood had to be carried down from the woods some four to five miles upcountry, making procuring it a "very troublesome laborious work" (Log, following 4 Feb 1779, p. 53). Since the British were about to leave, the wood had to be "purchas'd," as Edgar and many of his mates say. The amount thus obtained was substantial: two launch loads for the *Discovery* and three for the *Resolution.*

In a number of such respects Obeyesekere sets up a bogus scene of the crime, that is, in order to frame Cook. Another is that Cook must have put the marines up to entering the temple, as they could not have done so in the face of his (ostensible) orders to the contrary. "That ordinary marines would have been permitted to enter the temple is not likely. It is also highly unlikely that they would do so on their own volition, defying Cook's own orders by ransacking the temple of its images" (Ob. 115). First of all, it was an ordinary sailor's detail that gathered the wood, not the ships' (armed) marines. Second, there was no barrier to Cook's people entering the temple. On the contrary, the British had taken possession of two houses on the temple mound as a place for their sailmakers to work and, in part of one, as a hospital for their sick (Beaglehole 1967 : 508; Ledyard 1963 : 139; Anonymous of Mitchell 1781). Moreover, Ledyard's account (which plays a decisive part in Obeyesekere's) shows him entering into a Hawaiian gathering on the heiau (1963 : 125). In connection with the houses on the temple, Obeyesekere makes a sidewise try at blaming Cook for having them burnt down by the ships' people, or at least wanting to, which is bizarre anyhow because the British never did so. "Obviously," he wrote, "Cook could not actually set the temple on fire without adequate provocation: this was done later by the ships' crew in an act of retaliation for Cook's death" (Ob. 119). But the fire set by the British in the attack in Kealakekua of 17 February, after Cook's death, burned the houses *between* the cliff and the temple (Burney MSb, 17 Feb 1779). The two houses occupied by the British in the temple had already burned down on the night of 3 February. The British, however, had previously evacuated the place in preparation for their first departure. The fire was set by Hawaiians either searching for things the Haole may have left behind (ibid., 3 Feb 1779; Beaglehole 1967 : 520) or perhaps "thro' some superstitious notion they had among them" (Gilbert 1982 : 103). Ledyard also notes that the Hawaiians set the fire, although his notion that they did so because the British had used the temple of Hikiau without their consent and against their wishes is manifestly incorrect (Ledyard 1963 : 139).

Obeyesekere's interpretation of the removal of the temple palings and images, and the supposed effect on the Hawaiians, depends on devaluing Lieutenant King's account of the transaction and crediting instead that of John Ledyard. King says he was the one who negotiated with the priests on the matter and, rather to his surprise, there was no perceptible resentment on the Hawaiians' part; nor does he indicate there was any negative aftermath. Ledyard says that Cook negotiated the affair himself, and that it infuriated the priest Keli'ikea and outraged the Hawaiians who were about. Obeyesekere finds King's story suspicious, and believes it is a cover-up for Cook's sacrilege. Ledyard's account, on the other hand, he finds "extremely plausible"—twice over (Ob. 116, 118). The grounds for this critical reading seem to be that Ledyard's version agrees with his own interpretation, while King's contradicts it. The internal evidence does not particularly support the notion that King was lying to protect Cook, for a couple of reasons. One, that although this is the disposition King supposedly shows in writing the official account (that is, according to Obeyesekere), it is only in this official version that King says he had some initial doubts "about the decency of this proposal, and was apprehensive, that even the bare mention of it might be considered, by them, as a piece of shocking impiety" (Cook and King 1784, 3:25). He hastened to add, "I found myself mistaken." Second, although this reservation is not mentioned in King's private journal, the transaction is described there, innocently and as of no serious consequence. Since this was a daily journal, written while Cook was still alive and before King ever dreamed the presentation of the voyage to the public would devolve on him, there is no reason to suppose he was fabricating a story. Moreover, King was in a position to undertake the negotiation of the wood, as he was in charge of the observatory next to Hikiau and knew the priests well.

King's private journal is indeed all innocence. He says Cook "desird us" to see if the Hawaiians would sell the fence or not, as it looked like going to ruin anyhow, and they had sometimes taken off posts themselves. Hence "we did not seem to run any risk in being look'd upon as impious to propose the purchasing of it" (Beaglehole 1967:516). The Hawaiians readily agreed, without even asking compensation, though they were "very handsomely rewarded." Before King was aware, however, the sailors were also carrying away the semicircle of images. When he inquired, they said "the Natives told them to do so & assist'd." Apparently disturbed, King went to the head priest Ka'ō'ō, who merely asked that the small central figure of Kū be returned and two images at the center be left standing (ibid.). Apart from misdating the episode to the second of February, King in the published version adds that he specifically was detailed to treat with the priests, and that he was at first worried about the propriety of doing so. Again, however, he says that no surprise was expressed at the proposal. And not only had Hawaiians assisted in removing the images, but they "had not shewn any mark of resentment at it" (Cook and King 1784, 3:25). He repeats the sequel of the conversation with Ka'ō'ō, and indicates no further interest or concern with the matter.

The other contemporary accounts of this differ from King's, mostly in the matter of who negotiated for the wood. Burney, Law, Edgar, and Roberts variously say that Cook, Clerke, or both directly arranged the transaction. Law's account, like King's, suggests that the fear of sacrilege was indeed a European a priori; hence his contempt for Hawaiians who would "for the sake of a little iron . . . sell both church and burying ground" (Journal, 1 Feb 1779). It is not known whether these notices were based on direct observation. Ledyard, who was a corporal in the marines and stationed at the observatory, reports a different understanding of what transpired, although he also says Cook was personally engaged. Obeyesekere attempts to reconcile the differences by hypothesizing that Lieutenant King was at first charged with negotiating the fence but failed, which brought Cook in to do his own dirty work, as Ledyard then described it.

This description of Ledyard's is aberrant in the role it accords to Cook and in the supposed disagreement between him and the priest Keli'ikea. Neither feature can be corroborated from other accounts, and the second is clearly contradicted by later events. Ledyard says that Cook, "insensible of the daily decline of his greatness and importance in the estimation of the natives," came ashore to purchase the temple fence for firewood (1963:136). Sending for the priest "Kikinny" (Keli'ikea) and other chiefs, he offered them two iron hatchets for the fence, a proposal that astonished them—and not only for the inadequacy of the price—so they refused. The angry Cook ordered his men to break down the fence, "leading the way himself to enforce his orders" (ibid., 137). Without power to oppose these "sacrilegious [sic] depredations," the chiefs could only look on in dismay. They again refused Cook's offer of two hatchets. (Obeyesekere, incidentally, does not say why Cook was so anxious to compensate for an act that he took to wipe out his guilt and humiliation.) Still according to Ledyard, Cook then added a third hatchet, but Keli'ikea was now pale and trembling and refused again. So Cook simply thrust the hatchets into Keli'ikea's garment and went off.

Not wishing to touch them himself, Keli'ikea had some menials remove them from his clothing. Meanwhile, the islanders who had gathered under the walls of the temple were "very outrageous," and heaved the wood and images back as the British threw them down (ibid., 137). Thus Ledyard. The only other contemporary report anything like this is Zimmermann's, though we do not know if he was on the scene. He says the Hawaiians showed "signs of a secret annoyance," which they could not express, however, because their chief had given permission for the removal and had been mollified by a gift of six axes (1988:98).

Ledyard's description would therefore require us to disregard King and Zimmermann's reports that the transaction had been satisfactorily negotiated. Instead there would have been a contretemps between Cook and Keli'ikea that left the latter enraged—something that the other journalists, speaking merely of the purchase of wood for the ships, do not confirm. But then, neither does Keli'ikea's subsequent behavior show hostility to Cook *mā*—on the contrary, and this seems decisive. For it was Keli'ikea, the Lono priest—"our & esteemd and benevolent Kireekea," as Lieutenant King called him (Beaglehole 1967:563)—who consistently thereafter showed himself the friend of the British up to and after Cook's death. In word and deed and at some risk to his own safety, he acted in opposition to the king's party, who were responsible for that death, and subsequently engaged in open hostilities with the Haole.

When Cook fell on the 14th of February at Ka'awaloa, Keli'ikea was across the bay at Kealakekua. On hearing the news, he came to Lieutenant King at Hikiau temple, "with great sorrow and dejection in his countenance," to ask if it were true (Cook and King 1784, 3:56). Soon King and the British observatory party were besieged on the temple platform, where Keli'ikea and a few of his fellow priests remained with them. At King's request, the priests eventually arranged the truce that allowed the British to withdraw. According to several accounts, during the siege Keli'ikea procured water for King's people—giving drink to poor damned souls (Hey, that's Kipling! I know he wasn't there, but see Law Journal, 14 Feb 1779; Roberts Log, 16 Feb 1779). The "tabu man" who brought out a piece of Cook's body to the *Resolution* and warned the British not to trust the Ka'awaloa chiefs "was sent by our friend Kerrikae," as one report put it; others note he "belonged" to Keli'ikea; some (apparently incorrectly) say Keli'ikea himself came out that night (Anonymous of NLA, 13–14; Burney MSb, 15 Feb 1779; Clerke in Beaglehole 1967:542–43; Edgar Log, 16 Feb 1779; Samwell in Beaglehole 1967:1208; Law Journal, 16 Feb 1779). Gilbert says of this episode that the two who came to the *Resolution* were sent by a priest—whom he later identified as Keli'ikea—

> who had before always treated us with great hospitality. We learnt that Him and his adherents, still firmly attached to us, but were too few to declare it to their Countrymen, which was the reason of their coming in the dark that it might not be known. (1982:112–13)

Indeed, while the British were in conflict with the chiefs at Ka'awaloa, that is, until Cook's bones were returned, the Kealakekua priests kept the ships supplied with food (ibid., 117; Clerke in Beaglehole 1967:546). Again, it was from the "honest Kaireekea" that Samwell learned the names of the Ka'awaloa men who struck the first blows at Cook (Samwell 1957:23–24). And as late as 22 February, after the British had ostensibly made peace with the king's party, Keli'ikea was still warning them that,

> these people [the king and chiefs at Ka'awaloa] are not our friends and we have great reason to beli[e]ve him. On talking to him about the two Chiefs who killed Capt" Cook he asked us in a low Voice if we did not mean to get them into our hands and kill them before we went away. They are universally known, having acquired great Fame by the action. The Indians say that they thought Kariopoo would have been killed if he had gone on board with Capt" Cook. (Beaglehole 1967:1218)

None of this confirms Ledyard's story that Keli'ikea and the Lono priests who had charge of Hikiau temple were outraged by the removal of the fence and images, or that their anger was instrumental in Cook's death. On the contrary, their conduct remained friendly, even helpful and loyal, to the British. Nor was the temple desecrated by the affair of the firewood, since it was used for rituals twice afterwards and while the British were still at Kealakekua. Less than 48 hours after the removal of the fence, on the night of 2–3 February, a ceremony corresponding to a terminal rite of the Makahiki was held there. Drums were beaten, certain images were wrapped, and valuables were offered to one of them (King in Beaglehole 1967:620; see above, 74–77). On the 18th of February, the priests asked leave of the British to perform a ceremony at Hikiau, as the foreigners had posted some men there. On this occasion, Keli'ikea made the offering (Burney, MSb, 18 Feb 1779; Anonymous of NLA Account, 18). Occurring at the beginning of a lunar month—by our reckoning, 18 February 1779 was 2 lunar ($\pm$ 1 day) or the Kū tabu of the month of Kaulua (see Sahlins 1989)—this second ceremony corresponded to the resumption of ordinary temple rites (*haipule*) at the end of the Makahiki. "In the tabu period, Kū, of the month of Kaulua," Malo writes, "the king, chiefs, and all the people took up again their ordinary religious observances" (1951 : 152). This also helps explain certain notices of Hawaiian attitudes of indifference or even disrespect to the Hikiau images during the preceding weeks—attitudes that would also be consistent with their reported lack of concern at the British carrying them off, the image of Kū excepted. In his private journal as well as the published account, Lieutenant King had observed even on the first day at Kealakekua, when Cook was required to pay his respects to the Kū icon, the priest Koah appeared to offer some kind of slight or sneer to the other images as he led Cook past (Beaglehole 1967 : 505; Cook and King 1784, 3 : 7). It is true that such images were receptacles of the gods. But then, they would be so when and as they were ritually consecrated, a condition that would not obtain during the Makahiki, as ordinary rites were then in abeyance. Hence the indifference to images reported as a general rule by Lieutenant King in his résumé of observations at Hawaii (Cook and King 1784, 3 : 160). Samwell had remarked the like in his own journal:

> Tho' they look upon these Idols as their Gods they pay no great reverence to them, for when any of us laughed at them & treated with Contempt even those we supposed the most sacred among them, the Indians instead of being offended, would join with us in ridiculing them & seemed to think as lightly of them as we did, and there was none of them they would not sell even for trifles. (Beaglehole 1967 : 1185; n.b.: the last was not true of the Kū image)

So much for supposed sacrilege the unhinged Cook was led to commit out of guilt and humiliation. The further supposition that Cook added to the outrage by having Watman buried at Hikiau fares no better in the light of the documentary evidence. On the contrary, Obeyesekere characteristically compounds the inadequacies of his commonsense history of this episode by a neglect of the ethnography.

First, Obeyesekere has to make Cook responsible for the decision to bury Watman in Hikiau temple. No historical source even suggests this. Mainly the sources suggest that Watman was buried at Hikiau by Hawaiian request. Rickman, however, says it was according to Watman's "own desire" (1966 : 307). Ledyard, who borrows a lot from Rickman, agrees it was Watman's idea, to which Cook acceded, but before Cook could broach it to the Hawaiians, the priest Keli'ikea anticipated him by offering a place on Hikiau heiau (Ledyard 1963:124). Obeyesekere finds the notion that Watman would want to be buried in a heathen shrine improbable on the face of it, and for similar but inverse reasons does not think that Hawaiians would have wanted a common English seaman interred in their sacred royal temple.[1] However, with regard to the Hawaiian role in the decision, Ledyard at least agrees with Lieutenant King. In his private journal, King wrote: "The Chiefs knowing of [Watman's] death expressd a desire that he might be bury'd on shore, which he was accordingly upon the Morai" (Beaglehole 1967:517). In the official account: "At the request of the king of the island, he was buried on the Morai. . . . Old Kaoo [the priest] and his brethren were spectators" (Cook and King 1784, 3:24). Obeyesekere says the official account is implicitly contradicted by the absence of the king, Kalani'ōpu'u, from the ceremony. We are thus left to believe that Lieutenant King's (and Ledyard's) reports of Hawaiian interest in having Watman taken to Hikiau were concocted. Cook was presumably behind it all. What was not behind it all, according to Obeyesekere, who had long since dismissed the idea as "hard to believe," was the coincidence of Watman's death and the ritual prescription of a human sacrifice in the terminal ceremonies of the Makahiki. At a date in the ceremonial calendar that would occur at or about the Gregorian date of Watman's death, the king's human god, Kohoali'i, eats the eye of a man sacrificed at the temple used in the main Makahiki rites (Malo 1951:152).[2] The correspondences would not only explain Hawaiian interest in getting Watman's body to Hikiau, but the way Hawaiians acted during the interment.

Obeyesekere thinks the Hawaiians were boycotting the British ceremonies out of chagrin at this impious insult Cook was now adding to the

1. Obeyesekere thinks it not improbable that Watman wanted to be buried ashore, though not at Hikiau. But King's description of Watman's final illness would make it unlikely that the latter had cogitated on or communicated his wishes about burial. Watman had been convalescent when the British first came into Kealakekua and spent a few days on shore—that would be in the sick bay established in the temple. He seemed then to recover and returned to the ship at his own request. The day after, however, he was "taken with a paralytic stroke & in two days died" (Beaglehole 1967:516). As usual, Ledyard has his own, idiosyncratic version: "he died with a slow-fever that had partly been hastened if not brought on by intemperance" (1963: 123). If Ledyard is to be believed, Cook's purported dear old friend had a drinking problem. As for his low status disqualifying Watman for burial at the temple, Obeyesekere forgets that sacrificial victims are generally rebels, wrongdoers or so-called slaves (*kauwā*).

2. Watman was buried on 1 February 1779. This was the 14th day of the moon, the Hua tabu period of the full moon. On the Hua period of the month of Kaelo, the sacrifice is made. By the concordance here adopted (Sahlins 1989), this was the month of Kā'elo.

injuries he had already done to Hikiau temple. In part, he reads this from the disappointment of the British (at least as recounted by Ledyard) at the Hawaiian response to the grand procession they made with Watman's body from the landing place to the temple:

> When the Pennace landed with Watman's body we expected the curiousity of the natives would have been excited to come in crouds to see it and to observe our conduct upon the occasion—but it was quite otherwise, the people all shut themselves up in their houses, and nobody was seen but two or three men who attended Kikinny [Keli'ikea]. (Ledyard 1963:124)

Neither Ledyard nor Obeyesekere had reflected on the fact that the British had not been able to witness the disposal of the corpse in the two funerary ceremonies that took place during Cook's visit—the corpse having been (more or less literally) spirited away. And perhaps even more to the point here, when the priests hunt a human sacrifice and drag him to the temple, the people indeed shut themselves up in their houses (Malo 1951:172–73). The other evidence of the Hawaiians' avoidance of the ceremonies was the small number of them present. Obeyesekere takes Ledyard's mention of Keli'ikea and the two or three others who were seen at the procession as that small number. Lieutenant King speaks of Ka'ō'ō "& his brethern" as present at the ceremonies (Beaglehole 1967:517); Edgar spoke rather of "many Indians attending" (Log, 2 Feb 1779). Be that as it may, Obeyesekere seems to have forgotten that common people are not participants in ceremonies taking place in the royal (*luakini*) temples, which are restricted to high priests and chiefs. (At one attended by Vancouver, in 1794, there were about 30 such dignitaries present: Vancouver 1801, 5:36–39). Ignoring this ethnography allows Obeyesekere to consummate his pseudo-history of Cook's wrath with the invention of a Hawaiian pollution-removal ritual:

> One can reasonably interpret this Hawaiian boycott as a reaction to the pollution of the royal *heiau* by the burial of a commoner. . . . The priests were the only ones present and their ritual actions on this occasion had nothing to do with honoring Watman but were attempts to counter the effects of pollution or the violation of the temple taboos. (Ob. 195)

Obeyesekere is thus referring to the fact that after the Christian service was read, Ka'ō'ō *mā* proceeded to throw in a dead pig, some plantains, and coconuts. Indeed, reports King, they wanted to show their respect for

Watman by a great many of such articles, together with the ceremonies they repeated. And although "they were in some measure stop'd," yet for three nights "Kao & the rest of them surrounded the grave, killd hogs, sung a great deal, in which Acts of Piety & good will they were left undisturb'd" (Beaglehole 1967:517). Ledyard relates joining a company of 12 or 13 men on one of these nights. His understanding was that they gathered solely "to sacrifice (if I may so call it) to the manes of Watman" (1963:125). That this was in fact a ritual burial of importance to Hawaiians is corroborated by contemporary descriptions of two burial places, called by the British "Morais" (that is, the Tahitian *marae*, 'temple'), likewise the subject of offerings of pigs and plantains, and attended by priests. Edgar saw these on one of his inland excursions (Log, following 4 Feb 1779). Law describes them thus:

> We also saw two very Good Morais one of which I Examined & found it differing from the Taheiti ones, as People Expose the Body under a Shed Erected on Long Poles . . . & Erect a kind of Monument over the Tomb[.] on a *bye* Tree hanging was 2 pigs & a Bunch of Plantains. The Morai was Close Adjoining to a House which belong to a Priest Who I suppose had charge of the Dead Man. (Journal, 31 Jan 1779)

Beginning with the amphiboly of Cook's supposed prostration before the image of Kū, Obeyesekere's speculations on Cook's wrath give rise to an elaborate set of makeshift interpretations whose truth values range from the historically unknown to the ethnographically unwarranted, passing by way of the textually disproven.

The Language Problem

lthough, as in the case of Lieutenant Rickman, Obeyesekere can be dubious about the linguistic competence of the Cook journalists, at other points he is able to accept uncritically their specific understandings of what Hawaiians were saying or doing. So, according to Obeyesekere, not only does Rickman accurately report from Kealakekua that Kalaniʻōpuʻu is currently at Maui making peace but Samwell is able to make a subtle distinction (that escapes later Western academics) in noting that a certain ceremony conducted by priests at the House of Lono was merely intended to make Cook a sacred chief in the same capacity as Omeah, likewise known as "Lono." Again, Obeyesekere sometimes qualifies his judgments of Haole linguistic knowledge by confirming what they admitted themselves, that they did not have enough to decipher the local religious concepts. This is plainly true, but plainly also their ignorance can then be no argument against the Hawaiian understanding of Cook as a form of the Makahiki god.

Lieutenant King admitted that the British did not learn as much about Hawaii as they should have, despite that "we may be said to have a great advantage in knowing something of their Language" (Beaglehole 1967: 603). They knew something of the language in part because of their Tahitian experience, which in the case of certain people included participation in one or both of Cook's previous Pacific voyages. From the very first day of contact, off Kauaʻi, on the 19th of January 1778, the British picked up cognates of Tahitian in the speech of Hawaiians, from which they immediately concluded the two peoples were of the same "nation." But because the British spent only about a fifth of their three-and-a-half months in Hawaii on shore, and because the estimable observers Cook and Anderson died on this voyage, the report of things Hawaiian, according to Mr. King, came out poorer than it might have been.

All the same, many of the Cook chronicles show such detailed and verifiable comprehension of Hawaiian conditions and activities as could only come from "knowing something of their language." This includes Mr. King's own quite remarkable account of the politics of the several Hawaiian islands, including the genealogies, kinship and marriage relationships, and territorial claims and disputes of the ruling chiefs and their families (Beaglehole 1767: 614–17; see also the independent account in Ellis 1782, 2:184–87). The British learned that shortly before they appeared in November 1778 the Hawai'i king had been fighting in Maui on behalf of the claims of his son Kiwala'o to the royal succession in that island; they knew that the king's wife, Kalola, together with Kiwala'o, had been left at Maui when the Hawai'i army came into Kealakekua; they also knew in advance exactly when the king and warriors would arrive at Kealakekua. The British successfully arranged several inland excursions with the Lono priests of Kealakekua, guided and provisioned at the latter's command. Among other such arrangements were the use of Hikiau temple and its precincts by the Haole; and conversely on two occasions they, on request, gave over the temple to the priests for specific rituals. The British were guests of two "entertainments" staged for them by Hawaiians, the plans for which were communicated to them—after they had communicated to Hawaiians the date of their departure. When the observatory party under Lieutenant King was beseiged at Hikiau after Cook's death, they were able to effect a cease fire by appealing to the Lono priests—to whom they had at first denied that Cook was dead. Thereafter, over several days, the British would successfully negotiate for the return of Cook's body. But then, from the first day at Kealakekua, they had effectively communicated with the chiefs (Palea and Kanaina) who came on board the ships to regulate the movements of Hawaiians on deck; and when they wished the ships cleared of Hawaiians (or of Hawaiian men) these two saw to it. The Haole at Kealakekua were also able to make shrewd observations about the antagonisms subsisting between the local priests and the king's party at Ka'awaloa, observations entirely consistent with later historical relationships between Lono priests and Hawai'i royals. The British also learned that Lono resided in the heavens and the king's god lived in their own country (Beretane). They observed the phonetic shift from *t* to *k* in the Hawaiian language passing from the leeward to the windward part of the archipelago. Samwell provided a "specimen" word list of more than 140 words and phrases, including 21 of human body parts, 18 verbs or verb phrases, and several sentences (Beaglehole 1967:1230–34). One could go on for some time. But enough said, perhaps, for the historiographic conclusion that no statement about Hawaiian speech or action on the part of the Cook chroniclers can be dismissed a priori on the grounds of their supposed linguistic incompetence. Everything that is said about Hawaii in these journals has to be evaluated in relation to the accumulated knowledge of Hawaiian history and culture.

Kamakau's Gods

Obeyesekere was not forewarned by Dorothy Barrère's critical comments on just this aspect of Kamakau's work—the assimilation of Hawaiian to Christian concepts of god and man—although he quotes it himself:

> Kamakau was an ardent, vehement, and highly vocal Christian convert, and his own well-founded knowledge of the traditions of his people concerning their gods and their creation myths *led him into willful interpretations and equations in his zeal to show a comparable background of belief between the Hawaiian and Christian concepts of god and man.* (Barrère in Kamakau 1964 : viii; my emphasis)

The 1838 *Mooolelo* original of Kamakau's story of Cook's advent, as well as the Pogue version of 1858, repeatedly draw the conclusion that Cook was an actualization of Lono, on the kinds of empirical bases we have been discussing. These texts speak of judgments that presuppose a humanized cosmos and the immanence of spirit, including the logical synthesis thereof, the appearance of gods in human forms. At Maui, Cook *mā* "were gods; they were volcanoes because fire burned in their mouth" (Kahananui 1984 : 170; n.b. the connection to Lonomakua, keeper of volcanic fires). Or at Kaua'i: "And that night guns were fired and fire leaped skyward. The people thought it was a god. They named it Lonomakua—Father Lono" (ibid, 168). So far as can be determined, the British did not fire their big guns at Kaua'i on their initial visit. The motivation of this text, its Hawaiian logic, appears to be that expressed by the Ni'ihau or Kaua'i chief to Rickman the next year: "pointing to the sun, [he] seemed to suppose we should visit that luminary in our course, and that the thunder and lightning of our guns, and that which came from the heavens were both derived from the same source" (Rickman 1966 : 332). Other such structural motivations of Hawaiian memories will be noted momentarily.

With regard to the flexibility of Hawaiian interpretations of Cook, there are indeed explicit and implicit disagreements in the older texts as well as in Kamakau. They are of the kind that have been discussed here concerning the politics of Lono beliefs and the relations of different groups to the god. Disputes appear about whether or not to fight the god or to steal from the god. In the texts the disputes are notably resolved by the powers-that-be: priests and ruling chiefs, people who "could bring structure to bear on matters of opinion, and by rendering Cook the tributes of Lono, practically engaged the people in this religion of which they were the legitimate prophets" (Sahlins 1985a : 122). The early Hawaiian texts suggest a diversified "structure of the conjuncture," at times echoing the famous "party matters" that the journalists of Cook's voyage had observed. But, for all that, the early *Mooolelo* accounts are not equivocal about Cook's identification with Lono. He was Lono all right—in the Makahiki form, Lonomakua (Kahananui 1984 :168). The only point on which they correspond to Kamakau's Christian suppositions is the famous business at Cook's death, when the warrior decides Cook was not a god because he cried out and fell (ibid., 174). Again, the deduction supposes that up to that moment, the people believed he was Lono.

Other arguments alleged by Kamakau to have been made against Cook's divine status are evident permutations of the *Mooolelo* story as well as of the Hawaiian conceptions it purveys. Thus Kamakau tries to make out that when Cook slept with the daughter of the ranking Kaua'i woman, Kamakahelei, and the British sailors likewise slept with Hawaiian women, this convinced the people that the Haole were mere men, because Hawaiian gods do not do such things. This would be a peculiar statement for Kamakau to make in any case, since two or three years later he spoke of just such unions as a main source of family gods (*'aumākua*):

> The *'aumākua*, ancestral deities of the family, were the ancient source gods "from time immemorial" (*akua kumu kahiko mai na kupuna mai*)—the gods from whom the ancestors implicitly believed they had come, or one from whom they had actually descended. If a god had mated among them, and a human had come forth, this god was an *'aumākua* of theirs, and a *kumupa'a*, a "fixed origin." . . . An *akua 'aumākua* . . . was

a god who was deeply venerated. . . . The *akua 'aumākua* spoken of by
the ancestors were Kane, Kanaloa, Ku, and Lono. (Kamakau 1964:28;
originally published in 1870)

Of course there is the well-known story that Lono had descended from
heaven to mate with the high ranking woman of Puna (Hawai'i). And it is
precisely such dimensions of the Lono tradition that appear in the *Mooolelo*
version of Cook's advent, including the disagreements about how one should
relate to this Lono. At the Makahiki, Lono returns for his lost wife, or, in a
cosmic register, to fructify the land. And although Cook did not sleep with
Kamakahelei's daughter, so far as anyone can tell, the Hawaiian tradition of
the *Mooolelo* says that he did—exactly in his capacity as Lono. Moreover,
the *Mooolelo* sets this event in an argument among Hawaiians that entails the
other aspect of Lono's return, also related to his searching for the wife,
namely the battle with the people that ensues. When the Kaua'i people saw
the fire of ship's guns and decided this was Lonomakua,

> The natives [*kānaka*] thought they should fight. A certain chiefess—
> Kaumuali'i's mother—whose name was Kamakahelei, said, "Don't urge
> war against our god, placate him so that the god will be kind to us."
> Then Kamakahelei gave her own daughter as companion for Lono—
> Captain Cook. Lelemahoalani was the name of said woman. She was
> Kaumuali'i's older sister. (Kahananui 1984:168)

    Kamakau's intellectual work was frequently distinguished by a competi-
tive emulation of Malo and other Lahainaluna colleagues. His story of Captain Cook clearly tries to one-up the *Mooolelo* of 1838 in two ways. One was
this attempt to undermine the credibility of Cook's Lono identity by ascribing the skepticism of Christian conceptions to the old Hawaiians, as if they
likewise could not believe the man was the god. (The aspects that Obeyesekere deems the flexibility of Hawaiian beliefs were the contributions, courtesy of Kamakau, of Christian inflexibilities.) The other and opposite com-
petitive disposition consists of Kamakau's elaboration of the indigenous
logic of the concrete. Kamakau goes beyond his Hawaiian predecessors by
multiplying the empirical resemblances between the foreigners and divine
beings of received myths. This empirically motivated mytho-poesis is actually the more salient aspect, as Kamakau had to account for the main events
of Cook's Hawaiian career—not to mention that he was writing for a Hawaiian audience. Thus,

> When they went out to the ship, seeing some of the strangers peering
> out of the holes at the back one man said, "Those are the gods of the

upland of Mouths-shining-with-fat (Kanukuhinuhinu), Peep (Ki'ei) and Peer (Halo)." Seeing one of the strangers with a telescope they said, "Long-eyes (Maka-loa) and Eyes-that-rove (Na-maka-oka'a) the stargazers who see the heavens and the earth. . . . When they saw the strangers letting out ropes the natives called them Ku-of-the-tree-fern (Ku-pulupulu) and Coverer-of-the-island (Moku-hali'i). These were gods of the canoe builders in the forest. (Kamakau 1961:98–99)

Kamakau's text, including practically the whole debate about Cook's status, is developed in these mytho-practical terms. And the main conclusion was that "the people said, 'It is true, this is Lono, our god! This is Lono, our god!'" (ibid., 100).

Atua in the Marquesas
and Elsewhere

In his early account of the Marquesas, W. P. Crook wrote:

> They assert their ancestors were visited by Atuas from some of these
> islands [among the 41 named in sacred songs]. This Title they now
> give indiscriminately to all Europeans, & Foreigners of every descrip-
> tion. The Stories they relate, concerning some of their ancient Visi-
> tors, require them indeed, to have been something supernatural.
> (1800:30)

There seems to have been some misunderstanding of Dening's reading
of Marquesan historical ethnography on such matters. Obeyesekere wrote:
"Greg Dening in a personal communication tells me that this extension of
atua/akua for whites was very common among the Marquesans but it should
not be translated as 'god'" (Ob. 198). Dening explains the difficulty:

> Dr. Obeyesekere's citation of my personal communication to him on
> the use of the term *atua* in the Marquesas does not catch the meaning
> of what I wrote to him and certainly, in my opinion, does not support
> the point he made of it. He had written inquiring amongst other
> things about a footnote of mine in *The Marquesan Journal of Edward
> Robarts 1797–1824* (Honolulu: University Press of Hawaii, 1974),
> p. 74. The footnote read: "atua. The name given by the Marquesans
> to Europeans (Porter, 1882, II:52; Crook, 'Account': 30; Coulter,
> 1845; 204). The name and consequent privileges of deification were
> applied to other members of Marquesan society (Crook, 'Account':
> 35). Whether Robarts was categorised as an *atua* in this sense, we do
> not know." Obeyesekere was speculating at that time whether the use
> of the term *atua* for European intruders was a consequence of Cook's

death, not independent of it. My knowledge of the Marquesas suggested he was on the wrong track. The William Pascoe Crook manuscript, although composed by Samuel Greethead, the London Missionary Society intellectual, was made up from Crook's reminiscences of his year-long stay in the Marquesas in 1797 and the supportive evidence of the young Marquesan, Temouteitei, whom Crook had brought back to England. The Crook manuscript manifestly demonstrates that the Marquesan categorisation of the Europeans as *atua* was of their own making. This is what I wrote to Obeyesekere, January 29, 1991: "Crook (in reality Samuel Greethead) gives a list of islands (mostly unidentifiable in their ancient names) and then says: 'They [the Marquesans] assert that their ancestors were visited by Atuas from some of these islands. This title they now give indiscriminately to all Europeans, and foreigners of every description.' It has long been a contention of mine that the concept 'gods' for *atua* does not nearly give the meaning, or rather that the European presumptions that what is 'gods' to them is what *atua* means are skewed."

I suppose that I should have said quite explicitly that I thought that by using the term *atua* the Marquesans were invoking all their own mythic context of the word. I cannot see that the Marquesan mythic context would include all the Euro-American mythic content of their word "gods" as well. But I am just as sure it would not be contained by what the Euro-Americans would conceive of as "ordinary men." (Greg Dening, personal communication, quoted by permission)

The misunderstanding probably has its source in the use of *atua* as an unmarked term for spiritual being, in which function it includes many specific forms, as well as beings—including human beings—Europeans would not consider divine. Handy's ethnography of the Marquesans explains the matter thus:

Deities in the Marquesas may be grouped in the following classes: gods of myth and creation; departmental gods, including gods of nature and the elements, patrons of occupations, and gods of sickness; and tutelary deities, including personal, family, and tribal ancestral spirits. There was also what may be regarded as a class of demi-gods, including legendary heroes, and other characters. Such a classification must not be regarded as exact in the sense that every god will fit conveniently into one and only one class. For instance, Tana-oa is at one and the same time a mythical figure, a legendary hero, a god of the elements, and the patron of occupations. All gods of all classes were ancestral.

The term *etua* or *atua* was applied to all grades of supernatural beings included in the above classes, except the legendary characters whom the natives refer to, for the most part, as men *(enata)*. The native does not distinguish supernatural and natural, as we do. *Atua* were simply beings with powers and qualities of the same kind as those of living men *(enata)*, but greater. Some men and women were *atua* in this life; most became *atua* after death. (Handy 1923:244)

Reminiscences of the eponym of the modern Cook Islands are like those of New Zealand Maori: relatively brief, later accounts—in this case mainly second generation, collected by William Wyatt Gill—which speak of this passing visit of a certain god, or demi-god or "godlike race" (Gill 1984:258). The last occurs in a historical song from Mangaia, where contact was made only aboard ship—"Tangaroa has sent a ship, / Which has burst through the solid blue vault" (ibid., 255). Gill also records the speculations voiced about the spirit-world origin of the ship before anyone ventured out. One chief "oracularly declared that it was the great (god) Motoro himself come up from paying a visit to Vatea [ancestor of gods and men]" (Gill 1876:87). Local tradition at Atiu has it that Lieutenant Gore was asked a question of similar implication when he landed on the island:

"Are you one of the glorious sons of Tetumu? Are you a son of the Great Root or Cause, whose children are half divine, half human?" According to their mythology, Tetumu (= Root, Origin or Cause) was the father of gods and men and the maker of all things. The white complexion of the visitors, their wonderful clothing and weapons, all indicated, in their opinion, a divine origin. To these inquiries no reply was given. (Gill 1984:260)

The most noteworthy aspect of the British accounts of the relationships with the Atiu people (for our purposes) are: (1) Cook's astonishment that the local people conceived the Sheep and Goats as "some strange birds"; whereas (2) Omai, the Tahitian on board the *Resolution*, reciprocated the honors supposedly accorded the foreigners by calling the island "Wenua no Eatua, that is a land of gods" (Beaglehole 1967:83, 87). The first represented the common Polynesian classification of birds and land animals as *manu-manu*—which for Cook was an empirical scandal:

It will appear rather incredible how any set of men could conceive a Sheep or Goat to be a bird, as there is not the least similarity between them; but these people could have no idea of there being any other land animals but Hogs, Dogs and Birds; they must see they were not of the two first and therefore conceived they must be some species of the latter they had not seen before. (Ibid., 83)

Omai explained that he called Atiu a land of gods because "there were a great many men in it who were possessed with the Spirit of the Eatua, a kind of franticness, very common, as he says, at Otaheite and the neighboring isles" (ibid., 87).

Note that it is common in Western Polynesia and certain parts of eastern Melanesia for the designation referring to Europeans to have intimations of divine origin—as the famous *papalangi*, or *palangi*, which can be glossed 'heavenly people' or 'sky-breakers' (see Meleisea 1987:42). Maurice Leenhardt's reflections on the phenomenon in New Caledonia are like many others. Explaining the apparent inattention of the Caledonians to the movements of their early British visitors, Leenhardt wrote:

This was neither indolence nor indifference on the part of the Caledonians but an attitude of complete anticipation toward the extraordinary visit of human beings arriving from the empty horizon. Were they authentic human beings? The Caledonians were convinced of their inauthenticity. They refused to give the name of *Kamo* to this camouflaged man. More than a hundred and fifty years have passed since then, but even today, if you meet a Caledonian entering a store in the city of Nouméa and ask him in his language what he is shopping for, he says he is going to buy a *kara bao*, that is, he is going to buy a god-skin. Since the time of Cook and his successors, European dress has been called 'god-skin.' So the first white men to land on the island were confused with the deified defunct, ghosts returning to visit their old homes, not *kamos* but *baos*. (Leenhardt 1979:27)

There are many such traces of "first contact" all around Polynesia and environs. Their inscriptions in local speech do not suggest that the conception of the advent of the foreigners as a spiritual irruption was a European myth.

Bibliography

Abbreviations

ABCFM/L   Letters of Hawaiian missionaries to the American Board of Commissioners for Foreign Missions. Hawaiian Mission Children's Society Library, Honolulu.

ABCFM/MJ   Sandwich Islands Mission Journal, Hawaii Papers of the American Board of Commissioners for Foreign Missions. Hawaiian Mission Children's Society Library, Honolulu.

ABCFM/ML   Missionary Letters, Correspondence of American Board Missionaries in Hawaii. Hawaiian Mission Children Society Library, Honolulu.

AH   Archives of the State of Hawaii, Honolulu.

AH/GB   Genealogy Books, Archives of the State of Hawaii, Honolulu.

BM   British Library. British Museum, London.

BM/GB   Genealogy Books, Bernice P. Bishop Museum.

HEN   Hawaiian Ethnographic Notes, Bernice P. Bishop Museum, Honolulu.

Kuokoa   *Ka Nupepa Kukoa.* Hawaiian-language newspaper.

Ko Hawaii   *Ko Hawaii Pae Aina.* Hawaiian-language newspaper.

LC/FT   Foreign Testimony, Land Commission Records of the Department of Land and Natural Resources, Kingdom of Hawaii. Archives of Hawaii, Honolulu.

LC/NR   Native Register, Land Commission Records of the Department of Land and Natural Resources, Kingdom of Hawaii. Archives of Hawaii, Honolulu.

LC/NT   Native Testimony, Land Commission Records of the Department of Land and Natural Resources, Kingdom of Hawaii. Archives of Hawaii, Honolulu.

LMS   London Missionary Society (CWM) Journals, Library of the
               School of Oriental and African Studies, University College,
               London.

MH   *Missionary Herald* (Journal of the ABCFM).

MKP/GB   Genealogy Books, Mary Kawena Pukui, Church of the Latter
               Day Saints Library, Laie, Hawaii.

ML   Mitchell Library. Library of New South Wales, Sydney,
               Australia.

NLA   National Library of Australia, Canberra.

PRO/Adm   Public Records Office, Dept. of the Admiralty, London

Works Cited

An asterisk (*) indicates that a work is unpublished.

Adler, Alfred. 1982. *La mort est le masque du roi*. Paris: Payot.

Andrews, Lorrin. 1974 [1865]. *A dictionary of the Hawaiian language*. Rutland, Vt.:
    Charles E. Tuttle.

Anonymous of Kohala. 1916–17. "Relating to Amusements," in A. Fornander, *For-
    nander collection of Hawaiian antiquities and folklore*. Memoirs of the Bernice P. Bishop
    Museum, vol. 4, pt. 1, pp. 192–217.

*Anonymous of Mitchell. 1781. Copy of Letter to Mrs Strachan of Spithead, 23 Janu-
    ary 1781. Mitchell Library (Safe 1/67).

*Anonymous of NLA. "An Account of the Death of Cook, 9–22 February 1779, by
    an Eyewitness," National Library of Australia (MS 8).

*Appadurai, Arjun. 1991. "Culture, Cultures, Culturalism," Ford Lecture, Social Sci-
    ence Collegiate Division, University of Chicago, April 1991. Manuscript.

Ashmore, Malcolm, Derek Edwards, and Jonathan Potter. 1994. "The Bottom Line:
    The Rhetoric of Reality Demonstrations," *Configurations* 2:1–14.

Astley, Thomas (Collection). 1747. *A new general collection of voyages and travels*, vol. 4.
    London: Thomas Astley. (Also known as "Green's collection.")

Babadzan, Alain. 1993. *Les dépouilles des dieux: Essai sur la religion Tahitienne à l'époque de
    découverte*. Paris: Maison des Sciences de l'Homme.

Bachelot, Père Alexis. 1830. "Mission des Îles Sandwick [sic]," *Annales de la Propagation
    de la Foi*, 19:265–98.

*Ballard, Chris. 1992. "First Contact as Non-Event in the New Guinea Highlands,"
    Paper presented at the 91st Annual Meeting of the American Anthropological
    Association, San Francisco, 2–6 December 1992.

Barnard, F. M. 1969. Introduction. Pp. 3–60 in *J. G. Herder on social and political culture*,
    ed. and trans. F. M. Barnard. Cambridge: Cambridge University Press.

*Bayly, William. MSa. Log (11 June 1776–30 April 1779) and Journal (12 August
    1777–30 June 1778). Turnbull Library, Wellington.

*———. MSb. A Log and Journal, kept on Board His Majestes Sloop *Discovery* by
    Wm Bayly Astronomer. August 1, 1776–December 3, 1779. PRO Adm. 55/20.

Beaglehole, J. C. 1956. "On the Character of Captain James Cook," *The Geographical Journal* 122:417–19.

———. 1967. *The journals of Captain James Cook on his voyages of discovery, III: The voyage of the* Resolution *and* Discovery, *1776–1780*. Parts 1 and 2. Cambridge: Cambridge University Press (for the Hakluyt Society).

———. 1969. *The journals of Captain James Cook: The voyage of the* Resolution *and* Adventure, *1772–1775*. Cambridge University Press (for the Hakluyt Society).

Beckwith, Martha. 1919. "The Hawaiian Romance of Laieikawai by S. N. Haleole," *Bureau of American Ethnology Report* 33:285–366. Washington, D.C.: Government Printing Office.

———. 1932. *Kepelino's traditions of Hawaii*. Bernice P. Bishop Museum Bulletin 95. Honolulu: Bishop Museum.

———. 1970. *Hawaiian mythology*. Honolulu: University of Hawaii Press.

———. 1972. *The Kumulipo*. Honolulu: University of Hawaii Press.

Bell, Edward. 1929. "Log of the Chatham," *Honolulu Mercury* 1(4):7–26; 1(5):55–69; 1(6):76–96; 2(1):80–91; 2(2):119–29.

Bénéton, Philippe. 1975. *Histoire de mots: Culture et civilisation*. Travaux et Recherches de Science Politique, no. 35. Paris: Fondation Nationale des Sciences Politiques.

Beneveniste, Emile. 1971. *Problems in general linguistics*. Coral Gables, Fla.: University of Miami Press.

Bergendorff, Steen, Ulla Hasager, and Peter Henriques. 1988. "Mythopraxis and History: On the Interpretation of the Makahiki." *Journal of the Polynesian Society* 97:391–408.

Berlin, Brent. 1992. *Ethnobiological classification: Principles of categorization of plants and animals in traditional societies*. Princeton: Princeton University Press.

Berlin, Isaiah. 1976. *Vico and Herder: Two studies in the history of ideas*. New York: Vintage Books.

———. 1982. *Against the current: Essays in the history of ideas*. Harmondsworth: Penguin Books.

———. 1991. *The crooked timber of humanity*. New York: Alfred A. Knopf.

———. 1993. "The Magus of the North." *New York Review of Books* 40(17).

Berlin, Isaiah, and Ramin Jahanbegloo. 1991. *Conversations with Isaiah Berlin*. New York: Charles Scribner's Sons.

Berman, Morris. 1981. *The reenchantment of the world*. Ithaca: Cornell University Press.

Berndt, Ronald M. 1952–53. "A Cargo Movement in the Eastern Central Highlands of New Guinea." *Oceania* 23:41–64, 138–157, 203–34.

Besant, Walter. 1890. *Captain Cook*. London: Macmillan.

Best, Elsdon. 1924. *The Maori*. 2 vols. Wellington: Harry H. Tombs.

———. 1972 [1925]. *Tuhoe: The children of the mist*, vol. 1. Wellington: A. H. & A. W. Reed.

———. 1976. *Maori religion and cosmology*, pt. 1. Wellington: A. R. Shearer, Government Printer.

Bingham, Hiram. 1969 [1855]. *A residence of twenty-one years in the Sandwich Islands*. New York: Praeger.

Bloch, Marc. 1966. *French rural history*, trans. Janet Sondheimer. Berkeley: University of California Press.

————. 1983. *Les rois thaumaturges.* Paris: Gallimard.

*Bloxam, Andrew. Diary of A. R. Bloxam on H.M.S. Blonde, 1824–5. Typescript in Bernice P. Bishop Museum Collections.

*Bloxam, (Rev.) Richard. "A Narrative of a Voyage to the Sandwich Islands in H.M.S. Blonde, 1824–1825–1826. National Library of Australia (MS 4255).

Bordo, Susan. 1987. *The flight to objectivity: Essays on Cartesianism and culture.* Albany: State University of New York Press.

Brossard, Contre-amiral de. 1966. *Moana, océan cruel: Les dieux meurent à la grande Mer du Sud.* Paris: Éditions France-Empire.

Buck, Sir Peter [Te Rangi Hiroa]. 1945. "Cook's Discovery of the Hawaiian Islands." Report of the Director for 1944. Bernice P. Bishop Museum Bulletin 186. Honolulu: Bishop Museum.

————. 1938. *Mangarevan society.* Bernice P. Bishop Museum Bulletin, no. 157. Honolulu: Bishop Museum.

Bulmer, Ralph. 1967. "Why is the Cassowary not a Bird? A Problem of Zoological Taxonomy among the Karam of the New Guinea Highlands." *Man* (n.s.) 2:5–25.

————. 1968. "Worms that Croak and Other Mysteries of Karam Natural History." *Mankind* 6:621–39.

————1974. "Folk Biology of the New Guinea Highlands." *Social Science Information* 13:9–28.

————1979. "Mystical and Mundane in Kalam Classifications of Birds." Pp. 57–79 in *Classifications in their social context,* ed. Roy F. Ellen and David Reason. London: Academic Press.

Bulmer, R. H., and J. I. Menzies. 1972–73. "Karam Classification of Marsupials and Rodents." *Journal of the Polynesian Society* 81:472–99; 82:86–107.

Bulmer, R. N. H., and M. J. Tyler. 1968. "Karam Classification of Frogs." *Journal of the Polynesian Society* 77:333–85.

Bulmer, Ralph N. H., J. I. Menzies, and F. Parker. 1975. "Kalam Classification of Reptiles and Fishes." *Journal of the Polynesian Society* 84:267–308.

Burney, James. 1819. *Chronological History of North-eastern Voyages.* London: Payne & Foss.

*————. MSa. "Journal of Lieutenant James Burney with Captain Ja⁵ Cook, 1776–1780." BM Add MS 8955.

*————. MSb. "Journal of the Proceedings of His Maj^ies Sloop, the Discovery." ML.

Burrows, Edwin G. 1936. *Ethnology of Futuna.* Bernice P. Bishop Museum Bulletin 138.

Byron, Captain the Hon. Lord [George Anson]. 1826. *Voyage of H.M.S. Blonde to the Sandwich Islands, in the years 1824–1825.* Ed. Maria Graham, Lady Calcott. London: John Murray.

Caillot, A.-C. Eugène. 1914. *Mythes, légendes et traditions des Polynésiens.* Paris: Ernest Leroux.

Campbell, Archibald. 1967. *A Voyage round the world from 1806 to 1812 . . . with an account of the . . . Sandwich Islands.* Honolulu: University of Hawaii Press.

Capell, A. 1938. "The Stratification of Afterworld Beliefs in the New Hebrides." *Folklore* 49:51–84.

Carruthers, Sir Joseph. 1930. *Captain James Cook, R.N., one hundred and fifty years after.* New York: Dutton.

Certeau, Michel de. 1991. "Travel Narratives of the French to Brazil: Sixteenth to Eighteenth Centuries." *Representations* 33:221–26.

*Chamberlain, Levi. Journals of Levi Chamberlain. Typescript. HMCS Library.

Chamisso, Adelbert von. N.d. *Chamissos Werke. Fünfter Teil: Reise um die Welt II*, ed. Max Sydow. Berlin, Leipzig, Wien, Stuttgart: Deutsches Verlagshales Bony & Co.

Chanel, Pierre. 1960. *Ecrits du Père Pierre Chanel, Missionaire Mariste à Futuna.* Publications de la Société des Océanistes, no. 9. Paris: Musée de l'Homme.

Charlot, John. 1987. Review of Valerio Valeri, *Kingship and sacrifice. Pacific Studies* 10: 107–47.

———. 1991. "The Feather Skirt of Nahi'ena'ena." *Journal of the Polynesian Society* 100: 199–265.

*Charlton, William. Journal, 10 February 1776–28 November 1779. PRO-Adm 51/4557/191–93.

*Clerke, James. Log and Proceedings, 10 February 1776–12 February 1779. PRO-Adm 55/22, 23.

Colnett, James. 1968. *Colnett's journal aboard the* Argonaut. New York: Greenwood Press.

*———. The Journal of James Colnett aboard the *Prince of Wales* and *Princess Royal.* . . . PRO-Adm 55/146.

Conklin, Harold C. 1962a. "Ethnobotanical Problems in the Comparative Study of Folk Taxonomy." *Proceedings of the Ninth Pacific Science Congress of the Pacific Science Association, 1957,* 4:299–301.

———. 1962b. "Lexicographical Treatment of Folk Taxonomies." Pp. 119–41 in *Problems in lexicography*, ed. F. Householder and S. Saporta. Indiana University Research Center in Anthropology, Folklore and Linguistics, Publication no. 21.

Conner, Daniel, and Lorraine Miller. 1978. *Master mariner: Captain James Cook and the peoples of the Pacific.* Seattle: University of Washington Press.

Connolly, Bob, and Robin Anderson. 1987. *First contact.* New York: Viking Penguin.

Cook, James, and James King. 1784. *A voyage to the Pacific Ocean . . . on His Majesty's Ships* Resolution *and* Discovery. 3 vols. Dublin: Chamberlaine et al. Maps 1.1 and 1.3 and fig. 1.2 of the present work are reproduced from a London edition of the same year (pub. W. and A. Strachan for G. Nicol and T. Cadell, 1784).

Cooper, Michael. 1965. *They came to Japan: An anthology of European reports on Japan, 1543–1640.* Berkeley and Los Angeles: University of California Press.

Craig, Barry. 1990. "The Telefomin Murders: Whose Myth?" Pp. 115–50 in *Children of Afek*, ed. Barry Craig and David Hyndman. Sydney: University of Sydney.

*Crook, William Pascoe. 1800. Account of the Marquesas Islands. Typescript copy of ML (C 111).

Dampier, Robert. 1971. *To the Sandwich Islands on H.M.S. Blonde.* Honolulu: University of Hawaii Press.

Davis, Eleanor Harmon. 1979. *Abraham Fornander: A biography.* Honolulu: University of Hawaii Press.

Deane, Herbert A. 1963. *The political and social ideas of St. Augustine.* New York: Columbia University Press.

Dibble, Sheldon. 1909 [1843]. *A history of the Sandwich Islands.* Honolulu: Thos. G. Thrum.

Diderot, Denis. 1972. *Le neveu de Rameau et autres textes*. Paris: Le Livre de Poche.

*Dimsdell, J. L. Account of the Death and Remains of Capt. Cook—at Owhyhee recd from Joshua Lee Dimsdell Quarter Master of the *Gunjara* Capt. James Barber. 1801. Dixson Library (MS Q 154).

Dixon, George. 1789. *A voyage round the world . . . in 1785, 1786, 1787 and 1788*. 2d ed. London: George Goulding.

Dominguez, Virginia R. 1992. "Invoking Culture: The Messy Side of 'Cultural Politics.'" *South Atlantic Quarterly* 91, no. 1 (Winter): 19–42.

Dumézil, Georges. 1948. *Mitra-Varuna: Essai sur deux représentations Indo-Européenes de la souveraineté*. Paris: Gallimard.

Dumont, Louis. 1986. "Are Cultures Living Beings? German Identity in Interaction." *Man* (n.s.) 21 : 587–604.

Durkheim, Émile. 1947. *The elementary forms of the religious life*. Glencoe, Ill.: The Free Press.

Eco, Umberto. 1986. *Art and beauty in the Middle Ages*. New Haven: Yale University Press.

*Edgar, Thomas. A Log of the Proceedings of His Majesty's Sloop Discovery, Charles Clerke, Commander. PRO-Adm 55/21, 55/24.

*———. A Journal of a Voyage undertaken to the South Seas by His Majesty's Ships Resolution and Discovery. BM Add MS 37528.

Elias, Norbert. 1978. *The civilizing process: History of manners*. New York: Urizen Books.

Ellen, R. F. 1986. "Ethnobiology, Cognition and the Structure of Prehension: Some General Theoretical Notes." *Journal of Ethnobiology* 6 : 83–98.

Ellis, William (Reverend). 1833. *Polynesian researches*. 4 vols. New York: J. & J. Harper.

*———. Journal of William Ellis, Sandwich Islands (1823). London Missionary Society (World Council of Missions) Papers. School of Oriental and African Studies, University College London, Library (South Seas, Journals, Box 5).

Ellis, William (Surgeon). 1782. *An authentic narrative of a voyage performed by Captain Cook and Captain Clerke. . . . 1776–80*. 2 vols. London: Robinson, Sewell and Dobrett.

*Emerson, J. S. (Collection). J. S. Emerson Collection, in HEN, vol. 1. Honolulu: Bishop Museum.

Emerson, Nathaniel B. 1893. *Long voyages of the ancient Hawaiians*. Hawaiian Historical Society Paper no. 5.

Farnham, Thomas J. 1846. *Life and adventures in California, and scenes in the Pacific Ocean*. New York: Graham.

Feachem, Richard. 1972–73. "The Religious Belief and Ritual of the Raiapu Enga." *Oceania* 43 : 259–85.

Feld, Steven. 1982. *Sound and sentiment: Birds, weeping, poetics and song in Kaluli expression*. Philadelphia: University of Pennsylvania Press.

Finney, Ben R., Ruby K. Johnson, Malcolm N. Chun, and Edith K. McKinzie. 1978. "Hawaiian Historians and the First Pacific History Seminar." In Neil Gunson, ed., *The changing Pacific: Essays in honour of H. E. Maude*. Melbourne: Oxford University Press.

Firth, Raymond. 1970. *Rank and religion in Tikopia*. London: George Allen and Unwin.

Fornander, Abraham. 1916–20. *Fornander collection of Hawaiian antiquities and folklore*, T. A. Thrum, ed. Memoirs of the Bernice Pauaki Bishop Museum, vols. 4–6.

———. 1969 [1878–85]. *An account of the Polynesian race.* 3 vols. Rutland, Vt.: Tuttle.

Foucault, Michel. 1973. *The order of things.* New York: Vintage Books.

Frankfort, Henri. 1948. *Kingship and the gods.* Chicago: University of Chicago Press.

Frankfort, H., and H. A. Frankfort. 1946. "The Emancipation of Thought from Myth." Pp. 363–88 in *The intellectual adventure of ancient man,* by H. Frankfort, H. A. Frankfort, John A. Wilson, Thorkild Jacobsen, and William A. Irwin. Chicago: University of Chicago Press.

Freud, Sigmund. 1961. *Civilization and its discontents.* New York: W. W. Norton.

Freycinet, Louis Claude de Saulses de. 1978. *Hawaii in 1819: A narrative account.* Trans. Ella Wiswell, ed. Marion Kelly. Pacific Anthropological Records 26. Honolulu: Bishop Museum.

Friedman, Jonathan. 1988. "No History is an Island." *Critique of Anthropology* 8:7–39.

Funkenstein, Amos. 1986. *Theology and the scientific imagination from the middle ages to the seventeenth century.* Princeton: Princeton University Press.

Gast, Ross H., and Agnes Conrad. 1973. *Don Francisco de Paula Marin.* Honolulu: Hawaiian Historical Society.

Geertz, Clifford. 1961. *The social history of an Indonesian town.* Cambridge: MIT Press.

———. 1973. *The interpretation of cultures.* New York: Basic Books.

Gell, Alfred. 1975. *Metamorphosis of the cassowaries.* London: Athlone Press.

Gilbert, George. 1982. *Captain Cook's final voyage: The journal of Midshipman George Gilbert.* Honolulu: The University of Hawaii Press.

*———. Journal of George Gilbert [Cook's Third Voyage]. BM Add MS 38580.

Gill, William Wyatt. 1876. *Life in the southern isles.* London: The Religious Tract Society.

———. 1984. *From darkness to light in Polynesia.* Institute of Pacific Studies, University of the South Pacific. Apia: Commercial Printers Ltd. (Reprint of the 1894 edition.)

Gordon, R. L., ed. 1981. *Myth, religion and society: Structuralist essays by M. Detienne, L. Gernet, J.-P. Vernant and P. Vidal-Naquet.* Cambridge: Cambridge University Press.

Gould, Lt.-Cmdr. Rupert T. 1928. "Some Unpublished Documents of Cook's Death." *The Mariner's Mirror* 14:301–19.

*Hammatt, Charles. Journal of Charles H. Hammatt, Sandwich Islands, 6 May 1823–9 September 1825. Baker Library, Harvard University.

Handy, E. S. Craighill. 1923. *The native culture in the Marquesas.* Bernice P. Bishop Museum Bulletin 9.

———. 1927. *Polynesian religion.* Bernice P. Bishop Museum Bulletin 34.

———. 1940. *The Hawaiian planter, Volume 1: His plants, methods and areas of cultivation.* Bernice P. Bishop Museum Bulletin 161.

———. 1968. "Traces of Totemism in Polynesia." *Journal of the Polynesian Society* 77:43–56.

Handy, E. S. Craighill, and Elizabeth Green Handy. 1972. *Native planters in old Hawaii: Their life, lore, and environment.* Bernice P. Bishop Museum Bulletin 233.

Handy, E. S. Craighill, and Mary Kawena Pukui. 1972. *The Polynesian family system in Ka-'u, Hawaii.* Rutland, Vt.: Charles E. Tuttle.

*Harvey, William. Log of the *Resolution.* PRO Adm 55/121.

Helvétius, Claude Adrien. 1795. *Oeuvres complètes*. Paris: Garnery.

Henry, Teuira. 1928. *Ancient Tahiti*. Bernice P. Bishop Museum Bulletin 48.

Herder, Johann Gottfried. 1966. "Essay on the Origin of Language." In Jean-Jacques Rousseau and Johan Gottfried Herder, *On the origin of language*. New York: Ungar.

——. 1968. *Reflections on the philosophy of the history of mankind*, ed. Frank E. Munuel. Chicago: University of Chicago Press.

——. 1969. *J. G. Herder on social and political culture*, ed. and trans. F. M. Barnard. Cambridge: Cambridge University Press.

de Heusch, Luc. 1982. *Rois nés d'un coeur de vache*. Paris: Gallimard.

——. 1985. *Sacrifice in Africa*. Bloomington: University of Indiana Press.

*Home, Alexander. Log Book of Captain Alex. Home, R.N. . . . while with Captain Cook on His Last Voyage. Typescript, NLA (MS 690).

Hough, Richard. 1979. *The murder of Captain James Cook*. London: Macmillan.

Huizinga, Johan. 1954. *The waning of the Middle Ages*. New York: Doubleday, Anchor Books.

Humphreys, Clarence Blake. 1926. *The southern New Hebrides*. Cambridge: Cambridge University Press.

Ii, John Papa. 1890. "Ancient Idolatrous Customs and Kapus of the Hawaiian People." Pp. 59–62 in *Hawaiian Annual for 1890*.

——. 1959. *Fragments of Hawaiian history*. Honolulu: Bishop Museum press.

Indices of Awards Made By the Board of Commissioners to Quiet Land Titles in the Hawaiian Islands. 1929. Honolulu: Star-Bulletin Press.

Izard, Michel, and Pierre Smith. 1979. *La fonction symbolique*. Paris: Gallimard.

——. 1982. *Between Belief and Transgression: Structuralist Essays in Religion, History, and Myth*, trans. John Leavitt. Chicago: University of Chicago Press. (English translation of Izard and Smith 1979.)

Johansen, J. Prytz. 1958. *Studies in Maori rites and myths*. Historisk-filosofiske Meldelelser 37(4). Copenhagen.

Judd, Laura Fish. 1966. *Honolulu: Sketches of life in the Hawaiian Islands from 1828 to 1861*. Chicago: Lakeside Press.

Kaempfer, Engelbertus. 1728. *The history of Japan*. 2 vols. London: Woodward.

Kahananui, Dorothy M., ed. 1984. *Ka Mooolelo Hawaii*. Trans. and ed. from the 1838 edition by Dorothy M. Kahananui. Honolulu: University of Hawaii, Committee for the Preservation and Study of Hawaiian Language, Art and Culture.

Kahiolo, G. W. 1978. *He Mooolelo no Kamapuaa: The story of Kamapuaa*. Trans. Esther T. Mookini and Erin C. Neizmen. Honolulu: Hawaiian Studies Program, University of Hawaii.

Kamakau, Kelou [Kamakau o Kaawaloa]. 1919–20. "Concerning Ancient Religious Ceremonies." Pp. 2–45 in A. Fornander, *Fornander collection of Hawaiian antiquities and folklore*, vol. 6, pt. 1. Honolulu: Memoirs of the Bernice P. Bishop Museum.

Kamakau, Samuel Manaiakalani. 1867. "Ia John Kaimola." *Ka Nupepa Kuokoa* (Hawaiian newspaper), 6 April 1867.

——. 1961. *Ruling chiefs of Hawaii*. Honolulu: Kamehameha Schools Press.

——. 1964. *Ka Po'e Kahiko: The people of old*. Trans. Mary Kawena Pukui, ed. Dorothy Barrère. Honolulu: Bishop Museum Press.

————. 1976. *The works of the people of old*, ed. D. Barrère. Bernice P. Bishop Museum Special Publication 61. Honolulu: Bishop Museum Press.

————. 1991. *Tales and traditions of the people of old: Nā Moʻolelo a ka Poʻe Kahiko*, trans. Mary Kuwena Pukui; ed. Dorothy B. Barrère. Bernice P. Bishop Museum Special Publication 90. Honolulu: Bishop Museum Press.

Kapiti, Pita (dictated to Mohi Turei). 1912. "The History of 'Horouta' Canoe, and the Introduction of the kumara into New Zealand." *Journal of the Polynesian Society* 21:152–63.

Kelly, Marion. 1983. *Nā Māla o Kona: Gardens of Kona. A history of land use in Kona, Hawaii.* Department of Anthropology Report 83–2; Bernice Pauahi Bishop Museum. Honolulu: Bishop Museum.

Kelly, Raymond C. 1977. *Etoro social structure: A study in structural contradiction.* Ann Arbor: The University of Michigan Press.

Kennedy, Donald Gilbert. 1931. "Field Notes on the Culture of Vaitapu, Ellice Islands." *Journal of the Polynesian Society* 41:217–319.

*Kepelino, Zepherino. Sundry Antiquarian Matters by Kepelino. In Emerson Collection, HEN, 1:113–25.

*King, James. Log and Proceedings [of Cook's Third Voyage]. PRO-Adm 55/116 (Photostat, Cook Collection, AH).

Kirtley, Basil F., and Esther T. Mookini, eds. and trans. 1977. "Kepelino's Hawaiian Collection; His Hooiliili Hawaii, Pepa I, 1858," *Hawaiian Journal of History* 11:39–68.

Koskinen, Aarne A. 1960. *Ariki, the first-born: An analysis of a Polynesian chieftain title.* Folklore Fellows Communications No. 181, Helsinki.

Kotzebue, Otto von. 1821. *A voyage of discovery into the South Sea . . . in the years 1815–1818.* 3 vols. (Volume 3 by Adelbert von Chamisso and others). London: Longman et al.

————. 1830. *A new voyage round the world, in the years 1823, 24, 25, 26.* London: Henry Colburn and Richard Bentley.

Kriger, Martin H. 1994. "Making Physical Objects: The Law of the Excluded Middle, Dumbing-Up the World, & Handles, Tools, and Fetishes." *Configurations* 2:107–17.

Kroeber, Alfred, and Clyde Kluckhohn. 1952. *Culture: A critical review of concepts and definitions.* New York: Vintage Books.

Kulick, Don. 1992. *Language shift and cultural reproduction: Socialization, self, and syncretism in a Papua New Guinean village.* Cambridge: Cambridge University Press.

Kuykendall, Ralph S. 1968. *The Hawaiian kingdom, Volume I: 1778–1854.* Honolulu: University of Hawaii Press.

Lach, Donald F., and Edwin J. Van Kley. 1993. *Asia in the making of Europe*, vol. 3. Chicago: University of Chicago Press.

Laval, P. Honoré. 1938. *Mangareva: L'Histoire ancienne d'un peuple polynésien.* Braine-le-Comte: Maison des Pères des Sacrés-Coeurs.

*Law, John. Journal of John Law. BM Add MS 37, 327.

Lawrence, Peter. 1984. *The Garia: An ethnography of a traditional cosmic system in Papua New Guinea.* Manchester: Manchester University Press.

Ledyard, John. 1963. *John Ledyard's journal of Captain Cook's last voyage,* ed. James Kenneth Munford. Corvallis: Oregon State University Press.

Leenhardt, Maurice. 1979. *Do kamo: Person and myth in the Melanesian world,* trans. Bsia Miller Gulati. Chicago: University of Chicago Press.

LeGoff, Jacques. 1988. *Medieval civilization.* Oxford: Basil Blackwell.

*Lepowsky, Maria. 1992. "Islanders, Ancestors and Europeans on the Coral Sea Frontier." Paper presented at the 91st annual meeting of the American Anthropological Association, San Francisco, 2–6 December 1992.

Lévi-Strauss, Claude. 1966a. *The savage mind.* Chicago: University of Chicago Press.

———. 1966b. "Introduction à l'oeuvre de Marcel Mauss." In Marcel Mauss, *Sociologie et anthropologie.* Paris: Presses Universitaires de France.

Lisiansky, Urey. 1814. *A voyage around the world in the years 1803, 1804, 1805, and 1806.* London: Booth.

Little, George. 1843. *Life on the Ocean; or Twenty Years at Sea.* Baltimore: Armstrong and Berry.

*Loomis, Elisha. Journal of Elisha Loomis, 1824–1826. Typescript copy of "original owned by Dr. Wm. D. Westervelt and placed in the University of Hawaii." AH.

Lovejoy, Arthur O. 1948. *Essays in the history of ideas.* Baltimore: Johns Hopkins Press.

*Lyons, Lorenzo. Letter to Rufus Anderson. Correspondence in ABCFM/L. Typescript copy, Hawaiian Mission Children's Society Library.

MacGregor, John. 1970. *Tibet: A chronicle of exploration.* New York: Praeger.

Macpherson, Crawford Brough. 1962. *The political theory of possessive individualism.* Oxford: Clarendon Press.

Majnep, I. S., and R. N. H. Bulmer. 1977. *Birds of My Kalam Country.* Auckland: University of Auckland Press.

Makemson, Maud. 1938. "Hawaiian Astronomical Concepts." *American Anthropologist* 40:370–83.

Makemson, Maud W. 1941. *The morning star rises.* New Haven: Yale University Press.

Malo, David. 1951. *Hawaiian antiquities,* trans. and ed. Nathaniel B. Emerson. Bernice P. Bishop Museum Special Publication no. 2.

*———. Ka Moolelo Hawaii. In MH. University of Hawaii Libraries.

Manby, Thomas. 1929. "Journal of Vancouver's Voyage to the Pacific Ocean." *Honolulu Mercury* 1(1):11–15; 1(2):33–45; 1(3):39–55.

Manuel, Frank E. 1968. Editor's introduction. Pp. ix–xxv in Johann Gottfried von Herder, *Reflections on the philosophy of the history of mankind,* trans and ed. Frank E. Manuel. Chicago: University of Chicago Press.

Manwaring, G. E. 1931. *My friend the Admiral: The life, letters and journals of Rear-Admiral James Burney, F.R.S.* London: George Routledge & Sons.

Marcus, George. 1989. "Chieftainship." Pp. 175–209 in *Developments in Polynesian ethnology,* ed. Alan Howard and Robert Borofsky. Honolulu: University of Hawaii Press.

Martin, John, ed. 1817. *An account of the natives of the Tonga Islands . . . from the extensive communications of Mr. William Mariner.* 2 vols. London: Murray.

Marx, Karl. 1961 [1844]. *Economic and philosophical manuscripts of 1844.* Moscow: Foreign Languages Publishing House.

Mathison, Gilbert Farquhar. 1825. *Narrative of a visit to Brazil, Chile, Peru and the Sandwich Islands, during the Years 1821 and 1822....* London: Charles Knight.

McDowell, Nancy. 1991. *The Mundugumor, from the field notes of Margaret Mead and Reo Fortune.* Washington, D.C.: Smithsonian Institution Press.

McKinzie, Edith Kawelohea. 1986. *Hawaiian genealogies, Extracted from Hawaiian language newspapers,* vol. 2. Laie, Hawaii: Institute for Polynesian Studies, Brigham Young University–Hawaiian Campus.

Meares, John. 1790. *Voyages made in the years 1788 and 1789, from China to the north west coast of America....* London: Logographic Press.

Meleisea, Malama. 1987. *Lagaga: A short history of western Samoa.* Suva, Fiji: University of the South Pacific.

Menzies, Archibald. 1920. *Hawaii nei 128 years ago.* Honolulu: W. F. Wilson.

*———. Journal of Vancouver's Voyages. BM Add. MS 32641.

Meyer, Alfred G. 1952. "Historical Notes on Ideological Aspects of the Concept of Culture in Germany and Russia." Pp. 403–13 in *Culture: A critical review of concepts and definitions,* ed. A. L. Kroeber and Clyde Kluckhohn. New York: Vintage Books.

Mikloucho-Maclay, Nikolai Nikolaevich. 1975. *New Guinea diaries, 1871–1883,* trans. C. L. Sentinella. Madang (P.N.G.): Kristen Press.

Moerenhaut, Jacques-Antoine. 1837. *Voyages aux îles au Grand Océan....* 2 vols. Paris: Bertrand.

Montaigne, Michel de. 1958. *The complete essays of Montaigne,* trans. Donald M. Frame. Stanford: Stanford University Press.

Montanas, Arnoldus. 1680. *Ambassades memorables de la Compagnie des Indes Orientales des Provinces Unies, vers les Empereurs du Japon.* Amsterdam: Jacob de Meurs.

Montesquieu, Baron de. 1966. *The spirit of the laws.* New York: Hafner.

———. 1973. *Persian letters.* London: Penguin Books.

Morris, Brian. 1984. "The Pragmatics of Folk Classification." *Journal of Ethnobiology* 4: 45–60.

Morrison, James. 1935. *The journal of James Morrison, Boatswain's mate of the Bounty,* ed. Owen Rutter. London: The Golden Cockerel Press.

Murray, A. W. 1862. *Missions in eastern Polynesia.* London: John Snow.

Murray-Oliver, Anthony. 1975. *Captain Cook's Hawaii, as seen by his artists.* Wellington: Millwood Press.

Newman, T. Stell. 1970. *Hawaiian fishing and farming on the island of Hawaii in A.D. 1778.* State of Hawaii, Dept. of Land and Natural Resources, Division of State Parks.

Nidditch, Peter H. 1975. Foreword. Pp. vii–xxvi in John Locke, *An Essay Concerning Human Understanding.* Oxford: Clarendon Press.

Nilles, John. 1953. "The Kuman People: A Study of Cultural Change in a Primitive Society in the Central Highlands of New Guinea." *Oceania* 24: 1–27.

Obeyesekere, Gananath. 1984. *The cult of the goddess Pattini.* Chicago: University of Chicago Press.

———. 1990. *The work of culture.* Chicago: University of Chicago Press.

———. 1992. *The apotheosis of Captain Cook: European mythmaking in the Pacific.* Princeton: Princeton University Press.

Oliver, Douglas. 1974. *Ancient Tahitian society.* 3 vols. Honolulu: University of Hawaii Press.

Padgen, Anthony. 1982. *The fall of natural man: The American Indian and the origins of comparative ethnology.* Cambridge: Cambridge University Press.

Péron, François. 1824. *Mémoires du Capitaine Péron sur ses voyages. . . .* Paris: Brissot-Thivars.

*Poepoe, Joseph. Kamehameha I: The conqueror of the Nation of Hawaii, The Lion of the Pacific. Typescript copy of translation from *Ka Na'i Aupuni* (newspaper), 1905–6.

Pogue, Rev. John F. 1978. *Mooolelo of ancient Hawaii,* trans. Charles W. Kenn. Honolulu: Topgallant.

Portlock, Nathaniel. 1789. *A voyage around the world . . . in 1785, 1786, 1787, and 1788.* London: Stockdale.

Posey, Darrell Addison. 1984. "Hierarchy and Utility in a Folk Biological Taxonomic System: Patterns in Classification of Arthopods by the Kayapo Indians of Brazil." *Journal of Ethnobiology* 4 : 123–39.

Pouillon, Jean. 1993. *Le cru et le su.* Paris: Seuil.

Prout, E. 1843. *Memoir of the life of the Rev. John Williams.* New York: Allen, Morrill and Wardwell.

*Puget, Peter. Fragment of a Journal, March 1792. BM (Add MSS 17, 547).

*———. Journals of the Proceedings of the *Chatham,* January 1794–September 1795. BM (Add MSS 17, 548).

*———. A Log of the Proceedings of His Majesty's Armed Tender *Chatham.* 2 vols. PRO Adm. 55/27, PRO Adm/27.

*———. Papers Relating to the Voyage of the *Discovery* and *Chatham,* 1790–1795. BM (Add MSS 17, 552).

*Pukui, Mary Kawena. "Makahiki Hou." In HEN, 1 : 1294–1297. Bernice P. Bishop Museum Library.

Pukui, Mary Kawena, and Samuel H. Elbert. 1957. *Hawaiian dictionary.* Honolulu: University of Hawaii Press.

Purchas, Samuel. N.d. [1625]. *Purchas his pilgrimes in Japan,* ed. Cyril Wild. Kobe: J. L. Thompson & Co.

Putilov, B. N. 1982. *Nikolai Miklouho-Maclay: Traveller, scientist, and humanist.* Trans. Glenys Ann Kozlov. Moscow: Progress Publishers.

Putnam, Hilary. 1975. *Mind, language and reality,* vol. 2. Cambridge: Cambridge University Press.

Remy, Jules. 1859. *Récits d'un vieux sauvage pour servir à l'histoire ancienne de Havaii.* Chalons-sur-Marne: E. Laurent.

Rickman, John. 1966. *Journal of Captain Cook's Last Voyage to the Pacific Ocean.* U.S.A.: Readex Microprint.

*Riou, Edward. A Log of the Proceedings of His Majesty's Sloop *Discovery,* Book 3d, 4 August 1778–17 January 1779. PRO Adm 51/4529/43.

Robarts, Edward. 1974. *The Marquesan journal of Edward Robarts, 1797–1824,* ed. G. M. Dening. Canberra: Australian National University Press.

*Roberts, Henry. A Log of the Proceedings of His Majesties Sloop *Resolution* on Discoveries, toward the South North Pole. James Cook Esqr Commander. Dixson Library, Library of New South Wales (MS Q/51–2).

Robbins, Lionel. 1952. *An essay on the nature and significance of economic science.* London: Macmillan.

Robertson, H. A. 1902. *The Martyr Isle Erromanga.* New York: A. C. Armstrong and Son.

Rousseau, Jean-Jacques. 1984. *A discourse on inequality,* trans. with an Introduction and Notes by Maurice Cranston. Harmondsworth: Penguin Books.

Sahlins, Marshall. 1976. "Colors and Cultures." *Semiotica* 16: 1–22.

———. 1977. "The State of the Art in Social/Cultural Anthropology." Pp. 14–32 in *Perspectives on anthropology,* ed. Anthony F. C. Wallace et al. American Anthropological Association, Special Publication no. 10.

———. 1978. "The Apotheosis of Captain Cook." *Kroeber Anthropological Society Papers,* nos. 53/54: 1–31. (Reprinted in Izard and Smith, 1982.)

———. 1979. "L'Apothéose du capitaine Cook." Pp. 306–43 in *La fonction symbolique,* ed. Michel Izard and Pierre Smith. Paris: Gallimard.

———. 1981. *Historical metaphors and mythical realities: Structure in the early history of the Sandwich Island kingdom.* Ann Arbor: University of Michigan Press.

———. 1982. "The Apotheosis of Captain Cook." Pp. 73–102 in *Between belief and transgression,* ed. Michel Izard and Pierre Smith. Chicago: University of Chicago Press.

———. 1983. "Other Times, Other Customs: The Anthropology of History." *American Anthropologist* 85: 517–44.

———. 1985a. *Islands of history.* Chicago: University of Chicago Press.

———. 1985b. "Hierarchy and Humanity in Polynesia." Pp. 195–214 in *Transformations of Polynesian culture,* ed. Antony Hooper and Judith Huntsman. Auckland: The Polynesian Society.

———. 1988. "Deserted Islands of History: A Reply to Jonathan Friedman." *Critique of Anthropology* 8: 41–51.

———. 1989. "Captain Cook at Hawaii." *Journal of the Polynesian Society* 98: 371–425.

———. 1991. "The Return of the Event, Again." Pp. 37–100 in *Clio in Oceania: Toward a historical anthropology,* ed. Aletta Biersack. Washington, D.C.: Smithsonian Institution Press.

———. 1992. *Historical ethnography.* Vol. 1 of Patrick V. Kirch and Marshall Sahlins, *Anahulu: The anthropology of history in the kingdom of Hawaii.* Chicago: University of Chicago Press.

———. 1993. "Goodbye to *Tristes Tropes:* Ethnography in the Context of Modern World History." *The Journal of Modern History* 65: 1–25.

———. 1994. "The Discovery of the True Savage." Pp. 41–95 in *Dangerous liaisons: Essays in honour of Greg Dening,* ed. D. Merwick. Melbourne: Melbourne University Press.

*———. MS. Manuscript summaries of Cook voyage to Hawaii, Makahiki and Calendrical Data. Special Collections, Regenstein Library, University of Chicago.

Salisbury, Richard. 1962. *From stone to steel: Economic consequences of a technological change in New Guinea.* London: Cambridge University Press.

Salmond, Anne. 1991. *Two worlds: First meetings between Maori and Europeans, 1642–1772.* Honolulu: University of Hawaii Press.

Saussure, Ferdinand de. 1966. *Course in general linguistics.* New York: McGraw-Hill.

Schiefflin, Edward L., and Robert Crittendon. 1991. *Like people you see in a dream.* Stanford: Stanford University Press.

Schmidt, Alfred. 1971. *The concept of nature in Marx.* London: NLB.

Schrempp, Gregory. 1992. *Magical arrows: The Greeks, the Maori and the folklore of the universe.* Madison: University of Wisconsin Press.

Shineberg, Dorothy. 1967. *They came for sandalwood.* Melbourne: Melbourne University Press.

Sillitoe, Paul. 1979. *Give and take: Exchange in Wola society.* New York: St. Martin's Press.

Smith, Bernard. 1979. "Cook's Posthumous Reputation." Pp. 159–85 in *Captain James Cook and his times,* ed. Robin Fisher and H. Johnston. Seattle: University of Washington Press.

Smith, Jean. 1974. *Tapu removal in Maori religion.* Wellington: The Polynesian Society.

Stocking, George W., Jr. 1968. *Race, culture, and evolution: Essays in the history of anthropology.* New York: The Free Press.

———. 1987. *Victorian anthropology.* New York: The Free Press.

Stokes, John F. G. 1931. "Origin of the Condemnation of Captain Cook in Hawaii."Pp. 68–104 in *39th Annual Report of the Hawaiian Historical Society for the Year 1930.* Honolulu.

Strathern, Andrew. 1984. *A line of power.* London: Tavistock.

Tambiah, S. J. 1969. "Animals are Good to Think and Good to Prohibit." *Ethnology* 8:423–59.

*Taylor, Andrew B. Journals of A. B. Taylor on the *Prince of Wales* Commanded by J. Colnett, 1786–1788. ML (A 2106).

Thomas, Nicholas. 1990. *Marquesan societies: Inequality and political transformation in Eastern Polynesia.* Oxford: Clarendon Press.

Thrum, Thomas G. 1909. "Tales from the Temples, Part 3." Pp. 44–54 in *Hawaiian Annual for 1909.*

———. 1927. "The Paehumu of Heiaus Non-Sacred." Pp. 56–57 in *35th Annual Report of the Hawaiian Historical Society.*

*———. Ancient Hawaiian Mythology. Sinclair Library, University of Hawaii.

Titcomb, Margaret. 1972. *Native use of fish in Hawaii* (with the collaboration of Mary Kawena Pukui). Honolulu: University of Hawaii Press.

Todorov, Tzvetan. 1984. *The conquest of America.* New York: Harper & Row.

Traeger, Edward. 1969. *The Maori-Polynesian comparative dictionary.* Oosterhout N.B. (Netherlands): Anthropological Publications.

*Trevenan, James. Marginal annotations to the published account (Cook and King) of Cook's third voyage. Typescript copy in Sinclair Library, University of Hawaii.

*——— (attributed). A Log of the Proceedings of His Majesty's *Sloop Resolution,* James Cook Esquire Commander, from Nov. 16th, 1778 to Feb. 15th, 1779. . . . PRO Adm 55/123.

Turnbull, John. 1805. *A voyage round the world in the years 1800, 1801, 1802, 1803, and 1804. . . .* 3 vols. London: Richard Phillips.

Turner, Rev. George. 1861. *Nineteen years in Polynesia.* London: Snow.

―――. 1884. *Samoa a hundred years ago and long before.* London: Macmillan.

Turner, Terence. 1993. "Anthropology and Multiculturalism: What is Anthropology that Multiculturalists Should Be Mindful of It?" *Cultural Anthropology* 8:411–25.

Tyerman, Daniel, and George Bennet. 1831. *Journal of voyages and travels.* 2 vols. London: Westley and Davis.

―――. 1832. *Journal of voyages and travels . . . in the South Sea Islands . . . between the years 1821 and 1829.* Boston: Crocker and Brewster. (An American edition of the preceding work.)

Valeri, Valerio. 1985. *Kingship and sacrifice: Ritual and society in ancient Hawaii.* Chicago: University of Chicago Press.

―――. 1987. "Response." *Pacific Studies* 10:148–214.

―――. 1990. "Diarchy and History in Hawaii and Tonga." In *Culture and history in the Pacific,* ed. J. Siikala. Transactions of the Finnish Anthropological Society, Helsinki.

―――. 1991. "The Transformation of a Transformation: A Structural Essay on an Aspect of Hawaiian History (1809 to 1819)." Pp. 101–64 in *Clio in Oceania: Toward a historical anthropology,* ed. Aletta Biersach. Washington, D.C.: Smithsonian Institution Press.

Vancouver, Captain George. 1801. *A voyage of discovery to the North Pacific Ocean . . . in the years 1790, 1791, 1792, 1793, 1794, and 1795.* New ed., 5 vols. London: Stockdale.

Varigny, C. de. 1874. *Quatorze ans aux îles Sandwich.* Paris: Hachette.

Vyerberg, Henry. 1989. *Human nature, cultural diversity, and the French Enlightenment.* New York: Oxford University Press.

*Watts, John. Proceedings of His Majesty's Sloop Resolution, Ap. 23, 1776–Nov. 29, 1779. PRO Adm 51/4559.

Webster, E. M. 1984. *The Moon Man: A biography of Nicolai Mikluoho-Maclay.* Berkeley and Los Angeles: University of California Press.

Whitman, John B. 1979. *An account of the Sandwich Islands: The Hawaiian journal of John B. Whitman, 1813–1815,* ed. John Dominus Holt. Honolulu: TopGallant and the Peabody Museum of Salem.

*Whitney, Samuel. The Journal of Samuel Whitney. Hawaiian Mission Children's Society Library, Honolulu.

Williams, Francis Edward. 1941. *Natives of Lake Kutubu, Papua, Oceania.* Monographs, no. 6. Sydney: Australian National Research Council.

Williams, Francis Edgar. 1976. *'The Vailala madness' and other essays,* ed. Erik Schwimmer. London: C. Hurst.

*Williams, (Rev.) John W. "Papeiha's Description of Idols." In LMS, South Seas no. 57.

Williamson, Robert W. 1924. *The social and political systems of central Polynesia.* 3 vols. Cambridge: Cambridge University Press.

Wolpe, Hans. 1957. *Raynal et sa machine de guerre: L'Histoire des deux Indes et ses perfectionnements.* Stanford: Stanford University Press.

Zimmermann, Heinrich. 1781. *Reise um die Welt, mit Captain Cook.* Mannheim: C. F. Schwan.

―――. 1988 *The third voyage of Captain Cook.* Fairfield, Wash.: Ye Galleon Press.

Index

and Dixon account of, 212–13;
primary documents on, 208; and
Sahlins's Frazer lecture, 3; temple
refurbishing, 77; timing of celebrations of, 27n; Vancouver party on,
213–15, 221, 222; and veneration
of Cook in the nineteenth century,
96, 97, 98. See also *kāliʻi;* Makahiki
image
Makahiki image: appearance of, 27–
29; at ceremonial boxing matches,
77, 78; Colnett on, 89; Cook imi-
tating at Hikiau ceremony, 53, 55,
56, 60; drawings of, 28, 78, 89;
Hikiau temple as starting point of
circuit of, 48; *kabu,* 138, 138n;
kaʻupu skins used in, 27, 28n;
Kahoaliʻi watching over, 30–31,
147; as the long god, 29n.16; Lono
embodied in, 22; and Lonoikamakahiki, 28n, 106; net house of Kahoaliʻi, 31; net of Maoloha, 31; at
Oʻahu in 1788, 88n.4; Obeyesekere
on, 230–31; Taylor on, 90–91. *See
also* Lonomakua
Makaliʻi, 31
Malo, David: on the bonito ceremonies,
214; on deifying a deceased king,
144–45; depiction of Makahiki
image, 28, 230; on *hānaipū,* 58n;
on the interdiction on pork, 46n;
on the king meeting Lono, 225; on
Makahiki economics, 218, 219; on
the net of Maoloha, 31; on the
priestly genealogies, 256; on the
purification ceremonies, 46; on sacred chiefs, 253; as source on the
Makahiki, 208, 211, 212; on the
termination rituals, 75
mana, 127, 127n, 128–29
mana of Kū, 126
Manby, Thomas, 96, 96n.9
Mangaia, 71, 284
Mangareva, 252
Maoloha, net of, 31
Maori: ceremonies that pollute the

gods, 84; creation myths, 164,
164n.16; gods of, 120n, 284; mythical categorization in, 249–50;
myths of Europeans, 115; rituals
compared to Makahiki, 22n.8, 77
Mariner, William, 97–98, 178
Marquesans, 178, 254, 282–85
Martin, John, 97, 98
Mathison, Gilbert, 113, 113n, 218
Maui: conquered by Kamehameha,
215; Cook's people considered as
gods at, 278; Cook's arrival off, 33,
34, 211; Kalaniʻōpuʻu's attack on, 35,
36–37, 37n.21; map of eastern, 35
Mauss, Marcel, 96n.10
Meares, John, 87
Melanesia: first contacts with Westerners, 179–80, 180n, 188; New Caledonia, 285; New Guineans, 157–
58, 160–62, 177, 180–87
Menzies, Archibald, 141–42
Menzies, J. I., 162
Mikado, 135–36
Mikloucho-Maclay, Nikolai Nikolaevich, 181–82, 251
"milk of the father, the," 7
Miller, Lorraine, 55
missionaries: Bennet and Tyerman,
102, 102n.15, 254; Bingham, 103,
104–5, 122, 137n.12; Dibble, 21,
38n.23, 41–43, 103; Lyons, 114; as
source of Cook as Lono myth, 4–6,
8, 41, 101–5, 124n. *See also* Ellis,
Reverend William
Moana, 48
Moho, 176, 176n.27
Montaigne, Michel de, 11n
Mooolelo Hawaii, Ka: on Cook as Lono,
22, 33, 36, 41–42, 103, 278, 279;
on Cook sleeping with Kamakahelei's daughter, 279; on Cook's death,
240; Hawaiian description of the
British, 183; on Hawaiian reaction
to the British, 66; on Kalaniʻōpuʻu's
welcome of Cook, 68–69; Kamakau's role in, 48n, 106; method of